FIERCE

PAJAMAS

FIERCE

PAJAMAS

AN ANTHOLOGY OF HUMOR WRITING
FROM *THE NEW YORKER*

EDITED BY DAVID REMNICK

AND HENRY FINDER

RANDOM HOUSE | NEW YORK

LIBRARY OF CONGRESS CATALOGING-IN-PUBLICATION DATA

Fierce pajamas: an anthology of humor writing from the New Yorker/edited by David
Remnick and Henry Finder.
p.   cm.
ISBN 0-375-50475-3
1. American wit and humor. I. Remnick, David. II. Finder, Henry. III. New Yorker.
PN6165 .F54   2001
817′.508—dc21   2001031775

Random House website address: www.atrandom.com
Printed in the United States of America on acid-free paper
24689753
First Edition
Book design by JoAnne Metsch

To John Updike

CONTENTS

THE FRENZY OF RENOWN

THE WAR BETWEEN MEN AND WOMEN

THE WRITING LIFE

A FUNNY THING HAPPENED

INTRODUCTION

FOR all that has been written about the origins of The New Yorker, the significance of one fact has been overlooked: its main backer owed his fortune to yeast. To be founded upon yeast is different from being founded upon soap, or steel, or natural gas, and, surely, the source of this seed money—spore money?—set the tone for all that followed. Our first editor, Harold Ross, wanted a publication that would be consistently leavened by comedy. It was his constant refrain: "We need words like the art"—prose that matched the spirit of the cartoons. "Humor was allowed to infect everything," E. B. White, a singularly contagious soul, would write. And Ross's efforts paid off: New Yorker humor, like Dole pineapples and Microsoft operating systems, represents a deep alliance of product and institution.

It was a serious business, putting out what Ross called his "comic weekly." Lois Long, an early contributor, described daily staff meetings that consisted of craps games, and an editor whose wont was "to move the desks about prankishly in the dead of night." (Some things never change.) To start naming the magazine's contributors in its earliest years is to explain how Ross achieved his objectives. There was Dorothy Parker, who, as Constant Reader, concluded a review of Dreiser's memoir *Dawn* with the couplet "Theodore Dreiser / Should ought to write nicer." There was Robert Benchley, for a decade the magazine's chief drama critic, who ascribed to John Barrymore's Hamlet "the smile of an actor who hates actors, and who knows that he is going to kill two or three before the play is over." There was Lois Long herself on fashion; Ring Lardner on radio; George Ryall (Audax Minor) on the racetrack; and Alexander Woollcott on whatever popped into his head. If humor infected everything, it was because it wasn't quarantined to humor

pieces, or "casuals," as they came to be known. An undercurrent of jok-
iness ran through the reviews and the commentary. (That tradition has
lasted—from the unfailing urbanity of Brendan Gill and the unfailing
anti-urbanity of Pauline Kael down to the spring-loaded wit of such
writers as Nancy Franklin and Anthony Lane, who have kept the art of
the comic review very much alive.) After the arrival, in the thirties, of
Joseph Mitchell and A. J. Liebling, Ross got long-form journalism with
matching brio and brilliance. The comic weekly had come of age.

Still, if there was such a thing as *New Yorker* humor—as distinct from
humor in *The New Yorker*—the credit must go largely to E. B. White
and James Thurber. White, a master of understatement, could creep
along so quietly you might not realize that he was stalking prey, and that
you were it. Thurber was perhaps a more belligerent soul, but then his
favorite quarry was himself. Both worked in every comic form and invented new ones; and their touch was so pervasive that, in the words of
Brendan Gill, "the persona of the magazine [was] White-Thurber." Yet
White and Thurber had a particular genius for creating personas of their
own. In 1927, Thurber published "An American Romance," which
opens, "The little man in an overcoat that fitted him badly at the shoulders had had a distressing scene with his wife. He had left home with a
look of serious determination and had now been going around and
around in the central revolving door of a prominent department store's
main entrance for fifteen minutes." With this, "Little Man" humor, as it
came to be called, was launched—tales of ineffectual men victimized by
the world, by women, by nagging suspicions of their own absurdity.

Another comic specialty of the magazine was what Benchley dubbed
"dementia praecox" humor: monologues, basically, of the unstrung and
the unhinged—"The Tell-Tale Heart" with laughs. It was a mainstay of
Benchley's repertory, and so was the news-clipping conceit: the piece
that started with some scrap of news and elaborated on the premise ad
absurdum. In the thirties, the humorous reminiscence, too, became a
staple of *The New Yorker*. It began, more or less, with a notable series of
pieces by Clarence Day, a former stockbroker who, confined to his
apartment by severe arthritis, set about writing affectionately satiric
anecdotes about life with his father. Shortly after Day's first piece appeared, in 1933, Thurber started publishing bits of autobiography
about his Ohio upbringing, eventually collected under the title *My Life
and Hard Times*. Thus primed, the pump soon yielded memoirs by
Ludwig Bemelmans, H. L. Mencken, and Ruth McKenney. As an old
bit of magazine wisdom has it, you get what you publish.

Sometimes—blessedly—you get even what you don't publish. To editors, as custodians of standards, work that broke the rules could seem just broken. A recent chronicler of the magazine, Ben Yagoda, has extracted from the archives an exchange of memos among three of its most illustrious editors—Katharine S. White, Wolcott Gibbs, and John Mosher—in reaction to a 1933 submission called "The Island of Dr. Finkle," apparently inspired by the recently released film version of *The Island of Dr. Moreau.* Here's a sample.

WHITE: "Not having seen the Island of Dr. What's His Name I don't know whether this is any good. He seems to be burlesquing a dozen things at once also??"

GIBBS: "I didn't know there was any such book. Thought this was just a burlesque of those old clubmen talking about India stories. . . . Object to one or two of the worst gags, but other wise O.K. By the way, Donald Stewart and Thurber have both done things like this, if it matters."

MOSHER: "Awful humor—this dry, synthetic stale style—central idea about island is rather funny perhaps. . . . I can't stand these trick phrasings—jumpy nervous nasty things."

In a letter of rejection to the author, Ross offered the following counsel: "I think you ought to decide when you write a piece whether it is going to be a parody, or a satire, or nonsense. These are not very successfully mixed in short stuff; that has been my experience." Though the advice went unheeded, a few years later Ross hired Sidney Joseph Perelman anyway. In an introduction to a 1937 Perelman collection, Robert Benchley himself graciously declared that the Brooklyn-born interloper now owned the "dementia praecox field": "Any further attempts to garble thought-processes sounded like imitation-Perelman." Perhaps determined to keep such imitators at bay, Perelman went on to flood the market with the real thing, contributing three hundred casuals over the next four decades. In 1952—when about a hundred and thirty of them had so far seen print—W. H. Auden pronounced *The New Yorker* "the best comic magazine in existence."

Persistence was one way past the praetorian guards, but there were other routes, too. Prospective contributors may wish to study the example of Peter De Vries. De Vries, who grew up in Chicago, came to *The New Yorker*'s attention from *Poetry* magazine via James Thurber; and he came to Thurber's attention via a flattering essay he had published entitled "James Thurber: The Comic Prufrock." It is just possible to imagine that his career trajectory would have been different had he published, instead, "Ed Sullivan: The Comic Prufrock."

Students of the magazine have pointed out that the fifties saw the addition of relatively few new comic voices. There are various theories to account for this. Some conjecture that if only people like Stanley Elkin, Terry Southern, or Joseph Heller had published something along the lines of "James Thurber: The Comic Prufrock," they, too, might have found their way into the magazine. Others blame the growing allure of Hollywood—the maw of Tinseltown. Yet, as was the case with Benchley, Perelman, and Parker, the traffic between the coasts goes both ways. Sensitive artists, moreover, have always found this world of glitz and glamour something of a hardship post, what with being ordered around by besuited philistines and having their words hacked at by an army of anonymous interlopers. Which is not to say that Hollywood is any better.

In the event, the lean years were followed by fat: in the sixties, new arrivals included Calvin Trillin, Pauline Kael, Donald Barthelme, and Woody Allen. They published journalism, criticism, fiction, and casuals, and they were funny, in ways slightly different from the way people used to be funny. In the seventies and eighties, some of the magazine's most distinctive voices—including Garrison Keillor, Veronica Geng, George W. S. Trow, and Ian Frazier—devoted themselves to reinventing the casual. (To read Frazier's "A Reading List for Young Writers" is to inoculate oneself against writing sonorously about literature.) And in the past decade a new generation of contributors—but why mention names you'll find in the issues on your coffee table?—both extend and pay homage to a tradition arduously achieved, and do it in ways that can be stunningly original, or stunningly not. As the poet said, there's tradition, and there's the individual talent, and a collection like this one helps you appreciate how intertwined the two are—how eerily contemporary some of the old stuff seems, how venerable some of the new.

WHY did we choose what we chose? On the whole, the basis for our selections was visceral: Was a piece funny? Is it still? Did it make us gasp with admiration and an apprehension of the sublime? (This last was optional.) Yes, you'll find the odd concession—sometimes *very* odd—to literary history. But basically pieces are here because they made us laugh. A very few are here because they're weird, ethereal, and beautiful, and would have made us laugh if we were better people. Sophisticates may object that we have included pieces they consider overexposed, excessively familiar. Behind this objection, we submit, is a fetching misunderstanding of contemporary American culture. "Overexposed" may describe a Pepsi commercial with Britney Spears; it does not describe "The Night the Ghost Got In."

What taxed our ingenuity wasn't so much deciding what to put in as deciding what not to. "Humor was allowed to infect everything," as White had observed, and, for an anthologist, that's just the problem. A collection of humor writing from *The New Yorker* can't be a collection of humorous writing from *The New Yorker*—a category that would include perhaps the greater part of the magazine's output. To keep the book to a compassable length, we resorted to firm, if arbitrary rules. In the end, the essential principle of inclusion, for any given candidate, was simple: did we fail to come up with some excuse for excluding it?

Most "humor pieces"—casuals, or the sort of piece that in today's *New Yorker* runs under the rubric Shouts & Murmurs—are short: canapés, not steaks. These are mostly what you'll find here: pieces that have some specific density of wit or are governed by a comic premise. And yet some of the finest instances of humor are, one might say, incidental (though incidental in an integral way) to a work of journalism. These are nonfiction narratives where, in the words of Calvin Trillin, "the jokes sometimes are suspended for the lamentable necessity of transferring a little information to the reader." Our decision to scant such pieces means that some of our funniest contributors aren't represented. We've already beaten ourselves up over this, so don't feel you have to. Likewise, we generally gave a cold shoulder to short stories. We did so out of the kind of anxiety that inspires trade quotas: if we opened our doors to their authors, we'd be inundated with scarily deserving contenders—from Sally Benson to George Saunders—and hardworking native humorists would be put out of work. Hence our recourse to such protectionist edicts as would put the Hawley-Smoot Act to shame. Having established these firm ground rules, naturally, we proceeded to violate them, dutifully proving the rule with its necessary exceptions.

Rules, anyway, get you only so far. Occasionally, we found that a comic tour de force required a slightly greater familiarity with Van Wyck Brooks or Frank Harris than could now be assumed; nor do we apologize for omitting a dead-on parody of James Branch Cabell. There were instances in which reclamation would have amounted to cruelty, in a whatever-happened-to-Baby-Jane sort of way. Some classics are best appreciated in the diffuse, amber light of distant recollection, and we honored them by not disturbing their repose. And, of course, a great deal of the most ingenious and uproarious work is, by design, topical; it belongs to a particular place and time. This is not said invidiously. The vaunted "test of time" is a circular one: all the test of time really tells you is whether something has survived the test of time. Unless strontium 90 is to be preferred to sunflowers, perishability is no disgrace. But these concerns applied only to a minority of cases. In truth, there were hundreds of pieces we'd love to have included, had we not—*vide* deforestation, the greenhouse gases—loved the planet more. "I must get back to the office and reject," John Mosher used to say to his lunch companions. The poor fellow. We thought about him a lot.

"WHEN you are creeping through the literary underbrush hoping to bag a piece of humor with your net, nothing seems funny," Russell Baker wrote in a preface to an anthology of American humor that he compiled. "The thing works the other way around. Humor is funny when it sneaks up on you and takes you by surprise."

Yes, funny writing is funny that way. Defying the laws of nature, humor is often diluted by concentration. So you might be ill-advised to read this book straight through. Consider this, rather, a prescription of antibiotics, to be rationed out over a period of time, not knocked back all at once. Consider it a fridge full of food, and put yourself on a diet. Print is a perilous medium, so precautions must be taken. When stand-up comedians play to a club, there's usually a two-drink minimum, which means they're extracting laughs from a pleasantly sozzled audience. Are *you* pleasantly sozzled? We worry about these things. We worry about the sated reader who turns pages out of obligation, as stone-faced as an Easter Island *moai*.

This collection is divided into categories that reflect a few salient preoccupations of the contributors. We'd like to pretend these categories represent a definitive taxonomy. In truth, given the amount of overlap, the exercise was more like assigning students to a homeroom. Still, one distinction did seem useful: we wanted to segregate pieces that are basically witty but truthful essays or recollections from those that are basically fictive conceits (as most of them are). You don't want to have to get to the fourth paragraph to figure out that the voice is the author's, not some apparently soigné narrator whose lofty tones will devolve into utter lunacy before the piece is over. Reflections and recollections, however various, have thus been placed in administrative custody for their own protection and yours. But beyond this? We laboriously organized the contents in a cunning, intricate sequence so that you could enjoy the transgressive thrill of reading them *out of order.*

IN gathering these pieces, we somehow racked up more debts than a first-term congressman. Thanks, first and foremost, are due C. S. Ledbetter, one of the institution's true stalwarts, who made his way through the depths of the *New Yorker* archives like a foraging Egyptologist equipped with hand trowel and toothbrush. Mr. Ledbetter is alert even to ironies pitched beyond the normal range of human hearing. Thanks, also, to Susan Morrison, for her stewardship of the Shouts & Murmurs department and her attentive egg-candling of the magazine's more recent offerings. To Pamela Maffei McCarthy and Edward Klaris, for ensuring that these pieces could be reprinted legally and by a publishing house, rather than illegally and by a campus-based file-sharing system. To Alice Quinn, for her sensitive sifting through of the magazine's light and lightish and not all that light verse. To Christopher Shay and Erin Overbey of the magazine's library, for assistance of every variety. We're particularly indebted to Leo Carey, Dana Goodyear, and Brenda Phipps, who were responsible for the Notes on Contributors (assisted by Jacob Goldstein, Chuck Wilson, and Austin Kelley), and who kept the project on the rails.

This book of humor writing further benefited from the advice of some of the most distinguished practitioners of the art: Roger Angell, Nancy Franklin, Ian Frazier, Adam Gopnik, Charles McGrath, Calvin Trillin, and John Updike. We are also grateful to Daniel Menaker, a *New Yorker* veteran as well as the book's editor at Random House. To have counsellors and kibbitzers of such distinction is indeed a privilege: it means we can claim responsibility for all remaining oversights, confident that readers will see through our affected modesty and assign the blame elsewhere.

FIERCE

PAJAMAS

SPOOFS

WOLCOTT GIBBS

DEATH IN THE RUMBLE SEAT

WITH THE USUAL APOLOGIES TO ERNEST HEMINGWAY,

WHO MUST BE PRETTY SICK OF THIS SORT OF THING

MOST people don't like the pedestrian part, and it is best not to look at that if you can help it. But if you can't help seeing them, long-legged and their faces white, and then the shock and the car lifting up a little on one side, then it is best to think of it as something very unimportant but beautiful and necessary artistically. It is unimportant because the people who are pedestrians are not very important, and if they were not being *cogido* by automobiles it would just be something else. And it is beautiful and necessary because, without the possibility of somebody getting *cogido*, driving a car would be just like anything else. It would be like reading "Thanatopsis," which is neither beautiful nor necessary, but hogwash. If you drive a car, and don't like the pedestrian part, then you are one of two kinds of people. Either you haven't very much vitality and you ought to do something about it, or else you are yellow and there is nothing to be done about it at all.

IF you don't know anything about driving cars you are apt to think a driver is good just because he goes fast. This may be very exciting at first, but afterwards there is a bad taste in the mouth and the feeling of dishonesty. Ann Bender, the American, drove as fast on the Merrick Road as anybody I have ever seen, but when cars came the other way she always worked out of their terrain and over in the ditch so that you never had the hard, clean feeling of danger, but only bumping up and down in the ditch, and sometimes hitting your head on the top of the car. Good drivers go fast too, but it is always down the middle of the road, so that cars coming the other way are dominated, and have to go in the ditch themselves. There are a great many ways of getting the effect of danger, such as staying in the middle of the road till the last minute and then swerving out of the pure line, but they are all tricks, and afterwards you know they were tricks, and there is nothing left but disgust.

The cook: I am a little tired of cars, sir. Do you know any stories?

I know a great many stories, but I'm not sure that they're suitable.

The cook: The hell with that.

Then I will tell you the story about God and Adam and naming the animals. You see, God was very tired after he got through making the world. He felt good about it, but he was tired so he asked Adam if he'd mind thinking up names for the animals.

"What animals?" Adam said.

"Those," God said.

"Do they have to have names?" Adam said.

"You've got a name, haven't you?" God said.

I could see—

The cook: How do *you* get into this?

Some people always write in the first person, and if you do it's very hard to write any other way, even when it doesn't altogether fit into the context. If you want to hear this story, don't keep interrupting.

The cook: O.K.

I could see that Adam thought God was crazy, but he didn't say anything. He went over to where the animals were, and after a while he came back with the list of names.

"Here you are," he said.

God read the list, and nodded.

"They're pretty good," he said. "They're all pretty good except that last one."

"That's a good name," Adam said. "What's the matter with it?"

"What do you want to call it an elephant for?," God said.

Adam looked at God.

"It looks like an elephant to me," he said.

The cook: Well?

That's all.

The cook: It is a very strange story, sir.

It is a strange world, and if a man and a woman love each other, that is strange too, and what is more, it always turns out badly.

In the golden age of car-driving, which was about 1910, the sense of impending disaster, which is a very lovely thing and almost nonexistent, was kept alive in a number of ways. For one thing, there was always real glass in the windshield so that if a driver hit anything, he was very definitely and beautifully *cogido*. The tires weren't much good either, and often they'd blow out before you'd gone ten miles. Really, the whole car was built that way. It was made not only so that it would precipitate accidents but so that when the accidents came it was honestly vulnerable, and it would fall apart, killing all the people with a passion that was very fine to watch. Then they began building the cars so that they would go much faster, but the glass and the tires were all made so that if anything happened it wasn't real danger, but only the false sense of it. You could do all kinds of things with the new cars, but it was no good because it was all planned in advance. Mickey Finn, the German, always worked very far into the other car's terrain so that the two cars always seemed to be one. Driving that way he often got the *faender*, or the clicking when two cars touch each other in passing, but because you knew that nothing was really at stake it was just an empty classicism, without any value because the insecurity was all gone and there was nothing left but a kind of mechanical agility. It is the same way when any art gets into its decadence. It is the same way about s-x—

The cook: I like it very much better when you talk about s-x, sir, and I wish you would do it more often.

I have talked a lot about s-x before, and now I thought I would talk about something else.

The cook: I think that is very unfortunate, sir, because you are at your best with s-x, but when you talk about automobiles you are just a nuisance.

1932

E. B. WHITE

DUSK IN FIERCE PAJAMAS

RAVAGED by pink eye, I lay for a week scarce caring whether I lived or died. Only Wamba, my toothless old black nurse, bothered to bring me food and quinine. Then one day my strength began to return, and with it came Wamba to my bedside with a copy of *Harper's Bazaar* and a copy of *Vogue*. "Ah brought you couple magazines," she said proudly, her red gums clashing.

In the days that followed (happy days of renewed vigor and reawak-ened interest), I studied the magazines and lived, in their pages, the gracious lives of the characters in the ever-moving drama of society and fashion. In them I found surcease from the world's ugliness, from dis-array, from all unattractive things. Through them I escaped into a world in which there was no awkwardness of gesture, no unsuitability of line, no people of no importance. It was an enriching experience. I realize now that my own life is by contrast an unlovely thing, with its disease, its banalities, its uncertainties, its toil, its single-breasted suits, and its wine from lesser years. I am aware of a life all around me of gracious-ness and beauty, in which every moment is a tiny pearl of good taste, and in which every acquaintance has the common decency to possess a good background.

Lying here in these fierce pajamas, I dream of the *Harper's Bazaar* world, the *Vogue* life; dream of being a part of it. In fancy I am in Mrs. Cecil Baker's pine-panelled drawing-room. It is dusk. (It is almost al-ways dusk in the fashion magazines.) I have on a Gantner & Mattern knit jersey bathing suit with a flat-striped bow and an all-white buck shoe with a floppy tongue. No, that's wrong. I am in chiffon, for it is the magic hour after bridge. Suddenly a Chippendale mahogany hors-d'œuvre table is brought in. In its original old blue-and-white Spode compartments there sparkle olives, celery, hard-boiled eggs, radishes—evidently put there by somebody in the employ of Mrs. Baker. Or per-haps my fancy wanders away from the drawing-room: I am in Mrs. Baker's dining-room, mingling unostentatiously with the other guests, my elbows resting lightly on the dark polished oak of the Jacobean table, my fingers twiddling with the early Georgian silver. Or perhaps I am not at Mrs. Baker's oak table in chiffon at all—perhaps instead I am at Mrs. Jay Gould's teakwood table in a hand-knitted Anny Blatt en-semble in diluted tri-colors and an off-the-face hat.

It is dusk. I am dining with Rose Hobart at the Waldorf. We have lifted our champagne glasses. "To sentiment!" I say. And the haunting dusk is shattered by the clean glint of jewels by Cartier.

It is dusk. I am seated on a Bruce Buttfield pouf, for it is dusk.

Ah, magazine dreams! How dear to me now are the four evenings in the life of Mrs. Allan Ryan, Junior. I have studied them one by one, and I feel that I know them. They are perfect little crystals of being—static, precious. There is the evening when she stands, motionless, in a mag-nificent sable cape, her left arm hanging gracefully at her side. She is ready to go out to dinner. What will this, her first of four evenings, bring of romance, or even of food? Then there is the evening when she just sits on the edge of a settee from the Modernage Galleries, the hard bright gleam of gold lamé topping a slim, straight, almost Empire skirt. I see her there (the smoke from a cigarette rising), sitting, sitting, waiting. Or the third evening—the evening with books. Mrs. Ryan is in chiffon; the books are in morocco. Or the fourth evening, standing with her dachshund, herself in profile, the dog in full face.

So I live the lives of other people in my fancy: the life of the daughter of Lord Curzon of Kedleston, who has been visiting the Harold Talbotts on Long Island. All I know of her is that she appeared one night at dinner, her beauty set off by the lustre of artificial satin and the watery fire of aquamarine. It is all I know, yet it is enough; for it is her one perfect moment in time and space, and I know about it, and it is mine.

It is dusk. I am with Owen Johnson over his chafing dish. It is dusk. I am with Prince Matchabelli over his vodka. Or I am with the Countess de Forceville over her bridge tables. She and I have just pushed the tables against the wall and taken a big bite of gaspacho. Or I am with the Marquis de Polignac over his Pommery.

How barren my actual life seems, when fancy fails me, here with Wamba over my quinine. Why am I not to be found at dusk, slicing black bread very thin, as William Powell does, to toast it and sprinkle it with salt? Why does not twilight find me (as it finds Mrs. Chester Burden) covering a table with salmon-pink linens on which I place only white objects, even to a white salt shaker? Why don't I learn to simplify my entertaining, like the young pinch-penny in *Vogue,* who has all his friends in before the theatre and simply gives them champagne cocktails, caviar, and one hot dish, then takes them to the show? Why do I never give parties after the opera, as Mr. Paul Cravath does, at which I have the prettiest women in New York? Come to think of it, why don't the prettiest women in New York ever come down to my place, other than that pretty little Mrs. Fazaenzi, whom Wamba won't let in? Why haven't I a butler named Fish, who makes a cocktail of three parts gin to one part lime juice, honey, vermouth, and apricot brandy in equal portions—a cocktail so delicious that people like Mrs. Harrison Williams and Mrs. Goodhue Livingston seek him out to get the formula? And if I *did* have a butler named Fish, wouldn't I kid the pants off him?

All over the world it is dusk! It is dusk at Armando's on East Fifty-fifth Street. Armando has taken up his accordion; he is dreaming over the keys. A girl comes in, attracted by the accordion, which she mistakes for Cecil Beaton's camera. She is in stiff green satin, and over it she wears a silver fox cape which she can pull around her shoulders later in the evening if she gets feeling like pulling a cape around her shoulders. It is dusk on the Harold Castles' ranch in Hawaii. I have risen early to shoot a goat, which is the smart thing to do in Hawaii. And now I am walking silently through hedges of gardenias, past the flaming ginger flowers, for I have just shot a goat. I have on nothing but red sandals and a Martex bath towel. It is dusk in the Laurentians. I am in ski togs. I feel warm and safe, knowing that the most dangerous pitfall for skiers is *color*, knowing that although a touch of brilliance against the snow is effective, too much of it is the sure sign of the amateur. It is the magic hour before cocktails. I am in the modern penthouse of Monsieur Charles de Beistegui. The staircase is entirely of cement, spreading at the hem-line and trimmed with padded satin tubing caught at the neck with a bar of milk chocolate. It is dusk in Chicago. I am standing beside Mrs. Howard Linn, formerly Consuelo Vanderbilt, formerly Sophie M. Gay, formerly Ellen Glendinning, formerly Saks–Fifth Avenue. It is dusk! A pheasant has Julian Street down and is pouring a magnificent old red Burgundy down his neck. Dreams, I'm afraid. It is really dusk in my own apartment. I am down on my knees in front of an airbound radiator, trying to fix it by sticking pins in the vent. Dusk in these fierce pajamas. Kneeling here, I can't help wondering where Nancy Yuille is, in her blue wool pants and reefer and her bright red mittens. For it is dusk. I said *dusk*, Wamba! Bring the quinine!

1934

E. B. WHITE

ACROSS THE STREET

AND INTO THE GRILL

THIS is my last and best and true and only meal, thought Mr. Pirnie as he descended at noon and swung east on the beat-up sidewalk of Forty-fifth Street. Just ahead of him was the girl from the reception desk. I am a little fleshed up around the crook of the elbow, thought Pirnie, but I commute good.

He quickened his step to overtake her and felt the pain again. What a stinking trade it is, he thought. But after what I've done to other assistant treasurers, I can't hate anybody. Sixteen deads, and I don't know how many possibles.

The girl was near enough now so he could smell her fresh receptiveness, and the lint in her hair. Her skin was light blue, like the sides of horses.

"I love you," he said, "and we are going to lunch together for the first and only time, and I love you very much."

"Hello, Mr. Pirnie," she said, overtaken. "Let's not think of anything."

A pair of fantails flew over from the sad old Guaranty Trust Company, their wings set for a landing. A lovely double, thought Pirnie, as he pulled. "Shall we go to the Hotel Biltmore, on Vanderbilt Avenue, which is merely a feeder lane for the great streets, or shall we go to Schrafft's, where my old friend Botticelli is captain of girls and where they have the mayonnaise in fiascos?"

"Let's go to Schrafft's," said the girl, low. "But first I must phone Mummy." She stepped into a public booth and dialled true and well, using her finger. Then she telephoned.

As they walked on, she smelled good. She smells good, thought Pirnie. But that's all right, I add good. And when we get to Schrafft's, I'll order from the menu, which I like very much indeed.

THEY entered the restaurant. The wind was still west, ruffling the edges of the cookies. In the elevator, Pirnie took the controls. "I'll run it," he said to the operator. "I checked out long ago." He stopped true at the third floor, and they stepped off into the men's grill.

"Good morning, my Assistant Treasurer," said Botticelli, coming forward with a fiasco in each hand. He nodded at the girl, who he knew was from the West Seventies and whom he desired.

"Can you drink the water here?" asked Pirnie. He had the fur trapper's eye and took in the room at a glance, noting that there was one empty table and three pretty waitresses.

Botticelli led the way to the table in the corner, where Pirnie's flanks would be covered.

"Alexanders," said Pirnie. "Eighty-six to one. The way Chris mixes them. Is this table all right, Daughter?"

Botticelli disappeared and returned soon, carrying the old Indian blanket.

"That's the same blanket, isn't it?" asked Pirnie.

"Yes. To keep the wind off," said the Captain, smiling from the backs of his eyes. "It's still west. It should bring the ducks in tomorrow, the chef thinks."

Mr. Pirnie and the girl from the reception desk crawled down under the table and pulled the Indian blanket over them so it was solid and good and covered them right. The girl put her hand on his wallet. It was cracked and old and held his commutation book. "We are having fun, aren't we?" she asked.

"Yes, Sister," he said.

"I have here the soft-shelled crabs, my Assistant Treasurer," said Botticelli. "And another fiasco of the 1926. This one is cold."

"Dee the soft-shelled crabs," said Pirnie from under the blanket. He put his arm around the receptionist good.

"Do you think we should have a green pokeweed salad?" she asked. "Or shall we not think of anything for a while?"

"We shall not think of anything for a while, and Botticelli would bring the pokeweed if there was any," said Pirnie. "It isn't the season." Then he spoke to the Captain. "Botticelli, do you remember when we took all the mailing envelopes from the stockroom, spit on the flaps, and then drank rubber cement till the foot soldiers arrived?"

"I remember, my Assistant Treasurer," said the Captain. It was a little joke they had.

"He used to mimeograph pretty good," said Pirnie to the girl. "But that was another war. Do I bore you, Mother?"

"Please keep telling me about your business experiences, but not the rough parts." She touched his hand where the knuckles were scarred and stained by so many old mimeographings. "Are both your flanks covered, my dearest?" she asked, plucking at the blanket. They felt the Alexanders in their eyeballs. Eighty-six to one.

"Schrafft's is a good place and we're having fun and I love you," Pirnie said. He took another swallow of the 1926, and it was a good and careful swallow. "The stockroom men were very brave," he said, "but it is a position where it is extremely difficult to stay alive. Just outside that room there is a little bare-faced highboy and it is in the way of the stuff that is being brought up. The hell with it. When you make a breakthrough, Daughter, first you clean out the baskets and the half-wits, and all the time they have the fire escapes taped. They also shell you with old production orders, many of them approved by the general manager in charge of sales. I am boring you and I will not at this time discuss the general manager in charge of sales as we are unquestionably being listened to by that waitress over there who is setting out the decoys."

"I am going to give you my piano," the girl said, "so that when you look at it you can think of me. It will be something between us."

"Call up and have them bring the piano to the restaurant," said Pirnie. "Another fiasco, Botticelli!"

They drank the sauce. When the piano came, it wouldn't play. The keys were stuck good. "Never mind, we'll leave it here, Cousin," said Pirnie.

THEY came out from under the blanket and Pirnie tipped their waitress exactly fifteen per cent minus withholding. They left the piano in the restaurant, and when they went down the elevator and out and turned in to the old, hard, beat-up pavement of Fifth Avenue and headed south toward Forty-fifth Street where the pigeons were, the air was as clean as your grandfather's howitzer. The wind was still west.

I commute good, thought Pirnie, looking at his watch. And he felt the old pain of going back to Scarsdale again.

1950

JOHN UPDIKE

ON THE SIDEWALK

(AFTER READING, AT LONG LAST,

"ON THE ROAD," BY JACK KEROUAC)

I WAS just thinking around in my sad backyard, looking at those little drab careless starshaped clumps of crabgrass and beautiful chunks of some old bicycle crying out without words of the American Noon and half a newspaper with an ad about a lotion for people with dry skins and dry souls, when my mother opened our frantic banging screendoor and shouted, "Gogi Himmelman's here." She might have shouted the

Archangel Gabriel was here, or Captain Easy or Baron Charlus in Proust's great book: Gogi Himmelman of the tattered old greenasgrass knickers and wild teeth and the vastiest, most vortical, most insatiable wonder-filled eyes I have ever known. "Let's go, Lee," he sang out, and I could see he looked sadder than ever, his nose all rubbed raw by a cheap handkerchief and a dreary Bandaid unravelling off his thumb. "I know the WAY!" That was Gogi's inimitable unintellectual method of putting it that he was on fire with the esoteric paradoxical Tao and there was no holding him when he was in that mood. I said, "I'm going, Mom," and she said, "O.K.," and when I looked back at her hesitant in the pearly mystical UnitedStateshome light I felt absolutely sad, thinking of all the times she had vacuumed the same carpets.

His scooter was out front, the selfsame, the nonpareil, with its paint scabbing off intricately and its scratchedon dirty words and its nuts and bolts chattering with fear, and I got my tricycle out of the garage, and he was off, his left foot kicking with that same insuperable energy or even better. I said, "Hey wait," and wondered if I could keep up and probably couldn't have if my beltbuckle hadn't got involved with his rear fender. This was IT. We scuttered down our drive and right over Mrs. Cacciatore's rock garden with the tiny castles made out of plaster that always made me sad when I looked at them alone. With Gogi it was different; he just kept right on going, his foot kicking with that delirious thirtyrevolutionsasecond frenzy, right over the top of the biggest, a Blenheim six feet tall at the turrets; and suddenly I saw it the way he saw it, embracing everything with his unfluctuating generosity, imbecile saint of our fudging age, a mad desperado in our Twentieth Century Northern Hemisphere Nirvana deserts.

We rattled on down through her iris bed and broke into the wide shimmering pavement. "Contemplate those holy hydrants," he shouted back at me through the wind. "Get a load of those petulant operable latches; catch the magic of those pickets standing up proud and sequential like the arguments in Immanuel Kant; boom, boom, bitty-boom BOOM!" and it was true.

"What happens when we're dead?" I asked.

"The infinite never-to-be-defiled subtlety of the late Big Sid Catlett on the hushed trap drums," he continued, mad with his own dreams, imitating the whisks, "Swish, swish, swishy-swish SWOOSH!"

The sun was breaking over the tops of Mr. Linderman's privet hedge, little rows of leaves set in there delicate and justso like mints in a Howard Johnson's roadside eatery. Mitzi Leggett came out of the house, and Gogi stopped the scooter, and put his hands on her. "The virginal starchblue fabric; printed with stylized kittens and puppies," Gogi explained in his curiously beseechingly transcendent accents. "The searing incredible *innocence!* Oh! Oh! Oh!" His eyes poured water down his face like broken blisters.

"Take me along," Mitzi said openly to me, right with Gogi there and hearing every word, alive to every meaning, his nervous essence making his freckles tremble like a field of Iowa windblown nochaff barley.

"I want to," I told her, and tried to, but I couldn't, not there. I didn't have the stomach for it. She pretended to care. She was a lovely beauty. I felt my spokes snap under me; Gogi was going again, his eyes tight-shut in ecstasy, his foot kicking so the hole in his shoesole showed every time, a tiny chronic rent in the iridescent miasmal veil that Intrinsic Mind tries to hide behind.

Wow! Dr. Fairweather's house came up on the left, delicious stucco like piecrust in the type of joints that attract truckers, and then the place of the beautiful Mrs. Mertz, with her *canny* deeprooted husband bringing up glorious heartbreaking tabourets and knickknacks from his workshop in the basement, a betooled woodshavingsmelling fantasy worthy of Bruegel or Hegel or a seagull. Vistas! Old Miss Hooper raced into her yard and made a grab for us, and Gogi Himmelman, the excruciating superbo, shifted to the other foot and laughed at her care-worn face. Then the breathless agape green space of the Princeling mansion, with its rich calm and potted Tropic of Cancer plants. Then it was over.

Gogi and I went limp at the corner under a sign saying ELM STREET with irony because all the elms had been cut down so they wouldn't get the blight, sad stumps diminishing down the American perspective whisperingly.

"My spokes are gone," I told him.

"Friend—ahem—*zip, zip*—parting a relative concept—Bergson's in-valuable marvelchocked work—tch, tch." He stood there, desperately wanting to do the right thing, yet always lacking with an indistinguish-able grandeur that petty ability.

"Go," I told him. He was already halfway back, a flurrying spark, to where Mitzi waited with irrepressible womanwarmth.

Well. In landsend despair I stood there stranded. Across the asphalt that was sufficiently semifluid to receive and embalm millions of star-sharp stones and bravely gay candywrappers a drugstore twinkled arti-ficial enticement. But I was not allowed to cross the street. I stood on the gray curb thinking, They said I could cross it when I grew up, but what do they mean grown up? I'm thirty-nine now, and felt sad.

1959

MIKE NICHOLS

SAVE MY SEAT

THERE is a still newer wave of films on its way from Italy. Here are some synopses, so that you can plan your weekends.

"THE OCCURRENCE"

Giovanna has lost her thimble. For the first two and three-quarters hours of the film, she and her friends look for it. In the final ten minutes, she is raped, and we are left with a sense of loss.

"The Occurrence" is the first film made by the cruel and talented Dominic Fabiani, and stars his good friend and constant companion Fabiana Dominici.

"CARLO AND HIS BROTHERS"

"Carlo and His Brothers" is the odyssey of Carlo and his brothers, Niccolo, Giacomo, Ottorino, Gioacchino, Giuseppe, Vittorio, Gaetano, Ruggiero, Cesare, and Pietro, who emigrate from the suburbs of Rome to midtown Rome. In the course of the conflicts brought about by the crude uprooting forced on them by the Industrial Revolution, Niccolo becomes deeply obsessed with Giulietta, who loves Ruggiero and Pietro. Gaetano marries Francesca, whose affair with Giuseppe has caused him heartlessly to leave Gina, who, in her bitterness, impulsively tells Cesare that Floria has been carrying on a liaison with Goldfine.

At the big family reunion, Antonietta, unable to contain her unhappiness, reveals her pregnancy. In their grief, the brothers visit the childlike Sylvana, who for all of them has been their only contact with the soil from which they have been uprooted. They rape her, and we are left with a sense of loss.

"Carlo and His Brothers" is the first film from the perverse and talented Penuche Marchesi, and stars his good friend and constant companion Gérard Durain.

"MOTHER AND DAUGHTER"

Gia and Maria, mother and daughter, walk the length of wartime Italy to present their last pair of stockings to the Pope. The stockings are lost in Torino, where they settle to look for them. After Torino is devastated by American bombs, Gia and Maria are raped by the Army, and we are left with a sense of loss.

This is the twenty-seventh film about war-torn Italy by the bitter and successful Carissimo De Vita; it stars his good friends and constant companions Lucia Vengerini and Patsy Harkness.

1961

WOODY ALLEN

HASSIDIC TALES, WITH A GUIDE

TO THEIR INTERPRETATION BY THE

NOTED SCHOLAR

A MAN journeyed to Chelm in order to seek the advice of Rabbi Ben Kaddish, the holiest of all ninth-century rabbis and perhaps the greatest *noodge* of the medieval era.

"Rabbi," the man asked, "where can I find peace?"

The Hassid surveyed him and said, "Quick, look behind you!"

The man turned around, and Rabbi Ben Kaddish smashed him in the back of the head with a candlestick. "Is that peaceful enough for you?" he chuckled, adjusting his *yarmulke.*

In this tale, a meaningless question is asked. Not only is the question meaningless but so is the man who journeys to Chelm to ask it. Not that he was so far away from Chelm to begin with, but why shouldn't he stay where he is? Why is he bothering Rabbi Ben Kaddish—the Rabbi doesn't have enough trouble? The truth is, the Rabbi's in over his head with gamblers, and he has also been named in a paternity case by a Mrs. Hecht. No, the point of this tale is that this man has nothing better to do with his time than journey around and get on people's nerves. For this, the Rabbi bashes his head in, which, according to the Torah, is one of the most subtle methods of showing concern. In a similar version of this tale, the Rabbi leaps on top of the man in a frenzy and carves the story of Ruth on his nose with a stylus.

RABBI RADITZ of Poland was a very short rabbi with a long beard, who was said to have inspired many pogroms with his sense of humor. One of his disciples asked, "Who did God like better—Moses or Abraham?"

"Abraham," the Zaddik said.

"But Moses led the Israelites to the Promised Land," said the disciple.

"All right, so Moses," the Zaddik answered.

"I understand, Rabbi. It was a stupid question."

"Not only that, but you're stupid, your wife's a *meeskeit,* and if you don't get off my foot you're excommunicated."

Here the Rabbi is asked to make a value judgment between Moses and Abraham. This is not an easy matter, particularly for a man who has never read the Bible and has been faking it. And what is meant by the hopelessly relative term "better"? What is "better" to the Rabbi is not necessarily "better" to his disciple. For instance, the Rabbi likes to sleep on his stomach. The disciple also likes to sleep on the Rabbi's stomach. The problem here is obvious. It should also be noted that to step on a rabbi's foot (as the disciple does in the tale) is a sin, according to the Torah, comparable to the fondling of matzos with any intent other than eating them.

A MAN who could not marry off his ugly daughter visited Rabbi Shimmel of Cracow. "My heart is heavy," he told the Rev, "because God has given me an ugly daughter."

"How ugly?" the Seer asked.

"If she were lying on a plate with a herring, you wouldn't be able to tell the difference."

The Seer of Cracow thought for a long time and finally asked, "What kind of herring?"

The man, taken aback by the query, thought quickly and said, "Er—Bismarck."

"Too bad," the Rabbi said. "If it was Maatjes, she'd have a better chance."

Here is a tale that illustrates the tragedy of transient qualities such as beauty. Does the girl actually resemble a herring? Why not? Have you seen some of the things walking around these days, particularly at resort areas? And even if she does, are not all creatures beautiful in God's eyes? Perhaps, but if a girl looks more at home in a jar of wine sauce than in an evening gown she's got big problems. Oddly enough, Rabbi Shimmel's own wife was said to resemble a squid, but this was only in the face, and she more than made up for it by her hacking cough—the point of which escapes me.

RABBI ZWI CHAIM YISROEL, an Orthodox scholar of the Torah and a man who developed whining to an art unheard of in the West, was unanimously hailed as the wisest man of the Renaissance by his fellow-Hebrews, who totalled a sixteenth of one per cent of the population. Once, while he was on his way to synagogue to celebrate the sacred Jewish holiday commemorating God's reneging on every promise, a woman stopped him and asked the following question: "Rabbi, why are we not allowed to eat pork?"

"We're *not?*" the Rev said incredulously. "Uh-oh."

This is one of the few stories in all Hassidic literature that deals with Hebrew law. The Rabbi knows he shouldn't eat pork; he doesn't care, though, because he *likes* pork. Not only does he like pork, he gets a kick out of rolling Easter eggs. In short, he cares very little about traditional Orthodoxy and regards God's covenant with Abraham as "just so much chin music." Why pork was proscribed by Hebraic law is still unclear, and some scholars believe that the Torah merely suggested not eating pork at certain restaurants.

RABBI BAUMEL, the scholar of Vitebsk, decided to embark on a fast to protest the unfair law prohibiting Russian Jews from wearing loafers outside the ghetto. For sixteen weeks, the holy man lay on a crude pallet, staring at the ceiling and refusing nourishment of any kind. His pupils feared for his life, and then one day a woman came to his bedside and, leaning down to the learned scholar, asked, "Rabbi, what color hair did Esther have?" The Rev turned weakly on his side and faced her. "Look what she picks to ask me!" he said. "You know what kind of a headache I got from sixteen weeks without a bite!" With that, the Rabbi's disciples escorted her personally into the *sukkah*, where she ate bounteously from the horn of plenty until she got the tab.

This is a subtle treatment of the problem of pride and vanity, and seems to imply that fasting is a big mistake. Particularly on an empty stomach. Man does not bring on his own unhappiness, and suffering is really God's will, although why He gets such a kick out of it is beyond me. Certain Orthodox tribes believe suffering is the only way to redeem oneself, and scholars write of a cult called the Essenes, who deliberately went around bumping into walls. God, according to the later books of Moses, is benevolent, although there are still a great many subjects he'd rather not go into.

RABBI YEKEL of Zans, who had the best diction in the world until a Gentile stole his resonant underwear, dreamed three nights running that if he would only journey to Vorki he would find a great treasure there. Bidding his wife and children goodbye, he set out on a trip, saying he would return in ten days. Two years later, he was found wandering the Urals and emotionally involved with a panda. Cold and starving, the Rev was taken back to his home, where he was revived with steaming soup and flanken. Following that, he was given something to eat. After dinner, he told this story: Three days out of Zans, he was set upon by wild nomads. When they learned he was a Jew, they forced him to alter all their sports jackets and take in their trousers. As if this were not humiliation enough, they put sour cream in his ears and sealed them with wax. Finally, the Rabbi escaped and headed for the nearest town, winding up in the Urals instead, because he was ashamed to ask directions.

After telling the story, the Rabbi rose and went into his bedroom to sleep, and, behold, under his pillow was the treasure that he originally sought. Ecstatic, he got down and thanked God. Three days later, he was back wandering in the Urals again, this time in a rabbit suit.

The above small masterpiece amply illustrates the absurdity of mysticism. The Rabbi dreams *three* straight nights. The Five Books of Moses subtracted from the Ten Commandments leaves five. Minus the brothers Jacob and Esau leaves *three*. It was reasoning like this that led Rabbi Yitzhok Ben Levi, the great Jewish mystic, to hit the double at Aqueduct fifty-two days running and still wind up on relief.

1970

HOWARD MOSS

THE ULTIMATE DIARY

(FURTHER DAILY JOTTINGS OF A CONTEMPORARY COMPOSER)

MONDAY

Drinks here. Picasso, Colette, the inevitable Cocteau, Gide, Valéry, Ravel, and Larry. Chitchat. God, how absolutely dull the Great can be! I know at least a hundred friends who would have given their eyeteeth just to have had a *glimpse* of some of them, and there I was bored, incredible lassitude, *stymied.* Is it me? Is it them? Think latter. Happened to glance in mirror before going to bed. Am more beautiful than ever.

TUESDAY

Horrible. After organ lesson at C's, he burst into tears and confessed that he loved me. Was mad about me, is how he put it. I was embarrassed. I respect him, he is a great *maître* and all that, but how could I reciprocate when I, myself, am so involved with L? I tried to explain.

He said he thought it would be better if we discontinued our lessons. How am I ever going to learn to play the organ? Came home upset. Finished *Barcarolles, Gigue, Danse Fantastique,* and *Cantata.* Writing better than ever. Careful of self-congratulations. So somebody said. John Donne? Fresh mushrooms. Delicious.

WEDNESDAY

Drunk at the dentist's. He removed a molar, and cried when I said it hurt. *Très gentil.* I think he has some feeling for me. The sky was like a red blister over the Dome. Streaks of carmine suffused the horizon. Sometimes I wonder if I shouldn't have been a writer. Drunk as I was, I caught a glimpse of myself in a bakery window. No wonder so many people love me!

THURSDAY

Arletty said something profound at lunch. "The trouble with homosexuals is that they like men." She sometimes gets to the heart of the matter with all her superficiality. She is leaving M. Talked and talked about it. I found my attention wandering, and kept seeing the unfinished pages of the *Symphony.* It is a great hymn to world peace, a kind of apotheosis of calmness, though it has a few fast sections. Drank a lot, and can't remember much after lunch. Woke up in Bois. Think something happened. But what? To relieve depression, dyed my hair again. Must say it looks ravishing. *Ravissant.*

FRIDAY

Calls from Mauriac and Claudel. Why don't they leave me alone?

FRIDAY, LATER

Larry back from Avignon. Seems changed. Felt vague feeling of disgust. To camouflage, worked all day and finished *Pavane, Song Cycles,* and *Sonata.* Dedicated latter—last?—to Princesse de N. She sent me a Russian egg for my name day. How know? Malraux, Auric, Poulenc, and Milhaud dropped by.

SATURDAY

Stravinsky angry with me, he said over phone. I must never stop working, working. What about sex? L has left. Should I call C? Thinking of it.

Press clippings arrived. Is there any other composer under seventeen whose works are being played in every capital of Asia? Matisse said, jokingly at lunch, that I was too beautiful to live. Genius is not a gift; it is a loan.

SATURDAY, LATER

At state banquet for de Gaulle, misbehaved. Slapped his wife in face during coffee. Drunk. Terribly depressed, but am I not also not a little proud? Contrite but haughty, sorry but pleased? Can't remember issue. Something about Monteverdi? Sent her a dozen white roses as apology. The Princesse says I should get out of town for a while. I WILL NOT RUN AWAY! C back. We are both more gorgeous than ever. Finished *War and Peace*. A good book.

SUNDAY

Pneumatique from Mallarmé. I will not answer. C and I had pique-nique. Fell asleep on Seine bank. Dream: Mother in hippopotamus cage, crying. She said, "If music be the feast . . ." and then gobbled up by crowd of angry deer. What mean? Shaken. C bought me drink at Deux Magots. Sweet. Told me he thought there had never been a handsomer man placed on this earth. Forced to agree, after catching tiny glimpse of myself in café window. How often are genius and beauty united? They will hate me when they read this diary, but I tell the truth. How many can say as much?

MONDAY

A name even *I* cannot mention. . . . And he wants me to spend the summer in Africa with him! C angry. Finished *Concerto Grosso* and *Hymn to the Moon*, for female voices. Something new, a kind of rough susurration, here and there, a darkening of strings. It is raining. Sometimes I think we are more ourselves in wet weather than in dry. Bought linen hat.

TUESDAY

Gertrude, Alice, James, Joyce, Henry Green, Virginia Woolf, Eliot, Laforgue, Mallarmé (all is forgiven!), Rimbaud's nephew, Claudel's niece, Mistinguett, Nadia, Marais, Nijinska, Gabin, and the usual for drinks. I did it with Y in the pantry while the party was going on! Ashamed but exhilarated. I think if THEY knew they would have approved. Finished *Sixty Piano Pieces for Young Fingers*. Potboiler. But one has to live!

WEDNESDAY

Snow. Hideous hangover. Will never drink again. Deli dinner with Henry Miller.

THURSDAY

Half the Opéra-Comique seems to have fallen in love with me. I cannot stand any more importuning. Will go to Africa. How to break with C? Simone de Beauvoir, Simone Signoret, Simone Weil, and Simone Simon for drinks. They didn't get it!

FRIDAY

C left. Am bruised but elated. Dentist. I was right. I wonder if he'll dare send me a bill. *Now,* I mean. Tea with Anaïs. *Enchantant.*

SATURDAY

René Char and Dior for lunch. Interesting. Clothes are the camouflage of the soul. Leave for Africa with X tomorrow. Had fifty tiny Martinis. Nothing happened.

SUNDAY

Barrault, Braque, Seurat, Mayakovski, Honegger, and René Clair saw us off. Very gala. I think I am really in love for the first time. I must say I looked marvellous. Many comments. Wore green yachting cap and cinnamon plus fours. Happy.

WEDNESDAY

Dakar: Tangled in mosquito netting. Getting nowhere with *Chanson d'Afrique.*

SATURDAY

Back in Paris. God, what a fool I've been! Someday I will write down the whole hideous, unbelievable story. Not now. Not when I am so close to it. But I will forget *nothing.* Leaving tonight for Princesse

de N's country place. Green trees, green leaves. The piercing but puri-
fying wind of Provence! Or is it Normandy? Packed all afternoon.
Long bath, many thoughts. Proust called. . . .

1975

MARSHALL BRICKMAN

_____

THE ANALYTIC NAPKIN

R ECENT work by Frimkin and Eliscu has brought to light valuable
new material about the origin and development of the analytic
napkin. It is not generally realized outside of psychoanalytic circles that
the placement by the analyst of a small square of absorbent paper at the
head of the analysand's chair or couch at the start of each session is a
ritual whose origins are rooted in the very beginnings of analysis, even
predating the discovery of infant sexuality. Indeed, references to a
"sticky problem" ("*eines Entführung bezitsung*") appear as early as 1886,
in a letter the young Freud wrote to his mentor Breuer:

> I am convinced that "hysterical symptoms," so-called, are nothing but
> the emergence of long-buried psycho-neurotic conflicts [*bezitsunger
> Entführung*]. Does that sound crazy? More important, how can I keep
> the back of the patient's chair from becoming so soiled [*ganz gesch-
> mutzig*]? They come in, they put their heads back—one week and al-
> ready my upholstery has a spot the size of a *Sacher Tarte*.
>
> *With warm regards, Freud*

Breuer's reply is not known, of course, because of the curious manner
in which he conducted his correspondence. (Breuer was unreasonably
afraid that samples of his handwriting might fall into the hands of his
"many powerful enemies;" therefore, upon receiving a letter, he would
carefully draft a reply, take it to the addressee's home, read it aloud to
him, and then tear it to shreds. He claimed that this behavior saved him
a fortune in postage, although Mrs. Breuer opined that her husband's

head was lined with "wall-to-wall kugel.") Breuer's only public statement on the napkin question was made during a demonstration of hypnosis, when he remarked that "a patient in a trance can be induced to stand on his feet for an entire treatment and never know the difference."

It is perhaps ironic—or, as Ernest Jones put it, "not ironic at all"—that the napkin problem should have emerged at a time when the antimacassar was attaining universal acceptance by the East European intelligentsia. Freud, however, abhorred simplistic solutions, and sought more profound answers. Failing to find these, he sought more complicated questions. In any event, he rejected the use of antimacassars as "Victorian, confining, and repressive—everything I am fighting against. Besides, they are too bumpy." The extent of the problem, however, can be inferred from a perusal of Freud's professional expenses incurred for April, 1886, his first month of private practice:

WAITING ROOM
    3 coat hooks @ 5 kreuzer . . . . .15 kr.
    2 chairs @ 20 gulden . . . . .40 fl.
    1 ashtray . . . . .8 kr.
    16 issues *Viennese Life* magazine, 1861–77 period . . . . .2 fl., 8 kr.
    1 framed Turner reproduction, "Cows in a Field" . . . . .16 fl.
CONSULTING ROOM
    3 doz. medium-hard pencils . . . . .18 kr.
    9 writing tablets, unlined, in "easy-eye green" . . . . .2 fl., 14 kr.
    Certificates & diplomas, framing and mounting . . . . .7 fl.
    "Complete Works of Goethe" (18 vols.) . . . . .40 fl.
    "Works of Nietzsche" (abridged, 20 vols.) . . . . .34 fl.
    "Simple Card Tricks You Can Do" (pocket edition) . . . . . . .20 kr.
    1 clock . . . . .8 fl.
    Dry-cleaning and spotting upholstery . . . . .240 fl.

"At this rate," Freud wrote to Koller, "every neurasthenic I treat this year should set me back in the neighborhood of four hundred gulden. Pretty soon, *I'll* be needing some treatment, eh? Ha, ha." On the advice of Charcot, Freud had his housekeeper apply a solution of nux vomica and lye to his consulting chair after each session—a remedy that was hastily abandoned when a patient, Theo F., brought a legal complaint of massive hair loss directly traceable to consultations with the young neurologist. Freud managed to mollify the unfortunate man with a sampler of marzipan and a warm fur hat, but his reputation in Vienna had been shaken.

THE early practitioners of psychoanalysis devised artful stopgap solutions to the problem of the napkin. For a time, Jung met his patients at a furniture store, where, under the pretext of inspecting a couch, he would conduct an analytic session. After fifty minutes, patient and doctor would depart, Jung explaining to the salesman that they wanted to "shop around a little more." By contrast, Ferenczi required his patients to lie face down on the consulting couch—a procedure that eliminated all stains but a small nose smudge. However, the patients' constant mumblings into the upholstery caused Ferenczi to become enraged, and he finally abandoned this technique. Klein, claiming that he was only trying to "lighten up" what was "an already dreary enough business," asked his patients to wear cone-shaped party hats during their session hours. The real reason, of course, was to protect Klein's couch, a flamboyant chesterfield covered in pale-lemon bombazine.

Freud launched his own systematic research program by scouring Vienna for fabric samples, which he placed on the upper portion of his couch, a different sample being assigned to each patient. One case, that of a man who was analyzed on a folded barbecue apron, became the subject of an extended monograph of Freud's on hallucinations and hysteria. The apron had been presented to Freud by Charcot, and bore the legend "*König von die Küche*" ("King of the Kitchen"). An apparently severe olfactory hallucination (old cabbage) reported by the patient during his analysis eventually proved to have its source in the apron, and Freud was forced to withdraw his paper. To conceal his disappointment, he invited the man to a coffeehouse, but at the last moment changed his mind and instead sent Adler to meet him. Unfortunately, Adler became distracted in the process of flattening kreuzer on the trolley tracks and arrived a day late. (This episode was often referred to sarcastically by Freud, and provided the basis for the later break between him and Adler.)

In a series of unattended lectures (May, 1906), Freud crystallized the need for a resolution of the "sofa problem," as he termed it. "Something small and protective, yet flexible," he wrote in his notes, "ought to be placed beneath (or possibly wrapped around) the patient's head. Perhaps a small rug or some sort of cloth." It was several decades before the notion of a napkin would surface, but during a summer visit to Manchester, England, during which Freud presented his half sister with a bookend, he purchased a bolt of Japanese silk, which he sent to Vienna and caused to be cut up into small squares. The new material seemed to be working admirably, until an unexpected occurrence shattered his illusions. From his notebook:

> October 8. Especially crisp fall day. Treating Otto P., a petty official of the Bureau of Wursts. Classic psycho-neurosis: inability either to go to sleep or remain awake. Patient, while recounting significant dream, thrashed about on the couch. Because of the extremely cool climate, extensive static electricity caused the silk to cling to the patient's hair when he rose to leave at the end of the session. Analytic propriety, plus the delicacy of the transference, prevented me from mentioning the situation and I merely bade him good day.

Upon reaching home, Otto P. was mortified to find a square of cloth adhering to the back of his head, and he publicly accused Freud of insensitiveness and willful japery. An anti-Semitic journalist claimed that Freud had attempted to impose his own ethnic customs on a patient. The outcry raged for months, severely taxing Freud's energies, and only after it had abated could he enter in his journal, with wry insight: "Clearly, silk is not the answer—unless perhaps it is first dampened."

Freud's tentative moves in the direction of an all-purpose analytic napkin inspired others to ponder the matter. At the Weimar Congress, Bleuler called for a standardization of napkin technique. A lively debate ensued, with a variety of shapes, sizes, and materials finding ready champions. Abraham favored classical antimacassars, while Jung was partial to jute placemats, which he imported from a private source in Africa. The purist Holtz (it was he who in 1935 criticized Freud for not being Freudian enough) ridiculed the whole notion of a napkin and advocated "six couches, to be changed daily, like underwear." Liebner, who detested Holtz, suggested that the material of the napkin vary with the patient's complaint; Freud then recalled that he had had no success in treating the celebrated "Wolf Man" until he tried a scrap of terry cloth, to which the patient developed a massive transference. In a culminating speech at Weimar, Freud outlined his vision of the ideal solution: "Hygienic, disposable, inexpensive, and without any referential value whatsoever. I dream of a totally affect-less napkin that every analyst can afford."

Freud's experimental early napkins (many of which are still in private collections) show this drive toward simplicity and clarity—swatches of wool, gabardine, madras, burlap, and unbleached muslin, and, finally, a double layer of cheesecloth. He was making notes on the use of blotting paper when the Anschluss forced him to leave for London. Later that week in Vienna, the Nazis publicly burned most of his napkin file, including an irreplaceable sampler knitted by Lionel Walter, the Baron Rothschild.

The enormous current popularity of psychoanalysis in the United States is easily explained by the napkin historian. American technological know-how, plus the easy availability of materials, provided the answer Freud and his early disciples searched for but never found. In 1946, after extensive research at Mount Sinai Hospital, a team of pillow scientists at the Kimberly-Clark paper company test-marketed a prototype napkin in the analytic communities of Boston, New York, and Los Angeles. It was a double-ply, semiabsorbent, bleached-wood-fibre product, with a forty-per-cent rag content and an embossed edge. The response was overwhelming, and the course of psychoanalysis was forever altered. As Dr. Neimann Fek said, expressing the gratitude of his colleagues, "It took seventy years before we perfected the beard and the fee. Now, finally, the napkin. No one need ever be crazy again."

1975

MARSHALL BRICKMAN

WHO'S WHO IN THE CAST

ANTHONY MOON (Zeckendorf) was born in England and attended Eton, Wibley, and Miss Gobbett's Academy, concluding his formal education at St. Vitus's College, Oxford, where he studied *moue* under the brilliant House Beamish. His first professional job was as Obadiah in the revue *A Pound of Cheese*, which ran for fifteen years at the Wee-Theatre-in-the-Bog, breaking all records for the West End and closing only when the cast set fire to the scenery. After joining the National Theatre, Mr. Moon was acclaimed for his performances as Rosalind in *As You Like It*, Monroe Parch in *Parsippany Place*, and Sir Giggling Fatbody in Sheridan's *The Wind-Sucker*. Mr. Moon is the author of *A Penn'orth of Rumply*, a fantasy for "children of all ages" based on the limericks of Albert Speer, which is currently in preparation for the 1977 season. His autobiography, *Scones at Eventide,* was a best-seller and will be filmed by the Rank Organisation, featuring Colin Ponce and Colin Headstrong-Jones as the twin bakers.

MISHRU FEK (Curley) in a long and distinguished theatrical career has appeared in over three thousand productions, from Second Avenue cabaret (*Don't Make Me Laugh, So Who Are You Kidding?, I'm Entitled,* and *You Should Live So Long*) to regional theatre (Chaim in *The Wild Mouse,* Vontz in *Crusts*) to Broadway, where he triumphed last season as the grief-stricken father in *Runteleh,* the Pulitzer Prize–winning musical drawn from the life of Eddie Carmel, the Jewish giant. In recent years, Mr. Fek has divided his time between *King Lear* ("twice a year, rain or shine") and Hollywood; his latest films include *Blood of the Face Eaters, Nostril from Outer Space,* and *Monster Beach Party.* His television credits include numerous specials, notably an abbreviated version of *Runteleh,* for which he won the coveted Emmeleh. The Department of State has engaged Mr. Fek to tour Europe with his phenomenal one-man show *Jews in Motion,* an entertainment based on the *responsa* of Chodish, the skating rabbi of Budapest.

MARY BETH NUMKINS (Nell Runcible) is a self-professed "stage kook" who has appeared in stock and regional theatre. Among her favorite roles are Molly in *Tom O'Monahoon's Chowder,* Sally in *The Misty Bog,* Wendy in *The Bosky Feu,* Peggy in *The Dusky Glen,* and Polly in *Poppa's Pockmark.* She appeared as Princess Tinkle-Beam in *Toast and Mrs. Toast* and won plaudits for her portrayal of the shepherdess in *The Bleat of My Heart.* She maintains that the theatre is a "special, magical place, made of fairy-webs and gossamer." She lives in New York City with her cat, Mister Cat, and a large colored man.

RAMON PELIGROSO (Parson Anders, Ziggy) was last seen in the role of the psychotic barber in *Don't Nobody Gonna Whup My Face,* presented last season at the Drainpipe Theatre. In addition, Mr. Peligroso has appeared as the addict in *No Horse for Handkerchief-Heads* and the sadistic orderly in *Enema.* He created the role of Goatberry Jones in the national company of *Harlan Peachtree's Massive Apparatus,* for which he won the Frobischer Award. His autobiographical play, *The Repositude of Naphthalene Catfish,* was presented last season by the Militant Playhouse.

LYDIA BUNTING (Mrs. Peahen) made her theatrical debut thirty years ago in Tennessee Williams' *For the Safety of the Passengers, the Driver Is Not Permitted to Change Any Bills Larger Than Five Dollars,* playing the harelip to Luther Dabchick's waterhead. After a hiatus of twenty-eight years, she returned to Broadway last season in the revival of *Perfervid Desires,* which closed during the first act, although the critics were unanimous about her performance. This marks Miss Bunting's first appearance in the legitimate theatre without a mobcap.

RENÉ CATAFALQUE (Beggars, Whores, Townspeople)

> To act is to be;
> To be is merely to seem.
> The truth is a hat.
> —HANS EKHARDT

O'BOB MACVOUT (Director) trained at L.A.M.D.A. and the Yale Drama School under Fleming Pease, directing revue and cabaret (*Redoubtable Antics of '62, Arty-Tarty*). After a spell in television, he directed the wildly successful nature film *Ring of Bright Beavers* ("Vapid family fun! Non-threatening!"—L.A. *Times*), which grossed six hundred million dollars worldwide and won him three Oscars, two Patsys, and the Distinguished Flying Cross. Last season he directed Sir Henry Wolfsbane in the highly acclaimed R.S.C. production of Congreve's *Pox; or, The Traducer Traduced,* which won both the Drama Circle Critics Citation Prize Award and the Award Circle Drama Critics Prize Citation.

LEON MATRIX (Sets and Lighting) is one of our most versatile designers, whose work ranges from the long-running *Leafy Green Vegetables* to the costumes for *Mary's Nose.* Trained under Schlemmer and Gropius, he did pioneering work at both the Bauhaus and the Bau-wau-haus, the avant-garde Theatre for Hounds he designed for Piscator in Berlin. More recently, he won the rarely awarded Mortimer for *Roach!,* the musical version of Kafka's *Metamorphosis,* which will be presented on Broadway every season by David Merrick. He is four feet tall.

ARNOLD BATFISH (Author) spent several years as an advertising copy-writer and burst upon the theatrical scene with a cathartic evening of one-acters: *Spearmint, Doublemint,* and *Excremint,* which won him both a Nudlicer and a Peavy. His dental trilogy, *Drill, Fill,* and *Rinse, Please,* was hailed as the finest American dental writing in fifty years and was compared to Gogol's *The Overbite* and Sophocles' *Oedipus in Pyorrhea.* Mr. Batfish resides with his wife, Laura, and her wife, Leslie, at Nutmeat College, North Carolina, where he holds the Robert Goulet Chair of Dramaturgy.

AHMET ERGOTAMINE (Producer) has been represented on Broadway by *Goodbye, My Toes* and the smash hit musical *Morons Over Manhattan,* currently in its third season. In association with Max Rubric he produced *The Man in the Paper Pants* and *The Smell of Shapiro* for the Colloid Center Theatre Group in Los Angeles. Mr. Ergotamine's reputation as a promotional genius dates from 1950, when he employed a chimpanzee in a miter to unicycle through the theatre district to publicize his knockabout religious farce, *Bishopzapoppin!* His innovative all-black production of *The Dance of Death* was followed by an equally successful all-male-Pakistani *Riders to the Sea* and an all-parrot *Importance of Being Earnest.* Next spring, he will produce *Death of a Salesman* in New Orleans with everyone (cast and audience) wearing giant papier-mâché Mardi Gras heads, borrowed from the Grand Krewe of the Knights of Toulouse.

1976

DANIEL MENAKER

HEALTH DEPARTMENT LISTS

RESTAURANT VIOLATIONS

SEPTEMBER 27—The New York City Health Department has cited the following restaurants, food shops, and other eating places for violations of the health code:

P. J. Murphy's, 1100 Second Avenue: early-seventies jukebox.

Au Contraire Restaurant, 79 East 54th Street: gross disproportion of foundation executives among clientele.

Tyrone X. Shabazz Nation of Islam Cafeteria, 79 West 148th Street: reverse-quota seating.

Joe's Spot Food Shop, 987 Amsterdam Avenue: abandoned automobile in kitchen.

Gang of Four Shanghai Restaurant, 37 Mott Street: makes hungry where most it satisfies.

One Man's Meat Antivegetarian Restaurant, 34–56¼ Flatbush Avenue, Brooklyn: trace elements of soybean extender in chopped round steak.

Zoom 'n' Dolly Avant-Garde Triplex Theatre Candy Stand, 9 Greenwich Avenue (third-floor hallway): no Jujubes.

Jekyll's Deli, 10 East 7th Street: dropping rodents.

The Upper Crust Penthouse Restaurant, 665 Fifth Avenue: overt ridiculing of tip.

Let's Eat Right to Get Off Health Food Café, 37 St. Marks Place: undernourished waiters.

Sauce for the Moose Alaskan Hideaway, Jerome Avenue and 210th Street: fused after-dinner mints.

VIOLATIONS CORRECTED

Mi-Mi-Mi Opera Café, 49 West 66th Street: "I Loves You, Porgy" dropped from singing waiters' repertoire.

Nadine's Bigshot Hangout, Third Avenue and 89th Street: Tongsun Park barred from premises.

INSPECTOR VANISHED

Punch Bowl S&M Diner, 294 11th Avenue.

1977

CHARLES McGRATH

THE DELTS OF VENUS

(SELECTIONS FROM ANOTHER VOLUME

OF EARLY WRITINGS BY ANISE NUN)

PREFACE

Gomez told me about the Collector. I was living in Paris, finishing up the eleventh installment of my memoirs of infantile sexuality, and I was so poor that for days on end I ate nothing but string and leaves. Gomez said that the Collector would pay a dollar a page for stories about sport.

"Well," I said, "we know a little about sport, eh, Gomez?"

What else was I to do? Arnold needed cash for some dental work, Helga needed wallpaper for her garret, and Lazlo wanted to hire a dozen convent girls for his experimental film. So Gomez told me the story of the Stewardess and the Swedish National Track Team, and I wrote it up for the Collector. A day or two later, the Collector called me on the telephone. "More action," he said. "Leave out that sex stuff and just give me the sport."

I swore that never again would I work for a man so cold and unfeeling—so insensitive to the true sport of love—but Arnold wanted money for opium, Helga's cat needed an operation, and Lazlo wanted to buy a dozen see-through middy blouses. Swallowing my pride, I wrote for the Collector the stories published here.

— ANISE NUN

EUGÉNIE AND THE BARON

When Eugénie awoke, it was late in the afternoon, the draperies were drawn, and the Baron was sitting in a velvet-covered chaise, smoking and regarding her coldly. He was wearing a soft peaked cap and a loosely cut suit of fine striped flannel, and his eyes had the fixed, hypnotic gaze of an animal, or of a man who has not slept for several months. There were furs on the floor, exotic plants in the window, and a replica of the American League pennant of 1975 hung from the ceiling.

When the Baron saw Eugénie begin to stir, he crushed out his cigarette, strode over to the bed, and pulled back the sheets. "Here, put this on," he said, handing her a catcher's mask. "And this, too." He slipped a chest protector over her chemise and began fastening the straps in back. Eugénie felt his warm breath on her shoulder and she quivered involuntarily. He smelled of stale popcorn.

"That's too tight," she said. Her skin was very sensitive, and she was afraid the leather would give her an equipment rash.

"They'll work themselves loose," the Baron said hoarsely, and then he held the mitt out to her. It was huge and fat, laced at the bottom, and had a deep, soft pocket. Burned into it were the words "Official Yogi Berra."

"Please," Eugénie said. "I don't feel like it right now."

The Baron said nothing but led her out into the long hallway and motioned for her to crouch. "Just give me a target," he whispered. "Give me a good target."

The Baron paced off sixty and one-half feet along the carpet, then turned and—softly at first, then faster and harder—began throwing to Eugénie a hard white ball, which she caught, reluctantly, and tossed back to him. After a while a light sweat broke out on the Baron's forehead, and Eugénie could hear him begin to breathe heavily. The throws came even faster now, and the ball began to move curiously, shooting down and to the inside, or else at times seeming to pause a moment and then soaring up and away. Eugénie was still tense and uncertain, but the shape of the Baron's leg, as he kicked it toward the ceiling just before delivery, was so graceful and the arc of the ball as it spun and curved through the air was so vivid and poignant that she felt a part of herself begin to thaw. Her left hand, inside the dark, odorous mitt, grew warm and then began to tingle with a kind of delicious pain, and, without entirely willing it, Eugénie found herself calling out, "Hum, baby, hum. Atta boy. No batter, no batter. Way to go, way to go, *babe!*"

MARIE

Marie had fallen into a way of life that caused her family and relatives to disown her. She lived above an all-night lanes in Montparnasse, and she liked to bowl for money. Her father, who was dying of consumption, prevailed on her to change her habits, and he obtained for Marie a position as a governess in a large house on the Rue Victor-Massé. The work was not arduous—it consisted simply of caring for a small boy named Pierre and wearing sheer black stockings and a garter belt so intricate that only the Master knew how to fasten it—but Marie soon grew restless. At night she had difficulty sleeping, and thrashed in bed for hours, practicing her four-step approach and her body English.

At last Marie could bear this state of craving no more, and early one morning, before the sun was up and while the rest of the house was still asleep, she stole into Pierre's room and gently shook him awake. "Pierre, darling, I have a surprise for you," she said softly, full of self-loathing and yet unable to help herself. "Something very nice."

She helped the boy off with his pajamas—his skin, as she allowed her hands to linger over it, was smooth and almost unnaturally cool, like the finish on a duckpin—and she dressed him in powder-blue Sans-a-Belt slacks and an open-collared satin shirt with the words "Café Joe" embroidered on the back.

"What a lovely boy you are!" said Marie. Breathlessly, she handed him a bowling ball. "Roll it," she whispered. "Let me see you roll it."

Pierre looked at her questioningly, and a faint blush came to his cheeks.

"Surely you must have bowled before," said Marie. "Perhaps with one of your little chums?"

"No," said the boy timidly.

"A big strong boy like you? Never been bowling? I don't believe it."

"No, really," said Pierre.

"But you know how, don't you?" Marie said gently. "Haven't the boys in school told you how?"

Pierre nodded shyly.

"Well, then!" Marie laughed. "Now I will teach you some things they *didn't* tell you. I will teach you some things even Papa doesn't know!"

Arranging ten of Pierre's lead soldiers in a triangle on the nursery floor, Marie showed the boy how to make the 4–10 split, how to handle the groove in a worn-down lane, and how to put a duck hook on the ball so that it slammed into the pocket from the Brooklyn side. "There!" she said, her bosom heaving. "Now you try, and if you're a very nice boy I'll tell you about Bowling for Francs."

MATHILDE, GEORG, AND THE KNICKS

Mathilde was young, wealthy, and very beautiful—she had many lovers—but she had never been to see the Knicks. The one man she wished to share this experience with, a tall Hungarian named Georg, for many weeks refused to oblige her. Finally, he yielded to her entreaties, and on a soft, rainy evening in March they took the A train together to Madison Square Garden, to catch the Knicks and SuperSonics.

The game proved to be all that Mathilde had hoped, with the Knicks jumping away to an early lead on three dazzling picks by Bob McAdoo, and before the end of the first quarter she had grown feverish with excitement. Her lips were moist, hoarse cries issued from her throat, and at crucial free throws her hand unconsciously sought out Georg's. Mathilde then understood why so many men refused to introduce their lovers to the Knicks: they feared awakening in them an insatiable passion. Georg, however, was behaving very strangely, almost as if he were afraid of her ardor, and in the last quarter she noticed that his eyes were tightly shut. On their way home in a cab after the game, Georg sighed and told Mathilde this story:

"When I was fourteen, and still innocent, my family lived in a dangerously overheated apartment in Budapest, which had a great many balconies. I was bored, with nothing to do but wander aimlessly back and forth from one balcony to the next, and one afternoon when I was doing this I noticed a woman shooting baskets across the courtyard. She was wearing filmy black knee socks, boxer shorts, and a halter made of feathers, and she was tossing two-handed jumpers into a basket that had been attached to a marble column. I felt sure she knew she was being watched, but she gave no sign; instead, she tried more and more difficult shots: hooks, driving layups, double pumps, and even a behind-the-back slam dunk. Observing her gave me the most intense pleasure imaginable. 'She must think I'm a scout,' I murmured to myself.

"The next day, I went out on the balcony carrying a clipboard and binoculars and wearing a whistle around my neck. As if by magic, the woman appeared again, clothed this time in a sweatsuit of diaphanous gauze, and rewarded me with a display of shot-making worthy of the great Doctor J himself. These scenes continued every day for more than a week, and then one morning when I stepped out onto my balcony I saw that the basket had been torn down and the woman's windows boarded up. My father had found out, you see. That evening, he sent me to my room for three years."

"Oh, poor darling," Mathilde said, covering Georg with kisses. "And you never saw the woman again?"

"Worse than that," Georg said, blushing furiously. "The truth is, I can take no pleasure in the Knicks unless I watch them with my binoculars on the television set of the doorman in the lobby across the street."

YVONNE, GISÈLE, THE BASQUE, AND THE CUBAN

It was a languid, febrile afternoon, and the Basque stirred with euphoria and anticipation. It seemed to him as he hurried along the Rue de Rivoli that all over Paris there were raised enclosures fenced with chicken wire, where people cavorted wantonly, and that every man he passed was carrying, like himself, a pair of sneaks and a dark wooden paddle suggestively perforated.

The Basque met Gisèle in the doorway of the English bookstore (she was wearing white fur warmups and a pair of extremely low-cut Adidas), and together they ascended the stairs that led to the rooftop. "My husband almost found us out," Gisèle whispered to the Basque, trembling and pressing herself against him. "He asked where I was going dressed up like this, and I told him I was just popping out for some absinthe."

"We will make it fast," said the Basque. "Who are our opponents today?"

"There's Yvonne, who was a friend of mine at school," said Gisèle. "She has mastered many unusual strokes, and you will like her very much, I know. And then the Cuban. I have never met him, but it is said he possesses a top-spin backhand taught to him by André Gide himself."

When Gisèle and the Basque came out on the roof, Yvonne and the Cuban were already on the court. They were dressed in identical silk kimonos, but the Cuban was also remarkable for his completely shaven head, which glistened in the Parisian sun. The Basque felt a sensual tremor of fear, a primitive dark anxiety. Quickly he said, "*Alors*, shall we warm up?"

They began rallying, and in the frenzy of their exertions the Basque soon forgot himself. His eyes grew brilliant, and his paddle threw off sparks whenever it nicked the wire. He lunged back and forth, attacking and retrieving, and even the caressing wind seemed to burn the heated flesh of his bare torso. He moved to the net, he moved to the baseline, and now he was climbing to the very top of the back fence to pick off a tricky lob. His fall, when it came, was greater than any he had ever known, because he had ventured so far into the game and had abandoned himself to it. He lay on the court for a moment, spent and shuddering, and then, half sobbing, half laughing, he called out to the Cuban, "All right—serve it up!"

Gisèle and the Basque won the first three sets, 6–2, 6–4, 6–3. Then they changed partners.

1978

NOTES FROM THE EDGE CONFERENCE

LeFEBVRE, opening remarks:
Don't know all there is to know about edge. Do know: Misconceptions abound. Fixed? No. Plottable? No. Like line on map, where important things lie on either side? No.

"Sometimes my edge is a round edge." Now tongue, now groove.

Edge, as in: Lip. Verge. Pungency. To sidle. Advantage. "Near bound of nerves' end, inside of out."

(Mutterings.)

Registration packets: Should have been plenty. Ppl. who took more than one should return same.

•

Armentout, "Edges and Hedges: Things That Get in the Way":

Ppl. say, "I want to live out there close to the edge. But I don't want to look funny."

Cf. Gary Busey. Look at him first time: "Damn, no *way* that man can be a star." But: "Sure, the man looks funny at first—anybody they thought of to play Buddy Holly had to look a little funny right off. But next thing you know, hey, he's *out* there." *Beyond* a star. Where it is. Raising hell in the social notes. "Jumping into people's sets, man."

•

Hully, Perl, Tibbett Panel, "Getting Words in Edgewise":

"Outfit" self for E.? (Figurative goose down, asbestos.) Whole industry growing up. But is to gear for it to be not out close to it? Or to . . . temper it? Perhaps.

Out on E. for its own sake, or should we wait until propelled there by just cause? Hard question. Finally unanswerable.

Diff. ppl. higher/lower threshold of E.?

"I mean, I'll start a sentence sometimes and halfway have to stop— *skreek!*—not on the edge anymore. But the first half . . ."

"Would you be interested in approaching the edge again, possibly in a more definitive manner?"

"Well . . ."

"Or a less definitive one?"

"Ah!"

Diff. cultures, diff. E.s. Navaho: Whole notion of edge as maze. (Maize?)

•

Out on E., as compared to "hip":

Rohle: "Yeah, but whoever heard of 'The Razor's Hip'?"

Many ppl. hip. Well, to be fair, not *many*—not untold numbers. More aren't.

Basic point of hip: Certain people know you know what. "You know, it's a *social* thing."

Hip: Pick up on yet unassimilated Black English. "Come on over to the crib and we'll . . ." "This johnson." Call everything a "johnson."

For some ppl., hip not enough.

•

Van Roud II, on Loss of E.:

"Suddenly this sinking sensation. Put a foot out one way, and . . . solid ground.

"Put it out the other way, and . . . solid ground.

"I was in some kind of Kansas of the mind—Sunday afternoon of the soul. I said, 'Whoa, get back.' I was *upset*."

•

Stapenink, "Lines: Toward a Definition":

Where does closeness to E. begin? Is there fine line separating area within which one may be said to be out close to E. from area within which one may be said to be cut off from E.? In that case: Does E. have an e.?

That line past which being close to E. begins. Greater value in being on that line? On edge of that line?

E. an absolute, or gradations? Sort of close to E. Really really close to E. Marginally barely close to E. Nearly close to E.

(Grumblings.)

•

During mixer, overheard:

"My friend and I were talking. I'm saying like who is your best rock star and who is your best this star and that star and it hits us, all our best ones like live out near the edge. And we're talking you know and I go, 'That's why you like me. I'm out near the edge.'

"And he goes like he's not believing me, he goes, 'Yeah?'

"I go, 'Yeah.'

" 'So what's it look like over there?' he goes.

"I go, 'You put your toes out over it and look out and down and you feel something pressing up evenly on each one of your toes, toe toe toe toe toe, and you see somebody looking out and up at you.' Because—

"And I don't know what hit him, he goes like '*Yeah!* Oh, *yeah!* Oh *yeah*, Lori! Sure, Lori!' and goes out and rents this motel room somewhere and tears it up."

.

"Seeing the Humor of It"—Dr. Ardis Wickwire:

"How you like yr. edge?" "Which first, chicken or edge?" "Big butter and edge man."

Ha.

.

Grosjean, Three types *not* near edge:

(1) Don't know where edge is, never will. Don't even know what direction it's in. (Voice: "That's cool.")

(2) Grew up along the edge, or had one or more parents who were out close to it or named them something like Guava, and now want to spend their adult lives getting far from edges as possible. Beer on table, some art on walls that don't mess over their relaxation, nobody after them with knife. (Voice: "That's cool.")

(3) Don't believe there even *is* an edge. So-called "Round-Earthers." (Voice: "All *right!*")

.

Overheard conversation of electricians outside conf. rm.:

"Christ, my mom is dying and getting this S.S.I. Supplemental Security Income. You can only have fifteen hundred in the bank, so we took the rest of it out for her, put it in the house, and Christ the money come pouring in. For my mom, fine, but Christ how about all these guys who *won't* work. There's a limit. There's a limit. It's the middle-income guy—fifteen, eighteen, twenty thou, and you and me are paying for it. Christ my mom is dying and getting this S.S.I. . . . ."

(Poss. paper for next year: "Middle-Edge Spread"?)

•

Crits. of conf.:

(1) Missed most fundamental point.
(2) What those splotches up on Vu-Graph?
     a. Finger smudges
     b. Insect matter
     c. Eyesight
     d. Weren't any
(3) Same old crowd running.
(4) Ppl. screaming in ppl.'s ears.
(5) Should have been more registration packets. And more in them.
(6) Not out close to E.

•

LeFebvre, closing:
     Always "same old crowd running things," because when something
has to be done you find out pretty quickly there are only a few people
you can call on.
     Cutting/leading E. dichotomy? "So fine, can only be palped by sur-
prise."
     (Boos.)
     Banquet, installation new officers 8:30 in Ballroom C. (Thing of
throwing food: "Just obnoxious.")
     Proposals for new award categories *must* be in Sept. 1.

                                                        1979

LGA·ORD

Then, Beckett decided to become a commercial pilot . . .

"I think the next little bit of excitement is flying," he wrote to McGreevy. "I hope I am not too old to take it up seriously nor too stupid about machines to qualify as a commercial pilot."

—*"Samuel Beckett," by Deirdre Bair.*

GRAY bleak final afternoon ladies and gentlemen this is your captain your cap welcoming you aboard the continuation of Flyways flight 185 from nothingness to New York's Laguardia non non non non non non nonstop to Chicago's Ohare and on from there in the passing of gray afternoons to empty bleak eternal nothingness again with the Carey bus the credit-card machine the Friskem metal detector the boarding pass the in-flight magazine all returned to tiny bits of grit blowing across the steppe for ever

(Pause)

Cruising along nicely now.

(Pause)

Yes cruising along very nicely indeed if I do say so myself.

(Long pause)

Twenty-two thousand feet.

(Pause)

Extinguish the light extinguish the light I have extinguished the No Smoking light so you are free to move about the cabin have a good cry hang yourselves get an erection who knows however we do ask that while you're in your seats you keep your belts lightly fastened in case we encounter any choppy air or the end we've prayed for past time remembering our flying time from New York to Chicago is two hours and fifteen minutes the time of the dark journey of our existence is not revealed, you cry no you *pray* for a flight attendant you pray for a flight attendant a flight attendant comes now cry with reading material if you care to purchase a cocktail

(Pause)

A cocktail?

(Pause)

If you care to purchase a piece of carrot, a stinking turnip, a bit of grit our flight attendants will be along to see that you know how to move out of this airplane fast and use seat lower back cushion for flotation those of you on the right side of the aircraft ought to be able to see New York's Finger Lakes region that's Lake Canandaigua closest to us those of you on the left side of the aircraft will only see the vastness of eternal emptiness without end

(Pause)
(Long pause)
(Very long pause)
(Long pause of about an hour)

We're beginning our descent we're finished nearly finished soon we will be finished we're beginning our descent our long descent ahh descending beautifully to Chicago's Ohare Airport ORD ORD ORD ORD seat backs and tray tables in their full upright position for landing for ending flight attendants prepare for ending it is ending the flight is ending please check the seat pocket in front of you to see if you have all your belongings with you remain seated and motionless until the ending until the finish until the aircraft has come to a complete stop at the gate until the end

(Pause)

When we deplane I'll weep for happiness.

1980

VERONICA GENG

LOVE TROUBLE IS MY BUSINESS

Francis X. Clines, in the Sunday *Times* . . . : "President Reagan resembled a bashful cowboy the other day when he was asked about the apparent collapse of the 'Star Wars' talks with the Soviet Union. . . . At his side, murmuring something through the fixed smile that seems required of American political spouses, Mrs. Reagan was overheard prompting him: 'We're doing

everything we can.' . . . Out there in . . . the President's mountainside retreat, subjects such as the Soviet Union seem to haunt Mr. Reagan the way
vows to read Proust dog other Americans at leisure."

This may be the only time in history in which the words "Mr. Reagan"
and "read Proust" will appear in the same sentence.

—*Geoffrey Stokes in the* Village Voice.

GLANCED over at the dame sleeping next to me, and all of a sudden
I wanted some other dame, the way you see Mr. Reagan on TV and
all of a sudden get a yen to read Proust. Not that she wasn't attractive,
with rumpled blond curls and a complexion so transparent you could
read Proust through it—that is, as long as her cute habit of claiming a
tax deduction for salon facials didn't turn up in a memo to Mr. Reagan
from some I.R.S. stool pigeon. It was taking her a little more time to
wake up than it would take Mr. Reagan's horse to read Proust. After I'd
showered and shaved and put on an old pair of pants that wouldn't lead
anybody to believe my tailor was unduly influenced by having read
Proust, I went back over to the bed, where I wasn't exactly planning to
say my prayers—Mr. Reagan or no Mr. Reagan.

"Mr. . . . Reagan . . . ?" she whispered, fluttering her lashes, and I
trusted the dazed quizzical act about as much as if she'd told me she
could read Proust without moving her lips.

I slugged her a couple of times, and I'd have slugged her a couple of
more times if something hadn't told me I'd get a colder shoulder than a
cult nut insisting you could read Proust as anagrams predicting the end
of the world during the Administration of Mr. Reagan.

She chuckled insanely, like Mr. Reagan looped on something you
wouldn't want to drink while you read Proust. Then she touched me,
with the practiced efficiency of a protocol officer steering some terribly
junior diplomat through a receiving line to meet Mr. Reagan; funny, but
I got the idea she wasn't suggesting we curl up and read Proust. As her
hand slid along my thigh, I noticed that she wore a ring with a diamond
the size of the brain of a guy who read Proust all the time, and if I'd been
Mr. Reagan I'd have been dumb enough to buy her another one to go
with it. But the distance between a private eye's income and Mr. Reagan's was a gaping chasm big enough to crawl into and read Proust.

I wondered if Mr. Reagan worked this hard for his dough, as I ma-
neuvered her into the Kama Sutra position known as "Too Busy to
Read Proust."

I WOKE to the phone shrilling in my ear like the hot line warning Mr. Reagan that ten thousand Russian missiles hurtling over Western Europe weren't R.S.V.P.ing for a let's-get-together-once-a-week-and-read-Proust party. I let it ring, hoping the caller would decide to quit and go reread Proust, and wondering why dames always ran out on me without saying goodbye—why they didn't stick around with loyal wifely fixed smiles the way they did for hotshots like Mr. Reagan. Then I found myself getting a little weepy at a sentimental popular tune that was drifting through the venetian blinds:

> The connoisseur who's read Proust does it,
> Mr. Reagan with a boost does it,
> Let's do it, let's fall in love.

> Read Proust, where each *duc* and *comte* does it,
> Mr. Reagan with a prompt does it,
> Let's do it, let's fall in love.

> I've read Proust wished that he had done it
> Through a small aperture,
> Has Leningrad done it?
> Mr. Reagan's not sure.

> Some who read Proust say Odette did it,
> Mr. Reagan with a safety net did it,
> Let's do it, let's fall in love.

"*Cherchez la femme,*" I said to myself—a phrase I'd picked up on a case where the judge gave clemency to a homicidal maniac for having read Proust—and then I went out in the rain to a bookstore where I usually browsed for dames, and found one perusing Mr. Reagan's latest autobiography. Just for fun, I looked over her shoulder and read:

For a long time, before I met Nancy, I used to go to bed early.

1984

IN THE NEW CANADA,

LIVING IS A WAY OF LIFE

THE cabin attendant on our Air Canada flight answers a request for the correct time in almost perfectly unaccented English. She will not be the last Canadian in this new Canada of hers to try meeting a question with an answer, to make a reply her way of dealing with a query.

●

Below us, so vast that only a tiny portion is visible from the aircraft window, is Canada. Could any land be more aptly named? The name "Canada," after all, derives from the ancient Indian word "kanata," meaning, as luck would have it, "Canada."

●

Now visible as our plane descends toward the airport are the familiar antlike legions of motor-powered cars that are the sole means of private transport for most Canadians. They swarm across the landscape in columns so regimented that none dares stray from its place on the paved strip laid down by the authorities to head off across the open country all around.

These are the new Canadians, on their way to work in this, the new Canada.

●

The dinner party goes on almost until bedtime. The conversation has blithely looped and skimmed all evening around the subject of Baffin Island, as if that icebound mass of a hundred and eighty-three thousand square miles simply did not exist. For these citizens of the new Canada, at this dinner party, Baffin Island does *not* exist.

●

The Ross Farquaharsons (as they shall be called here) dwell, like most families in this new Canada, indoors. Yet for all the official government statistics "proving" a huge leap in living standards since confederation, in 1867, the Farquaharsons live little differently from the way Canadians have lived for most of this century.

Ross Farquaharson, his wife, Helen, and teen-age daughter, Kelly, all share a single living room without running water. To use the only swimming pool requires a trip outdoors. Dogs roam freely indoors, begging scraps from the meals taken communally at a table hewn from a piece of wood.

But there is no wood to burn in the fireplace. "Ran out in May," Ross Farquaharson says with a shrug. May is now three months past.

·

The rickety old bus full of bawling infants and caged chickens never comes; we must take a gleaming new one instead. There is no time to quibble. We have come to a wide river, and no ferryboat is available to take us across. Instead, government engineers have thrown a bridge of sorts across from the near to the far bank. It is just four lanes wide, and only a shoulder-high concrete retaining wall, a wire fence, and a few iron stanchions on either side prevent wayward vehicles or pedestrians from plunging into the rapids below.

The bus makes the two-thousand-foot crossing in thirty seconds that seem like half a minute. Yet there is no cheering from the passengers as we finally gain firm ground on the other side.

·

The plane approaches the airport runway slowly, cautiously, even tentatively, as if the Canadian pilot were unwilling to risk landing until his airspeed was throttled back to almost nothing and his wheels were fully down.

·

Everywhere the same gradations of blue and green and yellow and red and brown and orange and purple and taupe and mauve and pink and beige; city and countryside, summer and winter, in this new Canada, the only color is that of a single spectrum attempting to encompass all the hues of the rainbow.

·

The story of "Jack" (real name: John) typifies life as it is lived today in this, the new Canada. He had no choice after graduating from elementary school but to attend high school, and after high school no choice but to attend university, and after university no choice but to go to work. "It's the system," he confides, without evident bitterness. Jack is twenty-eight.

If he "keeps his nose to the grindstone," in the painfully graphic phrase Canadians are wont to use in describing toil, Jack may one day earn as much as two hundred thousand Canadian dollars per year in his job as a physician, a princely income in this new nation—not yet a nation when Pickett charged at Gettysburg—where sixteen ounces of prime sirloin steak can cost the average worker a fraction of his weekly wage.

·

In this land of the musk-ox, the beaver, and the moose, there is no musk-ox or beaver or moose meat to be had. The man behind the counter at the meat store is little more than a butcher. The remains of cows and sheep and pigs are all he has to sell.

·

It is a Saturday night in Coboconk. Like so many towns in this new Canada, Coboconk is too small to be a city and too large to be a village. The citizenry has learned to treat this not as a paradox but as a fact of life. And life, in Coboconk, as all across this vast land with more letters in its name than India but less than one-thirtieth the population, goes on.

·

The sight is far from uncommon: uniformed men are removing the furniture from a suburban house and manhandling it piece by piece into a huge van parked on the street nearby. No one protests or attempts to restrain them—not even the family whose possessions these are.

The house is soon stripped bare. The van is bolted and locked and rumbles away. A few minutes later, the former occupants of the now deserted house are bundled into a waiting red Volvo station wagon, and it, too, moves off down the street and out of sight.

"Well," sighs a neighborhood woman who has been watching all along, "we'll never see *them* again."

·

"They say we'll get some rain today."

"They tell us you're up here from the States, eh?"

"They never let you park in that spot without a permit."

Who are "They," who seem to know all, to control all, in this new Canada? The Canadian we ask blurts out the answer we expect. "I don't know what the heck you're talking about," he sputters, careful not to *not* look us straight in the eye.

·

The church, save for the minister, the choir, the sexton, and perhaps a hundred parishioners huddled in a space easily large enough to accommodate a hundred and thirty or more, is empty. The stone walls lack paint. Bits and pieces of colored glass serve as windows. Music is provided not by an orchestra but by a lone pipe organ. Men shuffle among the worshippers soliciting coins and paper currency—anything anyone can afford to give. There is no talking, no playing checkers, no smoking allowed.

·

There are no schoolchildren with bouquets to see us off at the airport, as there had been no folk dancers to greet us when we arrived. This is the new Canada.

·

"Friendly, familiar, foreign, and near." That was the old Canada. No such four glib adjectives could today limn this new Canada; or could they? Is it merely the same old Canada but full of new Canadians? A new Canada but full of old Canadians? Somewhere in between—as, indeed, most of the new Canada lies somewhere in between the Pacific on one side and the Atlantic on the other?

What is this thing we call the new Canada; and, equally important, what isn't it? More important still, has our foray, shorter by far than all of Frobisher's and Franklin's voyages of discovery combined, helped unravel the enigma of a nation-cum-riddle only now coming to terms with changes that not even Canadians pretend to know have yet occurred? To these quintessentially American questions, can there ever be truly Canadian answers? Perhaps it is too early—or too late—to ask.

1985

CORRECTIONS

January 14

BECAUSE of an editing error, an article in Friday's theatre section transposed the identifications of two people involved in the production of "Waiting for Bruce," a farce now in rehearsal at the Rivoli. Ralph W. Murtaugh, Jr., a New York attorney, is one of the play's financial backers. Hilary Murtaugh plays the ingénue. The two Murtaughs are not related. At no time during the rehearsal visited by the reporter did Mr. Murtaugh "sashay across the stage."

March 25

BECAUSE of some problems in transmission, there were several errors in yesterday's account of a symposium held by the Women's Civic Forum of Rye on the role played by slovenliness in cases of domestic violence. The moderator of the symposium, Laura Murtaugh, is not "a divorced mother of eight." Mrs. Murtaugh, the president of the board of directors of the Women's Civic Forum, is married to Ralph W. Murtaugh, Jr., an attorney who practices in Manhattan. The phrase "he was raised with the hogs and he lived like a hog" was read by Mrs. Murtaugh from the trial testimony of an Ohio woman whose defense against a charge of assault was based on her husband's alleged slovenliness. It did not refer to Mrs. Murtaugh's own husband. Mr. Murtaugh was raised in New York.

April 4

AN article in yesterday's edition on the growing contention between lawyers and their clients should not have used an anonymous quotation referring to the firm of Newton, Murtaugh & Clayton as "ambulance-chasing jackals" without offering the firm an opportunity to reply. Also, the number of hours customarily billed by Newton, Murtaugh partners was shown incorrectly on a chart accompanying the article. According to a spokesman for the firm, the partner who said he bills clients for "thirty-five or forty hours on a good day" was speaking ironically. There are only twenty-four hours in a day. The same article was in error as to the first name and the background of one of the firm's senior partners. The correct name is Ralph W. Murtaugh, Jr. There is no one named Hilary Murtaugh connected with the firm. Ralph W. Murtaugh, Jr., has at no time played an ingénue on Broadway.

April 29

BECAUSE of a computer error, the early editions on Wednesday misidentified the person arrested for a series of armed robberies of kitchen-supply stores on the West Side of Manhattan. The person arrested under suspicion of being the so-called "pesto bandit" was Raymond Cullom, twenty-two, of Queens. Ralph W. Murtaugh III, nineteen, of Rye, should have been identified as the runner-up in the annual Squash for Kids charity squash tournament, in Rye, rather than as the alleged robber.

May 18

BECAUSE of an error in transmission, a four-bedroom brick colonial house on Weeping Bend Lane, in Rye, owned by Mr. and Mrs. Ralph W. Murtaugh, Jr., was incorrectly listed in Sunday's real-estate section as being on the market for $17,500. The house is not for sale. Also, contrary to the information in the listing, it does not have flocked wallpaper or a round bed.

June 21

IN Sunday's edition, the account of a wedding that took place the previous day at St. John's Church in Rye was incorrect in a number of respects. The cause of the errors was the participation of the reporter in the reception. This is in itself against the policy of this newspaper, and should not have occurred. Jane Murtaugh was misidentified in two mentions. She was neither the mother of the bride nor the father of the bride. She was the bride. It was she who was wearing a white silk gown trimmed in tulle. The minister was wearing conventional ministerial robes. Miss Murtaugh should not have been identified on second mention as Mrs. Perkins, since she will retain her name and since Mr. Perkins was not in fact the groom. The number of bridesmaids was incorrectly reported. There were eight bridesmaids, not thirty-eight. Their dresses were blue, not glued. The bridegroom's name is not Franklin Marshall. His name is Emory Barnswell, and he graduated from Franklin and Marshall College. Mr. Barnswell never attended Emory University, which in any case does not offer a degree in furniture stripping. Mr. Barnswell's ancestor was not a signer of the Declaration of Independence, and was not named Hector (Boom-Boom) Bondini. The name of the father of the bride was inadvertently dropped from the article. He is Hilary Murtaugh.

1990

CHRISTOPHER BUCKLEY

STARDATE 12:00 12:00 12:00

"I watch science-fiction movies. . . . I like to watch them on tape, so I can examine them closely. There's only one problem: I still can't figure out my VCR."

—*William Shatner, in* TV Guide.

CAPTAIN KIRK: Captain's log, stardate 7412.6 . . . hello? The red light still isn't going on. Testing, 1-2-3-4. Chekov, it's not recording.

CHEKOV: I know, Keptin. Perhaps a negative function with the clock-timer.

UHURA: Captain, I'm getting indications of a Klingon presence.

KIRK: Mr. Spock?

SPOCK: I confirm at least six Imperial Klingon warships, Captain, and heading toward our position at Warp 7.

KIRK: No, the Captain's log. Why won't it record?

SPOCK: Might I suggest, Captain, that we first remove ourselves to a more secure sector and then address the matter of your log? That would be the . . . logical approach.

KIRK: There's nothing logical about this instruction manual. Chekov?

CHEKOV: Keptin?

KIRK: Try this. "With the Rec-On day flashing, press the 5 key."

CHEKOV: I did already, Keptin. *Still* negative function.

SULU: Captain, I'm having difficulty holding course.

KIRK: Shut down engines. Chekov, "Press the number for the day. For Sunday, press the 1 key, for Monday, the 2 key, and so on."

CHEKOV: Affirmative, Keptin. Still negative function. Perhaps ve should go back to page 15, vere it said to press Rec-Off time and enter two digits for hour.

SPOCK: Captain, the Klingons are arming their photon torpedoes.

KIRK: Engineering.

SCOTTY: Aye, Captain?

KIRK: Mr. Scott, we've got a malfunction in the log. We're going to need full deflector power while we get it fixed.

SCOTTY: I canna guarantee it, Captain. The systems are overloaded as it is.

CHEKOV: Keptin, the flashing 12:00 disappeared!

KIRK: Good work, Chekov!

CHEKOV: Den it came right back.

KIRK: Damn it. Analysis, Mr. Spock.

SPOCK: It would appear, Captain, that this instruction manual that you and Mr. Chekov have been attempting to decipher was written in Taiwan.

KIRK: Taiwan?

SPOCK: A small island in the Pacific Rim Sector, formerly inhabited by a determined people who believed that the adductor muscles in giant clams, *Tridacna gigas,* conferred sexual potency. In the later twentieth century, they became purveyors of early video equipment to what was then the United States. They were able to successfully emasculate the entire U.S. male population by means of impenetrable instruction manuals. It was this that eventually led to the Great Conflict.

KIRK: But this is 7412.6. How did a Taiwanese instruction manual get aboard the Enterprise?

SPOCK: It is possible that a Taiwanese computer virus was able to infiltrate Star Fleet Instruction Manual Command and subtly alter the books so that not even university-trained humans could understand them.

KIRK: It's diabolical.

SPOCK: On the contrary, it is perfectly logical. Their strategy was based on an ancient form of Oriental persuasion known as water torture. In this case, instead of water a digital rendering of the hour of twelve o'clock is flashed repeatedly and will not disappear until the unit is correctly programmed.

KIRK: And for that you need a manual you can understand.

SPOCK: Precisely. Unless . . .

KIRK: Spit it out, Spock.

SPOCK: You have Star Log Plus. A small device that permitted the Americans to bypass the instruction manuals and program their units so that they would not end up with six hours of electronic snow instead of "Masterpiece Theatre" or, more likely, "American Gladiators."

KIRK: Could you make one of these things, Spock?

SPOCK: It would take more than the one minute and twenty seconds that we have until we are within range of Klingon weapons.

DR. MCCOY: Jim, you know I hate to agree with Spock, but he's right. We've got to get out of here. There are hundreds of people on this ship, young people, with homes and families and futures, and pets—little hamsters on treadmills, Jim. You can't sacrifice them just because you can't figure out how to program your damn log!

KIRK: I know my responsibilities, Bones. Spock, would it be possible to beam the flashing 12:00 into the Klingons' control panel?

SPOCK: Theoretically, yes.

KIRK: Do it.

UHURA: Captain, I'm picking up a Klingon transmission.

KIRK: Put it on screen.

KLINGONS: QI'yaH, majegh!

KIRK: Translation, Spock.

SPOCK: It appears to have worked, Captain. They are surrendering.

KIRK: Take us home, Mr. Sulu. Mr. Chekov, try pressing the OTR button twice.

1993

GLENGARRY GLEN PLAID

EXCERPTS FROM THE NEW LAND HO! CATALOGUE,

AS IT WOULD BE WRITTEN BY DAVID MAMET

OUR FLANNEL SHIRTS ARE AS WARM AS A CUP OF COCOA!

The great flannel shirts you had, what do you remember about them? Not the pattern. Not the sleeves. Maybe it was the collar, the way it caressed your neck. Maybe it made a smell. Maybe it was the easy way it hung on you, like a drunk temp at an office party. Friend, *this* is a flannel. Most flannel shirts weigh eight ounces, they're crap. This weighs *ten* ounces. When it's so cold outside your balls shrink up like croutons, those extra two ounces are ounces of *gold*.

But you can't have these shirts.

They are not for the likes of you. These shirts are for *preferred customers*. If you called last year, you could have bought one, maybe, but not now. It's too late, they're sold out. They won't be avail— Huh? What's that, Gladys? We do have a few in stock? *Tonight only?* Well, pal, you just got lucky. You've got eight hours to get in on the ground floor. Of course, you can talk it over with your wife. How many should I put you down for? Seven? Nine? AND THE ALL-COTTON FABRIC GUARANTEES COMFORT!

ALL HAIL CHINOS! EVERYONE SHOULD OWN A PAIR!

You think chinos are queer? Let me tell you something: Everybody's queer. So what? You cheat on your wife? Live with it. You own a pair of bell-bottoms? Deal with it. At least these chinos have a fly that stays up, and you're not paying a hundred dollars for some piece of puke-colored polyester. Right now, you're asking, What do I want from a pair of pants? Comfort? Durability? A name? *An investment?* Listen: When you're in the accident, and they're cutting off your blood-stained trousers in that emergency room, who cares if you're wearing an expensive label? MACHINE WASHABLE, TOO!

OUR STIRRUP PANTS DON'T COST AN ARM AND A LEG!

You bitched about our stirrup pants. We heard you. Christ Almighty, everybody in the state heard you. We trimmed the legs, so, even with your fat thighs, you won't look like a Buick. We stitched up the back to prevent pulling. You guys know what *pulling* is? It's when the pants pull down on a chick's ass, because the things are strapped to her goddam *feet*. Smart, eh? Like all anybody needed was a strap to hold pants *down*. What ever happened to straps that held pants *up*? Ever hear of belts? Broads. Don't get me started. Look, this isn't about backstitching, or yuppie fashions, or why a nickel is bigger than a dime. It's about *men and women*. Screw it. I need a drink. AND THE SEAMLESS STIRRUPS MEAN EXTRA COMFORT!

MEET OUR MOCK: THE TURTLE WITH A LITTLE LESS HUG!

You don't like turtlenecks? You say they're too tight? What are you, some wussy? Can't handle the pressure from a fifty-fifty blend? What do *you* know from pressure? You sit there in your chintzy house and *you can't deal with a turtleneck?* Jesus Christ.

You know, this pisses me off. You don't know squat about running a business or about publishing a catalogue. You just sit there, looking at all the shiny, pretty pictures, and when you do finally call, you are the Customer, and the Customer Is Always Right, so the Customer can screw around and waste the time of men who bust their balls for a living, and it doesn't matter that the Customer Is Full of Shit. Who taught you to buy clothes? You stupid, lard-assed deadbeat.

That's it. I've had it. I don't care whose nephew you are. I don't care who you're boffing. You drive everybody goddam nuts. This catalogue costs big money, but what do you care? *You* get it for free. That's the problem. You don't respect what you cannot buy. Well, buy *something*, asshole. AND IT'S MADE IN THE U.S.A.!

1994

GUM

(Fade in old-timey fiddle music.)
Title: "Something Like a Candy"
(Slow zoom on single shot of eight-year-old boy, in mid-chew.)

NARRATOR: It started as an idle pursuit: a way to pass the time, to occupy the slackened jaw of street urchin and steel magnate alike. *(Hold on various stills of farmhands, factory workers, men in bowler hats.)* But even in its infancy, when America wakened to its unfurling power like a slumbering giant whose nap had been cut short by the ambulance cry of its own withered soul, when gnashing, nattering demons fought for the very plinth of this great land, when the corn was as high as an elephant's eye—even then it served as a salve to the spirit, a lulling reminder that there would still be a tomorrow, even if tomorrow never came.

FYVUSH FINKEL: I used to take my penny down to the candy store every Friday. This is in New York City, on the Lower East Side, which could be a very rough place back then—not like it's a big picnic basket today—and if you didn't get run over by a pushcart on your way to the store, or beaten up by the Ukrainian gangs over on Cherry Street, which happened about every other day, you'd give your penny to the man behind the counter, and if he wasn't the kind of fellow to rob you blind, which most of them were, you'd get, I don't know, six or seven pieces of candy, and usually in there would be a stick of gum.

(Hold on shots of tropical foliage, migrant laborers.)
NARRATOR: The resin of the sapodilla tree was made to yield a chewable substance that could produce a kind of refreshment lasting all the livelong day. Mixed first with lye, then with iodine, and finally with sugar, it soon filled the mouths of schoolboys and stumblebums, of pugilists and prostitutes from Portland, Maine, to Portland, Oregon.

SUSAN SONTAG: You have to understand, gum was very much frowned upon by the rising merchant class, who saw it as a kind of repudiation of all that they had done to distance themselves from their very provincial, very backwoods sorts of backgrounds. So what you had was this tremendous excitement, this wonderful violation of the social code, whenever someone would "pop in a stick," as they'd say. It was all really very exciting, really.

(Hold on shots of robber-baron types.)

NARRATOR: With the rise of "gumming" came the gum lords. They were ruthless men: cold, overbearing, quick to anger, bad of breath, unfriendly, rude, and, more often than not, not nice. They would hold the burgeoning gum world by its wrapper for more than three decades. It would be more than thirty years before the world of gum would be loosed from their very sticky and unpleasant grip.

KEANU REEVES: "I intend to build me a gumworks the likes of which has not been seen east of the Mississippi, nor north of the Ohio, nor west of the Allegheny, nor south of Lake Huron. I will set it in the city of Chicago, for that is the place where I live, though not in summer, for it is too blessed hot."—Colonel Harry A. Beech-Nut.

NARRATOR: Men with names like Wrigley, Dentyne, and Bazooka would seek control of what quickly grew to be a multibillion-dollar-a-year industry (*hold on shots of bubble-popping contests, kids at candy counters*) built on the pennies of boys with names like Tommy, Frank, and Ken, and girls with names like Laura, Sandy, and Jo. Day after day, they came to stores with names like Pop's, Morry's, and the Pit Stop, to buy gum with names like Juicy Fruit, Beeman's, and Big Red.

SHELBY FOOTE: The mere fact that you could *chew* gum for so long, that it would last and last and not lose its flavor—although all gum would *eventually* lose its flavor—that fact alone made it a kind of metaphor for all that was regenerative in American life, the sense that you could go away and the place you left would *still be there*, it wouldn't be gone like some vaporous illusion—it was the same with gum, you could go out, bowl a few frames, make a phone call, get back in your car, and you'd still be chewing *the same piece of gum.* That was tremendously important in establishing the whole entire gum mystique, which is to say legend.

MARTIN SCORSESE: Sure, I saw all the gum pictures, uh, all the great, great gum-chewing heroes. Sam Spade, of course, comes to mind. The Thin Man, William Powell, Cool Hand Luke—What? They didn't? Are you sure? It's really very funny, because I always associate them with, uh, with gum.

(Shots of clouds gathering, sound of thunderclaps.)

NARRATOR: But a dark cloud hovered on the horizon: a bubble-gum-versus-chewing-gum conflagration that would rend the land asunder.

Brother would be set against brother, in what came to be known as the Big Gum War.

(Station break.)

ANNOUNCER: The twenty-seven-part television event "Gum" will return in a moment with Part Two: "Bubble Trouble."

1994

MICHAEL GERBER AND JONATHAN SCHWARZ

WHAT WE TALK ABOUT WHEN WE

TALK ABOUT DOUGHNUTS

MY friend Jim Forrer was talking. Jim Forrer is a professional fish measurer, and sometimes that gives him the right.

We were sitting around the kitchen table drinking gin and smoking. There was Jim and me and his wife, Elizabeth—Lisa, we called her, or sometimes Frank—and my wife, Carol.

There was a bowl of peanuts sitting on the table, but nobody ate many of them, because we were drinking and smoking. We were talking to ourselves like this: "Some of us are drinking more than we are smoking, and some of us are smoking more than we are drinking. Some of us are drinking and smoking about the same amount."

We went on drinking and smoking for a while, and somehow we got on the subject of doughnuts. Jim thought that real doughnuts were nothing less than spiritual doughnuts. He said he had spent ten minutes at a seminary before he had gone to fish-measuring school. He said he still looked back on those ten minutes as the most important minutes of his life.

Lisa said that the man she lived with before Jim had really liked doughnuts. She said he liked them so much that sometimes he would shoot at them with his gun, or flush them down the toilet. Sometimes, she said, he would put them on the living-room rug, climb up on the coffee table, and then jump off directly on top of them.

"It was scary," she said.

Carol and I smiled at each other.

Just then I dropped a peanut on the floor. It rolled behind the refrigerator. It was hard to get it out. It was very hard. But not so hard as other things. Other things had been harder.

"I LIKE doughnuts as much as anyone," said Jim. He took a sip of his drink. "I like them at breakfast, and sometimes lunch."

"Now, hon, you know that's not true," said Lisa.

"What do you mean?" said Jim. "I like doughnuts a lot."

"No, you don't," said Lisa. "And I've never seen you eat a doughnut at lunch."

"Has it ever occurred to you once in your goddam life that I might not always tell you when I eat a goddam doughnut? Has that ever occurred to you once?" said Jim. *"Christ."*

He took a sip from his drink, and then stopped, so he could smoke.

Jim's dog was scratching at the door, but we couldn't let him out. We were drinking and smoking.

WHEN I met Jim he was still married to Nancy, his forty-fifth wife. They had been very much in love, but one day she inhaled too much helium and just floated away. Then he met Lisa.

When I introduced Jim to Carol he said that she was "a real person." I was glad, because my college girlfriend, Hillary, was a facsimile person. She was warm and loving, and with the proper equipment could be sent across the country in seconds. But things didn't work out.

"Has anyone ever seen a really big doughnut?" said Carol. "I did once. At a pawnshop in Maine." She paused. But she didn't say anything afterward, so actually it was less like a pause and more like a full stop.

"No," said Jim, taking a sip of his drink, "but I ate some miniature doughnuts once." He took a sip of the gin he was drinking. "I ate ten or twelve of them." Jim leaned back, rubbed his temples, and took a sip from his glass. "I thought," he said, pausing to take a sip of his drink, "that they were pretty," he continued, sipping from his drink, "good." Jim took one last sip, this time of my drink.

WE reminisced about the best doughnuts we had had in our lives.

"The best doughnut I ever had," said Jim, "was when I was working for Harry Niven. Do you remember Harry, honey?"

"Of course," said Lisa.

"Compared to him I can't measure fish at all," said Jim. "I mean, there was a man who could measure a fish!"

We went on talking.

"The best doughnut I ever had," said Lisa, "was when I was dating Daniel." We all knew about Daniel. They had been deeply in love and on the brink of marriage when Lisa realized that he was a hologram.

"Hold on a second, hon," Carol said to Lisa. She turned to me. "Do you want to get divorced?"

"O.K.," I said.

Carol and I left and got divorced. Then we came back with our new spouses, Dave and Terri.

We all sat there talking, the six of us in the dark. We went on talking and talking, even after the gin ran out. Talking about doughnuts. Talking about doughnuts in the dark.

1999

PAUL RUDNICK

TEEN TIMES

PEOPLE, *Vogue*, and *Cosmopolitan* have each recently introduced a separate teen edition, aimed at a friskier demographic. It's only a matter of time before other magazines follow, offering their own youthful rethinks, complete with age-appropriate cover lines.

TEEN SCIENTIFIC AMERICAN

If the Universe Keeps Expanding, What Will It Wear?
Cancer: Shut *Up!*
Are the Ice Caps Melting? Blame Enrique!
Penis Grafting—Is It the Answer for N'Sync?
Is the Earth Over Two Billion Years Old—Like Your Dad?

TEEN TIKKUN

Make Your Own Wailing Wall—Just Styrofoam and Post-its!
Five Pounds by Purim—Lose That Arafat!
Are All Jewish Girls as Pretty as Their Parents Claim? Our Survey
  Says Yes!
Which Backstreet Boy's Facial Hair Could Almost Be Orthodox?
Intermarriage: What If He's Only a Paralegal?

TEEN U.S. NEWS & WORLD REPORT

Ethnic Deep Cleansing: Kiss Albanians and Blemishes Goodbye!
Britney vs. the Taliban: Oops, They Stoned Her to Death
Milosevic—Now He's Got Time for You!
Famine—Does the Weight *Stay* Off?
Is the Pope Catholic? Your Surprising Letters!

TEEN NATIONAL GEOGRAPHIC

Tribal Makeovers: It's Called Clothing
The Strange, Ugly People of Other Countries
Australia—Is It Too Far Away?
The Elephants of India—Of Course They're Lonely
The Pygmy Prom—Don't Worry About Your Hair

TEEN NATIONAL REVIEW

Sex with a Republican—Your Best Ten Seconds Ever!
Abortion: You Could Be Killing Ricky Martin, Jr.
Sweatshops: Can't They Make Our Clothes Without Touching Them?
Don't Ask, Don't Tell—How It Saved My Parents' Marriage
12 Ways to Make Him Buy You a Handgun

TEEN PSYCHOLOGY TODAY

Why Everybody Hates You—Duh, It's Called "They're Jealous"
Eating Disorders—Which Ones Really Work
Electroshock and Split Ends—We Tell You the Truth
Attention Deficit Disorder: The Article You Won't Finish

2000

THE

FRENZY

OF

RENOWN

PRESS AGENTS I HAVE KNOWN

T HE little fellow climbed upon my lap and tugged me gently by the
beard. "Tell me, grandfather," he said, "about your first press
agent."

I gazed into the fire. Unknowingly, the child had touched a tender
spot. It had been years since I even thought of the affair. But now something within me stirred. My whole body seemed on fire. I seemed to
catch a faint odor of hyacinth. Ah, youth! Those moonlit nights! Those
first interviews! Those passionate scenes! Those notes! Those notes—

(From the Spokane *Spokesman*)

Groucho Marx, a member of the Four Marx Brothers, spends his
spare time collecting pipes. He now has 762 pipes of all sizes and varieties. When asked about his hobby, Mr. Marx said slyly, with a twinkle
in his eye, "Yes, I collect pipes. Let me show you a rare piece of lead
pipe."

I claim to be an authority on press agents. As soon as I have finished
my present opus, "My Fifty Years on the American Stage," or, "From
Weber and Fields to an Institution," I intend to write the long-awaited
work, "Press Agents I Have Known, or Regretted." These few notes
will constitute my introduction:

First of all, there is the stunt press agent. The fellow who pops into
your dressing-room, all smiles, and says, "What are you doing tomorrow afternoon?"

"Fixing the coil on my still," I say, all hope abandoned.

"Oh, no, you're not," he insists cheerily. "You're going to sit on top of
the flagpole on the Paramount Building with a sign on your back: 'Hello
Mars! The Marx Brothers in "Animal Crackers" send greetings.' "

"But my lumbago—"

"It's all arranged. I'm going to have fourteen reporters, a flock of cameramen and the ship-news reporters. What a break it'll be! It'll go all over the world! For the good of the show!"

That always gets me. I don't know why it should after all these years, but it does. . . . After I get vertigo reaching the top of the Paramount Building, I find that the reporters have been called away to cover a big fire and the flock of cameramen consists of two disagreeable little fellows who seem quite bored with the whole proceeding.

"Climb a little higher," they tell me. "Can't you do better than that?—this will make a terrible picture."

They probably figure that if I climb any higher they won't have to use their plates at all. They are right about one thing. It makes a terrible picture. Two weeks later, the press agent comes bounding into the dressing-room, waving the evidence of his genius. The picture is published on page 34 of *The Billboard*. That's the way it goes all over the world. The caption reads:

CLIMBS FLAGPOLE

G. Merks, of the Three Merks Brothers, vaudeville acrobats, climbed the Paramount flagpole last month to pay an election bet.

Let's consider another species—the press agent who keeps phoning you: "Wait until you see what I have to show you! Articles in seven newspapers and each one different!"

They are. He finally struts around to show you the stories. The first one starts: "*Les frères Marx, maintenant*—" (That's all I can read—it's in the Paris *Matin*.) The next article begins: "*Die Marx Brüder,*" and is in the Berlin *Tageblatt*. You get the idea—he gets us swell publicity in some of the world's greatest newspapers, including the Stockholm *Svenborgen*, the Portugal *Estrada*, and the Riga *Raschgitov*. Nice little articles for the scrapbook, to read before the fire some rainy night.

Then there is the highbrow press agent who spends weeks interviewing me. He corners me for hours at a stretch to ask me such questions as, "But, Mr. Marx, don't you feel that Pinero was undoubtedly influenced by Aeschylus?" I'm all a-twitter when he tells me he has placed the interview. It finally appears in the *Dial*, which comes out once a month and is great for business.

Then there is the fellow who has been a circus press agent and can't forget his early training. He's a dangerous character. No weather is too bad for him to lead you out to Central Park to be photographed with the animals. After risking my life trying to appear as if I were teaching a hippopotamus to sing (the press agent cleverly gets the hippopotamus to open his mouth by holding out a frankfurter—from the other side of the fence), the animal always gets the credit. The picture appears with the hippopotamus covering seven-eighths of the space and my picture looking like the frankfurter. And the caption reads:

CHARLIE, CENTRAL PARK HIPPO, RECEIVES CONGRATULATIONS ON HIS THIRD BIRTHDAY. Picture shows Charlie receiving the best wishes from one of his admirers, a well-known Broadway hoofer.

And then there is the press agent who *schmeichels* you into doing his work. "Mr. Marx, I could get stories about you in any paper in New York, but I know perfectly well I can't write as well as you can. So why don't you dash off one of your brilliant articles for the *Times,* a clever autobiography for the *Sun,* and one of your screamingly funny pieces for the *American.* I'll take them around myself to make sure they get in."

Then the press agent who never gets you in the papers unless you play at least three benefits a week and appear at the opening of a new butcher shop to throw out the first chop.

And the press agent who gets you all steamed up about the story he landed for you in the *Tribune.*

"What's it like?" you ask, all agog.

"Wait till you see it."

He finally sends you a copy. The story runs like this:

Among those present at the dance of the Mayfair Club at the Ritz on Saturday night were Eddie Cantor, Mary Eaton, Gertrude Lawrence, Beatrice Lillie, Walter Woolf, Peaches Browning, Ethel Barrymore, Will Rogers, Lenore Ulric, Alice Brady, Katharine Cornell, Tammany Young and one of the Marx Brothers.

I mustn't forget the press agent who gets such wonderful publicity for himself. After getting me all on edge about the interview he has landed, I buy a paper and read the following:

AN INTERVIEW WITH GROUCHO MARX
BY ALAN J. WURTZBURGER

I'll admit that I was terribly excited when I knocked on Mr. Marx's door, ready to interview him. My heart pounded rapidly. Then I recalled the time I interviewed Otis Skinner, my *tête-à-tête* with Pavlowa and my heart-to-heart talk with Doug Fairbanks.

So I walked boldly in. Mr. Marx received me cordially and after asking me to sit down, admired my cravat. "I always wear that tie when I'm interviewing a celebrity," I told him, to make him feel at ease. "I'll tell you an interesting story about that cravat—"

And so on for two columns about that fascinating fellow, Alan J. Wurtzburger.

ALL these varieties of press agents are pretty bad, but the fellow I had last spring was positively vicious. He used to drop into my dressing-room, smoke my cigars, and spend his time, not in interviewing me, but giving me advice on the market. The only things worse than my cigars were his tips. He was the reason I had to spend the summer delighting audiences in motion-picture houses.

Maybe I'm unduly hopeful, but I'm still looking for a press agent who will get me some publicity without making me roller-skate down Broadway to demonstrate that STAGE STAR SOLVES TRAFFIC PROBLEM BY SKATING TO THEATRE. I want a press agent like Hoover's got. Look at the stuff that chap landed for Hoover during the election. And I'll bet Hoover didn't climb any flagpoles either.

1929

JAMES THURBER

———————

THE GREATEST MAN IN THE WORLD

LOOKING back on it now, from the vantage point of 1940, one can only marvel that it hadn't happened long before it did. The United States of America had been, ever since Kitty Hawk, blindly constructing the elaborate petard by which, sooner or later, it must be hoist. It was inevitable that some day there would come roaring out of the skies a national hero of insufficient intelligence, background, and character successfully to endure the mounting orgies of glory prepared for aviators who stayed up a long time or flew a great distance. Both Lindbergh and Byrd, fortunately for national decorum and international amity, had been gentlemen; so had our other famous aviators. They wore their laurels gracefully, withstood the awful weather of publicity, married excellent women, usually of fine family, and quietly retired to private life and the enjoyment of their varying fortunes. No untoward incidents, on a worldwide scale, marred the perfection of their conduct on the perilous heights of fame. The exception to the rule was, however, bound to occur and it did, in July, 1935, when Jack ("Pal") Smurch, erstwhile mechanic's helper in a small garage in Westfield, Iowa, flew a second-hand, single-motored Bresthaven Dragon-Fly III monoplane all the way around the world, without stopping.

NEVER before in the history of aviation had such a flight as Smurch's ever been dreamed of. No one had ever taken seriously the weird floating auxiliary gas tanks, invention of the mad New Hampshire professor of astronomy, Dr. Charles Lewis Gresham, upon which Smurch placed full reliance. When the garage worker, a slightly built, surly, unprepossessing young man of twenty-two, appeared at Roosevelt Field early in July, 1935, slowly chewing a great quid of scrap tobacco, and announced "Nobody ain't seen no flyin' yet," the newspapers touched briefly and satirically upon his projected twenty-five-thousand-mile flight. Aëronautical and automotive experts dismissed the idea curtly, implying that it was a hoax, a publicity stunt. The rusty, battered, second-hand plane wouldn't go. The Gresham auxiliary tanks wouldn't work. It was simply a cheap joke.

Smurch, however, after calling on a girl in Brooklyn who worked in the flap-folding department of a large paper-box factory, a girl whom he later described as his "sweet patootie," climbed nonchalantly into his ridiculous plane at dawn of the memorable seventh of July, 1935, spit a curve of tobacco juice into the still air, and took off, carrying with him only a gallon of bootleg gin and six pounds of salami.

WHEN the garage boy thundered out over the ocean the papers were forced to record, in all seriousness, that a mad, unknown young man—

his name was variously misspelled—had actually set out upon a preposterous attempt to span the world in a rickety, one-engined contraption,
trusting to the long-distance refuelling device of a crazy schoolmaster.
When, nine days later, without having stopped once, the tiny plane appeared above San Francisco Bay, headed for New York, spluttering and
choking, to be sure, but still magnificently and miraculously aloft, the
headlines, which long since had crowded everything else off the front
page—even the shooting of the Governor of Illinois by the Capone
gang—swelled to unprecedented size, and the news stories began to
run to twenty-five and thirty columns. It was noticeable, however, that
the accounts of the epoch-making flight touched rather lightly upon
the aviator himself. This was not because facts about the hero as a man
were too meagre, but because they were too complete.

Reporters, who had been rushed out to Iowa when Smurch's plane
was first sighted over the little French coast town of Serly-le-Mer, to
dig up the story of the great man's life, had promptly discovered that
the story of his life could not be printed. His mother, a sullen short-
order cook in a shack restaurant on the edge of a tourists' camping
ground near Westfield, met all inquiries as to her son with an angry
"Ah, the hell with him; I hope he drowns." His father appeared to be in
jail somewhere for stealing spotlights and laprobes from tourists' automobiles; his young brother, a weakminded lad, had but recently escaped
from the Preston, Iowa, Reformatory and was already wanted in several
Western towns for the theft of money-order blanks from post offices.
These alarming discoveries were still piling up at the very time that Pal
Smurch, the greatest hero of the twentieth century, blear-eyed, dead for
sleep, half-starved, was piloting his crazy junkheap high above the region in which the lamentable story of his private life was being unearthed, headed for New York and a greater glory than any man of his
time had ever known.

The necessity for printing some account in the papers of the young
man's career and personality had led to a remarkable predicament. It
was of course impossible to reveal the facts, for a tremendous popular
feeling in favor of the young hero had sprung up, like a grass fire, when
he was halfway across Europe on his flight around the globe. He was,
therefore, described as a modest chap, taciturn, blond, popular with his
friends, popular with girls. The only available snapshot of Smurch,
taken at the wheel of a phony automobile in a cheap photo studio at an
amusement park, was touched up so that the little vulgarian looked
quite handsome. His twisted leer was smoothed into a pleasant smile.

The truth was, in this way, kept from the youth's ecstatic compatriots; they did not dream that the Smurch family was despised and feared by its neighbors in the obscure Iowa town, nor that the hero himself, because of numerous unsavory exploits, had come to be regarded in Westfield as a nuisance and a menace. He had, the reporters discovered, once knifed the principal of his high school—not mortally, to be sure, but he had knifed him; and on another occasion, surprised in the act of stealing an altarcloth from a church, he had bashed the sacristan over the head with a pot of Easter lilies; for each of these offences he had served a sentence in the reformatory.

Inwardly, the authorities, both in New York and in Washington, prayed that an understanding Providence might, however awful such a thing seemed, bring disaster to the rusty, battered plane and its illustrious pilot, whose unheard-of flight had aroused the civilized world to hosannas of hysterical praise. The authorities were convinced that the character of the renowned aviator was such that the limelight of adulation was bound to reveal him, to all the world, as a congenital hooligan mentally and morally unequipped to cope with his own prodigious fame. "I trust," said the Secretary of State, at one of many secret Cabinet meetings called to consider the national dilemma, "I trust that his mother's prayer will be answered," by which he referred to Mrs. Emma Smurch's wish that her son might be drowned. It was, however, too late for that—Smurch had leaped the Atlantic and then the Pacific as if they were millponds. At three minutes after two o'clock on the afternoon of July 17, 1935, the garage boy brought his idiotic plane into Roosevelt Field for a perfect three-point landing.

IT had, of course, been out of the question to arrange a modest little reception for the greatest flier in the history of the world. He was received at Roosevelt Field with such elaborate and pretentious ceremonies as rocked the world. Fortunately, however, the worn and spent hero promptly swooned, had to be removed bodily from his plane, and was spirited from the field without having opened his mouth once. Thus he did not jeopardize the dignity of this first reception, a reception illumined by the presence of the Secretaries of War and the Navy, Mayor Michael J. Moriarity of New York, the Premier of Canada, Governors Fanniman, Groves, McFeely, and Critchfield, and a brilliant array of European diplomats. Smurch did not, in fact, come to in time to take part in the gigantic hullabaloo arranged at City Hall for the next day. He was rushed to a secluded nursing home and con-fined in bed. It was nine days before he was able to get up, or to be more exact, before he was permitted to get up. Meanwhile the greatest minds in the country, in solemn assembly, had arranged a secret conference of city, state, and government officials, which Smurch was to attend for the purpose of being instructed in the ethics and behavior of heroism.

On the day that the little mechanic was finally allowed to get up and dress and, for the first time in two weeks, took a great chew of tobacco, he was permitted to receive the newspapermen—this by way of testing him out. Smurch did not wait for questions. "Youse guys," he said—and the *Times* man winced—"youse guys can tell the cock-eyed world dat I put it over on Lindbergh, see? Yeh—an' made an ass o' them two frogs." The "two frogs" was a reference to a pair of gallant French fliers who, in attempting a flight only halfway round the world, had, two weeks be-fore, unhappily been lost at sea. The *Times* man was bold enough, at this point, to sketch out for Smurch the accepted formula for inter-views in cases of this kind; he explained that there should be no arro-gant statements belittling the achievements of other heroes, particularly heroes of foreign nations. "Ah, the hell with that," said Smurch. "I did it, see? I did it, an' I'm talkin' about it." And he did talk about it.

None of this extraordinary interview was, of course, printed. On the contrary, the newspapers, already under the disciplined direction of a secret directorate created for the occasion and composed of statesmen and editors, gave out to a panting and restless world that "Jacky," as he had been arbitrarily nicknamed, would consent to say only that he was very happy and that anyone could have done what he did. "My achieve-ment has been, I fear, slightly exaggerated," the *Times* man's article had him protest, with a modest smile. These newspaper stories were kept from the hero, a restriction which did not serve to abate the rising malevolence of his temper. The situation was, indeed, extremely grave, for Pal Smurch was, as he kept insisting, "rarin' to go." He could not much longer be kept from a nation clamorous to lionize him. It was the most desperate crisis the United States of America had faced since the sinking of the *Lusitania*.

ON the afternoon of the twenty-seventh of July, Smurch was spirited away to a conference-room in which were gathered mayors, governors, government officials, behaviorist psychologists, and editors. He gave them each a limp, moist paw and a brief unlovely grin. "Hah ya?" he said. When Smurch was seated, the Mayor of New York arose and, with obvious pessimism, attempted to explain what he must say and how he must act when presented to the world, ending his talk with a high tribute to the hero's courage and integrity. The Mayor was followed by Governor Fanniman of New York, who, after a touching declaration of faith, introduced Cameron Spottiswood, Second Secretary of the American Embassy in Paris, the gentleman selected to coach Smurch in the amenities of public ceremonies. Sitting in a chair, with a soiled yellow tie in his hand and his shirt open at the throat, unshaved, smoking a rolled cigarette, Jack Smurch listened with a leer on his lips. "I get ya, I get ya," he cut in, nastily. "Ya want me to ack like a softy, huh? Ya want me to ack like that — — baby-face Lindbergh, huh? Well, nuts to that, see?" Everyone took in his breath sharply; it was a sigh and a hiss. "Mr. Lindbergh," began a United States Senator, purple with rage, "and Mr. Byrd—" Smurch, who was paring his nails with a jackknife, cut in again. "Byrd!" he exclaimed. "Aw fa God's sake, *dat* big—" Somebody shut off his blasphemies with a sharp word. A newcomer had entered the room. Everyone stood up, except Smurch, who, still busy with his nails, did not even glance up. "Mr. Smurch," said someone, sternly, "the President of the United States!" It had been thought that the presence of the Chief Executive might have a chastening effect upon the young hero, and the former had been, thanks to the remarkable coöperation of the press, secretly brought to the obscure conference-room.

A great, painful silence fell. Smurch looked up, waved a hand at the President. "How ya comin'?" he asked, and began rolling a fresh cigarette. The silence deepened. Someone coughed in a strained way. "Geez, it's hot, ain't it?" said Smurch. He loosened two more shirt buttons, revealing a hairy chest and the tattooed word "Sadie" enclosed in a stencilled heart. The great and important men in the room, faced by the most serious crisis in recent American history, exchanged worried frowns. Nobody seemed to know how to proceed. "Come awn, come awn," said Smurch. "Let's get the hell out of here! When do I start cuttin' in on de parties, huh? And what's they goin' to be *in* it?" He rubbed a thumb and forefinger together meaningly. "Money!" exclaimed a state senator, shocked, pale. "Yeh, money," said Pal, flipping his cigarette out of a window. "An' big money." He began rolling a fresh cigarette. "Big money," he repeated, frowning over the rice paper. He tilted back in his chair, and leered at each gentleman, separately, the leer of an animal that knows its power, the leer of a leopard loose in a bird-and-dog shop. "Aw fa God's sake, let's get some place where it's cooler," he said. "I been cooped up plenty for three weeks!"

Smurch stood up and walked over to an open window, where he stood staring down into the street, nine floors below. The faint shouting of newsboys floated up to him. He made out his name. "Hot dog!" he cried, grinning, ecstatic. He leaned out over the sill. "You tell 'em, babies!" he shouted down. "Hot diggity dog!" In the tense little knot of men standing behind him, a quick, mad impulse flared up. An unspoken word of appeal, of command, seemed to ring through the room. Yet it was deadly silent. Charles K. L. Brand, secretary to the Mayor of New York City, happened to be standing nearest Smurch; he looked inquiringly at the President of the United States. The President, pale, grim, nodded shortly. Brand, a tall, powerfully built man, once a tackle at Rutgers, stepped forward, seized the greatest man in the world by his left shoulder and the seat of his pants, and pushed him out the window.

"My God, he's fallen out the window!" cried a quick-witted editor.

"Get me out of here!" cried the President. Several men sprang to his side and he was hurriedly escorted out of a door toward a side-entrance of the building. The editor of the Associated Press took charge, being used to such things. Crisply he ordered certain men to leave, others to stay; quickly he outlined a story which all the papers were to agree on, sent two men to the street to handle that end of the tragedy, commanded a Senator to sob and two Congressmen to go to pieces nervously. In a word, he skillfully set the stage for the gigantic task that was to follow, the task of breaking to a grief-stricken world the sad story of the untimely, accidental death of its most illustrious and spectacular figure.

THE funeral was, as you know, the most elaborate, the finest, the solemnest, and the saddest ever held in the United States of America. The monument in Arlington Cemetery, with its clean white shaft of marble and the simple device of a tiny plane carved on its base, is a place for pilgrims, in deep reverence, to visit. The nations of the world paid lofty tributes to little Jacky Smurch, America's greatest hero. At a given hour there were two minutes of silence throughout the nation. Even the inhabitants of the small, bewildered town of Westfield, Iowa, observed this touching ceremony; agents of the Department of Justice saw to that. One of them was especially assigned to stand grimly in the doorway of a little shack restaurant on the edge of the tourists' camping ground just outside the town. There, under his stern scrutiny, Mrs. Emma Smurch bowed her head above two hamburger steaks sizzling on her grill—bowed her head and turned away, so that the Secret Service man could not see the twisted, strangely familiar leer on her lips.

1931

JAMES THURBER

THE INTERVIEW

WONDERFUL place you have here," said the man from the newspaper. He stood with his host on a rise of ground from where, down a slope to the right, they could see a dead garden, killed by winter, and, off to the left, spare, grim trees stalking the ghost of a brook.

"Everybody says that," said George Lockhorn. "Everybody says it's a wonderful place, to which I used to reply 'Thank you,' or 'I'm glad you think so,' or 'Yes, it is, isn't it?' At fifty-eight, Price, I say what I know. I say that you and the others are, by God, debasing the word wonderful. This bleak prospect is no more wonderful than a frozen shirt. Even in full summer it's no more wonderful than an unfrozen shirt. I will give you the synonyms for wonderful—wondrous, miraculous, prodigious, astonishing, amazing, phenomenal, unique, curious, strange. I looked them up an hour ago, because I knew you would say this is a wonderful place. Apply any of those words to that dahlia stalk down there."

"I see what you mean," said Price, who was embarrassed, and began looking in his pockets for something that wasn't there.

"I have known only a few wonderful things in my fifty-eight years," said Lockhorn. "They are easy to enumerate, since I have been practicing up to toss them off to you casually: the body of a woman, the works of a watch, the verses of Keats, the structure of the hyacinth, the devotion of the dog. Trouble is, I tossed those off casually for the Saint Louis *Post-Dispatch* man, or the Rochester *Times-Union* man. It's cold out here. Shall we go inside?"

"Just as you say," said the interviewer, who had reached for the copy paper and the pencil in his pocket, but didn't bring them out. "It's bracing out here, though."

"You're freezing to death, without your hat and overcoat, and you know it," said Lockhorn. "It's late enough for a highball— Do you drink cocktails?"

"No, sir. That is, not often," said Price.

"You're probably a liar," Lockhorn said. "Everybody replies to my questions the way they think I want them to reply. You can say that I say 'everybody-they;' I hate 'everybody-he.' 'Has everybody brought his or her slate?' a teacher of mine, a great goat of a woman, used to ask us. There is no other tongue in the world as clumsy as ours is—with its back to certain corners. That's been used, too—and don't make notes, or don't let me see you make notes. Never made a note in my life, except after a novel was finished. Plot the chapters out, outline the characters after the book has been published."

"That is extremely interesting," said Price. "What do you do with the notes?"

They had reached the rear of the house now. "We'll go in the back way," said Lockhorn. "I keep them around, tuck them away where my executor can find them if he's on his toes. This is the woodshed. We'll go through the kitchen. Some of my best character touches, some of the best devices, too, are in the notes. Anybody can write a novel, but it takes talent to do notes. We'll go through this door."

"This is wonderful," said Price. "I'm sorry. I mean—"

"Let it stand," said Lockhorn. "Wonderful in the sense of being astonishing, curious, and strange. Don't take the chair by the fire," he added as they reached the living room. "That's mine."

LOCKHORN dropped into the chair by the fireplace and motioned his guest into another. "Can I use that about the notes?" asked Price. "Mr. Hammer wants something new."

"Make us both a drink," Lockhorn said. "That's a bar over there. I drink bourbon, but there's Scotch and rye, too."

"I'll have bourbon," said Price.

"Everybody has what I have," Lockhorn growled. "I said Scotch, and the *Times-Union* man had Scotch; I said rye, and the *Post-Dispatch* man had rye. No, you can't use that about the notes. Tell it to everybody. Beginning to believe it myself. Have you gained the idea in your half hour here that I am a maniac?"

Price, noisily busy with bottles and glasses, laughed uncomfortably. "Everybody knows that your methods of work are unusual," he said. "May I ask what you are working on now?"

"Easy on the soda," said Lockhorn. "Martha will raise hell when she finds me drinking. Just bow at her and grin."

Price put two frightened squirts of soda in one glass and filled up the other. "Mrs. Lockhorn?" he asked, handing the strong highball to his host.

"What is this man Hammer like?" Lockhorn demanded. "No, let me tell you. He says 'remotely resembles,' he says 'flashes of insight.' He begins, by God, sentences with 'moreover.' I had an English teacher who began sentences with 'too.' 'Too, there are other factors to be considered.' The man says he's read Macaulay, but he never got past page six—Hammer, that is. Should have gone into real estate—subdivisions, opening up suburbs, and so on. This English teacher started every class by saying, 'None of us can write.' Hadn't been for that man, I would have gone into real estate—subdivisions, opening up suburbs, and so on. But he was a challenge. You can say my memoirs will be called 'I Didn't Want to Write.'" Lockhorn had almost finished his drink. "I'll have to see a proof," he said. "I'll have to see a proof of your article. Have you noticed that everybody says everything twice? They say everything twice. 'Yes, they do,' you'll say. 'Yes, they do.' Only contribution I've made to literature is the discovery of the duplicate statement. 'How the hell are you, Bill?' a guy will say. 'How the hell are you, anyway?' 'Fine,' Bill will say. 'Just fine.'"

"That's very interesting," said Price, and, feeling that his host expected it, he added, "That's very interesting."

Lockhorn held out his glass and Price carried it back to the bar. "The *Times* man, or whoever it was," Lockhorn went on, "put down that one of the things I regard as wonderful is the feminine anatomy. You can't get 'body of a woman' in the papers. The feminine anatomy is something that can be touched only with the mind, and you'll notice that in my list everything can be touched by the hand. A watch a man never held would not be wonderful."

"That's true," said Price, speculating on the factual aspect of devotion.

"There is only one thing I've never told an interviewer," Lockhorn said, after a pause. "I've never told any interviewer about the game.

'Don't tell the man about the game,' Mrs. Lockhorn always says. 'Promise me you won't tell the man about the game.' Let me ask you one thing—why would Martha ask me not to tell you about the game if there were no game?"

"She wouldn't, of course," said Price, taking a long slow sip of his drink to cover his embarrassment. The two men drank in silence for a while. "My second wife left me because of the game," Lockhorn said, "but you can't print that, because she would deny it, and I would deny it." Lockhorn took a great gulp of his drink and stared into the fire again. Two minutes of silence went by, during which Price found himself counting the ticks of the clock on the mantelpiece. "My memory is beginning to slip," Lockhorn said, "but if you print that, I'll sue Hammer's pants off. Maybe I'll sue his pants off anyway. Sunday editors are the worst vermin in the world. If you use that, credit it to Mencken. I don't know why the hell you boys want to interview me. I've said a great many sharp things in my life, but I can't remember which ones are mine and which ones were said by Santayana, or John Jay Chapman, or Bernard De Voto. You can say my memory is slipping—maybe it will arouse pity. I'm the loneliest man in the United States." Lockhorn had finished his drink very fast, and he got up and walked to the bar. Price's eyebrows went up as he heard the heavy slug of bourbon chortle into the glass. "Martha'll be sore as a pup," Lockhorn said with an owlish grin. "Just touch your forelock to her. You can't argue with her. She's my fourth wife, you know. The others were Dorothy, Nettie, and Pauline, not necessarily in that order." He came back to his chair and flopped into it. Price began to listen to the clock again. Lockhorn's head jerked up suddenly. "Going to call my memoirs 'I Had to Write,' " he said. "You can put that in your piece if you want to."

WHEN Mrs. Lockhorn came into the room, smiling her small, apprehensive smile, Price had just handed his host a seventh highball. "This is Pricey," said Lockhorn. Price, who had jumped to his feet, stood bowing and grinning at his hostess. She barely touched him with her smile. "One for the house," said Lockhorn, holding up his drink.

"It's early," said Mrs. Lockhorn. "It isn't five yet."

"I must be going," Price said. "May I make you a drink, Mrs. Lockhorn?"

"No, thank you," she said, in a tone that corked the bottles.

"Nonsense," said Lockhorn. "Sit down, Pricey. I've never, by God, known anything like the female timetable. They live by the clock. The purpose of 6 P.M. is to unlock their inhibitions about liquor. Sexual intercourse is for holidays—"

"George!" said Mrs. Lockhorn sharply.

Price began to babble. "Well, I guess it was us men—we men—who actually set a schedule for drinking, with that business about the sun over the yardarm, wasn't it, Mr. Lockhorn?"

"Sun over your grandma's thigh," said Lockhorn irritably, looking at Price but aiming the phrase at his wife. "Who called tea 'the five o'clock'? Women, French women. They don't even believe a man should smoke until he puts on his tuxedo. We are a prisoner of the hours, Pricey, and you know it." Price flushed and became vastly conscious of his hands.

"Finish your drink," said Martha Lockhorn to Price. "My husband is going to finish his, and then I'm afraid he must rest. The new book has taken a great deal out of him."

"You're goddam tootin' he's going to finish his," said Lockhorn, his fingers whitening on his glass, "and don't third-person me. Sit down, Pricey. We're just getting started." Price sat stiffly on the edge of his chair. He saw that Mrs. Lockhorn, who had moved behind her husband's chair, was trying to communicate with him by a shake of her head and a glance at the bar. "Don't let 'em third-person you, Pricey," said Lockhorn sternly. "Next comes the first person plural—they first-person-plural you to death. Then you might just as well go to bed and die. You might just as well go to bed and die."

"I hope he hasn't been entertaining you with imprecations all afternoon," said Mrs. Lockhorn.

"Oh, no indeed," exclaimed Price, picking up his glass and setting it down.

"She loves the happy phrase," said Lockhorn. "She spends more time on phrases than most women do on their hips."

"Don't be tiresome, George," said Mrs. Lockhorn. She turned to Price. "You see, he has been interviewed constantly," she told him. "It seems as if there has been an interviewer here every day since his novel came out. You all want something different, and then it never comes out the way he says it. It's all twisted and ridiculous."

"I hope to avoid that sin," said Price, noting that the famous author had closed his eyes but still kept his tight grip on his glass.

"He's terribly tired." Mrs. Lockhorn's voice was lowered to a whisper, as if they were in a sickroom. "He worked four years on 'The Flaw in the Crystal.' Some of the reviews have hurt him deeply."

"It's selling wonderfully," whispered Price.

Mrs. Lockhorn made a gesture with her hands, but its meaning was lost on him.

The novelist opened his eyes and quickly finished his drink. "I'll tell you some other wonderful things," he said. "A woman crying, children calling over the snow—across the snow—dogs barking at a distance, dogs barking far off at night." He put his empty glass on the floor and groped in the air for more wonders with his right hand. "Things I've wanted to do," he went on. "You can use this, Pricey. Bat baseballs through the windows of a firescraper from a lower roof across the street, spend—"

"Skyscraper," said Mrs. Lockhorn.

To Price's secret delight his host, after a slow stare at Mrs. Lockhorn, repeated with great authority, "Firescraper." He winked at Price. "I want to spend the night in Ovington's," he said. "I want to open a pigeon. All my life I've wanted to cut a dove open, looking for the goddamnedest omens in the history of the world. Like the Romans performing the ancient assizes. I want to find two hearts in one of the sons of bitches and go crying through the night, like another Whozis, 'Repent, ye sinners, repent. The world is coming to an end.'"

"George," said Mrs. Lockhorn, "the newspapers can't print things like that."

Lockhorn didn't hear her. He picked up the glass and drank the trickle of ice water in it. "Go down, ye sinners, to the sea," he said, with a wide gesture.

"Talk about your book," said his wife. "The newspapers want to know about your book."

Lockhorn looked at her. "They are all the same, Pricey," he said, "and they differ as the waves differ. Only in height. The blood of the dove, as they say, Pricey. I'll tell you about the book, drunk as I unexpectedly am, or get."

"He's terribly tired," cut in his wife.

"Spiritual hope!" bawled Lockhorn, so loudly Price started the ice tinkling in his glass. "Spiritual hope is my tiny stock in trade, to quote the greatest master of them all."

Mrs. Lockhorn, observing that the newspaperman looked puzzled, said, "He means Henry James," and then, to her husband, "I think he spoke of his *small* trade, George."

"The greatest master of them all," said Lockhorn again. "I always begin with a picture, a visual picture. Woman standing in the doorway with the evening sun in her hair. Dying rays of the evening sun in her hair, as Hockett would put it."

"Hockett?" asked Price, realizing, with a small cold feeling in his stomach, that he was not going to have anything to write.

"Your boss," said Lockhorn.

"Oh, Hammer," said Price.

"I beg your pardon?" said Mrs. Lockhorn.

The author jiggled what was left of the ice in his glass. "The women write backwards," he said, "beginning with their titles—'Never Dies the Dream,' 'Lonely Is the Hunting Heart.' "

"It's 'The Heart Is a Lonely Hunter,' " said his wife, but Lockhorn waved her away.

"I'm tired of the adult world seen through the eyes of a little girl," he said. "A woman forgets everything that happens to her after she is fourteen. I, too, have lived in Arcady, Pricey, but I'm tired of viewing the adult world through the great solemn eyes of a sensitive— What is that word like nipper?"

"Moppet?" asked Price.

"Sensitive moppet," said Lockhorn, closing his eyes, and sinking deeper in his chair.

Price attempted to make a surreptitious note on his copy paper.

"You can't use that," whispered Mrs. Lockhorn. "He's talking about one of his closest women friends."

The interviewer put his pencil and paper away as his host opened his eyes again and pointed a finger at him. "Henry James had the soul of an eavesdropper," he said. Price gave a laugh that did not sound like his own. "Everything he got, he got from what he overheard somebody say. No visual sense, and if you haven't got visual sense, what have you got?"

Price stood up as if to go, but Lockhorn waved him down again and grinned at his wife. "Pricey, here, has invented some remarkable game, Martha," he said. "Tell Martha about your game, son. It's all we've talked about all afternoon."

Price swallowed.

"What sort of game is it?" asked Martha.

"It's nothing, really," gurgled Price. He stood up again. "I must be running along," he said.

"Sit down for a moment," said Mrs. Lockhorn. "George, you better lie down awhile."

To Price's astonishment, the novelist got meekly to his feet and started for the door into the hall. He stopped in front of Price and stuck an index finger into his ribs, making a skucking sound with his tongue. "Is love worse living?" he said, and went out into the hall and closed the door behind him. He began to stomp up the carpeted stairs, shouting, "Dorothy! Nettie! Martha!"

Price, swallowing again, idiotically wondered what ever became of Pauline.

"As you see, he's really worn out," said Mrs. Lockhorn hastily. "He's not as young as he used to be, of course, and I wish he'd give up writing. After all, he's written eighteen books and he has a comfortable income."

From far upstairs Price heard a now faint shouting for the lost Pauline.

"Are you sure you won't have another drink?" asked Mrs. Lockhorn, not moving from the edge of her chair.

"A quick one, perhaps," said Price. "Just half a glass."

"Surely," said Mrs. Lockhorn with the hint of a sigh, taking his glass. "Bourbon?"

"Scotch, if you don't mind," said Price.

She made it very small, and very weak. "I know that you will use discretion," she said. "George has become a little reckless in some of the things he says, and I hope you were able to tell the truth from the things he just makes up."

Price finished half his drink. "I'm afraid I really haven't got anything," he said miserably. "Perhaps you could tell me something I could use."

Mrs. Lockhorn looked mysterious. "There are some wonderful things about the book," she said. "I mean about the way he wrote it and what had to be done by the publishers. He had actually written, word for word, a chapter from one of his earlier books into the new one. He hadn't copied it, you understand. It was simply there in his memory, word for word." Price got out his pencil and paper, but his hostess lifted her hand. "Oh, mercy!" she said. "You can't possibly print that. He would be furious if he found it out."

Price looked puzzled. "If he found it out?" he asked.

She stood up and Price got to his feet. "Oh, he doesn't remember writing it," she said. "It was just stuck in. The publishers had to take it out. But you mustn't mention it. Please don't even tell Mr. Hockett."

Price set his glass down on the table beside his chair. "I believe my hat and overcoat—" he began.

"I'll get them," she said. "They must be in the hall closet."

They went to the closet. There was no sound from upstairs. Price got into his coat, and Mrs. Lockhorn went with him to the front door and opened it. "I'm sorry," she said. "I'm afraid it's been something of a wild-goose chase."

"I'm afraid it has," said Price, a little grimly.

Mrs. Lockhorn gave him her best hostess smile. "George gets mixed up when he's tired," she explained, "or he wouldn't have said 'Is love worse living?' "

Price matched her smile with one just as artificial. "He was quoting one of the most famous lines ever written by James Joyce," he said. He went out and got into his car. "Goodbye, Mrs. Lockhorn," he said.

"Goodbye, Mr. Pricey," she called to him. Her smile was gone. "I'm sorry you didn't have time to tell me about your game."

"Some other time, maybe," said Price, whose smile was also gone, and he started the engine.

Mrs. Lockhorn closed the front door.

When Price had driven a few hundred yards from the house, he took the copy paper from his pocket and threw it out of the window. Then, suddenly, he reached for his pencil and threw it out of the window, too.

1950

BRUCE JAY FRIEDMAN

LET'S HEAR IT FOR A BEAUTIFUL GUY

Sammy Davis is trying to get a few months off for a complete rest.
—*Earl Wilson, February 7, 1974.*

I HAVE been trying to get a few months off for a complete rest, too, but I think it's more important that Sammy Davis get one. I feel that I can scrape along and manage somehow, but Sammy Davis always looks so strained and tired. The pressure on the guy must be enormous. It must have been a terrific blow to him when he switched his allegiance to Agnew and Nixon, only to have the whole thing blow up in his face. I was angry at him, incidentally, along with a lot of other fans of his, all of us feeling he had sold us down the river. But after I had thought it over and let my temper cool a bit, I changed my mind and actually found myself standing up for him, saying I would bet anything that Agnew and Nixon had made some secret promises to Sammy about easing the situation of blacks—ones that the public still doesn't know about. Otherwise, there was no way he would have thrown in his lot with that crowd. In any case, I would forgive the guy just about anything. How can I feel any other way when I think of the pleasure he's given me over the years, dancing and clowning around and wrenching those songs out of that wiry little body? Always giving his all, no matter what the composition of the audience. Those years of struggle with the Will Mastin Trio, and then finally making it, only to find marital strife staring him in the face. None of us will ever be able to calculate what it took out of him each time he had a falling-out with Frank. Is there any doubt who Dean and Joey sided with on those occasions? You can be sure Peter Lawford didn't run over to offer Sammy any solace. And does anyone ever stop to consider the spiritual torment he must have suffered when he made the switch to Judaism? I don't even want to talk about the eye. So, if anyone in the world does, he certainly deserves a few months off for a complete rest.

Somehow, I have the feeling that if I met Sammy, I could break through his agents and that entourage of his and convince him he ought to take off with me and get the complete rest he deserves. I don't want any ten per cent, I don't want any glory; I just feel I owe it to him. Sure he's got commitments, but once and for all he's got to stop and consider that it's one time around, and no one can keep up that pace of his forever.

The first thing I would do is get him out of Vegas. There is absolutely no way he can get a few months' rest in that sanatorium. I would get him away from Vegas, and I would certainly steer clear of Palm Springs. Imagine him riding down Bob Hope Drive and checking into a hotel in the Springs! For a rest? The second he walked into the lobby, it would all start. The chambermaids would ask him to do a chorus of "What Kind of Fool Am I," right in the lobby, and, knowing Sammy and his big heart, he would probably oblige. I think I would take him to my place in New York, a studio. We would have to eat in, because if I ever showed up with Sammy Davis at the Carlton Delicatessen, where I have my breakfast, the roof would fall in. The owner would ask him for an autographed picture to hang up next to Dustin Hoffman's, and those rich young East Side girls would go to town on him. If they ever saw me walk in with Sammy Davis, that would be the end of his complete rest. They would attack him like vultures, and Sammy would be hard put to turn his back on them, because they're not broads.

We would probably wind up ordering some delicatessen from the Stage, although I'm not so sure that's a good idea; the delivery boy would recognize him, and the next thing you know, Sammy would give him a C note, and word would get back to Alan King that Sammy had ducked into town. How would it look if he didn't drop over to the Stage and show himself? Next thing you know, the news would reach Jilly's, and if Frank was in town—well, you can imagine how much rest Sammy would get. I don't know if they're feuding these days, but you know perfectly well that, at minimum, Frank would send over a pure-bred Afghan. Even if they were feuding.

I think what we would probably do is lay low and order a lot of Chinese food. I have a hunch that Sammy can eat Chinese takeout food every night of the week. I know I can, and the Chinese takeout delivery guys are very discreet. So we would stay at my place. I'd give him the sleeping loft, and I'd throw some sheets on the couch downstairs for me. I would do that for Sammy to pay him back for all the joy he's given me down through the years. And I would resist the temptation to ask him to sing, even though I would flip out if he so much as started humming. Can you imagine him humming "The Candy Man"? *In my apartment?* Let's not even discuss it.

Another reason I would give him the sleeping loft is that there is no phone up there. I would try like the devil to keep him away from the phone, because I know the second he saw one he would start thinking about his commitments, and it would be impossible for the guy not to make at least one call to the Coast. So I'd just try to keep him comfortable for as long as possible, although pretty soon my friends would begin wondering what ever happened to me, and it would take all the willpower in the world not to let on that I had Sammy Davis in my loft and was giving him a complete rest.

I DON'T kid myself that I could keep Sammy Davis happy in my loft for a full couple of months. He would be lying on the bed, his frail muscular body looking lost in a pair of boxer shorts, and before long I would hear those fingers snapping, and I would know that the wiry little great entertainer was feeling penned up, and it would be inhuman to expect him to stay there any longer. I think that when I sensed that

Sammy was straining at the leash, I would rent a car—a Ford LTD (that would be a switch for him, riding in a Middle American car)—and we would ride out to my sister and brother-in-law's place in Jersey. He would probably huddle down in the seat, but somehow I have the feeling that people in passing cars would spot him. We'd be lucky if they didn't crash into telephone poles. And if I know Sammy, whenever someone recognized him he wouldn't be able to resist taking off his shades and graciously blowing them a kiss.

The reason I would take Sammy to my sister and brother-in-law's house is not only that it's out of the way but also because they're simple people and would not hassle him—especially my brother-in-law. My sister would stand there with her hands on her hips, and when she saw me get out of the Ford with Sammy, she would cluck her tongue and say, "There goes my crazy brother again," but she would appear calm on the surface, even though she would be fainting dead away on the inside. She would say something like "Oh, my God, I didn't even clean the floors," but then Sammy would give her a big hug and a kiss, and I'm sure that he would make a call, and a few weeks later she would have a complete new dining-room set, the Baby Grand she always wanted, and a puppy.

She would put Sammy up in her son's room (he's away at graduate school), saying she wished she had something better, but he would say, "Honey, this is just perfect." And he would mean it, too, in a way, my nephew's bedroom being an interesting change from those $1,000-a-day suites at the Tropicana. My brother-in-law has a nice easygoing style and would be relaxing company for Sammy, except that Al does work in television and there would be a temptation on his part to talk about the time he did the "Don Rickles Show" and how different and sweet a guy Don is when you get him offstage. If I know Sammy, he would place a call to C.B.S.—with no urging from any of us—and see to it that Al got to work on his next special. If the network couldn't do a little thing like that for him, the hell with them, he would get himself another network. Sammy's that kind of guy.

One danger is that my sister, by this time, would be going out of her mind and wouldn't be able to resist asking Sammy if she could have a few neighbors over on a Saturday night. Let's face it, it would be the thrill of a lifetime for her. I would intercede right there, because it wouldn't be fair to the guy, but if I know Sammy he would tell her, "Honey, you go right ahead." She would have a mixed group over—Italians, an Irish couple, some Jews, about twelve people tops—and she would wind up having the evening catered, which of course would lead to a commotion when she tried to pay for the stuff. No way Sammy would let her do that. He would buy out the whole delicatessen, give the delivery guy a C note, and probably throw in an autographed glossy without being asked.

Everyone at the party would pretend to be casual, as if Sammy Davis wasn't there, but before long the Irish space salesman's wife (my sister's crazy friend, and what a flirt *she* is) would somehow manage to ask him to sing, and imagine Sammy saying no in a situation like that. Everyone would say just one song, but that bighearted son of a gun would wind up doing his entire repertoire, probably putting out every bit as much as he does when he opens at the Sands. He would do it all—"The Candy Man," "What Kind of Fool Am I," tap-dance, play the drums with chopsticks on an end table, do some riffs on my nephew's old trumpet, and work himself into exhaustion. The sweat would be pouring out of him, and he would top the whole thing off with "This Is My Life" ("and I don't give a damn"). Of course, his agents on the Coast would pass out cold if they ever got wind of the way he was putting out for twelve nobodies in Jersey. But as for Sammy, he never did know anything about halfway measures. He either works or he doesn't, and he would use every ounce of energy in that courageous little show-biz body of his to see to it that my sister's friends—that mixed group of Italians, Irish, and Jews—had a night they'd never forget as long as they lived.

OF course, that would blow the two months of complete rest, and I would have to get him out of Jersey fast. By that time, frankly, I would be running out of options. Once in a while, I pop down to Puerto Rico for a three- or four-day holiday, but, let's face it, if I showed up in San Juan with Sammy, first thing you know, we would be hounded by broads, catching the show at the Flamboyan, and Dick Shawn would be asking Sammy to hop up onstage and do a medley from "Mr. Wonderful." (He was really something in that show, battling Jack Carter tooth and nail, but too gracious to use his bigger name to advantage.)

Another possibility would be to take Sammy out to see a professor friend of mine who teaches modern lit. at San Francisco State and would be only too happy to take us in. That would represent a complete change for Sammy, a college campus, but as soon as the school got wind he was around, I'll bet you ten to one they would ask him to speak either to a film class or the drama department or even a political-science group. And he would wind up shocking them with his expertise on the Founding Fathers and the philosophy behind the Bill of Rights. The guy reads, and I'm not talking about "The Bette Davis Story." Anyone who sells Sammy Davis short as an intellectual is taking his life in his hands.

In the end, Sammy and I would probably end up in Vermont, where a financial-consultant friend of mine has a cabin that he never uses. He always says to me, "It's there, for God's sakes—use it." So I would take Sammy up there, away from it all, but I wouldn't tell the financial consultant who I was taking, because the second he heard it was Sammy Davis he would want to come along. Sammy and I would start out by going into town for a week's worth of supplies at the general store, and then we would hole up in the cabin. I'm not too good at mechanical things, but we would be sort of roughing it, and there wouldn't be much to do except chop some firewood, which I would take care of while Sammy was getting his complete rest.

I don't know how long we would last in Vermont. Frankly, I would worry after a while about being able to keep him entertained, even though he would be there for a complete rest. We could talk a little about Judaism, but, frankly, I would be skating on thin ice in that area, since I don't have the formal training he has or any real knowledge of theology. The Vermont woods would probably start us batting around theories about the mystery of existence, but to tell the truth, I'd be a little bit out of my depth in that department, too. He's had so much experience on panel shows, and I would just as soon not go one-on-one with him on that topic.

Let's not kid around, I would get tense after a while, and Sammy would feel it. He would be too good a guy to let on that he was bored, but pretty soon he would start snapping those fingers and batting out tunes on the back of an old *Saturday Evening Post* or something, and I think I would crack after a while and say, "Sammy, I tried my best to supply you with a couple of months of complete rest, but I'm running out of gas." He would tap me on the shoulder and say, "Don't worry about it, babe," and then, so as not to hurt my feelings, he would say he wanted to go into town to get some toothpaste. So he would drive in, with the eye and all, and I know damned well the first thing he would do is call his agents on the Coast and ask them to read him the "N.Y. to L.A." column of a few *Varieties*. Next thing you know, I would be driving him to the airport, knowing in my heart that I hadn't really succeeded. He would tell me that any time I got to the Coast or Vegas or the Springs, and I wanted anything, *anything*, just make sure to give him a ring. And the following week, I would receive a freezer and a videotape machine and a puppy.

So I think I'm just not the man to get Sammy Davis the complete rest he needs so desperately. However, I certainly think someone should. How long can he keep driving that tortured little frame of his, pouring every ounce of his strength into the entertainment of Americans? I know, I know—there's Cambodia and Watergate, and, believe me, I haven't forgotten our own disadvantaged citizens. I know all that. But when you think of all the joy that man has spread through his night-club appearances, his albums, his autobiography, his video specials, and even his movies, which did not gross too well but were a lot better than people realized, and the things he's done not only for his friends but for a lot of causes the public doesn't know about—when you think of all that courageous little entertainer has given to this land of ours, and then you read that he's trying, repeat *trying*, to get a few months off for a complete rest and he can't, well, then, all I can say is that there's something basically rotten in the system.

1974

DONALD BARTHELME

THE KING OF JAZZ

WELL I'm the king of jazz now, thought Hokie Mokie to himself as he oiled the slide on his trombone. Hasn't been a 'bone man been king of jazz for many years. But now that Spicy MacLammermoor, the old king, is dead, I guess I'm it. Maybe I better play a few notes out of this window here, to reassure myself.

"Wow!" said somebody standing on the sidewalk. "Did you hear that?"

"I did," said his companion.

"Can you distinguish our great homemade American jazz performers, each from the other?"

"Used to could."

"Then who was that playing?"

"Sounds like Hokie Mokie to me. Those few but perfectly selected notes have the real epiphanic glow."

"The what?"

"The real epiphanic glow, such as is obtained only by artists of the calibre of Hokie Mokie, who's from Pass Christian, Mississippi. He's the king of jazz, now that Spicy MacLammermoor is gone."

Hokie Mokie put his trombone in its trombone case and went to a gig. At the gig everyone fell back before him, bowing.

"Hi Bucky! Hi Zoot! Hi Freddie! Hi George! Hi Thad! Hi Roy! Hi Dexter! Hi Jo! Hi Willie! Hi Greens!"

"What we gonna play, Hokie? You the king of jazz now, you gotta decide."

"How 'bout 'Smoke'?"

"Wow!" everybody said. "Did you hear that? Hokie Mokie can just knock a fella out, just the way he pronounces a word. What a intonation on that boy! God Almighty!"

"I don't want to play 'Smoke,' " somebody said.

"Would you repeat that, stranger?"

"I don't want to play 'Smoke.' 'Smoke' is dull. I don't like the changes. I refuse to play 'Smoke.' "

"He refuse to play 'Smoke'! But Hokie Mokie is the king of jazz and he says 'Smoke'!"

"Man, you from outa town or something? What do you mean you refuse to play 'Smoke'? How'd you get on this gig anyhow? Who hired you?"

"I am Hideo Yamaguchi, from Tokyo, Japan."

"Oh, you're one of those Japanese cats, eh?"

"Yes I'm the top trombone man in all of Japan."

"Well you're welcome here until we hear you play. Tell me, is the Tennessee Tea Room still the top jazz place in Tokyo?"

"No, the top jazz place in Tokyo is the Square Box now."

"That's nice. O.K., now we gonna play 'Smoke' just like Hokie said. You ready, Hokie? O.K., give you four for nothin'. One! Two! Three! Four!"

The two men who had been standing under Hokie's window had followed him to the club. Now they said:

"Good God!"

"Yes, that's Hokie's famous 'English sunrise' way of playing. Playing with lots of rays coming out of it, some red rays, some blue rays, some green rays, some green stemming from a violet center, some olive stemming from a tan center—"

"That young Japanese fellow is pretty good, too."

"Yes, he is pretty good. And he holds his horn in a peculiar way. That's frequently the mark of a superior player."

"Bent over like that with his head between his knees—good God, he's sensational!"

He's sensational, Hokie thought. Maybe I ought to kill him.

But at that moment somebody came in the door pushing in front of him a four-and-one-half-octave marimba. Yes, it was Fat Man Jones, and he began to play even before he was fully in the door.

"What're we playing?"

" 'Billie's Bounce.' "

"That's what I thought it was. What're we in?"

"F."

"That's what I thought we were in. Didn't you use to play with Maynard?"

"Yeah I was on that band for a while until I was in the hospital."

"What for?"

"I was tired."

"What can we add to Hokie's fantastic playing?"

"How 'bout some rain or stars?"

"Maybe that's presumptuous?"

"Ask him if he'd mind."

"You ask him, I'm scared. You don't fool around with the king of jazz. That young Japanese guy's pretty good, too."

"He's sensational."

"You think he's playing in Japanese?"

"Well I don't think it's English."

This trombone's been makin' my neck green for thirty-five years, Hokie thought. How come I got to stand up to yet another challenge, this late in life?

"Well, Hideo—"

"Yes, Mr. Mokie?"

"You did well on both 'Smoke' and 'Billie's Bounce.' You're just about as good as me, I regret to say. In fact, I've decided you're *better* than me. It's a hideous thing to contemplate, but there it is. I have only been the king of jazz for twenty-four hours, but the unforgiving logic of this art demands we bow to Truth, when we hear it."

"Maybe you're mistaken?"

"No, I got ears. I'm not mistaken. Hideo Yamaguchi is the new king of jazz."

"You want to be king emeritus?"

"No, I'm just going to fold up my horn and steal away. This gig is yours, Hideo. You can pick the next tune."

"How 'bout 'Cream'?"

"O.K., you heard what Hideo said, it's 'Cream.' You ready, Hideo?"

"Hokie, you don't have to leave. You can play too. Just move a little over to the side there—"

"Thank you, Hideo, that's very gracious of you. I guess I will play a little, since I'm still here. Sotto voce, of course."

"Hideo is wonderful on 'Cream'!"

"Yes, I imagine it's his best tune."

"What's that sound coming in from the side there?"

"Which side?"

"The left."

"You mean that sound that sounds like the cutting edge of life? That sounds like polar bears crossing Arctic ice pans? That sounds like a herd of musk ox in full flight? That sounds like male walruses diving to the bottom of the sea? That sounds like fumaroles smoking on the slopes of Mt. Katmai? That sounds like the wild turkey walking through the deep, soft forest? That sounds like beavers chewing trees in an Appalachian marsh? That sounds like an oyster fungus growing on an aspen trunk? That sounds like a mule deer wandering a montane of the Sierra Nevada? That sounds like prairie dogs kissing? That sounds like witchgrass tumbling or a river meandering? That sounds like manatees munching seaweed at Cape Sable? That sounds like coatimundis moving in packs across the face of Oklahoma? That sounds like—"

"Good God, it's Hokie! Even with a cup mute on, he's blowing Hideo right off the stand."

"Hideo's playing on his knees now! Good God, he's reaching into his belt for a large steel sword— Stop him!"

"Wow! That was the most exciting 'Cream' ever played! Is Hideo all right?"

"Yes, somebody is getting him a glass of water."

"You're my man, Hokie! That was the dadblangedest thing I ever saw!"

"You're the king of jazz once again!"

"Hokie Mokie is the most happening thing there is!"

"Yes, Mr. Hokie sir, I have to admit it, you blew me right off the stand. I see I have many years of work and study before me still."

"That's O.K., son. Don't think a thing about it. It happens to the best of us. Or it almost happens to the best of us. Now I want everybody to have a good time because we're gonna play 'Flats.' 'Flats' is next."

"With your permission, sir, I will return to my hotel and pack. I am most grateful for everything I have learned here."

"That's O.K., Hideo. Have a nice day. He-he. Now, 'Flats.' "

1977

VERONICA GENG

MY MAO

"Kay, would you like a dog? . . ." Ike asked.
"Would I? Oh, General, having a dog would be heaven!"
"Well," he grinned, "if you want one, we'll get one."
            —*"Past Forgetting: My Love Affair with Dwight D. Eisenhower."*

"I don't want you to be alone," he said after a while.
"I'm used to it."
"No, I want you to have a dog."
            —*"A Loving Gentleman: The Love Story of William Faulkner and Meta Carpenter."*

WHY this reminiscence, this public straining of noodles in the colander of memory? The Chairman despised loose talk. Each time we parted, he would seal my lips together with spirit gum and whisper, "Mum for Mao." During our ten-year relationship, we quarrelled only once—when I managed to dissolve the spirit gum with nail-polish remover and told my best friend about us, and it got back to a relative of the Chairman's in Mongolia. These things happen; somebody always knows somebody. But for one month the Chairman kept up a punishing silence, even though we had agreed to write each other daily when it was not possible to be together. Finally, he cabled this directive: "ANGRILY ATTACK THE CRIMES OF SILLY BLABBERMOUTHS." I knew then that I was forgiven; his love ever wore the tailored gray uniform of instruction.

UNTIL now, writing a book about this well-known man has been the farthest thing from my mind—except perhaps for writing a book about someone else. I lacked shirts with cuffs to jot memorandums on when he left the room. I was innocent of boudoir electronics. I failed even to record the dates of his secret visits to this country (though I am now free to disclose that these visits were in connection with very important official paperwork and high-powered meetings). But how can I hide while other women publish? Even my friends are at it. Fran is writing "Konnie!: Adenauer in Love." Penny and Harriet are collaborating on "Yalta Groupies." And my Great-Aunt Jackie has just received a six-figure advance for " 'Bill' of Particulars: An Intimate Memoir of William Dean Howells." Continued silence on my part would only lead to speculation that Mao alone among the greatest men of the century could not command a literate young mistress.

That this role was to be mine I could scarcely have foreseen until I met him in 1966. He, after all, was a head of state, I a mere spangle on the midriff of the American republic. But you never know what will happen, and then it is not possible to remember it until it has already happened. That is the way things were with our first encounter. Only now that it is past can I look back upon it. Now I can truly see the details of the Mayflower Hotel in Washington, with its many halls and doors, its carpeted Grand Suite. I can feel the static electricity generated by my cheap nylon waitress's dress, the warmth of the silver tray on which I hoisted a selection of pigs-in-blankets.

Chairman Mao was alone. He sat in the center of the room, in an upholstered armchair—a man who looked as if he might know something I didn't. He was round, placid, smooth as a cheese. When I bent over him with the hors d'oeuvres, he said in perfect English but with the mid-back-rounded vowels pitched in the typical sharps and flats of Shaoshan, "Will you have a bite to eat with me?"

"No," I said. In those days, I never said yes to anything. I was holding out for something better than what everybody had.

He closed his eyes.

By means of that tiny, almost impatient gesture, he had hinted that my way of life was wrong.

I felt shamed, yet oddly exhilarated by the reproof. That night I turned down an invitation to go dancing with a suture salesman who gamely tried to date me once in a while. In some way I could not yet grasp, the Chairman had renewed my sense of possibility, and I just wanted to stay home.

ONE evening about six months later, there was a knock at my door. It was the Chairman, cheerful on rice wine. With his famous economy of expression, he embraced me and taught me the Ten Right Rules of Lovemaking: Reconnoitre, Recruit, Relax, Recline, Relate, Reciprocate, Rejoice, Recover, Reflect, and Retire. I was surprised by his ardor, for I knew the talk that he had been incapacitated by a back injury in the Great Leap Forward. In truth, his spine was supple as a peony stalk. The only difficulty was that it was sensitive to certain kinds of pressure. A few times he was moved to remind me, "Please, don't squeeze the Chairman."

When I awoke the next morning, he was sitting up in bed with his eyes closed. I asked him if he was thinking. "Yes," he said, without opening his eyes. I was beginning to find his demeanor a little stylized. But what right did I have to demand emotion? The Cultural Revolution had just started, and ideas of the highest type were surely forming themselves inside his skull.

He said, "I want to be sure you understand that you won't see me very often."

"That's insulting," I said. "Did you suppose I thought China was across the street?"

"It's just that you mustn't expect me to solve your problems," he said. "I already have eight hundred million failures at home, and the last thing I need is another one over here."

I asked what made him think I had problems.

He said, "You do not know how to follow Right Rule Number Three: Relax. But don't expect me to help you. Expect nothing."

I wanted to ask how I was supposed to relax with a world figure in my bed, but I was afraid he would accuse me of personality cultism.

When he left, he said, "Don't worry."

I THOUGHT about his words. They had not been completely satisfying, and an hour after he had left I wanted to hear them again. I needed more answers. Would he like me better if I had been through something—a divorce, a Long March, an evening at Le Club? Why should I exhaust myself in relaxation with someone who was certain to leave? Every night after work I studied the Little Red Book and wrote down phrases from it for further thought: "women . . . certain contradictions . . . down on their knees . . . monsters of all kinds . . . direct experience."

My life began to feel crowded with potential meaning. One afternoon I was sitting in the park, watching a group of schoolchildren eat their lunch. Two men in stained gray clothing lay on the grass. Once in a while they moved discontentedly from a sunny spot to a shady spot, or back again. The children ran around and screamed. When they left, one of the men went over to the wire wastebasket and rifled the children's lunch bags for leftovers. Then he baited the other man in a loud voice. He kept saying, "*You* are not going downtown, Tommy. *We* are going downtown. *We* are going downtown."

Was this the "social order" that the Chairman had mentioned? It seemed unpleasant. I wondered if I should continue to hold out for something better.

AS it happened, I saw him more often than he had led me to expect. Between visits, there were letters—his accompanied by erotic maxims. These are at present in the Yale University Library, where they will remain in a sealed container until all the people who are alive now are dead. A few small examples will suggest their nature:

> My broom sweeps your dust kittens.
> Love manifests itself in the hop from floor to pallet.
> If you want to know the texture of a flank, someone must roll over.

WE always met alone, and after several years *dim sum* at my place began to seem a bit hole-in-corner. "Why don't you ever introduce me to your friends?" I asked. The Chairman made no reply, and I feared I had pushed too hard. We had no claims on each other, after all, no rules but the ones he sprang on me now and then. Suddenly he nodded with vigor and said, "Yes, yes." On his next trip he took me out to dinner with his friend Red Buttons. Years later, the Chairman would often say to me, "Remember that crazy time we had dinner with Red? In a restaurant? What an evening!"

Each time we met, I was startled by some facet of his character that the Western press had failed to report. I saw, for instance, that he disliked authority, for he joked bitterly about his own. No sooner had he stepped inside my bedroom than he would order, "Lights off!" When it was time for him to go, he would raise one arm from the bed as if hailing a taxi and cry, "Pants!" Once when I lifted his pants off the back of a chair and all the change fell out of the pockets, I said, "This happens a lot. I have a drawer full of your money that I've found on the floor."

"Keep it," he said, "and when it adds up to eighteen billion yuan, buy me a seat on the New York Stock Exchange." He laughed loudly, and then did his impersonation of a capitalist. "Bucks!" he shouted. "Gimme!" We both collapsed on the bed, weak with giggles at this private joke.

He was the only man I ever knew, this pedagogue in pajamas, who did not want power over me. In conversation, he was always testing my independence of thought. Once, I remember, he observed, "Marxism has tended to flourish in Catholic countries."

"What about China?" I said.

"Is China your idea of a Catholic country?"

"No, but, um—"

"See what I mean?" he said, laughing.

I had learned my lesson.

To divest himself of sexual power over me, he encouraged me to go dancing with other men while he was away. Then we held regular critiques of the boyfriends I had acquired. My favorite, a good-looking Tex-Mex poet named Dan Juan, provided us with rich material for instruction and drill.

"What is it you like about Dan Juan?" the Chairman asked me once.

"I'd really have to think about it," I said.

"Maybe he's not so interesting," said the Chairman.

"I see your point," I said. Then, with the rebelliousness of the politically indolent, I burst into tears.

The Chairman took my hand and brooded about my situation. I think he was afraid that helping me to enter into ordinary life—to go out with Dan Juan and then to learn why I should not be going out with him and so forth—might not be very much help at all.

Finally, he said, "I don't like to think you're alone when I'm not here."

"I'm not always alone."

"I'd like to give you a radio."

THE radio never reached me, although I do not doubt that he sent it. His only other gifts we consumed together: the bottles of rice wine, which we drank, talking, knowing that while this was an individual solution, it was simple to be happy. Now other women have pointed out to me that I have nothing to show for the relationship. Adenauer gave Fran a Salton Hotray. Stalin gave Harriet a set of swizzlesticks with little hammer-and-sickles on the tops. William Dean Howells gave my Great-Aunt Jackie a diamond brooch in the form of five ribbon loops terminating in diamond-set tassels, and an aquamarine-and-diamond tiara with scroll and quill-pen motifs separated by single oblong-cut stones mounted on an aquamarine-and-diamond band. That I have no such mementos means, they say, that the Chairman did not love me. I think they are being too negative, possibly.

THE Chairman believed that the most revolutionary word is "yes." What he liked best was for me to kiss him while murmuring all the English synonyms for "yes" that I could think of. And although neither of us believed in a life beyond this one, I feel to this day that I can check in with him if I close my eyes and say yes, yeah, aye, uh-huh, indeed, agreed, natch, certainly, okeydoke, of course, right, reet, for sure, you got it, well and good, amen, but def, indubitably, right on, yes sirree bob, sure nuff, positively, now you're talking, yep, yup, bet your sweet A, O.K., Roger wilco over and out.

1977

VERONICA GENG

OUR SIDE OF THE STORY

ANECDOTAL material has its place—neither Ed nor I is in a position to deny that. In fact, we got pretty deeply into that issue on our first date, drinking Rolling Rock beer at the Superba and telling all the stories we'd each heard about how horrible the other person was—stories that would curl your hair—and then finding out that while they weren't untrue, exactly, they hadn't been put into a full perspective. So we're highly aware that the anecdote in reportage, while useful, needs to be interpreted very, very cautiously.

That caution is exactly what we find lacking in the way people are now jumping to conclusions about us on the basis of these "eyewitness" reports being spread around by recent visitors to our Village apartment—not only journalists but private citizens who have come down here on junkets to see how our new regime is working out. Naturally, we hoped they would drum up popular support for our internal struggle to create a better life. We even hoped they might influence policy toward us. So much for hope. Their reports always begin with the person's breast-beating explanation of how painful it is for them to be honest about what they saw—how they had been our biggest supporters at first, and how their initial gush of sympathy gradually dried up as they were forced to confront the evidence of their senses. Far be it from us to question their sincerity, but a lot of their disillusionment is of their own creation, stemming from their original need to see me and Ed in mythic terms. Right off the bat they convinced themselves that Ed and I were going to demonstrate the impossible: that two people with bad reputations—I and Ed—could get together and be transformed overnight into a model relationship.

But I don't want to get bogged down in generalizations about what's wrong with *their* relationships to make them so desperate for a myth. Let me just take some of the specific stories they've been reporting, and deal with those. This one guy, a foreign correspondent who has actually moved into our building, has been saying he often sees a queue outside our apartment door—as he puts it, "like in Eastern Europe." From what we've heard, he goes into vivid detail about long lines of depressed-looking people shifting from foot to foot, wearing shabby clothes, carrying pathetic little parcels and lunchboxes, etc. He says one time a dowdy woman in a babushka, with a heartbreakingly small chicken she was dangling by the feet, told him tearfully that she'd been waiting outside our door for over two hours.

Now, Ed and I have been victims lately of a certain amount of economic sabotage—mainly from the Manhattan Cable TV company, Con Edison, and the phone company—and more than likely what this guy saw was a few repairmen, etc., who had failed to show up at the assigned time and then, hearing a radio or something in the apartment, assumed we were home and hung around trying to get in. As for the all too colorful touch of the woman with the undersized chicken: first of all, it was a Cornish game hen, Ed's favorite food; and second of all, the woman was his mother (who would be astonished to hear the word "dowdy" applied to herself, or "babushka" to the Hermès scarf she wears to cover her curlers). She had come over to cook dinner for Ed's birthday while we went to a movie, and she accidentally locked herself out when she went into the hall (absent-mindedly holding the game hen), thinking she heard a burglar.

It's true that Ed and I have some problems in the area of consumer goods. We wouldn't dream of minimizing that. And if some of our visitors get disenchanted when they see us using paper towels for napkins because we ran out—granted, they have a valid point, and we're working on a better-organized central system of supply. But lately one of Ed's ex-girlfriends—who of course claims that she always wished us the best and feels just awful being obliged to say anything negative about us—has been blabbing it around that we're so unhappy we don't even have enough faith in our relationship to invest in the basic necessities. She made her observations on a couple of transient visits to our place while I was away on business and Ed let her come over out of the goodness of his heart—and, I might add, her idea of "basic necessities" is a decadent bourgeois fantasy. She has gotten enormous mileage out of recounting how shocked she was when she saw that we don't have a toaster. For her information, we make toast in a frying pan because we prefer it that way.

Another thing these reports always mention is the bribes. They say Ed's and my relationship is corrupted by bribery at every level. One story that comes up over and over (always in the same words, curiously enough) is that I was seen going to various Village stores, buying stuff, and getting it wrapped up in pathetic little parcels, and then later that evening was seen giving the same parcels to Ed as a bribe to keep him at home. Again, the details are accurate as far as they go, but the story fails to mention that it was Ed's birthday eve, when (using money we could have spent on a toaster) we threw a huge birthday party, at which some of the guests apparently got too drunk to put what they saw into context. On top of which, when their own rowdiness provoked a noise complaint from upstairs, they went and reported the next day that Ed and I were destabilizing our neighbors.

Then there's the stuff about low morale—how Ed and I have such a demoralizing effect on each other that neither of us has been able to make a dentist's appointment for the entire year we've been together. The woman who's the source of this news may not have realized, as she flipped through our appointment books while Ed was in the bathroom, that we have our own priorities and are not in the habit of going to the dentist right around the time of Ed's birthday, or on other days when we have a lot on our minds—for example, when my birthday is coming up.

Oh, well—whatever we do or don't do is grist for their mill now that this revisionist line about us has set in. If Ed pinches me on the bottom in public, it's seen as evidence that we have a degenerate, sexist relationship—which makes us hypocrites into the bargain, since that's the kind of relationship we set out not to have. It doesn't occur to people that if Ed pinches me on the bottom, maybe he's doing it for exactly that reason—that he's being *ironic*.

I could go through every one of these stories—the one about us being seen drunk on the street (it was Ed's birthday, for heaven's sake!), the one about me being seen at midnight wearing dark glasses and looking "alienated" (I'd simply had too much to drink), etc. I could go bing bing bing, right down the list, but what good would it do? People just aren't skilled at interpreting what they see, and we can't spend the rest of our lives correcting them. If some intelligent, attractive person wants to move in with us for a few months and really observe us with an open mind, great. Otherwise, everybody who's interested can find out all they need to know by going to the Superba, where we still hang out, and looking at the front table, where recently Ed carved our initials in a heart. The heart was already there, along with a mess of other old carvings, and when Ed put our initials inside it, they looked raw and pale by comparison. He wanted to age them by rubbing them with cigarette ash, but I said no, I liked it that they looked fresh. I said all the other initials had probably been carved by people who hate each other now and are no longer even on speaking terms. Ed said I was right— that we were still new, even though the heart was old and ready-made.

1984

GEORGE W. S. TROW

DO YOU KNOW ME?

I WAS well known. I was so well known everyone knew me. I was the best-known person in the world. I put on my plaid shirt and my thick boots and the thin-wale corduroy pants and I was the best-known person in the world. And then I went slowly. I looked in the mirror. I wore the thin-wale corduroy pants because I think the thick-wale is effeminate. I went out my door. I went down the stairs. I lived on the second floor—no indoor entrance; I had to walk up and down outside stairs to get in and out. Outside stairs. My outside stairs. My weather-stained porch. Not a very pretty porch. No room for a nice chair. Paint peeling off, just like loneliness sloughing off the skin. Onto the sidewalk. I walked onto the sidewalk, watched the sidewalk, focussed on the sidewalk. I saw my thick boots only as a blur. So cracked, that sidewalk. The little shoots of grass, the roots of trees working the cement into dust. I was so well known that that sidewalk was well known.

I was quite well known when I was still quite young. I had many friends. Bobbi and Sammi and Tadi and Ronee and Bilye. I had so many friends. I liked friends who were girls but had boys' names, but ending in a different letter than a boy's name would. That was the kind of friend I wanted, and that was the kind of friend I had. That was my preference. My preference was for people just like that. I wanted to be specific. I wanted to be so specific that no one would have any doubts. That was the only reason I was that well known. Because it was so specific. Because there wasn't any doubt. People with a name like Sammi or Ronee or Jami or Tonee knew that kind of name was my preference. That made me well known.

Would you know me if I showed you my papers? Would you know me if I showed you my Bulldog Editions? Would you know me if I showed you my Special Home Editions? Would you let me show you the Blue Final and the Final Blue? Will you glance at my papers? Will you have a look? Do you know me when you have a look? Do you know me when I call you on the phone? Do you know me when I walk on the sidewalk, when I watch the cracks? Do you lie there and think, "It's him. He's on the sidewalk"?

Do you remember the texture of my nose? The slightly grainy texture, as though it had been rubbed and rubbed and rubbed? Do you have a general impression of my face—just that, a *general* impression? Nothing more than that? Just a vague feeling that the face is a type of face, a face of a type that a certain kind of person would have? Is it *abstract,* the way you feel, when I tried so hard to supply detail? I wanted everything so clear, so specific. I went to so much trouble. I dressed in a certain way. I dressed three times. I put on my clothes and then I took them off, and then I put them on and then I took them off, and then I put them on in a final way that was very specific. Then I walked slowly. Keeping my eye on the pavement. I made the pavement so specific. I made my friends so specific. Sometimes it happened that they thought they were general, but they were wrong. I made them specific, down to the details. I knew all the details and went over them three times. That was my preference.

Do you remember my preference? Do you remember the way I made them nervous? That was part of the preference. Do you remember the way I made them reluctant to wear their uniforms in public? That was part of my preference. So specific, my preference. So specific, the way the little uniforms looked under a big bulky coat. Would you know me if I wore a uniform? Would you know me if I wore a bulky coat? Would you know me if I moved a step closer? Would you know me if I took off my hat? Would you know me if I showed you a clipping? Would you know me if I took a clipping and circled my name so it would stand out, and then attached a small piece of white paper (with gum or mucilage) with my name typed out just like my name typed out on the Linotypes and on the wire services and on the special identification cards they require in so many places, typed out on plastic? Would you know me if I typed my name out? Would you know me if I asked you for a dime? Would you know me if I asked to walk you home?

1979

CHET WILLIAMSON

GANDHI AT THE BAT

History books and available newspaper files hold no record of the visit to America in 1933 made by Mohandas K. Gandhi. For reasons of a sensitive political nature that have not yet come to light, all contemporary accounts of the visit were suppressed at the request of President Roosevelt. Although Gandhi repeatedly appeared in public during his three-month stay, the cloak of journalistic silence was seamless, and all that remains of the great man's celebrated tour is this long-secreted glimpse of one of the Mahatma's unexpected nonpolitical appearances, written by an anonymous press-box denizen of the day.

YANKEE STADIUM is used to roaring crowds. But never did a crowd roar louder than on yesterday afternoon, when a little brown man in a loincloth and wire-rimmed specs put some wood on a Lefty Grove fastball and completely bamboozled Connie Mack's A's.

It all started when Mayor John J. O'Brien invited M. K. ("Mahatma") Gandhi to see the Yanks play Philadelphia up at "The House That Ruth Built." Gandhi, whose ballplaying experience was limited to a few wallops with a cricket bat, jumped at the chance, and 12 noon saw the Mayor's party in the Yankee locker room, where the Mahatma met the Bronx Bombers. A zippy exchange occurred when the Mayor introduced the Lord of the Loincloth to the Bambino. "Mr. Gandhi," Hizzoner said, "I want you to meet Babe Ruth, the Sultan of Swat."

Gandhi's eyes sparkled behind his Moxie-bottle lenses, and he chuckled. "Swat," quoth he, "is a sultanate of which I am not aware. Is it by any chance near Maharashtra?"

"Say," laughed the Babe, laying a meaty hand on the frail brown shoulder, "you're all right, kiddo. I'll hit one out of the park for you today."

"No hitting, please," the Mahatma quipped.

In the Mayor's front-row private box, the little Indian turned down the offer of a hot dog and requested a box of Cracker Jack instead. The prize inside was a tin whistle, which he blew gleefully whenever the Bambino waddled up to bat.

The grinning guru enjoyed the game immensely—far more than the A's, who were down 3–1 by the fifth. Ruth, as promised, did smash a homer in the seventh, to Gandhi's delight. "Hey, Gunga Din!" Ruth cried jovially on his way to the Yankee dugout. "Know why my battin' reminds folks of India? 'Cause I can really Bangalore!"

"That is a very good one, Mr. Ruth!" cried the economy-size Asian.

By the top of the ninth, the Yanks had scored two more runs. After Mickey Cochrane whiffed on a Red Ruffing fastball, Gandhi remarked how difficult it must be to hit such a swiftly thrown missile and said, "I should like to try it very much."

"Are you serious?" Mayor O'Brien asked.

"If it would not be too much trouble. Perhaps after the exhibition is over," his visitor suggested.

There was no time to lose. O'Brien, displaying a panache that would have done credit to his predecessor, Jimmy Walker, leaped up and shouted to the umpire, who called a time-out. Managers McCarthy and Mack were beckoned to the Mayor's side, along with Bill Dinneen, the home-plate umpire, and soon all of Yankee Stadium heard an unprecedented announcement:

"Ladies and gentlemen, regardless of the score, the Yankees will come to bat to finish the ninth inning."

The excited crowd soon learned that the reason for such a breach of tradition was a little brown pinch-hitter shorter than his bat. When the pin-striped Bronx Bombers returned to their dugout after the last Philadelphia batter had been retired in the ninth, the Nabob of Nonviolence received a hasty batting lesson from Babe Ruth under the stands.

Lazzeri led off the bottom of the stanza, hitting a short chop to Bishop, who rifled to Foxx for the out. Then, after Crosetti fouled out to Cochrane, the stadium became hushed as the announcer intoned, "Pinch-hitting for Ruffing, Mohandas K. Gandhi."

The crowd erupted as the white-robed holy man, a fungo bat propped jauntily on his shoulder, strode to the plate, where he remarked to the crouching Mickey Cochrane, "It is a very big field, and a very small ball."

"C'mon, Moe!" Ruth called loudly to the dead-game bantam batter. "Show 'em the old pepper!"

"I will try, Mr. Baby!" Gandhi called back, and went into a batting stance unique in the annals of the great game—his sheet-draped posterior facing the catcher, and his bat held high over his head, as if to clobber the ball into submission. While Joe McCarthy called time, the Babe trotted out and politely corrected the little Indian's position in the box.

The time-out over, Grove threw a screaming fastball right over the plate. The bat stayed on Gandhi's shoulder. "Oh, my," he said as he turned and observed the ball firmly ensconced in Cochrane's glove. "That *was* speedy."

The second pitch was another dead-center fastball. The Mahatma swung, but found that the ball had been in the Mick's glove for a good three seconds before his swipe was completed. "Stee-rike two!" Dinneen barked.

The next pitch was high and outside, and the ump called it a ball before the petite pundit made a tentative swing at it. "Must I sit down now?" he asked.

"Nah, it's a ball," Dinneen replied. "I called it before you took your cut."

"Yes. I *know* that is a ball, and I did swing at it and did miss."

"No, no, a ball. Like a free pitch."

"Oh, I see."

"Wasn't in the strike zone."

"Yes, I see."

"So you get another swing."

"Yes."

"And if you miss you sit down."

"I just *did* miss."

"Play ball, Mister."

The next pitch was in the dirt. Gandhi did not swing. "Ball," Dinneen called.

"Yes, it is," the Mahatma agreed.

"Two and two."

"That is four."

"Two balls, two strikes."

"Is there not but one ball?"

"Two balls."

"Yes, I see."

"And two strikes."

"And if I miss I sit down."

Ruth's voice came booming from the Yankee dugout: "Swing early, Gandy baby!"

"When is early?"

"When I tell ya! I'll shout '*Now!*'"

Grove started his windup. Just as his leg kicked up, the Bambino's cry of '*Now!*' filled the park.

The timing was perfect. Gandhi's molasses-in-January swing met the Grove fastball right over the plate. The ball shot downward, hit the turf, and arced gracefully into the air toward Grove. "*Run,* Peewee, *run!*" yelled Ruth, as the crowd went wild.

"Yes, yes!" cried Gandhi, who started down the first-base line in what can only be described as a dancing skip, using his bat as a walking stick. An astonished Grove booted the high bouncer, then scooped up the ball and flung it to Jimmie Foxx at first.

But Foxx, mesmerized by the sight of a sixty-three-year-old Indian in white robes advancing merrily before him and blowing mightily on a tin whistle, failed to descry the stitched orb, which struck the bill of his cap, knocking it off his head, and, slowed by its deed of dishabille, rolled to a stop by the fence.

Gandhi paused only long enough to touch first and to pick up Jimmie's cap and return it to him. By the time the still gawking Foxx had perched it once more on his head, the vital vegetarian was halfway to second.

Right fielder Coleman retrieved Foxx's missed ball and now relayed it to Max Bishop at second, but too late. The instant Bishop tossed the

ball back to the embarrassed Grove, Gandhi was off again. Grove, pan-
icking, overthrew third base, and by the time left fielder Bob Johnson
picked up the ball, deep in foul territory, the Tiny Terror of Tealand had
rounded the hot corner and was scooting for home. Johnson hurled the
ball on a true course to a stunned Cochrane. The ball hit the pocket of
Cochrane's mitt and popped out like a muffin from a toaster.

Gandhi jumped on home plate with both sandalled feet, and the
crowd exploded as Joe McCarthy, the entire Yankee squad, and even a
beaming Connie Mack surged onto the field.

"I ran home," giggled Gandhi. "Does that mean that I hit a run home?"

"A home run, Gandy," said Ruth. "Ya sure did."

"Well, technically," said Umpire Dinneen, "it was a single and an
overthrow and then—"

"*Shaddup,*" growled a dozen voices at once.

"Looked like a homer to me, too," the ump corrected, but few heard
him, for by that time the crowd was on the field, lifting to their shoulders a joyous Gandhi, whose tin whistle provided a thrilling trilling
over the mob's acclaim.

Inside the locker room, Manager McCarthy offered Gandhi a permanent position on the team, but the Mahatma graciously refused,
stating that he could only consider a diamond career with a different
junior-circuit club.

"Which club would that be, kid?" said the puzzled Bambino.

"The Cleveland Indians, of course," twinkled the Mahatma.

An offer from the Cleveland front office arrived the next day, but
India's top pinch-hitter was already on a train headed for points west—
and the history books.

1983

IAN FRAZIER

IGOR STRAVINSKY: THE SELECTED

PHONE CALLS

COMPOSER, conductor, critic, teacher, iconoclast, and grand old man, Igor Stravinsky bestrode this century like a colossus, with feet on two different continents. Already respected and popular in Europe for writing pieces like "Le Sacre du Printemps," he became equally if not more famous in his adopted country of America. The many friends he made here remember him as a man of breathtaking talent, whether he was composing an epochal symphony or playing shadow puppets in the candlelight after a small dinner party. Like many other geniuses, he was generous, almost profligate, with his gifts. He would write beautiful phrases of music on restaurant napkins and give them to friends, acquaintances, even passersby. Thoughts bubbled forth from him in such a torrent that often when he was sitting in his den writing a letter to a friend he would impulsively grab for the telephone, look up his friend's number in his address book while holding the phone to his ear with his shoulder, and dial. In a matter of seconds, he would be pouring out ideas that might have required days, even weeks, to travel through the mails. At the other end of the line, the friend would listen with delight as the great man went on, humming or singing at times, until finally he was "all talked out." Then Stravinsky would bid his grateful hearer goodbye, and, in the pleasant afterglow of inspiration,

	NO	DATE	TIME	PLACE	AREA-NUMBER	RATE APPLIED	MIN	AMOUNT
(A)	1	MAR 5	1101PM	TO NEW ORLEANS LA	504 555-6872	DIALED NIGHT	38	6.45
(B)	14	JUN 7	1037AM	TO CUSTER SD	605 555-9722	DIALED DAY	25	10.69
(C)	7	SEP 27	739PM	TO NEW YORK NY	212 555-0362	DIALED EVENING	104	31.24
(D)	15	FEB 8	833PM	FROM BOSTON MA	COL 555-1992	OPER EVENING	29	10.22
	5	JAN 7	330PM	TO SAN FRAN CA	415 555-7710	DIALED DAY	1	.29
	6	JAN 7	344PM	TO SAN FRAN CA	415 555-7710	" "	1	.29
(E)	7	JAN 7	403PM	TO SAN FRAN CA	415 555-7710	" "	1	.29
	8	JAN 7	418PM	TO SAN FRAN CA	415 555-7710	" "	1	.29

he would crumple up the unfinished letter, throw it in the wastebasket, and mix himself a cocktail.

Fortunately for us, his heirs, Stravinsky was a man aware of his place in history. With careful consideration for the students and biographers he knew would follow, he saved his telephone bills from year to year, and before his death he donated the entire corpus to the K-Tel Museum of the Best Composers Ever. What a fascinating picture these phone bills paint! With their itemized lists of long-distance calls and charges, they are like paper airplanes thrown to us from the past, providing a detailed record of the seasons of Stravinsky's mind in the multihued pageant of life as he lived it on a daily basis. And what better time for a close examination of the treasures his phone bills contain than this, the year after the centennial of Stravinsky's birth? (Actually, the centennial year itself would probably have been better, but even though this year might not be as good a time as last year, still, it is almost as good.) Now let us turn to the documents:

Ⓐ This call, made not long after Stravinsky moved to America and had his phone hooked up, shows him adjusting quickly to the ways of his new country. With scenes of Old World poverty fresh in his memory, he has prudently waited to place the call until 11:01 P.M., the very moment when the lowest off-peak rates go into effect. Such patience and calculation indicate a call that was professional rather than social in nature. Almost certainly, the recipient was Stravinsky's fellow-composer Arnold Schoenberg. It was common knowledge that Schoenberg often vacationed in New Orleans, where he enjoyed the food, the atmosphere, and the people. Stravinsky may have found out from a mutual friend where Schoenberg was staying and then surprised him with this call. Always one to speak his mind, Stravinsky probably began by telling Schoenberg that his dodecaphonic methods of musical composition were a lot of hooey. Very likely, Schoenberg would have bristled at this, and may well have reminded Stravinsky that great art, like the Master's own "Sacre," need not be immediately accessible. Stravinsky then probably made a smart remark comparing Schoenberg's methods to the methods of a troop of monkeys with a xylophone and some hammers. This probably made Schoenberg pretty mad, and it is a testament to the great (albeit hidden) regard each man had for the other that the call lasted as long as it did. Possibly, Schoenberg just held his temper and said something flip to defuse the situation, and then Stravinsky moved on to another subject. Inasmuch as they never spoke again, this intense thirty-eight-minute phone conversation may represent a seminal point in the history of twentieth-century music theory.

Ⓑ This call is of particular interest to the student because of its oddity. One is compelled to ask, "Who did Stravinsky know in Custer, South Dakota?" He never went there; none of his friends or relatives ever went there; the town has no symphony orchestra. So why did he call there? It is hard to believe that on a June morning the sudden urge for a twenty-five-minute chat with a person in Custer, South Dakota, dropped onto Stravinsky out of the blue. No, we must look elsewhere for an explanation. Two possibilities suggest themselves: (1) an acquaintance of the composer, perhaps an occasional racquetball partner, a fan, even a delivery boy from the supermarket, comes by the Stravinskys', sees no one is in, and takes the opportunity to make a long-distance call and stick someone else with the tab; or (2) the telephone company made an error. In either event, Stravinsky should not have paid the ten dollars and sixty-nine cents, and I believe it was taken from him unfairly, just as much as if a mugger had stolen it from him on the street.

Ⓒ Here we have a side of the composer's personality which we must face unflinchingly if we are to be honest. Every man has a dark side; this is his. On an evening in late September, just after dinner, Stravinsky placed a call to New York and talked for a hundred and four minutes. *A hundred and four minutes!* That's almost two hours! As one ear got tired and he switched the phone to the other, he obviously did not realize how inconsiderate he was being. It was as if he were the only person in the whole world who needed to use the phone. What if his wife wanted to make a call? What if somebody was trying to call him from a pay phone, dialling every five minutes, only to hear the busy signal's maddening refrain? Surely, after an hour or so he could have found a polite way to hang up. Surely, he could have at least made an effort to think of someone other than himself. But he didn't—he just kept yakking along, without a worry or a care, for over one hundred selfish minutes.

We should always remember that the perfection we demand of our heroes they cannot in reality ever attain.

Ⓓ Calling Stravinsky collect would seem to be the act of either a madman or a genius—or both. Yet here before us is the evidence that not only did someone pull such a stunt but Stravinsky actually went along with it and accepted the charges. In all likelihood, the caller was a young admirer, possibly a music student (Boston is known for its many music schools), who found himself in the middle of a creative crisis with nowhere else to turn. It shows how nice Stravinsky could be when he wanted to be that he gave the young man a shoulder to cry on, as well as some helpful encouragement. The disconsolate youth probably said that he despaired of ever finding an entry-level position as a composer, and that even if he did he was sure he would never make very much per week. Stravinsky may have gently reminded the lad that music is not a job but a vocation—which its true disciples cannot deny—and he may have added that a really good composer can earn a weekly salary of from eight hundred to one thousand dollars. Comforted, the student probably hung up and returned to his work with renewed dedication, and later went on to become Philip Glass or Hugo Winterhalter or André Previn. As success followed success, the young student (now adult) would always remember the time a great man cared enough to listen.

Ⓔ This delightful series of calls reveals the Master at his most puckish. The time is a drab afternoon in mid-winter; Stravinsky is knocking around the house at loose ends, possibly with a case of the post-holiday blahs. Maybe he starts idly leafing through a San Francisco telephone directory. Then, perhaps, a sudden grin crosses his face. He picks a number at random and dials. One ring. Two rings. A woman's voice answers. Stravinsky assumes a high, squeaky voice. "Is Igor there?" he asks. Informed that he has the wrong number, he hangs up.

Fourteen minutes pass. Then he calls back. In a low voice this time, he repeats his question: "Hi. Is Igor there?" Sounding a bit surprised, the woman again replies in the negative.

Nineteen minutes later, again Stravinsky dials the San Francisco number. Now his voice takes on a rich Southern accent: "Hello, Ma'am, is Igor there?"

"No, there's nobody by that name here," the woman says, by this time truly perplexed.

Stravinsky lets fifteen minutes go by. Then he is ready to deliver the classic punch line, which he has orchestrated as carefully as the crescendo in one of his most beautiful symphonies. He redials the number. The woman answers, a trace of annoyance coloring her tone. The great composer waits one beat; then, in his regular voice, he says, "Hello, this is Igor. Have there been any calls for me?"

An artist such as this comes along only once in a great while. Had he done nothing else but accumulate his remarkable portfolio of phone bills, he would merit our consideration. But, of course, he did much

more than that, in music as well as in other areas. We who are his contemporaries cannot presume to judge him in his totality; that task we
must leave for future ages blessed with a vision far greater than today's.

1983

GARRISON KEILLOR

WE ARE STILL MARRIED

ONE day last August after the vet said that Biddy had only
months to live, Willa and I took her for a cruise around Lake
Larson on our pontoon boat. She was listless and depressed from the
medication, and we thought the ride might cheer her up, but she sat
with her head in Willa's lap, her eyes closed, and when a flock of geese
flew down and landed alongside the boat she paid no attention. I felt
desolate to see her that way, and angry at other boats zipping around
without a care in the world, and so when we got home and I found a
message on the answering machine that said, "Hi, this is Blair Hague at
People magazine, and I'd like to come to Minnesota and do a piece
about your poor dog," I was relieved to know that someone cared.

Willa and I discussed it that night, and although she felt that a pet's
death is a private matter, eventually I convinced her that we should
agree to the story as a tribute to Biddy and also because, as Blair said on
the tape, our experience might help others who were going through the
same thing.

Blair arrived on Thursday with Jan, a photographer, and he explained
that they wanted to live with us, so they could do a better job. "You get
more nuance that way," he said. He had lived with a number of people
in order to write about them, including Joe Cocker, Jean Shepherd,
Merv Griffin, and the Pointer Sisters, he said. I could see his point, so
they moved in, and Jan set up a darkroom in the laundry, which was
fine with us—one thing we realized, with Biddy dying, was that we
didn't have many pictures of her—and Blair got to work gathering
background. Willa and I opened up our scrapbooks to him and Willa
even let him read her diary. I wondered about that, but she said, "Honesty is the only policy. There's a lot about Biddy in there."

We lived in a two-bedroom condominium overlooking Lake Larson, and although Blair and Jan were extremely pleasant and helped with the dishes and made their beds and kept the stereo turned down after ten o'clock, I started to feel crowded after a few days. I'd be shaving and Blair would stick his head in the bathroom door and ask, "How much do you earn a year, Earl? Do you consider yourself a religious person? Do you normally wear boxer shorts? Is that your real hair?" After work, when I like to sit down with a beer and watch television, he sat next to me. How would I describe myself? Had I ever wanted to be something other than a bus driver? How much beer did I consume per day, on the average? Was it always Bub's Beer? What were my favorite books? What was on my mind? What did I think of the future? What sorts of people made me angry?

I wanted to say, "People who ask too many questions," but I held my tongue. I did mention to Willa that I thought Blair was pushy. "The article is about Biddy, not us," I said. She thought Blair was doing an excellent job. She said, "I feel like he is helping me to understand a lot of things about us that I never thought about before."

Soon after they arrived, we noticed that Biddy was getting better. Her appetite improved, and she got so she liked to go for walks again. I told Willa I thought we should tell Blair that there was no story. She said, "There's a lot more story here than you know, Earl. Biddy is just the tip of the iceberg."

Two weeks passed, then three, and Blair wasn't running out of questions to ask. He kept coming back to the subject of our marriage. "Do you feel you have an excellent, good, average, or poor marriage? Do you regret not having had children? How many times per week do you have sexual relations? On the average—just a ballpark figure. Do you think Willa is happy?"

I said, "You ought to ask her."

"I have," he said.

Right up to the day they left, I had no idea he was going to write the story he did. Once, he said, "As so often happens, the story changes as a reporter works on it. You start out to do one thing and you wind up doing something entirely different." I thought he was referring to Biddy's improvement.

THE story was entitled "Earl: My Life with a Louse, by Willa Goodrich as told to Blair Hague, photographs by Jan Osceola," and the day it came out Willa took Biddy and moved to her mother's. I wasn't home so I didn't know she left. I was driving a charter to New Orleans. Some passengers picked up *People* in Des Moines, and as I drove South I could hear them whispering about me. In southern Missouri, a man came to the front and crouched down in the aisle beside me. "I thought you had a right to know this," he said, and he read me some parts. I couldn't believe the stuff Willa said about me! My personal grooming, my food preferences, my favorite TV shows, our arguments. And her referring to me as "stubborn and unreasonable"—why would she say that? In print!

In New Orleans, I discovered that the man had skipped some of the worst parts. Willa said she had often wanted to leave me. She said that I was uncaring and cold, that Biddy's illness didn't mean "beans" to me, and that I had talked about getting another dog soon. She said that I had "Victorian ideas about women and sex." She said I was often personally repulsive. To back her up, *People* printed three pictures with the story: me in my shorts, bending over to adjust the TV picture; me with my mouth open, full of baked potato; and me asleep on the La-Z-Boy recliner, in my shorts, with my mouth open.

I tried to reach Willa at her mother's, but she was in New York, and I saw her the next morning on "America, How Are You?" Essentially, she told Monica Montaine the same stuff, plus she said that I was "compulsive." She said, "He walks around humming the same tune over and over, usually 'Moon River.' He taps his fingers continuously, and he taps his foot in his sleep. He compulsively rips the labels off beer bottles. And at dinner he always eats all his meat first, then the potato, then the vegetable." Monica Montaine got a big kick out of that. "Sounds like he's missing the Up button," she said.

Two days later, someone from "Today" called and wanted me to get on a plane to New York and join Willa on the show for a dialogue. He said, "I think the country would like to hear your side, Earl." I told him I had no desire to engage in a public debate with my wife over matters I considered personal. Willa did the show herself, then a number of other daytime shows, and though I made a point of not watching, my friends were starting to ask questions. "Is it true about the almost total lack of any attempt at communication?" a guy at work wanted to know. "And you wearing socks in bed—any truth to that?" He said the story had given him a lot to think about.

In October, Willa testified before a House subcommittee, revealing new details about our marriage under oath. Several congressmen ex-

pressed shock at what she said about my lack of affection, my "utter in-
sensitivity" to her needs. "What was he *doing* all this time while you
were suffering?" one asked. She said, "He watched football on television. He played seven different types of solitaire. He carved a new stock
for his shotgun. He acted like I didn't exist." That was the quote they
used on "ABC World News Tonight."

I WAS lonely as winter approached. I'm not a man who can live by
himself. Some men are cut out for the single life, but not me. So I told
my boss I was available for all the charters I could get. I spent November and December mostly on the road, going to Orlando six times, Dis-
neyland four, making two runs to San Francisco. Meanwhile, I read in
People that Willa had sold her story to Universal Pictures and was in
California ironing out some wrinkles in the deal. The next week, she
got a call from the Pope, who expressed hope that efforts would be
made to reach a reconciliation. "I'm ready any time Earl is," she told the
Holy Father. She told him that although she was not a Catholic she respected the Church's view on marriage. "It's a two-way street, though,"
she said.

Finally, we met in New York, where I had driven a four-day "New
Year's Eve on the Great White Way" tour and was laying low at the Jay-
lor Hotel, and where she had rented a great apartment on the upper
West Side and was on her way to a cocktail party. We met at her place.
It was in a new building on Broadway, with a beautiful view from the
twenty-fifth floor. Biddy was living with her, of course. Biddy looked
wonderful, though she was a little hostile toward me. So were Willa's
three friends, who worked in publishing. "What do you do?" one man
asked, though I was sure he knew. The other man mentioned something about socks. The woman didn't talk to me at all. She kept telling
Willa, "We've got to get going—the invitation said five o'clock." Willa
kissed me goodbye. "Let's be friends," she said. "Call me sometime."

I did call her, four or five times, and we talked, mostly about her projects—she was writing a book, she was being considered as a substitute
host. We didn't talk about our marriage until one day in April, when
she mentioned that Biddy was sick again, and she said she missed me.
Biddy died a week later, and Willa brought the body back to Minnesota
for interment. She came to the condo for dinner one night and wound
up staying.

My friends can't believe I took her back after all those things she said about me, but I can't see where it's any of their business. I told her there was no need for her to apologize, so she hasn't. She did scrap the movie project and the book, though. The substitute-host deal fell through when the regular host decided he wasn't so tired after all. Except for our two dogs, Betty and Burt, we're almost where we were last summer. The ice has melted on Lake Larson, the lilacs and chokecherries are in bloom, soon the goslings will hatch and their mothers will lead them down to water, and everything will be as if none of this ever happened.

1984

GARRISON KEILLOR

MEETING FAMOUS PEOPLE

WHEN Big Tim Bowers just happened to turn to his left and see the little guy with the battered guitar case emerge limping from Gate 4A at the Omaha International Airport on July 12, 1985, he held out his big arms to greet his best friend, which, although they had never met in person, Sweet Brian surely was. *It was Sweet Brian himself! There! In Concourse C!* His "White Boy" album was what got Tim through the divorce from Deloyne after three loving months of marriage, when she notified him that he was hopeless and the next day upped and split for Cheyenne with a bald bread-truck driver (unbelievable), after which Tim lost his good job and apartment and would've lost his mind except for Sweet Brian, so of course he yelled, "Hey, you're my man! I got to shake your hand! Hiiiiya! Sweet Brian! Hey!"

Sweet Brian made a sharp right, climbed over a railing and a row of plastic chairs, and walked fast toward Baggage Claim, which didn't surprise Tim one bit. After all, the guy who wrote "Tie Me Loose" and "That Old Highway Suits Me Pretty Well, I Guess" and "Lovers Make Good Loners" is no Sammy Davis, Jr., and Tim respected him for the uncompromising integrity and privacy and sincerity of his art, which had been crucial to Tim when his own sense of self was chewed up by Deloyne, all of which Tim now needed to say to Sweet Brian. He galloped down the concourse after the fleeing singer-songwriter, who heard his two-hundred-and-sixty-two-pound fan and panicked and went through a door marked "No Admittance" and clattered down two flights of steel stairs, Tim's big boots whanging and whomping on the stairs above, convincing him that death was very near, and burst through a pair of swinging doors marked "Wear Earplugs" and headed across the tarmac, a man once nominated for a Grammy (for "Existential Cowboy") and once described as the Dylan of the late seventies, panting and limping around some construction barriers along the terminal wall toward a red door twenty yards away. Incredible, Tim was thinking. I come to the airport to hang around and maybe get an idea for a song—not to meet anybody or anything, just to think about something to write about, maybe about not having anybody to meet— and I meet *him*. Fantastic. Tim was six strides behind him when he burst through the red door. There was a second, locked door a few steps beyond, and then and there, in the tiny vestibule, Tim expressed a lifetime of appreciation. He hugged Sweet Brian from behind and said, "Hey, little buddy, I'm your biggest fan. You saved my life, man."

The star pushed Big Tim away and sneered, "You know, it's vampires like you who make me regret ever becoming a performer. You and your twenty-nine-cent fantasies. I don't know what you— You sicken me." And he slapped Tim.

At this point Tim wasn't thinking lawsuit at all. An apology would have been enough—e.g., "Sorry, pal. I'm under too darn much pressure right now. Please understand." He'd have said, "Fine, Sweet Brian. No problem. Just want you to know I love your music. That's all. Take care of yourself. Goodbye and God bless you." Instead, Sweet Brian said those terrible things and then *slapped him* and shoved him aside and went to the hotel and wrote an abusive song about him ("Your Biggest Fan") and sang it that night at the Stockyards, and that's how they wound up in U.S. District Court two years later.

TIM had lost quite a bit of weight in those two years, ever since he got a great job at NewTech, thanks to the company's excellent weight-loss program, which, in fact, Tim himself initiated (he's executive vice-president in charge of the entire Omaha and Lincoln operations, about eight thousand employees and growing daily since NewTech bought up SmetSys, ReinTal, and Northern Gas & Hot Water), and he looked blessedly happy at the courthouse, which might have had something to do with his new wife, Stephanie, a blond six-foot former *Vogue* model who accompanied him, leaning lovingly on him and smiling fabulously as photographers jockeyed for position. A handsome couple. Rumor said she was two months pregnant. They looked ecstatic. Young and rich and very much in love.

Inside, Tim's lawyer described Sweet Brian as a "candy-ass has-been who can't hit the notes and can't write the hits, so he hits his fans" and asked for a half million dollars in damages. The little guy sat twenty feet away from Tim, his ankles chained together. He looked bloated, sick. His cheap green sports coat wouldn't button in front. It had stains down the lapels. The story of his downfall was in all the papers. Sweet Brian and Tania Underwood had had to interrupt their Hawaiian honeymoon to fly to Nebraska for the trial and in Concourse C Brian was nabbed by the Omaha cops for possession of narcotics with a street value of three hundred and twenty-seven dollars. Tania was furious. She slapped him around in the police station and left town. It snowed three feet and his lawyer was stuck in L.A., and Sweet Brian sat in the clink for six days. That was when Tim saw him in court looking morose. "Can I help?" he asked, but the sullen singer turned away in anger. That night, a rodeo rider from Saskatchewan who was doing thirty days for bestiality beat the daylights out of Brian and knocked out four front teeth. Next morning, the county dentist, Dr. Merce L. Gibbons, had to drill out the stumps without Novocain. Brian bled so much he fainted and toppled forward, and the drill went through his cheek. The dentist panicked, thinking *malpractice suit,* and he tore his white smock slightly and roughed up his thin hair so as to claim that Brian had attacked *him,* and then he clubbed the former star hard, twice, with a mallet and yelled for the cops. They took Brian to the hospital and he got an infection from the blood test and died. Nobody came from L.A. for the body, and finally some reporters collected three hundred and ten dollars around the newsroom and Brian was buried in Omaha under a little headstone: "Brina Johnson, 1492–1987." The two typos weren't noticed until it was too late. So what could they do? A local columnist taped a note to the stone saying, "His name is Brian. Listen to his albums sometime. Not 'White Boy,' which is too pretty, too nostalgic, too *self-conscious,* but 'Coming Down from Iowa' is not bad. I think it's on the Argonaut label."

Tim was in Palm Beach when someone told him Brian was dead, and although he was extremely busy in meetings all day, he wondered, "Could this have been avoided if I had approached him differently, maybe been more low-key?"

"He was a big hero to me back then," he told Stephanie as they strolled along the beach toward The Palmery, where they were meeting some Florida associates for drinks and dinner. "I really wish we could have been friends."

EVEN today, after he settled out of court with the singer's estate for a rumored $196,000, Tim feels bad about the incident. He is not alone. Tens of thousands of people have approached very famous men and women intending to brighten the lonely lives of the great with a few simple words of admiration only to be rejected and abused for their thoughtfulness. To the stars, of course, such encounters are mere momentary irritations in their fast-paced sensational lives and are quickly forgotten, but for the sensitive fans personal rejection by an idol becomes a permanent scar. It could easily be avoided if, when approaching the celebrated, those who practically worship them would just use a little common sense:

1. Never grab or paw the famous. They will instantly recoil and you will never ever win their respect. Stand at least thirty-two inches away. If your words of admiration move him or her to pat your shoulder, then of course you can pat back, but don't initiate contact and don't hang on. Be cool.

2. Don't gush, don't babble, don't grovel or fawn. Never snivel. Be tall. Bootlicking builds a wall you'll never break through. A simple pleasantry is enough—e.g., "Like your work!" If you need to say more than that (*I think you're the most wonderful lyric poet in America today*), try to modify your praise slightly (*but your critical essays stink*). Or cough hard, about five times. That relieves the famous person of having to fawn back. The most wearisome aspect of fame is the obligation to look stunned by each compliment as if it were the first ever heard. That's why an odd remark (*Your last book gave me the sensation of being a horned toad lying on a hot highway*) may secretly please the famous person far more than a cliché (*I adore you and my family adores you and everyone I know in the entire world thinks you are a genius and a saint and I think I'm going to fall down on the sidewalk and just writhe around and foam for a while*). Be cool. Famous people *much* prefer a chummy insult to lavish nonsense: a little dig about the exorbitant price of tickets to the star's show, perhaps, or the cheesiness of the posters (*You design those yourself?*). Or a remark about the celebrity's pet (if any), like "How much

did you pay for that dog?" Personal stuff (*Do you have to shave twice a day? Do you use regular soap or what? What was it like when you found that out about her going out with him?*) can wait for later. For now, limit yourself to the dog. As it gazes up in mealymouthed brown-nosed, lickspittle devotion, glance down and say, "Be cool."

3. Autographs are fine, photos are fine, but be cool. Don't truckle (*Oh, please please please—I'll do anything—anything at all*), don't pander (*This is the high point of my life*), and never cringe or kowtow (*I know that this is just about the tackiest thing a person can do and it makes me sick with shame but . . .*), and never, never lie (*My mother, who is eighty-seven, is dying in Connecticut and it would mean the world to her if . . .*). Hand the famous person the paper and simply say, "I need you to sign this." Hand the camera to one of his hangers-on and say, "Take a picture of us."

4. When you are cool like this and don't fawn and don't grab and just go about your business as a fan and get that autograph and the photo and are businesslike about it, probably you are going to make such a big impression on the famous person that he or she will make a grab for *you* in that offhand way these people have (*Care to join Sammy and me for dinner, Roy?* or *Somebody find this guy a backstage pass, wouldja?*). Remember, these people are surrounded by glittering insincerity and false friendship and utter degradation of all personal values to such a degree that three cool words from you (*Like your work!*) will knock them for a loop. Suddenly the star recalls the easy camaraderie of a Southern small-town childhood and the old verities of love and loyalty in the circle of family, church, and community. Desperately he reaches out for contact with you (*Please. You remind me of a friend I once had. Many years ago and far away from here. Please*), wants your phone number, tries to schedule lunch with you on Thursday (*Anywhere, anytime. Early lunch, late lunch. You name it. I can send a car to pick you up. Thursday or Friday or Saturday or any day next week. Or Sunday if you'd rather. Or it doesn't have to be lunch. It could be breakfast or dinner. Or a late supper. Brunch*), tries to draw you into conversation (*You got a book you want published? Songs? Anyone in your family interested in performing? Got a favorite charity you need anyone to do a benefit for? Need a credit or job reference?*). Don't bite. Just smile and nod and say, "Nice to meet you," and walk away. He'll follow you (*What's your name? Please. I need you*). Walk faster. You don't want to get involved with these people. Thirty seconds can be interesting, but beyond two minutes you start to get entangled. They're going to want you to come to the Coast with them *that night* and involve you in such weird sadness as you can't believe. (*Please come with us.*

I mean it. There's something real about you that's been missing from my life for too long. Please. Just come and talk to me for three minutes.) Sorry. (*Please.*) No. (*Then let me come with you.*) No. (*Tell me why not.*) I'm sorry. I wish that it was possible, but it isn't, not at this time. I hope we can meet again very soon. Bye.

1988

FRANK GANNON

YO, POE

Consider [Sylvester Stallone's] pet project: a film biography of Edgar Allan Poe. "I am a student of his," says Stallone. "But people have this image of Poe as a crazy alcoholic and drug addict, and that's wrong. I'd like to set the record straight."

—Newsweek.

IT is with a lot of humility that I pen the first sentence of this work. It is almost accompanied by a sense of trembling awe that I approach the reader with this, the most dreamlike, the most solemn, the most difficult, the most buried-in-my-gut.

Hey, Ulalume, if I could sing and dance I wouldn't have to do this.

O strangely sent one, how your words touch my spirit! How well have we both learned the propensity of man to define the indefinable! How the strange happiness of our innermost souls has thus been magnified!

You really got lucky tonight, you know?

IT'S a quiet and still afternoon here. The leaves are all sere, whatever that means. But here inside the Spectrum it's a different story. Men are screaming, women are fainting, and the children—well, they're just being kids.

Right you are, Al. There's tumult everywhere, and with good reason. I've never seen anything quite like it.

No, Dick, I haven't either. You can almost feel the electricity in this arena. It's almost palpable.

I can't keep up with you, Al.

I've been going back to school, Dick. Heh, heh.

Excuse me for interrupting, but here he comes.

Making his way down the aisle with his entourage—Mister Edgar Allan Poe.

Some say his last name is Allan, some say it's Poe. There's quite a bit of controversy about that, Al.

All I know is he looks serious tonight, Dick.

Look at those eyes. Look at that expression.

He means business.

Yes, he does, Al. And there's that tie.

That trademark Edgar Allan Poe tie. He's still wearing it, and I guess he always will, Dick.

You can bet on that, Al.

But no raven tonight, Dick.

You're not going to get me to say "Nevermore," Al.

Heh, heh. You know, a lot of people don't know that Edgar Allan Poe was actually a very good broad jumper.

That's right, Al. A lot of critics feel that he may have symbolically put himself in his famous story "Hop-Frog."

You're a regular encyclopedia, Dick.

HELLO again, literature fans. Tonight we have a special treat on our post-fight show. Tonight's guest is Baudelaire, the unofficial manager of Edgar Allan Poe.

Edgar Poe. I always call him Edgar Poe. Please don't say "Edgar Allan Poe." I hate that. It makes me—how you say?—sick.

O.K., Beau, have it your way. Edgar Poe.

Gracias, amigo.

Let's get right to the big question. Why do you, the acknowledged champion of the symbolists, want to manage a guy like Poe, an alcoholic drug addict who marries little girls because he's a pervert. And on top of all that, he can't tie a tie.

Let me get this straight right away. And not just for you, Marv. For everybody. Edgar Poe is not a pervert. He is not an alcoholic. To my knowledge, the man has never taken a drink. He does not use drugs. He is not a "party" person.

How about the tie allegation?

I can't say anything about that. He's an individual, and like all individuals he has a right to his own tastes in neckwear.

You don't think he looks funny?

No. But let me say one thing.

Go right ahead.

My man was actually an excellent athlete.

You mean you're going to get into the broad-jumping thing and "Hop-Frog" and all of that?

Absolutely.

Good for you. And while we have you, you'll forgive another question, I'm sure. How is Rimbaud?

Loved it. I was on my feet cheering.

There you have it. Baudelaire, the self-styled king of the symbolist poets. Nothing if not controversial. Thank you for coming.

Gracias.

VIRGINIA. Yo, Virginia—wake up. I have something I want to tell you. I was just over to look at the poster they got of me. And you know what? They got the wrong tie. That's right. They got me wearing a club tie instead of this little one that I always tie funny.

I just want to say a couple of things. One, a lotta people probably think it was kinda weird for me to get married to you, on account of you being my cousin and only fourteen years old and like that. What they don't know is that for a guy like me beauty is incarnate only as an intellectual principle. Man is but a part of the great will that pervades the cosmos. In other words, when I hear somebody say something about my wife I tell him to get out of the car.

I got one more thing I want to say. Some of my early biographers, they got the idea that I was an alcoholic drug addict or something. That's just a bunch of you know what. I'm not a drug addict, I'm a poet. Keats, Shelley—they were poets and they died young. But it wasn't because they were drug addicts. It was because they didn't train.

Tonight I'll know one thing. If I hear that rapping, that rapping on my chamber door, and I'm sitting there. Still sitting there, pondering over a big pile of quaint and curious volumes. If I'm still sitting there, I'll know one thing: The record is now straight.

1985

MY LIFE: A SERIES OF PRIVATELY

FUNDED PERFORMANCE-ART PIECES

1. BIRTH

As the piece opens, another performance artist, "Mom" (an affiliate of my private funding source) waits onstage, consuming tuna-noodle casseroles. Eventually, she leaves the initial performance site—a single-family Cape Cod decorated with amoeboid sofas, Herman Miller co-conut chairs, boomerang-print linoleum, and semi-shag carpeting—for a second site, a hospital. There she is joined by a sterile-clad self-realized figure of authority ("Sidney Jaffe, M.D.") who commands her to "push," and then externalizes through language and gesture his desire to return to the back nine. This tableau makes allusion to the deadening, depersonalizing, postwar "good life." "Mom" continues "pushing," and at last I enter—nude. I do this in a manner that confronts yet at the same time steers clear of all obscenity statutes.

2. COMING HOME EXTREMELY LATE BECAUSE I WAS MAKING SNOW ANGELS AND FORGOT TO STOP

Again, an ensemble piece. But unlike "Birth," which explores the universal codes of pleasure and vulnerability, "Coming Home Extremely Late" is a manifesto about rage—not mine but that of the protonuclear family. The cast includes "Mom," "David," "Debra," "Fluffy," and my private funding source. In "Coming Home," I become Object, rather than Subject.

The piece is also a metaperformance; the more sophisticated members of the audience will realize that I am "coming home extremely late" because of *another* performance: "Snow Angels," an earlier, gestural work in which, clothed in a cherry-red Michelin Man–style snowsuit, I lower myself into a snowbank and wave my arms up and down, leaving a winged-creature-like impression upon the frozen palimpsest. Owing to my methodology, I am better at it than anyone on the block. Note the megatextual references to Heaven, Superior Being–as-girl-child, snow-as-inviolable-purity, and time-as-irrelevancy. "Coming Home Extremely Late" concludes with a choral declaration from the entire cast (except for my private funding source, who has returned to reading the sports section), titled "You Are Grounded for a Month, Young Lady."

3. I GO THROUGH A GANGLY PERIOD

A sustained dramatic piece, lasting three to five years, depending on how extensively the performer pursues the orthodontia theme. Besides me, the cast includes the entire student population of Byron Junior High School, Shaker Heights, Ohio—especially the boys. In the course of "Gangly Period," I grow large in some ways, small in others, and, ironically, they are all the wrong ways. I receive weird haircuts. Through "crabby" behavior (mostly directed at my private funding source), my noncontextual stage image projects the unspeakable fear that I am not "popular." In a surreal trope midway through the performance, I vocalize to a small section of the cast ("Ellen Fisher," "Sally Webb," and "Heather Siegel") my lack of knowledge about simple sexual practices.

Throughout the piece, much commentary about time: how long it is, why certain things seem to take forever, why I have to be the absolutely last girl in the entire seventh grade to get Courrèges boots.

4. FINDING MYSELF

This piece is a burlesque—a comic four-year-long high art/low art exploration. As "Finding Myself" opens, I am on-site—a paradigmatic bourgeois college campus. After performing the symbiotic ritual of "meeting my roommates" and dialoguing about whether boyfriends can stay overnight in our room, I reject the outmoded, parasitic escape route of majoring in English, and instead dare to enroll in a class called "Low Energy Living," in which I reject the outmoded, parasitic escape route of reading the class material and instead build a miniature solar-powered seawater-desalinization plant. I then confront Amerika's greedy soullessness by enrolling in a class called "Future Worlds," walking around in a space suit of my own design, doing a discursive/nonlinear monologue on Buckminster Fuller and futurism.

Toward the end of "Finding Myself," I skip all my "classes"—spatially as well as temporally—and move into an alternative environment to examine my "issues." At this point, my private funding source actually appears in the piece and, in a witty cameo, threatens to withdraw my grant. Much implosive controversy. To close the performance, I sit on an avocado-green beanbag chair and simulate "applying to graduate school."

5. I GET MARRIED AND SHORTLY THEREAFTER TAKE A POUNDING IN THE REAL-ESTATE MARKET

A bifurcated work. First, another performance artist, "Peter," dialogues with me about the explicit, symbolic, and functional presentations of human synchronism. We then plan and execute a suburban country-club wedding (again, with assistance from my private funding source). Making a conceptual critique of materialism, I "register" for Royal Copenhagen china, Baccarat crystal, and Kirk Stieff sterling. Syllabic chants, fragments of unintelligible words like the screeches of caged wild birds gone mad—this megatonality erupts when I confront my private funding source about seating certain little-liked relatives. At the work's interactive climax, "Peter" and I explode the audience/performer dialectic and invite the audience to join as we "perform the ceremony."

The second part of the piece—a six-month-long open-ended manifesto on the specificity of place—culminates with "Peter" and me purchasing a four-and-a-half-room coöperative apartment with a good address in Manhattan. Conran's furniture, Krups appliances, task-specific gadgets (apple corers, pasta makers, shrimp deveiners), and other symbol-laden icons are arranged on-site. Curtain goes down on the performers facing each other on a sofa, holding a *Times* real-estate section between them, doing a performative discourse lamenting that they have "purchased the apartment at the peak of the market."

The series will continue pending refinancing.

1990

DAVID BROOKS

THE A-LIST E-LIST

I SPEND my days trying to contribute to a more just, caring, and environmentally sensitive society, but, like most Americans, I'm always on the lookout for subtle ways to make myself seem socially superior. So I was thrilled recently to learn about E-name dropping, a new and extremely petty form of one-upmanship made possible by recent strides in information technology.

I first became aware of this new status ploy when a colleague sent out a mass message. "Dear friends," his E-mail began. But before I could go on to the text my eye was drawn up to the list of other people it had been sent to. My friend had apparently sent this message—it was a request for help on an article—to his entire E-mail address book. There were three hundred and four names, listed alphabetically, along with their E-mail addresses. It was like a roster of young media meritocrats. There were newsweek.coms, wsj.coms, nytimes.coms, as well as your assorted berkeley.edus, stanford.edus, microsoft.coms, and even a UN.org.

I realized that I had stumbled across the *Social Register* of the information age. We all carry our own select social clubs on our hard drives, and when we send out a mass mailing we can flaunt our splendiferous connections to arouse the envy of friend and foe alike. It's as if you were walking down the street with your Rolodex taped to your lapel—only better, since having an E-mail friendship with someone suggests that you are trading chatty badinage, not just exchanging stiff missives under a formal letterhead.

So in theory a strategic striver could structure his E-mail address list to reveal the entire trajectory of his career ascent. He could include a few of his early thesis advisers—groton.org, yale.edu, oxford.ac.uk— then a few internship-era mentors—imf.org, whitehouse.gov—and, finally, a few social/professional contacts—say, davosconference.com or trilat.org. When he inflicts this list on his friends' in-boxes, they will be compelled, like unwilling list archeologists, to retrace his perfect life, triumph by triumph.

My friend with the three-hundred-and-four-name list hadn't exploited the full potentialities of the genre, so I cast about for other lists and began to analyze them. I learned a lot from these lists. For example, my view of *The Nation*'s columnist Eric Alterman has been transformed by the knowledge that he has just stopped using "Tomseaver" as part of his E-mail address. But, frankly, reading through the address lists of my friends, I found that there were longueurs. Entire passages were filled with names of insignificant people, such as family members I'd never heard of. I came to realize, as Capability Brown must have, that in the making of any beautiful vista pruning is key.

If Aristotle were alive, he would note that there are four types of E-mail lists. There are lists that remind you that the sender went to a better college than you did. There are lists that remind you that he has a better job than you do. There are those that remind you that he has more sex than you do. And, finally, there are those that remind you that he is better than you in every respect: spiritually, professionally, and socially.

I have begun fantasizing about assembling the mother of all E-mail lists, the sort that would be accumulated by a modern Renaissance man. Such a list would be studded with jewels (HisHoliness@vatican.com, QEII@windsor.org). But, more than that, it would suggest a series of high achievements across the full range of human endeavor. It would include whopping hints about mysterious other lives (coupboy@theagency.gov, Ahmed@mujahedin.com). It would reveal intimate connections with the great but socially selective (JDSal@aol.com, Solzhenits@archi.org). Of course, I wouldn't want only celebrities on my list; that would be vulgar. I would leave room for talk-show bookers, upper-bracket realtors, Sherpas, airline presidents, night-club publicists, rain-forest tour guides, underprivileged kids, members of the Gotti family, and a rotating contingent of the people I actually know, for whose edification the whole list has been constructed in the first place.

To take advantage of this list, I would need excuses to send out mass mailings as frequently as possible. I would have to change my address a lot ("From now on you can reach me at genius24@MacArthurgrant .com . . ."). I would send out a lot of general queries ("Does anybody know who is handling Ike Berlin's estate? I'm trying to find a first edition of the complete works of Hérzen . . ."). And I'd send out a few accidental mass mailings by hitting the Reply All button by "mistake" ("Your Holiness, it turns out I can't make it to Rome Tuesday. Maybe somebody else can bring the beer and soda . . .").

No longer would I be the ninety-eight-pound cyberweakling that I am now. Alec Baldwin would start sending me dirty jokes in hopes of making it onto my E-mail list. People would actually begin replying to my messages. The fact is, in the new information age, we can now be snobs on a scale never dreamed of by our ancestors. Is this a great time to be alive, or what?

1999

THE

WAR

BETWEEN

MEN

AND

WOMEN

MR. PREBLE GETS RID OF HIS WIFE

MR. PREBLE was a plump middle-aged lawyer in Scarsdale. He used to kid with his stenographer about running away with him. "Let's run away together," he would say, during a pause in dictation. "All righty," she would say.

One rainy Monday afternoon, Mr. Preble was more serious about it than usual.

"Let's run away together," said Mr. Preble.

"All righty," said his stenographer. Mr. Preble jingled the keys in his pocket and looked out the window.

"My wife would be glad to get rid of me," he said.

"Would she give you a divorce?" asked the stenographer.

"I don't suppose so," he said. The stenographer laughed.

"You'd have to get rid of your wife," she said.

MR. PREBLE was unusually silent at dinner that night. About half an hour after coffee, he spoke without looking up from his paper.

"Let's go down in the cellar," Mr. Preble said to his wife.

"What for?" she said, not looking up from her book.

"Oh, I don't know," he said. "We never go down in the cellar any more. The way we used to."

"We never did go down in the cellar that I remember," said Mrs. Preble. "I could rest easy the balance of my life if I never went down in the cellar." Mr. Preble was silent for several minutes.

"Supposing I said it meant a whole lot to me," began Mr. Preble.

"What's come over you?" his wife demanded. "It's cold down there and there is absolutely nothing to do."

"We could pick up pieces of coal," said Mr. Preble. "We might get up some kind of a game with pieces of coal."

"I don't want to," said his wife. "Anyway, I'm reading."

"Listen," said Mr. Preble, rising and walking up and down. "Why won't you come down in the cellar? You can read down there, as far as that goes."

"There isn't a good enough light down there," she said, "and anyway, I'm not going to go down in the cellar. You may as well make up your mind to that."

"Gee whiz!" said Mr. Preble, kicking at the edge of a rug. "Other people's wives go down in the cellar. Why is it you never want to do anything? I come home worn out from the office and you won't even go down in the cellar with me. God knows it isn't very far—it isn't as if I was asking you to go to the movies or some place."

"I don't want to *go!*" shouted Mrs. Preble. Mr. Preble sat down on the edge of a davenport.

"All right, all *right,*" he said. He picked up the newspaper again. "I wish you'd let me tell you more about it. It's—kind of a surprise."

"Will you quit harping on that subject?" asked Mrs. Preble.

"LISTEN," said Mr. Preble, leaping to his feet. "I might as well tell you the truth instead of beating around the bush. I want to get rid of you so I can marry my stenographer. Is there anything especially wrong about that? People do it every day. Love is something you can't control—"

"We've been all over that," said Mrs. Preble. "I'm not going to go all over that again."

"I just wanted you to know how things are," said Mr. Preble. "But you have to take everything so literally. Good Lord, do you suppose I really wanted to go down in the cellar and make up some silly game with pieces of coal?"

"I never believed that for a minute," said Mrs. Preble. "I knew all along you wanted to get me down there and bury me."

"You can say that now—after I told you," said Mr. Preble. "But it would never have occurred to you if I hadn't."

"You didn't tell me; I got it out of you," said Mrs. Preble. "Anyway, I'm always two steps ahead of what you're thinking."

"You're never within a mile of what I'm thinking," said Mr. Preble.

"Is that so? I knew you wanted to bury me the minute you set foot in this house tonight." Mrs. Preble held him with a glare.

"Now that's just plain damn exaggeration," said Mr. Preble, considerably annoyed. "You knew nothing of the sort. As a matter of fact, I never thought of it till just a few minutes ago."

"It was in the back of your mind," said Mrs. Preble. "I suppose this filing woman put you up to it."

"You needn't get sarcastic," said Mr. Preble. "I have plenty of people to file without having her file. She doesn't know anything about this. She isn't in on it. I was going to tell her you had gone to visit some friends and fell over a cliff. She wants me to get a divorce."

"That's a laugh," said Mrs. Preble. "*That's* a laugh. You may bury me, but you'll never get a divorce."

"She knows that; I told her that," said Mr. Preble. "I mean—I told her I'd never get a divorce."

"Oh, you probably told her about burying me, too," said Mrs. Preble.

"That's not true," said Mr. Preble, with dignity. "That's between you and me. I was never going to tell a soul."

"You'd blab it to the whole world; don't tell me," said Mrs. Preble. "I know you." Mr. Preble puffed at his cigar.

"I wish you were buried now and it was all over with," he said.

"Don't you suppose you would get caught, you crazy thing?" she said. "They always get caught. Why don't you go to bed? You're just getting yourself all worked up over nothing."

"I'm not going to bed," said Mr. Preble. "I'm going to bury you in the cellar. I've got my mind made up to it. I don't know how I could make it any plainer."

"Listen," cried Mrs. Preble, throwing her book down, "will you be satisfied and shut up if I go down in the cellar? Can I have a little peace if I go down in the cellar? Will you let me alone then?"

"Yes," said Mr. Preble. "But you spoil it by taking that attitude."

"Sure, sure, I always spoil everything. I stop reading right in the middle of a chapter. I'll never know how the story comes out—but that's nothing to you."

"Did I make you start reading the book?" asked Mr. Preble. He opened the cellar door. "Here, you go first."

"BRRR," said Mrs. Preble, starting down the steps. "It's *cold* down here! You *would* think of this, at this time of year! Any other husband would have buried his wife in the summer."

"You can't arrange those things just whenever you want to," said Mr. Preble. "I didn't fall in love with this girl till late fall."

"Anybody else would have fallen in love with her long before that. She's been around for years. Why is it you always let other men get in ahead of you? Mercy, but it's dirty down here! What have you got there?"

"I was going to hit you over the head with this shovel," said Mr. Preble.

"You were, huh?" said Mrs. Preble. "Well, get that out of your mind. Do you want to leave a great big clue right here in the middle of everything where the first detective that comes snooping around will find it? Go out in the street and find some piece of iron or something—something that doesn't belong to you."

"Oh, all right," said Mr. Preble. "But there won't be any piece of iron in the street. Women always expect to pick up a piece of iron anywhere."

"If you look in the right place you'll find it," said Mrs. Preble. "And don't be gone long. Don't you dare stop in at the cigarstore. I'm not going to stand down here in this cold cellar all night and freeze."

"All right," said Mr. Preble. "I'll hurry."

"And shut that *door* behind you!" she screamed after him. "Where were you born—in a barn?"

1933

JAMES THURBER

A COUPLE OF HAMBURGERS

IT had been raining for a long time, a slow, cold rain falling out of iron-colored clouds. They had been driving since morning and they still had a hundred and thirty miles to go. It was about three o'clock in the afternoon. "I'm getting hungry," she said. He took his eyes off the wet, winding road for a fraction of a second and said, "We'll stop at a dog-wagon." She shifted her position irritably. "I wish you wouldn't call them *dog*-wagons," she said. He pressed the klaxon button and went around a slow car. "That's what they are," he said. "Dog-wagons." She waited a few seconds. "*Decent* people call them *diners*," she told him, and added, "Even if you call them diners, I don't like them." He speeded up a hill. "They have better stuff than most restaurants," he said. "Anyway, I want to get home before dark and it takes too long in a restaurant. We can stay our stomachs with a couple of hamburgers." She lighted a cigarette and he asked her to light one for him. She lighted one deliberately and handed it to him. "I wish you wouldn't say 'stay our stomachs,' " she said. "You know I hate that. It's like 'sticking to your ribs.' You say that all the time." He grinned. "Good old American expressions, both of them," he said. "Like sow belly. Old pioneer term, sow belly." She sniffed. "My ancestors were pioneers, too. You don't have to be vulgar just because you were a pioneer." "Your ancestors never got as far west as mine did," he said. "The real pioneers travelled on their sow belly and got somewhere." He laughed loudly at that. She looked out at the wet trees and signs and telephone poles going by. They drove on for several miles without a word; he kept chortling every now and then.

"What's that funny sound?" she asked, suddenly. It invariably made him angry when she heard a funny sound. "What funny sound?" he demanded. "You're always hearing funny sounds." She laughed briefly. "That's what you said when the bearing burned out," she reminded him. "You'd never have noticed it if it hadn't been for me." "I noticed it, all right," he said. "Yes," she said. "When it was too late." She enjoyed bringing up the subject of the burned-out bearing whenever he got to chortling. "It was too late when *you* noticed it, as far as that goes," he said. Then, after a pause, "Well, what does it sound like *this* time? All engines make a noise running, you know." "I know all about that," she answered. "It sounds like—it sounds like a lot of safety pins being jiggled around in a tumbler." He snorted. "That's your imagination. Nothing gets the matter with a car that sounds like a lot of safety pins. I happen to know that." She tossed away her cigarette. "Oh, sure," she said. "You always happen to know everything." They drove on in silence.

"I WANT to stop somewhere and get something to *eat!*" she said loudly. "All right, all right!" he said. "I been watching for a dog-wagon, haven't I? There hasn't been any. I can't make you a dog-wagon." The wind blew rain in on her and she put up the window on her side all the way. "I won't stop at just any old diner," she said. "I won't stop unless it's a cute one." He looked around at her. "Unless it's a *what* one?" he shouted. "You know what I mean," she said. "I mean a decent, clean one where they don't slosh things at you. I hate to have a lot of milky coffee sloshed at me." "All right," he said. "We'll find a cute one, then. You pick it out. I wouldn't know. I might find one that was cunning but not cute." That struck him as funny and he began to chortle again. "Oh, shut up," she said.

FIVE miles farther along they came to a place called Sam's Diner. "Here's one," he said, slowing down. She looked it over. "I don't want to stop there," she said. "I don't like the ones that have nicknames." He brought the car to a stop at one side of the road. "Just what's the matter with the ones that have nicknames?" he asked with edgy, mock interest. "They're always Greek ones," she told him. "They're always Greek ones," he repeated after her. He set his teeth firmly together and started up again. After a time, "Good old Sam, the Greek," he said, in a singsong. "Good old Connecticut Sam Beardsley, the Greek." "You didn't see his name," she snapped. "Winthrop, then," he said. "Old Samuel Cabot Winthrop, the Greek dog-wagon man." He was getting hungry.

On the outskirts of the next town she said, as he slowed down, "It looks like a factory kind of town." He knew that she meant she wouldn't stop there. He drove on through the place. She lighted a cigarette as they pulled out into the open again. He slowed down and lighted a cigarette for himself. "Factory kind of town than *I* am!" he snarled. It was ten miles before they came to another town. "Torrington," he growled. "Happen to know there's a dog-wagon here because I stopped in it once with Bob Combs. Damn cute place, too, if you ask me." "I'm not asking you anything," she said, coldly. "You think you're *so* funny. I think I know the one you mean," she said, after a moment. "It's right in the town and it sits at an angle from the road. They're never so good, for some reason." He glared at her and almost ran up against a curb. "What the hell do you mean 'sits at an angle from the road'?" he cried. He was very hungry now. "Well, it isn't silly," she said, calmly. "I've noticed the ones that sit at an angle. They're cheaper, because they fitted them into funny little pieces of ground. The big ones parallel to the road are the best." He drove right through Torrington, his lips compressed. "Angle from the *road*, for God's sake!" he snarled, finally. She was looking out her window.

On the outskirts of the next town there was a diner called The Elite Diner. "This looks—" she began. "I see it, I see it!" he said. "It doesn't happen to look any cuter to me than any goddam—" She cut him off. "Don't be such a sorehead, for Lord's sake," she said. He pulled up and stopped beside the diner, and turned on her. "Listen," he said, grittingly, "I'm going to put down a couple of hamburgers in this place even if there isn't one single inch of chintz or cretonne in the whole—" "Oh, be still," she said. "You're just hungry and mean like a child. Eat your old hamburgers, what do I care?" Inside the place they sat down on stools and the counterman walked over to them, wiping up the counter top with a cloth as he did so. "What'll it be, folks?" he said. "Bad day, ain't it? Except for ducks." "I'll have a couple of—" began the husband, but his wife cut in. "I just want a pack of cigarettes," she said. He turned around slowly on his stool and stared at her as she put a dime and a nickel in the cigarette machine and ejected a package of Lucky Strikes. He turned to the counterman again. "I want a couple of hamburgers," he said. "With mustard and lots of onion. *Lots* of onion!" She hated onions. "I'll wait for you in the car," she said. He didn't answer and she went out.

He finished his hamburgers and his coffee slowly. It was terrible coffee. Then he went out to the car and got in and drove off, slowly, humming "Who's Afraid of the Big Bad Wolf?" After a mile or so, "Well," he said, "what was the matter with the Elite Diner, milady?" "Didn't you *see* that cloth the man was wiping the counter with?" she demanded. "Ugh!" She shuddered. "I didn't happen to want to eat any of the counter," he said. He laughed at that comeback. "You didn't even notice it," she said. "You never notice anything. It was filthy." "I noticed they had some damn fine coffee in there," he said. "It was swell." He knew she loved good coffee. He began to hum his tune again; then he whistled it; then he began to sing it. She did not show her annoyance, but she knew that he knew she was annoyed. "Will you be kind enough to tell me what time it is?" she asked. "Big *bad* wolf, big *bad* wolf—five minutes o' five—tum-dee-*doo*-dee-dum-m-m." She settled back in her seat and took a cigarette from her case and tapped it on the case. "I'll wait till we get home," she said. "If you'll be kind enough to speed up a little." He drove on at the same speed. After a time he gave up the "Big Bad Wolf" and there was deep silence for two miles. Then suddenly he began to sing, very loudly, "*H*-A-double-R-*I*-G-A-*N* spells *Harrr*-i-gan—" She gritted her teeth. She hated that worse than any of his songs except "Barney Google." He would go on to "Barney Google" pretty soon, she knew. Suddenly she leaned slightly forward. The straight line of her lips began to curve up ever so slightly. She heard the safety pins in the tumbler again. Only now they were louder, more insistent, ominous. He was singing too loud to hear them. "Is a *name* that *shame* has never been con-*nec*-ted with—*Harrr*-i-gan, that's *me!*" She relaxed against the back of the seat, content to wait.

1935

PETER De VRIES

FOREVER PANTING

S TILL, I have a certain ramshackle charm. So that when I took her young hands in mine across the restaurant table she did not immediately withdraw from my grasp, nor from the larger, bolder plan of action, which I now proceeded to sketch out for her benefit.

"What I'm going to do is, I'm going to declare moral bankruptcy," I said. "I mean, we keep using the term in that sense, why not follow it through? When a man can no longer discharge his financial obligations, we let him off the hook. Why not when he can no longer meet his ethical ones? I have too many emotional creditors hounding me, I tell you! That's all there is to it. A man simply cannot meet all the demands made on his resources, simply cannot be expected to keep his books balanced. It's too much. Everybody keeps talking about moral bankruptcy but nobody does anything about it. Well, I'm going to. I'm going to declare it. I'm going into receivership. I'm going to pay everybody so much on the dollar."

"In other words, Duxbury," she said, calling me by my last name as people affectionately do, "you want to tell your wife about us."

"I do," I said, "and I've spoken those words only once before in my life."

She gazed thoughtfully into her post-luncheon mint, stirring the icy sludge around a bit with her straw.

"How will you go about it?" she asked, at length. "I mean, how much will you pay everybody on the dollar, as you put it?"

I frowned into my third brandy as I mentally reviewed the scale of figures I had already more or less worked out. Proclaiming to the world that one is materially insolvent is a serious enough step; posting notice that one is no longer ethically liquid is an even graver one, especially if, as appeared to be true here, one is the first man in history to be doing so in a formal sense. The case would be precedent-setting. It might even become a *cause célèbre*, with all the attendant widespread publicity that I must be prepared to shoulder and to shoulder alone. I therefore weighed my words carefully.

"I figure I can pay fifty cents on the dollar," I said at last. "That will be all told and across the board. It will be divided up as fairly as I know how among the claimants. That is to say, half of what is expected of this man on all fronts is really all there is of him to go around. That's all there is, there ain't no more." Here I paused to ask, "You understand that I am talking about the *moral equivalent* of money, in the mart of human relationships." She nodded, sucking up the bright-green cordial with lips pursed into a scarlet bud. "All right, then," I went on. "I shall continue to make my disbursements—of loyalty, coöperation, et cetera—at that level; I mean, I intend to stay in business as a human being. There will never be any question about that, nor that my wife and family will come first, my friends next, and then such things as obligation to community and whatnot, in the ever-widening circles of responsibilities as one sees them—and prorated as I say."

"What about your parents, Duxbury?" she asked, looking up. "You admitted you haven't been back home to see them in over a year. I don't like that in a man. A man should be thoughtful and considerate about things like that."

"All right, I'll throw in another nickel for them, so to speak. I mean, I'll stretch a point in what I'll give, so the others concerned won't get less of my time and devotion. But that's my top figure. More than that can simply not be squeezed out of the orange."

"What about me? What do I get?"

"You get me. A man out from under at last, ready to make a fresh start free and clear. How's that? Ah, *macushla* . . ."

There was a silence, broken only by the hydraulic sounds of the last of the mint going up the translucent straw, which was finally put by with a dainty crimson stain on its tip. "Well, all right," she said. "I expect you'll want to get home early tonight and have it out. I'm glad I won't have to be there," she added with a little shudder. "I just hope it won't be like the sordid blowups you can hear through the walls of apartments. The couple next door to mine actually throw crockery at each other."

"Love is a many-splintered thing. Heh-heh-heh. Ah, baby, the fun we'll—"

"So why don't you call for the check?"

I flagged the waiter, still brooding over the various aspects of this thorny problem, which I am sure vexes every man from time to time— just how much of him there is to go around. "As for one's country," I said, "that's all well and good, but I doubt whether in peacetime a man owes it any more than is extorted from him in taxes to maintain God knows what proliferating bureaus and agencies going to make up what is still essentially an eleemosynary goddam government."

"You don't have to swear to show how limited your vocabulary is," she said, reaching for her gloves and bag with a hauteur well supported by the patrician profile that had from the very first struck me to the heart. She is a tawny girl with long legs and hair like poured honey. In her brown eyes is a vacancy as divine as that left in the last motel available to the desperate wayfarer. My knees turned to rubber as I read the check and produced the forty clams necessary to discharge my immediate obligations. "Keep the change," I told the waiter in a voice hoarse with passion.

"If you do have it out at home, then you'll be able to make it for dinner tomorrow instead of lunch, I expect?" she said, rising as the waiter swung the table aside for her exit.

"Name the place," I said, trailing in her wake.

"The Four Seasons is nice."

WHEN I got home, after the usual grimy and spasmodic ride on that awful railroad, my family were already at meat. My wife looked up from a gardening magazine she was reading as she ate, and waved cheerfully. Our sixteen-year-old son was paging through a motorcycle pamphlet over his own heaped plate, while his ten-year-old brother pored, fork in hand, over a comic book. The latter wore a switchman's cap with the visor behind. Dented beer cans were clamped to the heels of his shoes, and his bubble gum was on his wrist. It seemed as good a time as any to make my declaration. My eighteen-year-old daughter, a free spirit now apparently touring Europe or something, would, I knew, heartily applaud my action, if I could only locate her.

I helped myself to some food from a casserole keeping warm in the oven and joined them at the table. But I could not eat. Finally, I shoved my plate aside and said, "I have an announcement to make."

There was a rustle of turned pages and a nod or two.

"You have all no doubt read Ibsen's 'The Wild Duck,' " I said. "That anti-morality play, perhaps his best, in which he makes the point that we cannot always be pressed with the claims of the ideal. That we should not be forever dunned," I went on, consulting a frayed cuff on which I had jotted what I could remember of Relling's crucial speeches in that drama, "forever dunned for debts we cannot pay. Isn't that fine? Doesn't that make reasonable sense? All right, then. I take this to mean, therefore, that a person who has reached a certain point in the general drain on his resources may with impunity say, 'I herewith formally declare myself bankrupt. I am going into moral receivership. Creditors, take note—you will henceforth get so much on the dollar,' said creditors to include all those reasonably embraced by that corporate term 'society,' on whose Accounts Receivable we are all permanently enrolled: family, friends, community, and so on. Now then for the figure I am prepared to give you. The absolute maximum disbursement I can manage is, roughly, fifty cents on the dollar. Put in plain English, this means that in future I shall be half the husband I was, half the father, half the friend, and so on down the line. Well, there it is. What have you to say?"

My wife dropped her magazine and passed a plate of homemade rolls around the table.

"Why, if she's what you want, go to her," she said. "Go away with her even, for a while, if it will help get her out of your system."

I rose and shoved my chair back with a force that sent it clattering to the floor behind me.

"I wish you'd stop treating me as an individual in my own right," I exclaimed. "All of you! Nothing is more irritating than that, or more demoralizing. As though a man has to be humored like some damn kid!" With that I flung out of the room, slamming the door after me.

My resolve to leave was by now quite firm. I marched to my bedroom and, pausing only long enough to stand modestly before a wall glass and say, "You ain't nuttin' but a hound-dog," I packed three bags, which I carried, forever panting, along the corridor and down the stairs to the vestibule. There I momentarily dropped my luggage to recover my wind.

As I stood there, I sensed a footfall in the passage along which I had just come. Looking up the stairs, I saw my mother-in-law approaching, in velvet slippers and with the aid of her stout cane. Slightly indisposed, she had had a tray in her room, the door of which she had left open, as is her wont, so as not to isolate herself entirely from the life of the house. She paused at the head of the stairs and from under her white lace mobcap fixed me with a bright eye.

"I could not help overhearing," she said, "and with all due apologies, I should like to remind you of one person you have overlooked in your list of creditors, as you put it. Someone to whom you also owe something."

"Who might that be, Mother Bunshaft?" I asked.

"Yourself," she answered, smiling.

"Ah, Mother Bunshaft," I said, "the longer you live with us the more your wisdom—"

"Correction—I think you mean the longer you live with me." The house is in her name for legal reasons (she owns it). "The longer you live with me, the more I find I have to tell you, it seems. Now I suggest you owe it to yourself to pause a moment and count the cost. Of a second establishment, which I assume is in your mind—especially if we increase the cost of this one by starting to ask for rent again. The upkeep of two cars, the many other possessions bought on time. I expect we're quite the ticket out there in the big city"—here she humorously cocked the tip of her stick at me and sighted along its length as along the barrel of a rifle, at the same time making that chucking noise out of the side of her mouth that once was used to make horses giddyap but now conveys the idea of hot stuff—"but it might just pay us to take a good hard look at our bank balance, if any, our arrears with the loan company— Just a minute, I'm not finished," she called as I hurried out the front door without the bags.

Well, that's how the cookie crumbles. It took very little probing to make clear the scale of living the other woman had in mind—a single phone call from a public booth, in fact. Her response to my suggestion that we meet at some convenient Schrafft's or Stouffer's, instead of the Four Seasons, with all that nonsense about flaming skewers and telephones brought to the tables, alone did the trick.

So that seems to be the point of this whole incident in a nutshell, its moral, you might say, which I pass along to any man contemplating the same course of action I was. Before you start declaring moral bankruptcy, make damn sure you're in good shape financially.

1963

THE KUGELMASS EPISODE

KUGELMASS, a professor of humanities at City College, was un-happily married for the second time. Daphne Kugelmass was an oaf. He also had two dull sons by his first wife, Flo, and was up to his neck in alimony and child support.

"Did I know it would turn out so badly?" Kugelmass whined to his analyst one day. "Daphne had promise. Who suspected she'd let herself go and swell up like a beach ball? Plus she had a few bucks, which is not in itself a healthy reason to marry a person, but it doesn't hurt, with the kind of operating nut I have. You see my point?"

Kugelmass was bald and as hairy as a bear, but he had soul.

"I need to meet a new woman," he went on. "I need to have an affair. I may not look the part, but I'm a man who needs romance. I need soft-ness, I need flirtation. I'm not getting younger, so before it's too late I want to make love in Venice, trade quips at '21,' and exchange coy glances over red wine and candlelight. You see what I'm saying?"

Dr. Mandel shifted in his chair and said, "An affair will solve nothing. You're so unrealistic. Your problems run much deeper."

"And also this affair must be discreet," Kugelmass continued. "I can't afford a second divorce. Daphne would really sock it to me."

"Mr. Kugelmass—"

"But it can't be anyone at City College, because Daphne also works there. Not that anyone on the faculty at C.C.N.Y. is any great shakes, but some of those coeds . . ."

"Mr. Kugelmass—"

"Help me. I had a dream last night. I was skipping through a meadow holding a picnic basket and the basket was marked 'Options.' And then I saw there was a hole in the basket."

"Mr. Kugelmass, the worst thing you could do is act out. You must simply express your feelings here, and together we'll analyze them. You have been in treatment long enough to know there is no overnight cure. After all, I'm an analyst, not a magician."

"Then perhaps what I need is a magician," Kugelmass said, rising from his chair. And with that he terminated his therapy.

A couple of weeks later, while Kugelmass and Daphne were moping around in their apartment one night like two pieces of old furniture, the phone rang.

"I'll get it," Kugelmass said. "Hello."

"Kugelmass?" a voice said. "Kugelmass, this is Persky."

"Who?"

"Persky. Or should I say The Great Persky?"

"Pardon me?"

"I hear you're looking all over town for a magician to bring a little exotica into your life? Yes or no?"

"Sh-h-h," Kugelmass whispered. "Don't hang up. Where are you calling from, Persky?"

Early the following afternoon, Kugelmass climbed three flights of stairs in a broken-down apartment house in the Bushwick section of Brooklyn. Peering through the darkness of the hall, he found the door he was looking for and pressed the bell. I'm going to regret this, he thought to himself.

Seconds later, he was greeted by a short, thin, waxy-looking man.

"*You're* Persky the Great?" Kugelmass said.

"The Great Persky. You want a tea?"

"No, I want romance. I want music. I want love and beauty."

"But not tea, eh? Amazing. O.K., sit down."

Persky went to the back room, and Kugelmass heard the sounds of boxes and furniture being moved around. Persky reappeared, pushing before him a large object on squeaky roller-skate wheels. He removed some old silk handkerchiefs that were lying on its top and blew away a bit of dust. It was a cheap-looking Chinese cabinet, badly lacquered.

"Persky," Kugelmass said, "what's your scam?"

"Pay attention," Persky said. "This is some beautiful effect. I developed it for a Knights of Pythias date last year, but the booking fell through. Get into the cabinet."

"Why, so you can stick it full of swords or something?"

"You see any swords?"

Kugelmass made a face and, grunting, climbed into the cabinet. He couldn't help noticing a couple of ugly rhinestones glued onto the raw plywood just in front of his face. "If this is a joke," he said.

"Some joke. Now, here's the point. If I throw any novel into this cabinet with you, shut the doors, and tap it three times, you will find yourself projected into that book."

Kugelmass made a grimace of disbelief.

"It's the emess," Persky said. "My hand to God. Not just a novel, either. A short story, a play, a poem. You can meet any of the women created by the world's best writers. Whoever you dreamed of. You could carry on all you like with a real winner. Then when you've had enough you give a yell, and I'll see you're back here in a split second."

"Persky, are you some kind of outpatient?"

"I'm telling you it's on the level," Persky said.

Kugelmass remained skeptical. "What are you telling me—that this cheesy homemade box can take me on a ride like you're describing?"

"For a double sawbuck."

Kugelmass reached for his wallet. "I'll believe this when I see it," he said.

Persky tucked the bills in his pants pocket and turned toward his bookcase. "So who do you want to meet? Sister Carrie? Hester Prynne? Ophelia? Maybe someone by Saul Bellow? Hey, what about Temple Drake? Although for a man your age she'd be a workout."

"French. I want to have an affair with a French lover."

"Nana?"

"I don't want to have to pay for it."

"What about Natasha in 'War and Peace'?"

"I said French. I know! What about Emma Bovary? That sounds to me perfect."

"You got it, Kugelmass. Give me a holler when you've had enough." Persky tossed in a paperback copy of Flaubert's novel.

"You sure this is safe?" Kugelmass asked as Persky began shutting the cabinet doors.

"Safe. Is anything safe in this crazy world?" Persky rapped three times on the cabinet and then flung open the doors.

Kugelmass was gone. At the same moment, he appeared in the bedroom of Charles and Emma Bovary's house at Yonville. Before him was a beautiful woman, standing alone with her back turned to him as she folded some linen. I can't believe this, thought Kugelmass, staring at the doctor's ravishing wife. This is uncanny. I'm here. It's her.

Emma turned in surprise. "Goodness, you startled me," she said. "Who are you?" She spoke in the same fine English translation as the paperback.

It's simply devastating, he thought. Then, realizing that it was he whom she had addressed, he said, "Excuse me. I'm Sidney Kugelmass. I'm from City College. A professor of humanities. C.C.N.Y.? Uptown. I—oh, boy!"

Emma Bovary smiled flirtatiously and said, "Would you like a drink? A glass of wine, perhaps?"

She is beautiful, Kugelmass thought. What a contrast with the troglodyte who shared his bed! He felt a sudden impulse to take this vision into his arms and tell her she was the kind of woman he had dreamed of all his life.

"Yes, some wine," he said hoarsely. "White. No, red. No, white. Make it white."

"Charles is out for the day," Emma said, her voice full of playful implication.

After the wine, they went for a stroll in the lovely French countryside. "I've always dreamed that some mysterious stranger would appear and rescue me from the monotony of this crass rural existence," Emma said, clasping his hand. They passed a small church. "I love what you have on," she murmured. "I've never seen anything like it around here. It's so . . . so modern."

"It's called a leisure suit," he said romantically. "It was marked down." Suddenly he kissed her. For the next hour they reclined under a tree and whispered together and told each other deeply meaningful things with their eyes. Then Kugelmass sat up. He had just remembered he had to meet Daphne at Bloomingdale's. "I must go," he told her. "But don't worry, I'll be back."

"I hope so," Emma said.

He embraced her passionately, and the two walked back to the house. He held Emma's face cupped in his palms, kissed her again, and yelled, "O.K., Persky! I got to be at Bloomingdale's by three-thirty."

There was an audible pop, and Kugelmass was back in Brooklyn.

"So? Did I lie?" Persky asked triumphantly.

"Look, Persky, I'm right now late to meet the ball and chain at Lexington Avenue, but when can I go again? Tomorrow?"

"My pleasure. Just bring a twenty. And don't mention this to anybody."

"Yeah. I'm going to call Rupert Murdoch."

Kugelmass hailed a cab and sped off to the city. His heart danced on point. I am in love, he thought, I am the possessor of a wonderful secret. What he didn't realize was that at this very moment students in various classrooms across the country were saying to their teachers, "Who is this character on page 100? A bald Jew is kissing Madame Bovary?" A teacher in Sioux Falls, South Dakota, sighed and thought, Jesus, these kids, with their pot and acid. What goes through their minds!

Daphne Kugelmass was in the bathroom-accessories department at Bloomingdale's when Kugelmass arrived breathlessly. "Where've you been?" she snapped. "It's four-thirty."

"I got held up in traffic," Kugelmass said.

KUGELMASS visited Persky the next day, and in a few minutes was again passed magically to Yonville. Emma couldn't hide her excitement at seeing him. The two spent hours together, laughing and talking about their different backgrounds. Before Kugelmass left, they made love. "My God, I'm doing it with Madame Bovary!" Kugelmass whispered to himself. "Me, who failed freshman English."

As the months passed, Kugelmass saw Persky many times and developed a close and passionate relationship with Emma Bovary. "Make sure and always get me into the book before page 120," Kugelmass said to the magician one day. "I always have to meet her before she hooks up with this Rodolphe character."

"Why?" Persky asked. "You can't beat his time?"

"Beat his time. He's landed gentry. Those guys have nothing better to do than flirt and ride horses. To me, he's one of those faces you see in the pages of *Women's Wear Daily*. With the Helmut Berger hairdo. But to her he's hot stuff."

"And her husband suspects nothing?"

"He's out of his depth. He's a lack-lustre little paramedic who's thrown in his lot with a jitterbug. He's ready to go to sleep by ten, and she's putting on her dancing shoes. Oh, well . . . See you later."

And once again Kugelmass entered the cabinet and passed instantly to the Bovary estate at Yonville. "How you doing, cupcake?" he said to Emma.

"Oh, Kugelmass," Emma sighed. "What I have to put up with. Last night at dinner, Mr. Personality dropped off to sleep in the middle of the dessert course. I'm pouring my heart out about Maxim's and the ballet, and out of the blue I hear snoring."

"It's O.K., darling. I'm here now," Kugelmass said, embracing her. I've earned this, he thought, smelling Emma's French perfume and burying his nose in her hair. I've suffered enough. I've paid enough analysts. I've searched till I'm weary. She's young and nubile, and I'm here a few pages after Léon and just before Rodolphe. By showing up during the correct chapters, I've got the situation knocked.

Emma, to be sure, was just as happy as Kugelmass. She had been starved for excitement, and his tales of Broadway night life, of fast cars and Hollywood and TV stars, enthralled the young French beauty.

"Tell me again about O. J. Simpson," she implored that evening, as she and Kugelmass strolled past Abbé Bournisien's church.

"What can I say? The man is great. He sets all kinds of rushing records. Such moves. They can't touch him."

"And the Academy Awards?" Emma said wistfully. "I'd give anything to win one."

"First you've got to be nominated."

"I know. You explained it. But I'm convinced I can act. Of course, I'd want to take a class or two. With Strasberg maybe. Then, if I had the right agent—"

"We'll see, we'll see. I'll speak to Persky."

That night, safely returned to Persky's flat, Kugelmass brought up the idea of having Emma visit him in the big city.

"Let me think about it," Persky said. "Maybe I could work it. Stranger things have happened." Of course, neither of them could think of one.

"WHERE the hell do you go all the time?" Daphne Kugelmass barked at her husband as he returned home late that evening. "You got a chippie stashed somewhere?"

"Yeah, sure, I'm just the type," Kugelmass said wearily. "I was with Leonard Popkin. We were discussing Socialist agriculture in Poland. You know Popkin. He's a freak on the subject."

"Well, you've been very odd lately," Daphne said. "Distant. Just don't forget about my father's birthday. On Saturday?"

"Oh, sure, sure," Kugelmass said, heading for the bathroom.

"My whole family will be there. We can see the twins. And Cousin Hamish. You should be more polite to Cousin Hamish—he likes you."

"Right, the twins," Kugelmass said, closing the bathroom door and shutting out the sound of his wife's voice. He leaned against it and took a deep breath. In a few hours, he told himself, he would be back in Yonville again, back with his beloved. And this time, if all went well, he would bring Emma back with him.

At three-fifteen the following afternoon, Persky worked his wizardry again. Kugelmass appeared before Emma, smiling and eager. The two spent a few hours at Yonville with Binet and then remounted the Bovary carriage. Following Persky's instructions, they held each other tightly, closed their eyes, and counted to ten. When they opened them, the carriage was just drawing up at the side door of the Plaza Hotel, where Kugelmass had optimistically reserved a suite earlier in the day.

"I love it! It's everything I dreamed it would be," Emma said as she swirled joyously around the bedroom, surveying the city from their window. "There's F.A.O. Schwarz. And there's Central Park, and the Sherry is which one? Oh, there—I see. It's too divine."

On the bed there were boxes from Halston and Saint Laurent. Emma unwrapped a package and held up a pair of black velvet pants against her perfect body.

"The slacks suit is by Ralph Lauren," Kugelmass said. "You'll look like a million bucks in it. Come on, sugar, give us a kiss."

"I've never been so happy!" Emma squealed as she stood before the mirror. "Let's go out on the town. I want to see 'Chorus Line' and the Guggenheim and this Jack Nicholson character you always talk about. Are any of his flicks showing?"

"I cannot get my mind around this," a Stanford professor said. "First a strange character named Kugelmass, and now she's gone from the book. Well, I guess the mark of a classic is that you can reread it a thousand times and always find something new."

THE lovers passed a blissful weekend. Kugelmass had told Daphne he would be away at a symposium in Boston and would return Monday. Savoring each moment, he and Emma went to the movies, had dinner in Chinatown, passed two hours at a discothèque, and went to bed with a TV movie. They slept till noon on Sunday, visited SoHo, and ogled celebrities at Elaine's. They had caviar and champagne in their suite on Sunday night and talked until dawn. That morning, in the cab taking them to Persky's apartment, Kugelmass thought, It was hectic, but worth it. I can't bring her here too often, but now and then it will be a charming contrast with Yonville.

At Persky's, Emma climbed into the cabinet, arranged her new boxes of clothes neatly around her, and kissed Kugelmass fondly. "My place next time," she said with a wink. Persky rapped three times on the cabinet. Nothing happened.

"Hmm," Persky said, scratching his head. He rapped again, but still no magic. "Something must be wrong," he mumbled.

"Persky, you're joking!" Kugelmass cried. "How can it not work?"

"Relax, relax. Are you still in the box, Emma?"

"Yes."

Persky rapped again—harder this time.

"I'm still here, Persky."

"I know, darling. Sit tight."

"Persky, we *have* to get her back," Kugelmass whispered. "I'm a married man, and I have a class in three hours. I'm not prepared for anything more than a cautious affair at this point."

"I can't understand it," Persky muttered. "It's such a reliable little trick."

But he could do nothing. "It's going to take a little while," he said to Kugelmass. "I'm going to have to strip it down. I'll call you later."

Kugelmass bundled Emma into a cab and took her back to the Plaza. He barely made it to his class on time. He was on the phone all day, to Persky and to his mistress. The magician told him it might be several days before he got to the bottom of the trouble.

"How was the symposium?" Daphne asked him that night.

"Fine, fine," he said, lighting the filter end of a cigarette.

"What's wrong? You're as tense as a cat."

"Me? Ha, that's a laugh. I'm as calm as a summer night. I'm just going to take a walk." He eased out the door, hailed a cab, and flew to the Plaza.

"This is no good," Emma said. "Charles will miss me."

"Bear with me, sugar," Kugelmass said. He was pale and sweaty. He kissed her again, raced to the elevators, yelled at Persky over a pay phone in the Plaza lobby, and just made it home before midnight.

"According to Popkin, barley prices in Kraków have not been this stable since 1971," he said to Daphne, and smiled wanly as he climbed into bed.

THE whole week went by like that. On Friday night, Kugelmass told Daphne there was another symposium he had to catch, this one in Syracuse. He hurried back to the Plaza, but the second weekend there was nothing like the first. "Get me back into the novel or marry me," Emma told Kugelmass. "Meanwhile, I want to get a job or go to class, because watching TV all day is the pits."

"Fine. We can use the money," Kugelmass said. "You consume twice your weight in room service."

"I met an Off Broadway producer in Central Park yesterday, and he said I might be right for a project he's doing," Emma said.

"Who is this clown?" Kugelmass asked.

"He's not a clown. He's sensitive and kind and cute. His name's Jeff Something-or-Other, and he's up for a Tony."

Later that afternoon, Kugelmass showed up at Persky's drunk.

"Relax," Persky told him. "You'll get a coronary."

"Relax. The man says relax. I've got a fictional character stashed in a hotel room, and I think my wife is having me tailed by a private shamus."

"O.K., O.K. We know there's a problem." Persky crawled under the cabinet and started banging on something with a large wrench.

"I'm like a wild animal," Kugelmass went on. "I'm sneaking around town, and Emma and I have had it up to here with each other. Not to mention a hotel tab that reads like the defense budget."

"So what should I do? This is the world of magic," Persky said. "It's all nuance."

"Nuance, my foot. I'm pouring Dom Pérignon and black eggs into this little mouse, plus her wardrobe, plus she's enrolled at the Neighborhood Playhouse and suddenly needs professional photos. Also, Persky, Professor Fivish Kopkind, who teaches Comp Lit and who has always been jealous of me, has identified me as the sporadically appearing character in the Flaubert book. He's threatened to go to Daphne. I see ruin and alimony jail. For adultery with Madame Bovary, my wife will reduce me to beggary."

"What do you want me to say? I'm working on it night and day. As far as your personal anxiety goes, that I can't help you with. I'm a magician, not an analyst."

By Sunday afternoon, Emma had locked herself in the bathroom and refused to respond to Kugelmass's entreaties. Kugelmass stared out the window at the Wollman Rink and contemplated suicide. Too bad this is a low floor, he thought, or I'd do it right now. Maybe if I ran away to Europe and started life over . . . Maybe I could sell the *International Herald Tribune*, like those young girls used to.

The phone rang. Kugelmass lifted it to his ear mechanically.

"Bring her over," Persky said. "I think I got the bugs out of it."

Kugelmass's heart leaped. "You're serious?" he said. "You got it licked?"

"It was something in the transmission. Go figure."

"Persky, you're a genius. We'll be there in a minute. Less than a minute."

Again the lovers hurried to the magician's apartment, and again Emma Bovary climbed into the cabinet with her boxes. This time there was no kiss. Persky shut the doors, took a deep breath, and tapped the box three times. There was the reassuring popping noise, and when Persky peered inside, the box was empty. Madame Bovary was back in her novel. Kugelmass heaved a great sigh of relief and pumped the magician's hand.

"It's over," he said. "I learned my lesson. I'll never cheat again, I swear it." He pumped Persky's hand again and made a mental note to send him a necktie.

THREE weeks later, at the end of a beautiful spring afternoon, Persky answered his doorbell. It was Kugelmass, with a sheepish expression on his face.

"O.K., Kugelmass," the magician said. "Where to this time?"

"It's just this once," Kugelmass said. "The weather is so lovely, and I'm not getting any younger. Listen, you've read 'Portnoy's Complaint'? Remember The Monkey?"

"The price is now twenty-five dollars, because the cost of living is up, but I'll start you off with one freebie, due to all the trouble I caused you."

"You're good people," Kugelmass said, combing his few remaining hairs as he climbed into the cabinet again. "This'll work all right?"

"I hope. But I haven't tried it much since all that unpleasantness."

"Sex and romance," Kugelmass said from inside the box. "What we go through for a pretty face."

Persky tossed in a copy of "Portnoy's Complaint" and rapped three times on the box. This time, instead of a popping noise there was a dull explosion, followed by a series of crackling noises and a shower of sparks. Persky leaped back, was seized by a heart attack, and dropped dead. The cabinet burst into flames, and eventually the entire house burned down.

Kugelmass, unaware of this catastrophe, had his own problems. He had not been thrust into "Portnoy's Complaint," or into any other novel, for that matter. He had been projected into an old textbook, "Remedial Spanish," and was running for his life over a barren, rocky terrain as the word *tener* ("to have")—a large and hairy irregular verb—raced after him on its spindly legs.

1977

PARTNER*S*

MISS TEAS
WEDS FIANCÉ
IN BRIDAL

The marriage of Nancy Creamer Teas, daughter of Mr. and Mrs. Russell Ruckhyde Teas of Glen Frieburg, N.Y., and Point Pedro, Sri Lanka, to John Potomac Mining, son of Mr. Potomac B. Mining of Buffet Hills, Va., and the late Mrs. Mining, took place at the First Episcopal Church of the Port Authority of New York and New Jersey.

The bride attended the Bodice School, the Earl Grey Seminary, Fence Academy, Railroad Country Day School, and the Credit School, and made her début at the Alexander Hamilton's Birthday Cotillion at Lazard Frères. She is a student in the premedical program at M.I.T. and will spend her junior year at Cartier & Cie. in Paris.

The bridegroom recently graduated from Harvard College. He spent his junior year at the Pentagon, a military concern in Washington, D.C. He will join his father on the board of directors of the Municipal Choate Assistance Corporation. His previous marriage ended in divorce.

CABINET, DELOS
NUPTIALS SET

Ellen Frances Cabinet, a self-help student at Manifest Destiny Junior College, plans to be married in August to Wengdell Delos, a sculptor, of Tampa, Fla. The engagement was announced by the parents of the future bride, Mr. and Mrs. Crowe Cabinet of New York. Mr. Cabinet is a consultant to the New York Stock Exchange.

Mr. Delos's previous marriage ended in an undisclosed settlement. His sculpture is on exhibition at the New York Stock Exchange. He received a B.F.A. degree from the Wen-El-Del Company, a real-estate-development concern with headquarters in Tampa.

MISS BURDETTE
WED TO MAN

Pews Chapel aboard the Concorde was the setting for the marriage of Bethpage Burdette to Jean-Claude LaGuardia Case, an account executive for the Junior Assemblies. Maspeth Burdette was maid of honor for her sister, who was also attended by Massapequa Burdette, Mrs. William O. Dose, and Mrs. Hodepohl Inks.

The parents of the bride, Dr. and Mrs. Morris Plains Burdette of New York, are partners in Conspicuous Conception, an art gallery and maternity-wear cartel.

The ceremony was performed by the Rev. Erasmus Tritt, a graduate of Skidmore Finishing and Divinity School and president of Our Lady of the Lake Commuter Airlines. The Rev. Tritt was attended by the flight crew. The previous marriages he has performed all ended in divorce.

DAISY LAUDERDALE
FEATURED AS BRIDE

Daisy Ciba Lauderdale of Boston was married at the Presbyterian Church and Trust to Gens Cosnotti, a professor of agribusiness at the Massachusetts State Legislature. There was a reception at the First Court of Appeals Club.

The bride, an alumna of the Royal Doulton School and Loot University, is the daughter of Mr. and Mrs. Cyrus Harvester Lauderdale. Her father is retired from the family consortium. She is also a descendant of Bergdorf Goodman of the Massachusetts Bay Colony. Her previous marriage ended in pharmaceuticals.

Professor Cosnotti's previous marriage ended in a subsequent marriage. His father, the late Artaud Cosnotti, was a partner in the Vietnam War. The bridegroom is also related somehow to Mrs. Bethlehem de Steel of Newport, R.I., and Vichy, Costa Rica; Brenda Frazier, who was a senior partner with Delta, Kappa & Epsilon and later general manager of marketing for the U.S. Department of State; I. G. Farben, the former King of England; and Otto von Bismarck, vice-president of the Frigidaire Division of General Motors, now a division of The Hotchkiss School.

AFFIANCEMENT
FOR MISS CONVAIR

Archbishop and Mrs. Marquis Convair of Citibank, N.Y., have made known the engagement of their daughter, Bulova East Hampton Convair, to the Joint Chiefs of Staff of Arlington County, Va. Miss Convair is a holding company in the Bahamas.

All four grandparents of the bride-to-be were shepherds and shepherdesses.

1980

MARK SINGER

MY MARRIED LIFE:

THE WHOLE TRUTH THUS FAR

IT is true. I have been married quite a few times. There have been more marriages than, at certain moments, I can remember. Concentrating, however, I recall them all. Damn near half a million. The entire fleet heaves into view on the warm ocean of my memory. I am proud of all my marriages. I have gulped so often from the deep cup of life's pleasures. And each time I have come away stumbling drunk. Women, I have discovered, find my marrying moods irresistible. Frankly, I think I am a pretty good catch.

My first wife was Eos, goddess of the dawn. I have never been certain how long our union lasted. This was before the Greeks could agree upon the number of days in a month. Keeping track of time was difficult. Sustaining a marriage was difficult, too. Her career got in the way. Eos, her hair the red of turning maples, was a child of the sun and the wind and the pale pink velvet morn. I, on the other hand, am basically a night person. Often, I felt like a Tuesday or a Thursday evening out on the town. "Come, Eos," I would say. "Let us go eat Chinese and riot in Athens till the wee hours." But she would protest: Tomorrow was a workday. How could I expect her to carouse all night? How, on little or no sleep, could she possibly usher the pristine dawn across the metallic firmament? She had a point. Inevitably, other conflicts arose between us. Fortunately, there were no children. We parted amicably and then, as can happen, lost track of each other.

I remarried almost immediately. Repeatedly, in fact, I have remarried almost immediately. Some of my wives wore black mesh stockings. Several wore heavy eye makeup. Some drank. One carried a small firearm. Two studied *tae kwon do,* the Korean art of self-defense. Two were Korean but defenseless. A dozen—maybe fifteen at tops—lacked conspicuous physical beauty. Their hidden beauties, however, made them ravishing. I have always taken marriage seriously and have concentrated upon the one I am involved in at the moment. I have always discovered the hidden beauties.

I married no men—only women. Men, I believe, do not make decent wives. Men make good fishing buddies. Once, I was offered a lot of money to marry Judge Crater, in the hope that this would bring him back into public view. Of course, I declined. The people who were offering this money had about them an air of being up to no good.

In addition to my own marriage ceremonies, I have attended many others. I was with Tommy Manville all thirteen times he took the leap. I witnessed three of Barbara Hutton's nuptials. Mickey Rooney and I go back a long way together. To my regret, I had to miss Norman Mailer's fifth wedding, the one that took place recently and was followed by a quick divorce so that he could marry someone else. I would have been there but I was getting married that day.

I believe that all of my wives were faithful. I believe that all of my wives were faithful despite the rumors I heard about Susan and Doreen, of Provo. This was during the six-year period when I was busy marrying all of the women in Utah. The rumors about Susan and Doreen—first Susan and then, somewhat later, Doreen—made no sense to me. I made it a policy to be totally up-front with my wives. I hid nothing from them. A marriage to me was always an eyes-open proposition. It must have been a different Susan and a different Doreen, or perhaps Susan and Doreen when they had already become ex-wives.

I was married to many movie stars. Although I loved them all, I know that in a way some of these marriages were tainted by cynicism. Some of these actresses had careers that had stalled. They needed a little ink in the columns. I married them for that reason. But that was not the reason I married Ingrid Bergman. I married her for pure, unalloyed love. This was while she was married to Roberto Rossellini, the Italian filmmaker. So great was my love of Ingrid Bergman that I was willing to become Rossellini for two years. I was willing to interrupt my own important work to direct the films "Open City" and "Paisan." I perfected my Italian. I spoke English with a convincing inflection. Ingrid Bergman was shocked when, at last, I confessed to her that I was not, technically speaking, Rossellini. He seemed not to notice.

Briefly, I married a woman who now stars in a popular television comedy series. I will call her Angela. We met on a blind date. In fact, now that I think of it, it's a funny coincidence; Pam Dawber, who was then a total nobody but later went on to star in "Mork & Mindy," fixed us up. Angela and I met for lunch, on a day in early spring, asparagus time. Between the cold cucumber soup and the crabmeat salad, we became engaged. Our waiter, having overheard our pledges of troth, announced that he was a minister. Angela ordered a second carafe of the house white. Before coffee, the waiter performed the ceremony in a small alcove between the coat-check room and the pay phone. We tipped him extravagantly. As we were leaving, the coat-check lady casually mentioned that the waiter had not actually been ordained. Outside, Angela said that she was feeling vexed. I said never mind, if we consider ourselves married, we're married. But we quarrelled. The quarrel made us realize that perhaps our decision to marry had been made in haste. Again, of course, there were no children. I still get Christmas cards from Angela and often watch her on TV.

That was by no means my shortest marriage. One day I married an entire subway carful of gorgeous ladies. There were forty-three of them. It was an uptown B train during rush hour. Never before had I been on a subway car with that many women and no other men present. Being recently divorced, I saw no reason not to marry all of them right then and there. I officiated at these ceremonies myself and, afterward, catered the reception and took photographs. There was plenty to drink and plenty to eat—hot chafing dishes filled with sweetbreads in wine sauce, silver trays of tiny lamb chops, roast-beef carving stations at either end of the subway car. We rode together to 168th Street, the end of the line, and then all forty-three of my new wives changed to an uptown A train headed for the George Washington Bridge Terminal, where they boarded buses for New Jersey. In New Jersey, they had homes with back yards, children, and husbands. I have been told that these forty-three marriages don't count in the final standings. I couldn't disagree more. I loved these women well and wish them well. In my book, they all count.

1981

LIFE WITHOUT LEANN

B Y the time you receive this, it will have been more than five hundred days and nearly seventy-five weeks since Leann and I broke up, and, while I cannot proclaim our long ordeal ended, I am pleased to report some encouraging developments in that direction.

LEANN WATCHER OF THE WEEK . . . Kudos (and a two-year subscription to this newsletter) for Mike, of Evanston, Ill., who so eloquently and informatively captures a brief encounter he had with Leann on Jan. 6.

"Leann has lost some weight," Mike writes, "but she is no less beautiful for it. She says she has been exercising, taking classes, doing this, doing that. It appeared to me that she was struggling to fill some void. Your name didn't come up, but it wasn't so much what she said as what she didn't say."

THE STRUGGLE CONTINUES . . . If only it could all be such good news. But unfortunately, OPERATION: TERRIBLE MISTAKE has not been the success I anticipated, and I'm afraid a new strategy may be required.

As you may recall (LWL #57), the operation's objectives were to: (1) apply societal pressure; (2) foster emotional uncertainty; (3) precipitate reevaluation; and ideally (4) achieve reconciliation.

The following conversation starter was suggested:

LEANN, I WAS SO SORRY TO HEAR ABOUT YOU AND LARRY. YOU MAKE SUCH A WONDERFUL COUPLE. SO I DON'T MIND TELLING YOU, I THINK YOU ARE MAKING A TERRIBLE MISTAKE. THIS IS MY OWN PERSONAL OPINION ON THE MATTER.

Unfortunately, a number of well-meaning individuals took this suggestion rather more literally than intended, and repeated it verbatim to Leann, creating a cumulative effect other than the one desired.

I have now received word through an intermediary that Leann requests I "call off the zombies." I will honor her wishes, as always, though I must emphasize that I cannot be held responsible for the behavior of individuals acting on their own initiative.

LEANN ANONYMOUS . . . In our first meeting at Gatsby's, the bartender, Mark, graciously accommodated us by closing off the back room and supplying extra folding chairs. All in attendance praised the wisdom of moving these mutual support sessions from my apartment, which some had complained was not neutral territory, and which had become quite cramped in any case. (On a related matter, Mark told me privately that, while he appreciates our patronage, he'd prefer that in the future we try not to monopolize the jukebox, or at least play a variety of songs. He says that if he doesn't see some improvement the Hank Williams selections will have to go.)

We ordered a round, and at Tom's suggestion dispensed with the reading of the minutes. We proceeded immediately to old business, resuming debate on Leann's eyes and whether they are a turbulent sea green or a sand-flecked moon blue. It appeared there could be no middle ground on the issue, until Dick stood up and declared, "To paraphrase Elton John, 'Who cares if they're blue or if they're green, those are the sweetest eyes I've ever seen.' "

The motion to adopt Dick's language carried unanimously, and we collected more change for the jukebox.

We ordered another round, and the conversation turned naturally to the rest of Leann: her quirky perky nose, her funny sunny smile, the perfect curve of her neck, her soft shoulders, and so on, until petty jealousies precluded further discussion.

Soon thereafter, we took a break to order more refreshments, and then it was time to welcome new members. A stubby and not particularly attractive man, who had been spotted with Leann as recently as mid-November, stood up in the back of the room.

"My name is Harry," he said, "and I love Leann."

Harry then related his long, sad tale, the details of which were all too familiar, ending with that same old refrain.

"She met this guy," he said. "She says she's deliriously happy."

"Deliriously happy, eh?" Gunther said slowly, staring into his beer. "He's *doomed*."

Those of us who could still laugh did so.

"Really?" Harry said, cheering considerably. "So you think there's a chance I can win her back?"

This question prompted extensive debate, leading to the inevitable threats of violence and ceasing only when Quentin moved that we change the name of our group from Lovers of Leann to Victims of Leann. The motion was soundly defeated, and we voted to adjourn.

Elmo closed the meeting by singing "Oh, Leann," including a new verse that had recently come to him in a dream:

> Oh, Leann,
> I love you,
> Love you still,
> I love you,
> I love you,
> I love you still,
> I always will.

LEANN ALERT . . . My special friend Jane, who has been so supportive during this difficult time, has suggested there is a need for a group addressing the concerns of the lovers of the Lovers of Leann. Anybody who knows somebody who might be interested in such a group should have them write to Leann Anon at this address.

THIS WEEK'S LEANN CHALLENGE . . . Leann is what she eats, but how well do you know what she eats? Everybody knows Leann likes horseradish on her hamburgers, but how many of you know what *kind* of horseradish? (Here's a hint: She received a case of it for Christmas.)

The answer to last week's challenge: From left to right.

LEANN'S MAILBAG . . . The mail ran heavy this week with entries to the "Candid Leann" photo contest, and it's obvious I need to remind everyone that the rules clearly stipulate that Leann must be the only person shown in the photograph.

In consideration of those who may wish to resubmit, I've decided to extend the deadline two weeks, until Jan. 29. And remember, entries cannot be returned.

One of our foreign correspondents, Miles, writes from Windsor, Ontario, "I'm going to be in the States in the near future, and I was hoping to finally meet this Leann I've heard so much about. Do you have her phone number or an address where I can write her directly?"

No need for that, Miles. Just send your correspondence to Leann in care of this newsletter, and I'll make sure she gets it.

And finally, Reggie, of Buffalo Grove, Ill., writes in and asks:

"Larry, isn't it time you got on with your life? It's been nearly two years [sic] since Leann broke up with you [sic], and I hate to be the one to tell you, pal, but it's over. O-V-E-R [sic].

"But listen," Reggie continues, "there are a lot of other chicks in the sea, my friend, and they're yours for the picking. Go for it!"

Well, Reggie, I don't quite know how to answer that. It's difficult to determine exactly what it is you're driving at, since I'm afraid I do not share your bitter perspective or your particular gift for playground aphorisms. So please understand when I suggest this: You know nothing about love.

But thanks for the letter, Reg. Your "Larry Loves Leann" T-shirt is in the mail.

1990

GARRISON KEILLOR

ZEUS THE LUTHERAN

WHEN Hera's lawyer, Alan, had lunch with Zeus that Wednesday at the Acropol, it certainly crossed his mind that the ageless gentleman in the blue T-shirt and white shorts sitting across the table from him and smelling of juniper was the Father of Heaven (and of the Seasons, the Fates, and the Muses) and the father of Athena and Apollo and Artemis and Dionysus, plus the father of Hephaestus by Hera, his wife, and of Eros by his daughter Aphrodite—a guy who didn't take no for an answer. So Alan felt silly saying, "Hello. How are you?" He knew the answer: *Great, all-powerful.* For aeons, Zeus had done exactly as he wished, following the amorous impulses of his heart, changing himself into a swan or a horse or Lord knows what for the purpose of making love with whomever he wanted. Now Alan had been hired to talk some sense into him.

"I realize you're omniscient, but let me say what's on my mind," he said. "Enough with the mounting and coupling. Keep it in your pants. What are you trying to prove? You're a *god,* for Pete's sake. Be a little divine for a change. Knock it off with the fornication, O.K.?"

"You want to see a magic trick?" said Zeus. And right there at the table he turned the young lawyer into a pitcher of vinaigrette dressing and poured him over the spinach salad and told the waiter, "Take this garbage away, Dimitri, and feed it to the pigs. And bring me a beautiful young woman, passionate but compliant, with small, ripe breasts." It was his usual way of dealing with opposition: senseless violence followed by easy sex.

Hera was swimming laps in the pool at her summer house when she got the tragic news from Victor, Alan's partner. She was hardly surprised; Alan was her six-hundredth lawyer in fourteen centuries. She climbed out of the water, her great alabaster rump rising like Antarctica, and wrapped herself in a vast white towel. "Some god!" she said. "Omniscient except when it comes to himself." She had thought she understood Zeus' fascination with mortal women until the day he tried to explain it to her. "The spirit of love is the cosmic teacher who brings gods and mortals together, lighting the path of beauty, which is both mortal and godly, from one generation to the next," he offered. "One makes love so that people in years to come can feel passion at the sight of flowers."

She said, "You're not that drunk—don't be that stupid."

When Victor told her that Alan was gone, eaten by pigs, she vowed to avenge him, but the next day she was in Thebes, being adored, when Diane sailed into the harbor at Rhodes aboard the S.S. Bethel with her husband, Pastor Wes. Zeus, who was drinking coffee in a dockside café with the passionate, compliant woman and was a little bored with her breasts, which now seemed slightly too small and perhaps a touch overripe, saw Diane overhead as the Bethel tied up, and he felt the old, familiar itch in the groin—except sharper. He arose. Her strawberry-blond hair and great tan made his heart come over the top of the Ferris wheel. She stood at the rail, in a bright-red windbreaker, furious at the chubby man in the yellow pants who was laying his big arm on her shoulder—her hubby of sixteen years. She turned, and the arm fell off her. Zeus paid the check and headed for the gangplank.

Wes and Diane were on the final leg of a two-week cruise that the grateful congregation of Zion Lutheran Church in Odense, Pennsylvania, had given them in tribute to Wes's ten years of ministry, and last night, over a rack of lamb and a 1949 Bordeaux that cost enough to feed fifty Ugandan children for a week, they had talked about their good life back in Odense, their three wonderful children, their good health and good luck, their kind fellow-Lutherans, and had somehow got onto the subject of divine grace, and that led into a discussion of pretentious clergy Diane had known, and that led to a twelve-foot dropoff into the wild rapids of a bitter argument about their marriage. They leaned across the baklava, quietly yelling things like "How can you say that?" and "I always knew you felt that way!" until the diners nearby were studying the ceiling for hairline cracks. In the morning, Diane announced that she wanted a separation. Now Wes gestured at the blue sea, the white houses, the fishing boats. "This is the dream trip of a lifetime," he said. "We can't come all this way to Greece just to break up. We could have done that at home. *Why are you so angry?*" And then the god entered his body.

It took three convulsive seconds for Zeus to become Wes; it felt to the fifty-year-old minister like a fatal heart attack. *Oh, shit!* he thought. *Death.* And he had quit smoking three years before! All that self-denial and hard work—and for what? For zip. He was going to fall down dead anyway. Tears filled his eyes. Then Zeus took over, and the soul of Wes dropped into an old dog named Spiros, who lived on the docks and suffered from a bad hernia.

The transformation shook Zeus up, too. He grabbed at the rail and nearly fainted; in the last hour, Wes had consumed a shovelful of bacon and fried eggs and many cups of dreadful coffee. The god was nauseated, but he touched the woman's porcelain wrist.

"*What?*" she said.

The god coughed. He tried to focus Wes's watery blue eyes. "O Lady whose beauty lights the darkening western skies, your white face flashes when I close my eyes."

She sighed and looked down at the concrete dock. The god swallowed. He wanted to talk beautifully, but English sounded raspy, dull; it tasted like a cheap cigar.

"A face of such reflection as if carved in stone, and such beauty as only in great paintings shone. O Lady of light, fly no higher, but come into my bed and know eternal fire."

"Where'd you get that? Off a calendar? Be real," she said.

The dumb mustache, the poofy hair, the brass medallion, the collapsed chest, the wobbly gut, the big lunkers of blubber on his hips, the balloon butt. The arms were weak, the legs shaky. The brain seemed corroded, stuffed with useless, sad, remorseful thoughts. He wished he could change to somebody trim and taut, an athlete, but he could feel the cold, wiggly flesh glued on him and he knew that Hera had caught him in the naked moment of metamorphosis and with a well-aimed curse had locked him tight inside the flabby body, this clown sack. A god of grandeur and gallantry living in a dump, wearing a mask of pork.

Just below, the dog sat on his haunches—a professional theologian covered with filthy, matted fur, and with his breakfast, the rancid hindquarters of a rat, dangling from his mouth.

"Look. That poor old dog on the dock," said Diane.

"When you open your thighs, the soft clanging of bells is heard across the valley, O daughter of Harrisburg. Come, glorious woman, and let us waken the day with the music of your clamorous thighs."

"Grow up," she advised.

His innards rumbled, and a bubble of gas shifted in his belly—a fart as big as a child. He clamped his bowels around it and faced her and spoke: "Dear, dear Lady, O Sweetness—the cheerful face of amiable passion in a cold, dry place. To you I offer a thousand tears and lies, an earnest heart longing for the paradise that awaits us in a bed not far away, I trust. Look at me, Lady, or else I turn to dust." His best effort. But the language was so flat, and the pastoral voice so clunky and ponderous.

"I could swear that dog is human," she cried.

"Thank you, Diane," said the dog. "I don't know how I became schizophrenic, but I do know I've never loved you more." This came from his mouth as a whine, and then he felt the rubber boot of a vicious dockhand kick him in the middle of the hernia. The woman rushed down the gangplank and knelt and picked him up and cradled him in her arms. She crooned, "Oh, honey, precious, baby, sweetness, Mama gonna be so good to you, little darling." She had never said this to him before. He felt small and cozy in her arms.

THE dog, the woman, and the god rode a bus three miles over the mountain to the Sheraton Rhodes, the woman holding the dog's head on her lap. She'd leave Wes and go back to school for her degree in women's studies—the simple life of the student, a tonic after all these years of ordinary lying. The god vowed to fast until she surrendered to him. The dog felt no pain. He planned to find a pack of Luckies and learn how to smoke again.

The hotel room had twin beds and looked out on a village of stucco houses with small gardens of tomato plants and beans, where chickens strolled among the vines. Brown goats roamed across the brown hills, their bells clanging softly. Diane undressed in the bathroom, and slid into bed sideways, and lay facing the wall. Zeus sat on the edge of her bed and lightly traced with his finger the neckline of her white negligee. She shrugged. The dog lay at her feet, listening. Zeus was confused, trying to steer his passion through the narrow, twisting mind of Wes. All he wanted was to make love enthusiastically for hours, but dismal Lutheran thoughts sprang up: Go to sleep. Stop making a fool of yourself. You're a grown man. Settle down. Don't be ridiculous. Who do you think you are?

Zeus pulled in his gut and spoke. "Lady, your quiet demeanor mocks the turmoil in my chest, the rage, the foam, the wind blasting love's light ships aground. Surely you see this, Lady, unless you are the cruellest of your race. Surely you hear my heart pound with mounting waves upon your long, passive shore. Miles from your coast, you sit in a placid town, feeling faint reverberations from beneath the floor. It is your lover the sea, who can never rest until you come down to him."

"I don't know who you're trying to impress, me or yourself," she said. Soon she was snoring.

"This is not such a bad deal," said the dog. "For me, this is turning out to be a very positive experience on the whole. Becoming a dog was never my first choice, but now that I am one I see that, as a man, my sense of self was tied up with being an oppressor. I got separated from my beingness, my creaturehood. It is so liberating to see things from down here at floor level. You learn a lot about man's relentlessness."

They spent two sunny days at the Sheraton, during which Zeus worked to seduce Diane and she treated him like a husband. She laughed at him. The lines that had worked for him in the past ("Sex is a token of a deeper friendship, an affirmation of mutual humanity, an extension of conversation") made her roll her eyes and snort. She lay on a wicker lounge beside the pool—her taffy-colored skin in the two red bands of bikini, her perfect breasts, her long, tan legs with a pale golden fuzz. Her slender hands held a book called "The Concrete Shoes of Motherhood."

"Let's take a shower. They have a sauna. Let me give you a backrub. Let's lie down and take a nap," he said.

"Cheese it," she said. "Amscray. Make tracks. Get smaller."

Zeus could hear his fellow-gods hooting and cackling up on Olympus. (The Father of Heaven! Shot Down! Given the Heave-Ho! By a Housewife!) He lost eighteen pounds. He ran twenty-one miles every morning. He shaved off the mustache. She refused to look at him, but, being a god, he could read her thoughts. She was interested. She hiked over the dry brown hills and he walked behind and sang songs to her:

> Lady, your shining skin will slide on mine,
> Your breasts tremble with gladness.
> Your body, naked, be clad in sweet oils,
> And rise to the temple of Aphrodite,
> Where you will live forever, no more
> Lutheran but venerated by mortals.
> This I pledge.

She pretended not to hear, sweeping the horizon with her binoculars, looking for rare seabirds. Zeus thought, I should have been a swan. The dog trotted along, his hernia cured by love. She had named him Sweetness. "You go ahead and use my body as long as you like," he said to Zeus. "You're doing wonders for it. I never looked so good until you became me. No kidding."

They didn't make love until they got on the plane and were almost to America. They hit turbulence over Newfoundland. The plane bucked in the boiling black clouds, the seat-belt light flashed on, they tipped and plunged and rattled, people shrieked. "We're going to die," Diane said. "I love you. Let's take our laps around the track, big boy." So they undressed under the thin blankets, unfastened their seat belts, and made steady and joyous love, two travellers across life's tumultuous sky joined in life's great mutual gift, until, just as the plane hit the concrete at Kennedy and bounced and touched down and rolled to a stop, Diane shuddered and moaned and raked his back with her nails. She said nothing. She was clearly moved. Not until they were in the terminal and had got their bags and passed customs and come through the crowd did she whisper to him, "That was so nice I could do it again, I bet."

Zeus didn't think he could. He felt weak and listless. Diane carried the bags, and he led the dog, who emerged from the baggage room dopey and confused. Zeus collapsed into the back seat of a van driven by a burly man named Vern, who, Zeus gathered, was his brother. "Wes is pretty jet-lagged," Diane told him, but the man yammered on and on about virtually nothing. "Hope you had a good trip," he said. Yes, they said, they had. "Always wanted to go over there myself," he said. "But things come up. You know." He talked for many miles about what he had done instead of going to Greece: resodding, finishing the attic, adding on a bedroom, taking the kids to Yellowstone. *Do we have kids?* Zeus wondered. "Four," said the dog, beaming. "Great kids. I can't wait for you to meet them, Mister." Then he dropped his chin on the seat and groaned. "The littlest guy is murder on animals. One look at me, he'll have me in a headlock until my eyeballs pop." He groaned again. "I forgot about Mojo. Our black Lab." His big brown eyes filled with tears. "I've come home in disgrace to die like a dog," he said. "I feed Mojo for ten years and now he's going to go for my throat. It's too hard." The god told him to buck up, but the dog brooded all the way home, and when Vern pulled up to the garage behind the little green house and Diane climbed out, the dog tore off down the street and across a playground and disappeared. Vern and Zeus cruised the streets for half an hour searching for the mutt, Zeus with gathering apprehension, even panic. Without Wes to resume being Wes, he figured, he couldn't get out of Wes and back into Zeus.

Vern went home for a warm jacket (he said, but Zeus guessed he was tired and would find some reason not to come back). The god strode across yards, through hedges, crooning, "Sweetness! Sweetness!" The yards were cluttered with machines, which he threw aside. *Sweetness!*

The dog was huddled by an incinerator behind the school. He had coached boys' hockey here for ten years. "I'm so ashamed," he wept. The god held him tightly in his arms. "To be a dog in a foreign place is one thing, but to come home and have to crawl around—" He was a small dog, but he sobbed like a man—deep, convulsive cries.

Zeus was about to say, "Oh, it's not all that bad," and then he felt a feathery hand on his shoulder. Actually, a wing. It was Victor, Hera's old lawyer, in a blue pin-striped suit and two transparent wings like a locust's. Zeus tried to turn him into a kumquat, but the man only chuckled. "Heh, heh, heh. Don't waste my time. You wanna know how come you feel a little limp? Lemme tell ya. Hera is *extremely* upset, Mr. Z. Frankly, I don't know if godhood is something you're ever going to experience again. It wouldn't surprise me that much if you spent the rest of recorded time as a frozen meatball."

"What does she want?"

"She wants what's right. Justice. She wants half your power. No more, no less."

"Divide power? Impossible. It wouldn't be power if I gave it up."

"O.K. Then see how you like *these* potatoes."

He snatched up the dog, and his wings buzzed as he zoomed up, and over the pleasant rooftops of Odense.

"Wait!" the god cried. "Forty-five per cent!" But his voice was thin and whispery. On the way home, he swayed, his knees caved in, he had to hang on to a mailbox. For three days, Zeus was flat on his back, stunned by monogamy: what a cruel fate for a great man! Diane waited on him hand and foot; children hung around, onlookers at the site of a disaster. They clung to him, they squeezed in next to him on the couch, fighting over the choice locations. They stank of sugar. He could not get their names straight. Melissa and Donnie (or Sean or Jon), or Melinda and Randy, and the fat one was Penny, and the little one's name began with an "H". He called him Hector, and the little boy cried. "Go away," the god snapped. "You are wretched and vile and disgusting. I'm sorry. It's the truth. I'm dying, I think. Let me die in peace. Bug off." The older boy wept: something about a promise, a trip to see something, a purchase—Zeus couldn't understand him. "Speak up!" he said, but the boy blubbered and bawled, his soft lemurlike face slimy with tears and mucus. The god swung down his legs and sat up on the couch and raised his voice: "I am trapped here, a being fallen from a very high estate indeed—you have no idea—and what I see around me *I do not want.*"

Everybody felt lousy, except Diane. "It's only jet lag!" she cried, bringing in a tray of cold, greasy, repulsive food, which he could see from her smile was considered a real treat here. He ate a nugget of cheese and gagged.

"You'll feel better tomorrow," she said.

Later, Penny, the fat girl, asked him if Greece was as dirty as they said. She asked if he and Mom had had a big fight. She asked why he felt trapped. She wanted to hear all the bad news.

"I felt crazy the moment we landed in America. The air is full of piercing voices, thousands of perfectly normal, handsome, tall people talk-talk-talk-talk-talking away like chickadees, and I can hear each one of them all the time and they make me insane. You're used to this, I'm not. *What do you people have against silence?* Your country is so beautiful, and it is in the grip of invincible stupidity. The President is a habitual liar and a hack, and the Vice-President is a raging idiot," he said. "The country is inflamed with debt and swollen with blight and trash, and the government is in the hands of people who lack the brains and integrity to run a small plumbing shop, and they'll be in power until 1997, and then it won't matter much."

"How can you say that, Dad?"

"Because I'm omniscient."

"You are?"

"I know everything. It's a fact." She looked at him with a level gaze, not smirking, not pouting, an *intelligent* child. The only one prepared to understand him.

"Do my homework," she whispered. He whipped off dozens of geometry exercises, algebra, trigonometry, in a flash. He identified the nations of Africa, the law of averages, the use of the dative. "You are *so smart*," she said.

Diane packed the kids off to bed. "Now," she said, "where's that guy I rode home with on the plane?"

How could she understand? Passion isn't an arrangement, it's an accident, and the guy on the plane was history.

She wanted him to see a therapist, but Zeus knew he was going back to Olympus. He just had to talk Hera down a little.

HE drove to the church, with Penny snuggled at his side. The town lay in a river valley, the avenues of homes extending up and over the hills like branches laden with fruit. The church stood on a hill, a red brick hangar with a weathervane for a steeple, a sanctuary done up with fake beams and mosaics, and a plump secretary with piano legs, named Tammy. She cornered him, hugged him, and fawned like a house afire. "Oh, Pastor Wes, we missed you so much! I've been reading your sermons over and over—they're so spirit-filled! We've got to publish them in a book!" She squealed.

"Go home," said Zeus. "Put your head under cold water." He escaped from the sanctuary into the study and slammed the door. The dog sat in the big leather chair behind the long desk. He cleared his throat. "I'd be glad to help with the sermon for tomorrow," he said. "I think your topic has got to be change—the life-affirming nature of change, the Christian's willingness to accept and nurture change."

"That's a lot of balloon juice," said Zeus. He caught a look at himself in a long mirror that stood in a closet full of robes: a powerful, handsome, tanned fellow in a white collar. Not bad.

"You sure you want to leave tomorrow?"

"That's the deal I made with Victor. Didn't he tell you?"

"You couldn't stay until Monday? This town needs shaking up. I always wanted to do it and didn't know how, and now you could preach on Sunday and it'd be a wonderful experience for all of us."

"You're a fool," Zeus said. "This is not a TV show. You people are dying. This is not a long-term problem, and the answer to it is not the willingness to accept change. You need heart but you're Lutherans, and you go along with things. We know that from history. You're in danger and months will pass and it'll get worse, but you won't change your minds. You'll sit and wait. Lutherans are fifteen per cent faith and eighty-five per cent loyalty. They are nobody to lead to revolt. Your country is coming apart."

The dog looked up at the god with tears in his brown eyes. "Please tell my people," he whispered.

"Tell them yourself."

"They won't believe me."

"Neither do I."

"Love me," Diane told Zeus that night in bed. "Forget yourself. Forget that we're Lutheran. Hurl your body off the cliff into the dark abyss of wild, mindless, passionate love." But he was too tired. He couldn't find the cliff. He seemed to be on a prairie. In the morning, he hauled himself out of bed and dressed in a brown suit and white shirt. He peered into the closet. "These your only ties?" he asked the dog. The dog nodded.

Zeus glanced out the bedroom window to the east, to a beech tree by the garage, where a figure with waxen wings was sitting on a low limb. He said, silently, "Be with you in one minute." He limped into the kitchen and found Diane in the breakfast nook, eating bran flakes and reading an article in the Sunday paper about a couple who are able to spend four days a week in their country home now that they have a fax machine. He brushed her cheek with his lips and whispered, "O you woman, farewell, you sweet, sexy Lutheran love of my life," and jumped out of Wes and into the dog, loped out the back door, and climbed into Victor's car.

"She'll be glad to hear you're coming," said Victor. "She misses you. I'm sorry you'll have to make the return flight in a small cage, doped on a heavy depressant, and be quarantined for sixty days in Athens, both July and August, but after that things should start to get better for you."

At eleven o'clock, having spent the previous two hours tangled in the sheets with his amazing wife, Wes stood in the pulpit and grinned. The church was almost half full, not bad for July, and the congregation seemed glad to see him. "First of all, Diane and I want to thank you for the magnificent gift of the trip to Greece, which will be a permanent memory, a token of your generosity and love," he said. "A tremendous thing happened on the trip that I want to share with you this morning. For the past week, I have lived in the body of a dog while an ancient god lived with Diane and made love to her."

He didn't expect the congregation to welcome this news, but he was unprepared for their stony looks: they stood up and pointed and glared at him as if he were a criminal. They cried out, "Get down out of that pulpit, you filth, you!"

"Why are you so hostile?" he said.

Why are you so hostile? The lamp swayed as the ship rolled, and Diane said, "Why so hostile? Why? You want to know why I'm hostile? Is that what you're asking? About hostility? My hostility to you? O.K. I'll answer your question. Why I'm hostile—right? Me. Hostile. I'll tell you why. Why are you smiling?"

He was smiling, of course, because it was a week ago—they were in Greece, and God had kindly allowed him one more try. He could remember exactly the horrible words he'd said the first time, and this time he did not have to say them and become a dog. He was able to swallow the 1949 wine, and think, and say, "The sight of you fills me with tender affection and a sweet longing to be flat on my back in a dark, locked room with you naked, lying on top, kissing me, and me naked, too."

The lawyer and the dog rode to the airport in the limousine, and somewhere along the way Zeus signed a document that gave Hera half his power and promised absolute fidelity. "Absolute?" he woofed. "You mean 'total' in the sense of bottom line, right? A sort of basic faithfulness? Fidelity in principle? Isn't that what you mean here? The spirit of fidelity?"

"I mean *pure*," the lawyer said.

Zeus signed. The lawyer tossed him a small, dry biscuit. Zeus wolfed it down and barked. In the back of his mind, he thought maybe he'd find a brilliant lawyer to argue that the paw print wasn't a valid signature, but he wasn't sure. He thought about a twenty-four-ounce T-bone steak, and he wasn't sure he'd get that, either.

1990

SUSAN SONTAG

THE VERY COMICAL LAMENT

OF PYRAMUS AND THISBE

(AN INTERLUDE)

WALL: Thus have I, Wall, my part dischargèd so; And being done, thus Wall away doth go.

—A Midsummer Night's Dream, *Act V, Scene 1.*

THISBE: It's not here anymore.

PYRAMUS: It separated us. We yearned for each other. We grew apart.

THISBE: I was always thinking about it.

PYRAMUS: I thought you were thinking about me.

THISBE: Ninny! *(Gives him a kiss.)* How often have I reassured you. But I'm talking about what I didn't say. With every sentence I uttered, there was another, unspoken half sentence: "And the wall . . ." Example: I'm going to the Paris Bar.

PYRAMUS: "And the wall . . ."

THISBE: Example: What's playing at the Arsenal tonight?

PYRAMUS: "And the wall . . ."

THISBE: Example: It's terrible for the Turks in Kreuzberg.

PYRAMUS: "And the wall . . ."

THISBE: Exactly.

PYRAMUS: It was a tragedy. Will it be a comedy now?

THISBE: We won't become normal, will we?

PYRAMUS: Does this mean we can do whatever we want?

THISBE: I'm starting to feel a little nostalgic. Oh, the human heart is a fickle thing.

PYRAMUS: Thisbe!

THISBE: Not about you, belovèd! You know I'll always be yours. I mean, you'll be mine. But of course that's the same, isn't it? No, I'm thinking about . . . you know. I miss it a little.

PYRAMUS: Thisbe!

THISBE: Just a little. *(Sees* PYRAMUS *frowning.)* Smile, darling. Oh, you people are so serious!

PYRAMUS: I've suffered.

THISBE: So have I, in my way. Not like you, of course. But it wasn't always easy here, either.

PYRAMUS: Let's not quarrel.

THISBE: *We* quarrel? Never! *(Sound of wall-peckers.)* Listen! What an amazing sound!

PYRAMUS: I wish I'd brought my tape recorder. It's a Sony.

THISBE: I'm glad you can buy whatever you want now. I didn't realize you were *so* poor.

PYRAMUS: It was awful. But, you know, it was good for my character.

THISBE: You see? Even you can feel rueful. An American artist warned me last year, You'll miss this wall. *(She spies some wall-peckers spraying their hoard of pieces of the wall with paint.)* They're improving it.

PYRAMUS: Let's not be nostalgic.

THISBE: But you agree there's something to be said for it. It made us different.

PYRAMUS: We'll still be different.

THISBE: I don't know. So many cars. So much trash. The beggars. Pedestrians don't wait at corners for the green light. Cars parked on the sidewalk.

Enter the SPIRIT OF NEW YORK.

SPIRIT: O city, I recognize you. Your leather bars, your festivals of independent films, your teeming dark-skinned foreigners, your real-estate predators, your Art Deco shops, your racism, your Mediterranean restaurants, your littered streets, your rude mechanicals—

THISBE: No! Begone! This is the Berkeley of Central Europe.

SPIRIT: Central Europe: a dream. Your Berkeley: an interlude. This will be the New York of Europe—it was ever meant to be so. Only postponed for a mere sixty years.

SPIRIT OF NEW YORK *vanishes.*

THISBE: Well, I suppose it won't be too bad. Since New York isn't America, this city still won't be—

PYRAMUS: Sure, provided it stays shabby as well as full of unwelcome foreigners. *(Sighs.)* Let's not be too hopeful.

THISBE: Oh, let's be hopeful. We'll be rich. It's only money.

PYRAMUS: And power. I'm going to like that.

THISBE: We're not getting anything we don't deserve. We're together. We're free.

PYRAMUS: Still, everything is going too fast. And costing too much.

THISBE: No one can make us do what we don't want as long as we're together.

PYRAMUS: I'm having a hard time thinking of those less fortunate than we are. But sometimes we'll remember, won't we.

THISBE: I want to forget these old stories.

PYRAMUS: History is homesickness.

THISBE: Cheer up, darling. The world is divided into Old and New. And we'll always be on the good side. From now on.

PYRAMUS: Goethe said—

THISBE: Oh, not Goethe.

PYRAMUS: You're right.

THISBE: In Walter Benjamin's last—

PYRAMUS: Not Benjamin, either!

THISBE: Right. *(They fall silent for a while.)* Let's stroll.

They see a procession of venders, including some Russian soldiers, coming across an empty field.

PYRAMUS: And to think *that* was no man's land.

THISBE: What are they selling?

PYRAMUS: Everything. Everything is for sale.

THISBE: Do say it's better. Please!

PYRAMUS: Of course it's better. We don't have to die.

THISBE: Then let's go on celebrating. Have some champagne. Have a River Cola.

They drink.

PYRAMUS: Freedom at last.

THISBE: But don't toss your can on the ground.

PYRAMUS: What do you take me for?

THISBE: Sorry. It's just that—I'm sorry. Yes, freedom.

CURTAIN.

1991

OFF-RAMP

I USED to speak the language of the patriarchy.

RICK, my stepfather, taught me Latin names for all the bones in his right foot. When I helped my first boyfriend with his high-school homework, he insisted I do it in baby talk.

And then there was Lyle. He came into the Carl's Jr. that Rick and my mom run near Flagstaff, Arizona, one day in late August. All summer we fed tourists after they were Grand Canyoned out. Hundreds— *thousands*—of exhausted, screaming kids and their zombified parents. I was nineteen. Lyle was sitting alone that afternoon, staring at me while I loaded French-fry bags.

"Tell that creep he's got to give up his table," Rick said. "He's been there fifteen minutes."

I went over to where Lyle was lounging. "My stepdad thinks it's impolite to digest your food," I told him.

Lyle looked deep into my eyes. "Doreen," he said, reading my nameplate. "I have news for you, Doreen. You are not who you think you are. You are not a fast-food server—you are an inspiration from the divine. You have made me want to create again."

"I have?" I said. "Are you an artist?"

"I could be," he said, "if you would be my muse." He paused and played with his straw. "Do you know what a muse is?" I shook my head. "A muse is a woman who makes it possible for a guy to carry out his life's work. But muses don't have names like Doreen."

He stood up and left. I ran after him.

"Then who am I?" I asked in the parking lot.

"Henceforth," he said, "you shall be Rawnee." He spelled it in the dust on his van.

I'D never been with anyone who lived for his art before. The people I knew all picked up after themselves. But Lyle couldn't function without me. And I thought I was discovering capabilities in myself I hadn't known were there, like paying bills.

We went through my junior-college savings fund in two weeks.

One night Lyle drove off without saying anything. I was terrified that he wouldn't come back, that he'd find another muse. At 3 A.M. he returned, carrying a huge cardboard box. "All the really creative people have to be subsidized," he explained. He knifed open the carton. Clothing labels spilled out onto the shag carpeting of the tiny house we were renting. "You and me are about to get a little grant from Mack Ropington," he said.

It was at the height of the Western-wear craze, and everyone was splurging on Ropington's designer clothes and furnishings. I knew that what we were about to do was wrong and, worse, that I could end up in jail.

"Do you think what *Ropington's* doing is right?" Lyle asked. "Making people think they're cowboys because they're wearing his hundred-dollar jeans or sleeping under his five-hundred-dollar horse blankets?"

"No, but—"

"I thought you loved me," Lyle said.

So, the next day I got up before dawn and drove out into the Verde Valley. I met up with my contact on a dirt road full of potholes. I paid him for his trunkful of men's cotton briefs—they were the kind you'd buy at K mart. Then I sat in my car and sewed in the tags. When I finished, it was 8 A.M., time to drive over to the Sedona off-ramp and set up shop. That day I cleared $169.52.

I was always selling something different. Sometimes it was ties, sometimes shirts, sometimes pillowcases, pot holders, or mittens. Whatever my supplier could get—and I never asked how. People would stop their cars to buy it as long as it said Ropington.

MY new career had its downside, too. I often had to change locations to avoid getting caught. And later, when the recession hit, the tourists started keeping their disposable income for vacation essentials such as motel childcare.

Lyle, however, was *always* having a hard time. "How can I create art when the world's so messed up?" he said one night. I was sitting on the bed, sewing labels into imitation-leather aprons. "I should be out making a difference," he said. "I should go leave tire tracks on the front lawn of the White House to let them know what I think of their energy policies."

"Lyle," I said, "you have to make things better where you can. And no improvement is too small."

He thought about this. "You're right, Rawnee," he said. "While you're doing that, take off your clothes."

"*Lyle,*" I said, "I'm *working.*" But I never could refuse him.

"The world's a better place already," he said.

ASTRA says that men have separated themselves from nature, and that's why in these last few years of this millennium Lyle can't create.

I was going to goddess therapy. I saw the ad for it in our newspaper. "Find the Power of Inspiration Within—Let the Muse Speak to *You,*" it said. I was sure this was what I needed to help Lyle.

We met every Tuesday evening at the public library, because it was over the strongest power vortex in our town. Unfortunately, the library closed that spring for lack of funding. We then got together at the Denny's on 89, which is on top of the second-strongest power vortex.

"This Astra is taking advantage of you," Lyle said. "She is leading you on, Rawnee, when she says that you can create art. Let me tell you, not everyone can create art. Even if you're an artist, it doesn't mean you can create art."

"Astra says that if you connect with the feminine you will achieve wholeness, and then you will create."

"Rawnee," he said, "the kind of wholeness *I* need to create art is matched pairs of socks in my drawer, and a refrigerator full of food. You've been neglecting things around here, especially me."

ASTRA felt I had it in me to perform my own ritual. I was nervous. The rituals that the other women had created were *so* impressive! One sat for three days in our local river. Another shaved her head and ate mud.

"Stop thinking and it will come to you," Astra said.

It was while I was selling at the Canyon de Chelly on-ramp that I had a revelation about what form my ritual must take. I phoned all the wo-men and invited them over to our house. Lyle was furious when I made him leave.

"I'm interested in getting in touch with my primordial wo-maness-ness," I announced. It was a suffocatingly hot July night. "So I'm going to turn off the air-conditioner."

We sweltered together for an hour, and then Astra spoke. "I don't mean to be hierarchical or anything," she said to me, "but I think you can do better."

SEPTEMBER 10th was a particularly bad day for me. My 5 A.M. contact could only get abalone shells. It took me forever to paste the Ropington tags into them. Then drivers just slowed down at the Moenkopi off-ramp and eyed me suspiciously. They didn't stop.

By noon I'd developed a halfway decent sales pitch. "Mack Ropington says the era of the West he's gaining the most inspiration from these days is when it was all underwater," I'd say. Not one sale.

Early that afternoon, a colleague set up beside me. I recognized him from various junctions and cloverleafs where he'd always dressed in old miner's gear. Now, he was wearing mirror shades, a poncho, and braids.

My heart sank when he propped up a dozen paintings on velvet. Sure enough, a man in an Infiniti screeched to a stop. He pointed to a picture of a chief offering a scalp to a naked squaw. "I really go for the Native American philosophy of life," the Infiniti man said.

"That's five per cent off the asking price for not calling us Indians," my competition said.

I got home around nine. All I wanted was to go straight to bed. When I opened the door, I didn't recognize my home. The furniture had been totally rearranged. And a woman I'd never seen before was draping herself on the couch *I'd* purchased.

"Who are you?" I demanded.

"Calm down," she said. "Nothing happened. Lyle and I are exploring the spiritual side of our relationship."

Lyle strolled into the room. He didn't say as much as hello to me.

"What's going on?" I said.

"Rawnee," he said, "meet Tawnee."

"Lyle," she whined, "I think it's time we advanced to touching. I'm getting achy in my shoulders from all the tension in the air."

He looked at me and sighed. "It's damn hard to be an artist in this house. On top of all *your* questions, now I have to give *her* a *massage*."

At that, I started packing my things.

When Lyle saw I was serious about leaving, he blocked the front door. "Rawnee," he said. "You can't abandon me. You know how much you mean to me. You are the air that gives me life, the water that sustains me—"

"And the earth you walk all over," I said.

I NEEDED a ritual that would transform my hurt into a mighty but sensitive sword. I drove high into the mesas with Astra and the others. We left our vehicles behind and climbed up a rock and into a cave. There we swept aside the used condoms and beer bottles.

"Let the wind and sky speak to you," Astra told me.

I tried.

"What are they saying?"

"I'm not sure," I said.

"You're thinking again," she said. "Don't think. Deep within you is the power to understand."

I listened again. This time I heard their voices.

"Forget that jerk," the voices said.

I HAVE left Rawnee behind, and I have no more need of Mack Ropington's name. I am Superba now, and I have my own resonant image.

TWO cars pull up to my stand. "Hey, that's you, isn't it?" the man in the white Bronco says. He casts his eyes on my wares: photos of me printed on T-shirts. "I'll take three of the ones with you topless."

The other driver gets out of his Hyundai. "Excuse me," he says. "Did I hear you say 'topless'? This is not a T-shirt with a photo on it of a topless woman. This is a T-shirt with a photo on it of a woman who has chosen to bare her breasts." This man turns to me. "I'm Coe," he says. "I'm white, I'm male, I'm heterosexual, and I'm sorry."

"I'm Superba," I tell him. "And I need to exorcise some submission forces arising in me upon meeting a man after being single for three months. I need to do this in a context in which I still honor my own power. So this is how it's going to be—you will pick a restaurant, drive us there, and pay for dinner."

WE are travelling along a winding mountain road. He relates the story of his quest to attain a genuine PMS state. His Hyundai begins to sputter. Moments later, we are out of gas.

Coe bursts into tears. "This is a metaphor for how the patriarchy's breaking down and me with it!" He clutches me and sobs. "Show me the way, Superba."

"Well," I say, "one of the first things I do when I get in a car is look at the gas gauge."

"You're a woman warrior!" he cries. He straightens up. "I've been reading Carl Jung. He says a man is nothing until he meets his anima. Please be my feminine principle and help me become whole again."

I pull him to me and kiss him.

"Wow," he says. "The way you're in charge of your sexuality is devastating to my male ego. But it's the only chance our planet has."

I kiss him again. Together we acknowledge the presence of nature. Snow is falling. The road is dark, and it doesn't appear likely that automobiles will pass by.

"What do we do now?" he asks.

"One of us must seek out a twenty-four-hour filling station and return with some gas."

"I lost my intuitive powers when my Fathers colonized your sex," he says. "We'll be doomed if *I* try to find one."

"You're right," I say. "You must stay here." I gather my purse, put on my jacket, and look over at Coe. He is trembling; there are holes in his sweater. The sight of him expressing his true male helplessness summons forth my inner voices. As Astra has taught me, I listen to them. "Remove your own parka and tuck it around him," the voices say.

I obey, then open the car door and step out. "You're my kind of goddess," he calls out from inside. "Hurry back."

The snow crunches under my sneakers. I am shivering, but that will pass. For I am the strong one.

1991

LISA WALKER

———————

BLOWN AWAY

"Actresses—especially those of the Sex Babe variety—are born with wiles that are always at work, beguiling and bedeviling. . . . Such women are not unaware of their impact. . . . They watch themselves drive men to despair."—*Interviewer Bill Zehme in* Rolling Stone, *the HOT 1992 issue.*

"Here in fact is how it goes, if you are Sharon Stone: . . . you are brighter than you look, since you look extraordinary."—*Bill Zehme, describing "America's Premier Sex Babe."*

"I've hit a few people, yes. I've knocked a couple of guys across the room."—*Sharon Stone, according to Zehme.*

"She can be seen as the Blonde in such works as 'Action Jackson,' 'Police Academy 4,' 'King Solomon's Mines' and 'Allan Quatermain and the Lost City of Gold,' . . . 'Above the Law,' 'Scissors' and 'He Said, She Said.' "—*Same interviewer, recapping Sharon Stone's career.*

"She can be very clever with words and hit you [with them]. . . . And if you're not careful she can be the victor."—*Director Paul Verhoeven on Sharon Stone.*

"Never play cards with a guy named Doc."—*One of the rules you live by if you are Sharon Stone.*

"You are skipped ahead in school, where you are still mostly bored."—*More of how it goes if you are Sharon Stone.*

"She owns two double-barreled, pump-action shotguns she will not hesitate to use and has known no greater joy than squeezing off rounds on an Uzi."—*About Sharon Stone.*

"I think you would have to be a really strong guy if you wanted to marry her, . . . otherwise, she'll blow you away."—*Director advising men who want to marry Sharon Stone.*

"Oh, it's *wonderful!* . . . You put it under your arm and hold it close to your body, and you feel the heat of the bullets as they pass out by your back!"—*Sharon on the joys of an Uzi.*

"My feeling is, if I could just stand alongside her and listen to her talk about her sex life once in a while, I would never have to date again!"—*Neurotic comedian Richard Lewis on overhearing Sharon Stone at the gym.*

"Murder is a very sexual thing. . . . And when two people commit murder together, that's the most bonding thing that there is, in a psychological sense."—*Quote from the actress Richard Lewis wants to listen to talk about sex.*

"She now owns the world."—*Bill Zehme, hailing the results of Sharon Stone's filming an interrogation scene without underwear on.*

"I think I oughta do what I wanna do."—*What Sharon Stone thinks.*

"You see her point always. She always *has* a point."—*Same Bill's assessment of Sharon.*

"Never eat at a place called Mom's."—*Sharon citing another of the rules she lives by.*

"She is a fight fan and a Lakers fan and aspires to act the way Magic Johnson passes."—*She is Sharon Stone.*

"I am for sure a Broad."—*Sharon Stone. For sure.*

"I've spent some quality time with her, yes."—*Michael Douglas to interviewer. Sounding tired.*

"You know, I'm a girl who really likes boys."—*Sharon. More on herself.*

"Here in fact is how it goes, if you are Sharon Stone: . . . Your IQ measures out as Einstein's superior."—*Fact.*

MOMS TUCKER (*proprietor of Mom's Place*): Maybe I'm just an old woman who don't know so much. I say this is a rule to live by: "You got cash, you don't need credit. You need credit, you got no cash." That's not exactly in the formal text of a rule, but it's my rule. I keep it taped to the front of my cash register for my customers to read and heed. Of course, I believe even though you've got a rule—or somebody else's rule—you live by, you have to be limber, like the wind. These are the wisdoms you acquire when you run a Mom's Place or eat at a Mom's Place.

Maybe this gal's just too young to have acquired this kind of reasoning. Then again, by the time I was her age I had nearly raised eight kids and already served two consecutive sentences. So she's probably got no excuse. But that's all right, because with age you do soften up.

GINGER HART (*Michael Douglas fan*): I think that Michael has really changed.

MARV ATLAS (*owner and master acting coach of the Magic Johnson Actor's Technique Studio*): She certainly wasn't the first to notice Magic's innate smoothness and natural sense of drama and climax. But she was the only student, male or non-male, I didn't have to explain the no-look-pass principles to.

I'll never forget the first day she walked into the studio. Heads were popping. It was clear she was the type to get bored very easy. She was a girl who really liked boys, and you could say I was beguiled by her desire to shock, but I get bored easy myself. All women should be so blessed. If I was a god, which I'm not, I would create all women in her image.

DOC (*card shark*): It's no exaggeration to say people have lost everything of meaning in a card game with me and then, without ever a hope of winning back what they've gambled away, begged me for one more round. When I ask, "Another hand?" I make them feel like it's their own idea, when in fact from the moment they sat across from me at the table they gave up any freedom they may have thought they had. And don't believe for a minute there's a person out there, man or woman, and I will emphasize "woman," who can refuse me. The slicker they are, the quicker they are to deal with. Hell, she's so easy it's almost not even sporting.

CASPER FINN (*owner of Casper's Survival Outfitters*): You've got your Uzi. Then there's the mini-Uzi and, shrunk even more, you've got your micro-Uzi. The micro has a cyclic rate of fire of 1250 rounds per minute. An itchy trigger finger can really wreak some destruction. Say your magazine holds twenty rounds, the micro can empty that in zero-point-nine-five of one second. Guaranteed respect when you've got a little buddy like this at your side. Course, you've got your rival machine guns. The Sterling L2A3—dependable, and I think the design is uncommonly graceful. The Beretta Model 12—smarter than it looks. Probably the most accurate baby is the Heckler & Koch MP5. Sophisticated weapon, intricate weapon.

There is a real selection, and almost every day the options widen—the MP5, the Spectre, the Steyr MPi 69 and 81. But I'd say for a woman of her calibre the Uzi is a good bet. A first-class piece of artillery for close-quarter combat.

CAROL (*of Charlie and Carol, two people who committed murder together*): We were in a bad mood. Charlie's dad wouldn't let him use the car, and we were both broke. Charlie never had money, because he spent his going to all the movies. My allowance had been suspended, because I slightly rearranged a letter my principal sent to my parents. He wrote them I had skipped school, and I slipped the words "ahead in" between "skipped" and "school." So what.

So anyway, you know how couples can get to taking things out on each other. Charlie and me, we'd been doing that for a while. Then there we were one day, just peckin' at each other, and it made me remember hearing how if you commit murder together, it's like the tightest thing you can do. So that's what we did. And now Charlie won't let me out of his sight, because he's afraid I'm unaware of my impact.

Some days I look back at what it was that got me to where I am right now. In an abandoned farmhouse with nothing but snakes and grasshoppers for outside company . . . except when Charlie eats the grasshoppers . . . just to make me mad. I try not to have regrets, but sometimes, usually when I'm hungry, I find myself wondering things. Like if Charlie had only been born with red hair. Then I never would have liked him to begin with, and I wouldn't be here now. Or if I really had been skipped ahead in school, then I would have been too old to go out with Charlie, and I wouldn't be here now. What if Charlie's dad had given him the car that day? Then Charlie would have gone on about with his regular plan, which was to two-time me with Ariel Stillwater. If only murder wasn't a love cure.

ANGEL PIÑERO (*phantom featherweight*): I used to see her at the matches. She couldn't see me—no one could see me, but after the bouts, when all the lights were out, they could hear me shadow-spar, an eerie echo in the ring. She didn't come to the fights before about a year ago. Then she started comin' regular. Usually always she was with these soft-bellies. That's standard quo for dolls type her. She would whistle at my boys when they'd derobe for the open. One time she was carryin' on, distracting the focus—added with the fact she was dressed in such a manner as to provoke undue attention. . . . So I made her spill her popcorn. She thought it was her date's fault, and she knocked him clear across the crowd. I felt sorry for the guy till he walked back over to her and said, "Sorry." Then I just felt like the dude got what was comin' to him. You don't let no woman treat you thataway.

Man! What a condition these folks are living in. I've been haunting these rings for thirty-some years, and I have seen a lot pass by. There are things you notice more when you're a phantom. So I see there is a definite shift in women's attitudes. You never used to see no unhaltered lady wearing a tight T-shirt with "I am for sure a broad" across it. Makes me glad to be nothing but a shadow of a man.

1992

DAVID OWEN

HERE'S A REALLY GREAT IDEA

IF you've been married for a really long time, as I have, you probably don't need me to tell you that marriage can get a little boring after a while. Oh, boy, can it get boring. But it doesn't have to! There are quite a few little tricks and other things you can do to make it a lot more exciting and just plain fun. Here's one of them: having sexual intercourse.

One of the things I like best about having sexual intercourse is that it really is an awful lot of fun. How much fun? Flying a kite, going to the circus, riding a horse, going out for ice cream—add all those things together and multiply by two. Seem like a lot? Sure does. But you're not even halfway to sexual intercourse. Go ahead, think all you want—you're just not going to come up with anything more fun than this.

Getting in the mood for sexual intercourse is easy. Drinking a lot of beer or going to a movie can do the trick, especially if the movie is rated R or higher. Popular fiction usually contains scenes that put one in a sexual-intercourse frame of mind. Sometimes a walk downtown or a trip to the beach can make you suddenly think, Whoops, I know what I want to do! (Or have.)

Don't worry—there's no right or wrong way to have sexual intercourse. Just start having it, and then take it from there! I like to have it this way, that way, any old way. And the more of it I have, the better—it's that much fun. You'll probably think of different ways to have it. If so, be my guest!

When is the best time to have sexual intercourse? How about any day of the week with a name that ends in "d-a-y." (See what I mean?) Try having it at night, before you go to sleep. You're already in bed and not wearing very much—so why not! Feeling bored? Having sexual intercourse is the perfect change of pace. Worried about work? Having sexual intercourse will take your mind off your job. Lost your keys? You don't need keys to have sexual intercourse.

And later that same night, if your keys are still lost . . . well, you get the idea!

But don't take my word for it. Try having sexual intercourse yourself and see if you don't agree. After all, it's more popular than ever. And I really think you're going to like it, too. If you don't, though, you'd better keep it to yourself, because I can tell you right now that I am honestly not going to believe you.

1999

THE

WRITING

LIFE

F. SCOTT FITZGERALD

A SHORT AUTOBIOGRAPHY

(WITH ACKNOWLEDGMENTS TO NATHAN)

1913

The four defiant Canadian Club whiskeys at the Susquehanna in Hackensack.

1914

The Great Western Champagne at the Trent House in Trenton and the groggy ride back to Princeton.

1915

The Sparkling Burgundy at Bustanoby's. The raw whiskey in White Sulphur Springs, Montana, when I got up on a table and sang, "Won't you come up," to the cowmen. The Stingers at Tate's in Seattle listening to Ed Muldoon, "that clever chap."

1916

The apple brandy nipped at in the locker-room at the White Bear Yacht Club.

1917

A first Burgundy with Monsignor X at the Lafayette. Blackberry brandy and whiskey with Tom at the old Nassau Inn.

1918

The Bourbon smuggled to officers' rooms by bellboys at the Seelbach in Louisville.

1919

The Sazzarac Cocktails brought up from New Orleans to Montgomery to celebrate an important occasion.

1920

Red wine at Mollat's. Absinthe cocktails in a hermetically sealed apartment in the Royalton. Corn liquor by moonlight in a deserted aviation field in Alabama.

1921

Leaving our champagne in the Savoy Grill on the Fourth of July when a drunk brought up two obviously Piccadilly ladies. Yellow Chartreuse in the Via Balbini in Rome.

1922

Kaly's crème de cacao cocktails in St. Paul. My own first and last manufacture of gin.

1923

Oceans of Canadian ale with R. Lardner in Great Neck, Long Island.

1924

Champagne cocktails on the Minnewaska, and apologizing to the old lady we kept awake. Graves Kressman at Villa Marie in Valescure and consequent arguments about British politics with the nursery governess. Porto Blancs at a time of sadness. Mousseux bought by a Frenchman in a garden at twilight. Chambéry Fraise with the Seldes on their honeymoon. The local product ordered on the wise advice of a friendly priest at Orvieto, when we were asking for French wines.

1925

A dry white wine that "won't travel," made a little south of Sorrento, that I've never been able to trace. Plot coagulating—a sound of hoofs and bugles. The gorgeous Vin d'Arbois at La Reine Pédauque. Champagne cocktails in the Ritz sweatshop in Paris. Poor wines from Nicolas. Kirsch in a Burgundy inn against the rain with E. Hemingway.

1926

Uninteresting St. Estèphe in a desolate hole called Salies-de-Béarn. Sherry on the beach at La Garoupe. Gerald M.'s grenadine cocktail, the one flaw to make everything perfect in the world's most perfect house. Beer and weenies with Grace, Charlie, Ruth, and Ben at Antibes before the deluge.

1927

Delicious California "Burgundy-type" wine in one of the Ambassador bungalows in Los Angeles. The beer I made in Delaware that had a dark inescapable sediment. Cases of dim, cut, unsatisfactory whiskey in Delaware.

1928

The Pouilly with Bouillabaisse at Prunier's in a time of discouragement.

1929

A feeling that all liquor has been drunk and all it can do for one has been experienced, and yet—*"Garçon, un Chablis-Mouton 1902, et pour commencer, une petite carafe de vin rosé. C'est ça—merci."*

1929

FRANK SULLIVAN

THE CLICHÉ EXPERT

TAKES THE STAND

Q—Mr. Arbuthnot, you are an expert in the use of the cliché, are you not?

A—Yes, sir, I am a certified public cliché expert.

Q—In that case would you be good enough to answer a few questions on the use and application of the cliché in ordinary speech and writing?

A—I should be only too glad to do so.

Q—Thank you. Now, just for the record—you live in New York?

A—I like to visit New York but I wouldn't live here if you gave me the place.

Q—Then where do you live?

A—Any old place I hang my hat is home sweet home to me.

Q—What is your age?

A—I am fat, fair, and forty.

Q—And your occupation?

A—Well, after burning the midnight oil at an institution of higher learning, I was for a time a tiller of the soil. Then I went down to the sea in ships for a while, and later, at various times, I have been a guardian of the law, a gentleman of the Fourth Estate, a poet at heart, a bon vivant and raconteur, a prominent clubman and man about town, an eminent—

Q—Just what is your occupation at the moment, Mr. Arbuthnot?

A—At the moment I am an unidentified man of about forty, shabbily clad.

Q—Now then, Mr. Arbuthnot, what kind of existence do you, as a cliché expert, lead?

A—A precarious existence.

Q—And what do you do to a precarious existence?

A—I eke it out.

Q—Have you ever been in a kettle of fish?

A—Oh, yes.

Q—What kind?

A—A pretty kettle of fish.

Q—How do you cliché experts reveal yourselves, Mr. Arbuthnot?

A—In our true colors, of course.

Q—And you expect to live to . . .

A—A ripe old age.

Q—What do you shuffle off?

A—This mortal coil.

Q—What do you thank?

A—My lucky stars.

Q—What kind of retreats do you like?

A—Hasty retreats.

Q—What do you do to hasty retreats?

A—I beat them.

Q—Regarding dogs, what kind of dog are you?

A—A gay dog.

Q—And how do you work?

A—Like a dog.

Q—And you lead?

A—A dog's life.

Q—So much for dogs. Now, Mr. Arbuthnot, when you are naked, you are . . .

A—Stark naked.

Q—In what kind of daylight?

A—Broad daylight.

Q—What kind of outsider are you?

A—I'm a rank outsider.

Q—How right are you?

A—I am dead right.

Q—What kind of meals do you like?

A—Square meals.

Q—What do you do to them?

A—Ample justice.

Q—What is it you do to your way?

A—I wend my way.

Q—And your horizon?

A—I broaden my horizon.

Q—When you buy things, you buy them for . . .

A—A song.

Q—How are you known?

A—I am familiarly known.

Q—You are as sober as . . .

A—A judge.

Q—And when you are drunk?

A—I have lots of leeway there. I can be as drunk as a coot, or a lord, or an owl, or a fool—

Q—Very good, Mr. Arbuthnot. Now, how brown are you?

A—As brown as a berry.

Q—Ever see a brown berry?

A—Oh, no. Were I to see a brown berry, I should be frightened.

Q—To what extent?

A—Out of my wits.

Q—How fit are you?

A—I'm as fit as a fiddle.

Q—How do you wax?

A—I wax poetic.

Q—How about the fate of Europe?

A—It is hanging in the balance, of course.

Q—What happens to landscapes?

A—Landscapes are dotted.

Q—How are you attired in the evening?

A—Faultlessly.

Q—What kind of precision are you cliché-users partial to?

A—Clocklike precision.

Q—And what kind of order?

A—Apple-pie order.

Q—When you watch a parade, you watch it from . . .

A—A point of vantage.

Q—And you shroud things . . .

A—In the mists of antiquity.

Q—What kind of threats do you make?

A—Veiled threats.

Q—And what kind of secrets do you betray?

A—Dark secrets.

Q—How about ignorance?

A—Ignorance is always abysmal.

Q—Times?

A—Times are usually parlous.

Q—What kind of succession do you prefer?

A—Rapid succession.

Q—When you travel, what do you combine?

A—I combine business with pleasure.

Q—And you are destined . . .

A—To go far.

Q—What kind of purposes do you have?

A—Express purposes.

Q—And what is it you save?

A—Wear and tear.

Q—What goes with "pure"?

A—Simple.

Q—The word "sundry"?

A—Divers.

Q—What are ranks?

A—Ranks are serried. Structures are imposing. Spectacles are colorful.

Q—Thank you, Mr. Arbuthnot. What kind of beauties do you like?

A—Raving beauties.

Q—How generous are you?

A—I am generous to a fault.

Q—How is corruption these days?

A—Oh, rife, as usual.

Q—What are you shot with?

A—I am shot with luck.

Q—When?

A—At sunrise.

Q—What time is it?

A—It is high time.

Q—How do you point?

A—I point with pride, I view with alarm, and I yield to no man.

Q—What do you pursue?

A—The even tenor of my way.

Q—Ever pursue the odd tenor of your way?

A—Oh, no. I would lose my standing as a cliché expert if I did that.

Q—As for information, you are . . .

A—A mine of information.

Q—What kind of mine?

A—A veritable mine.

Q—What do you throw?

A—I throw caution.

Q—Where?

A—To the winds.

Q—As a cliché-user, have you any pets?

A—Yes, I have pet aversions.

Q—Any tempests?

A—Oh, yes. In teapots. In china shops I have bulls.

Q—What kind of cunning do you affect, Mr. Arbuthnot?

A—Low, animal cunning.

Q—And when you are taken, you are taken . . .

A—Aback.

Q—I see. Well, Mr. Arbuthnot, I think that about covers the ground for the time being. I'm sure we're all very grateful to you for your co-operation and your splendid answers, and I think that everyone who has listened to you here today will be a better cliché-user for having heard you. Thank you very, very much.

A—Thank *you*, Mr. Steuer. It's been a pleasure, I assure you, and I was only too glad to oblige.

1935

THE CLICHÉ EXPERT TELLS ALL

Q—Mr. Arbuthnot, when you write a story for a newspaper in your capacity—

A—Pardon me, Mr. Dewey. My *official* capacity.

Q—To be sure. In your official capacity as a cliché expert, from what kind of source do you get your information?

A—From a reliable source.

Q—What kind of rumors do you deal in?

A—Persistent but unconfirmed.

Q—What do you do to rumors?

A—I noise them abroad, or bruit them about.

Q—What has been received?

A—Word has been received.

Q—How do you reply?

A—Either in the negative or in the affirmative.

Q—When a parade takes place, what do flags do?

A—Flags flutter.

Q—And what kind of steeds are in the parade?

A—Prancing steeds.

Q—What kind of scene is it?

A—It is a colorful scene, and a gala occasion. Bands blare, guns boom, treads are martial, uniforms are resplendent, the city roars a welcome to the returning hero, and police estimate that fully 750,000 spectators line the curbs along the route.

Q—What kind of spectators, please?

A—Cheering spectators.

Q—If the President is there, what do the police take?

A—Extra precautions.

Q—And what is it rain does?

A—Rain interrupts the festivities.

Q—Mr. Arbuthnot, what happens at railroad stations on holidays?

A—Well, there is what our Society of Cliché Experts likes to refer to as a holiday exodus. I mean to say, fully 1,500,000 pleasure-seekers leave the city, railroad officials estimate. Every means of transportation is taxed to its utmost capacity.

Q—I see. How are flowers arranged at a wedding?

A—Tastefully.

Q—And what does Society do?

A—Society turns out *en masse.*

Q—Why?

A—Because the bride and groom are popular members of the younger set.

Q—How about the first marriages of the bride and groom, if any?

A—They terminated in divorce.

Q—What kind of couples get married?

A—Happy couples.

Q—What kind of parents have children?

A—Proud parents.

Q—To what point do happy couples often come?

A—To the parting of the ways.

Q—Mr. Arbuthnot, tell me, to whom are testimonial dinners given?

A—Pardon me, Mr. Dewey, but testimonial dinners are never given. They are tendered.

Q—Thank you for setting me right on that.

A—I hope you don't think me rude or overprecious.

Q—Quite the opposite. I—

A—You see, I feel rather strongly about the cliché because I have devoted a great deal of time to perfecting myself in its use. I do think that if one is going in for them one might as well get them right, down to the last detail, mightn't one? You know the old saying, "Whatever is worth doing at all is worth doing well."

Q—And a world of truth there is in it, too.

A—You said a mouthful, Mr. Dewey. So that what I mean is, a testimonial dinner is tendered, and it is tendered to a valued guest of honor. At the testimonial dinner the guest of honor receives what our society calls a token of esteem, suitably inscribed. The guest of honor tries to express his appreciation, but is overcome by emotion.

Q—Thank you for a concise summary of the testimonial-dinner situation, Mr. Arbuthnot. Now, how about meetings? What happens at meetings?

A—Oh, plans are formulated, arrangements are made, initial steps are taken.

Q—How many kinds of citizens are there, Mr. Arbuthnot?

A—Our society recognizes only one kind—prominent. Of course, there are also well-known residents and outstanding figures.

Q—How many friends has a prominent citizen?

A—He has a host of friends.

Q—Why?

A—Because he is a highly respected member of the community.

Q—Mr. Arbuthnot, what kind of hopes do you have?

A—High hopes, and I don't have them; I entertain them. I express concern. I discard precedent. When I am in earnest, I am in deadly earnest. When I am devoted, I am devoted solely. When a task comes along, it confronts me. When I stop, I stop short. I take but one kind of steps—those in the right direction. I am a force to be reckoned with. Oh, ask me anything, Mr. Dewey, anything.

Q—All right. How about the weather? Where does weather occur?

A—You think you can stump me with that? Well, you can't. Weather occurs over widespread areas. Winter holds the entire Eastern seaboard in its icy grip. Snow blankets the city, disrupting train schedules and marooning thousands of commuters. Traffic is at a standstill—

Q—Hold on a minute, my friend. You've left out something.

A—I have not. What?

Q—Traffic is *virtually* at a standstill.

A—Oh, a detail, Mr. Dewey. All right, I concede you that. Ten thousand unemployed are placed at work removing the record fall as cold wave spells suffering to thousands. Old residents declare blizzard worst since '88—

Q—Mr. Arbuthnot—

A—Mayor fears milk shortage. Now, in the summer, things are different. Then the city swelters in record heat wave. Thousands flock to beaches to seek relief. Mercury continues to soar. In the spring, on the other hand, the first robin—

Q—Hold on, Mr. Arbuthnot. I concede you the weather clichés for all four seasons. I would like to ask you another question.

A—Go ahead, you can't stump me, Mr. Dewey. You would like to, though, wouldn't you?

Q—Well, it would be rather a feather—

A—Yes, I know. In your cap. Well, proceed.

Q—What kind of fires happen?

A—Fires don't happen. They occur. And they are frequently fires of undetermined origin.

Q—What do the victims do at fires?

A—They flee, scantily clad.

Q—What happens to the building?

A—It is completely gutted.

Q—If you fall off your horse, what kind of a spill do you take, Mr. Arbuthnot?

A—A nasty spill.

Q—And how do you escape from any accident?

A—Unscathed.

Q—If you don't escape unscathed, what happens?

A—I sustain cuts, contusions, and abrasions. Or maybe I suffer a fracture.

Q—What kind of fracture?

A—A possible fracture.

Q—How do they get a doctor for you if you have a possible fracture?

A—Our society recognizes only one approved method by which a doctor may be got. He is hastily summoned.

Q—And the ambulance?

A—The ambulance responds.

Q—Well, Mr. Arbuthnot, I must give you credit. You have passed through the ordeal of this cross-examination in a manner nothing short of admirable. I congratulate you, sir.

A—Thanks, Mr. Dewey. You know what I am, don't you?

Q—No. What?

A—I'm a foeman worthy of your steel. Goodbye.

1936

RUTH SUCKOW

HOW TO ACHIEVE SUCCESS

AS A WRITER

EVERY writer, having become a writer, should be able to answer a question which besets him on all sides: How can I become a writer? There may be several people now living in the United States to whom this question is of no moment. I have myself met one or two who went so far as to declare they couldn't be writers if they were to be paid for it. But such defeatists grow fewer day by day.

For the encouragement of the dauntless majority, there are always, of course, those newspaper interviews with successful authors who are only too ready to tell everybody else how to turn the trick. They all give the same advice: You can achieve success as a writer by writing. Obviously, if the questioners *could* be satisfied by such a simple answer as that, they wouldn't have asked in the first place. Still, I must confess that for many years I couldn't think of any better reply myself. Now, at last, I am convinced that I have the real solution to the problem and the very one that the inquirers have all been hoping to hear. The answer is, of course: You can achieve success as a writer by *not* being a writer.

It is plain to see that writers who aren't writers have it all over writers who are writers. In the first place, there is the saving in time. I have often had to spend several hours a day on writing while being a writer. If I had only kept myself busy at something else, such labor would have been unnecessary. Some other occupation, plus the consequent success in writing, is more profitable, besides. It is uphill work for a writer to sell his writings with only the narrow appeal of his own name as a writer, but if he were engaged in doing something quite different, he could be assured of a respectful audience. The surefire way to achieve success as a writer is to be a celebrity in any other line. The opportunities in other fields are so numerous, in fact, that the real difficulty lies in making a choice. A hasty glance through the publishers' lists will give a fascinating view of the range of occupations that really do lead to success in writing.

Aviation is a splendid preparation for writing, and is open to men and women alike. As soon as any flier reaches the end of his flight, he may find that he is a writer. Sport is a good line, on the whole. Tennis stars readily become writers by being tennis stars. Baseball stars, sprinters, swimmers, even prize-fighters, need have little or no trouble with their writing. Big-game hunters have still less.

Having been a Russian aristocrat is fine training for writing on any topic. Great scientists and big executives long ago entered what is sometimes known as the writing game. The latter, having learned the advantage of delegating power, were among the first to become writers by handing their writing over to some writer.

The government offers broad opportunities for success in writing by not being writers—to Presidents, ex-Presidents, First Ladies, ex-First Ladies; in fact, to all government officials and ex-government officials. Writers may wonder that a well-filled career as a government official, with all the social duties that follow in its wake, should bring with it more leisure for writing than they would have as writers. But that's because writers have started off on the wrong foot.

Nearly all the girls and boys of today hope to become movie stars. They could adopt no better method of achieving versatility as writers, although probably they aren't thinking about that. Once they are stars, beauty hints, health hints, hostess hints, fashion hints, and suggestions for interior-decorating will flow from their pens, putting the so-called experts to shame. They may write descriptions of Ideal Mates; authoritative discussions on love, sex, and marriage; articles telling what swell people other movie stars are who are playing in the same production, telling how it feels to be Mae West's leading man, telling why they'll never get divorced from their wives just before they get divorced from their wives. These suggestions only begin to indicate the possible range in subject matter. Nor is the field of belles-lettres closed to the cinema stars, if these other topics seem rather workaday. A movie star will have spare time to turn out a novel or two, and a bit of profound philosophy, along with a rhapsody on Lux toilet soap.

IF, however, the candidate for success in writing should be without qualifications in these or any other lines, he still need not attempt to become a writer by writing. If worst comes to worst, he can turn to crime, and find his gift right there. Criminal careers offer some of the finest training today in the art of narration. Or if a man prefers to stay on the side of the law, he can come into contact with outlaws as a warden, detective, G-man, or gas-station attendant, and thus develop talent as a writer.

In fact, celebrity in itself is not absolutely necessary. If it seems a little hard to attain, any touch with celebrity will do just about as well. The wives, sweethearts, mothers, and fathers of criminals are almost more likely to discover a bent for writing than the criminals themselves. The mothers, wives, ex-wives, sweethearts, and ex-sweethearts of movie stars can all become writers, or they can just tell their writings to some writer who does writing, if they feel a bit shy. Those who cannot claim any other relationship can cut the hair, design the clothes, slap off the extra pounds, foretell the future, or perform the marriage ceremonies of the stars, and so uncover their hidden gifts for writing. One very interesting way of getting in touch, and developing writing powers, is by acting as hostess to celebrities. The celebrities may even be writers.

But in this democratic country, even the everyday callings may be the roads to literary success. A doctor in the midst of active practice can turn out a column of writing a day, while if he were a columnist, he might find that writing his column alone took up far too much of his time. Any man who would or would not marry his wife, any woman who would or would not marry her husband (if the choice were open again), can do pretty well as a writer. Even as humble a person as a sharecropper would find excellent opportunities today. His appeal would not be so general as that of a murderer or a detective—a bit on the literary side, in fact—but worth considering, at that. It is not very up-and-coming of sharecroppers to let writers have share-cropping all to themselves, as seems now to be the case.

BUT what about the writer? Suppose he has followed the advice and started out to achieve success in writing by writing? There is an answer for him, too. He may just possibly succeed if he manages not to *look* like a writer. Today, for example, it is no longer advisable that a literary man look like Shelley. Indeed, to look like a poet, or even like a writer, is clearly an affectation. He may be mistaken for a businessman or, better still, for *any* businessman, thus proving his sincerity as a writer. Or he may resemble a sportsman or a gentleman farmer. English writers, however, have this down almost too pat. They look such thorough country gentlemen that it is becoming too easy to tell that they are writers. The American writer should be taken for some big, out-of-doors type—say a longshoreman, or a hunter. Then it will seem that here is a writer who is actually anything but a writer, thus pleasing both his readers and himself. If he is a novelist, though, it should be apparent that he is the main character of his own book, and has passed through the same interesting experiences. But he must never look "literary," an appearance too horrid to merit description. No matter what nature may have indicated in the matter, if he goes about it with a will to succeed, soon no one but the writer himself will remember the unpleasant fact that the writer is a writer.

So there it is. Either way, the prospects grow brighter and brighter: being somebody else to be a writer, and being a writer to be somebody else.

1936

LEONARD Q. ROSS

THE RATHER DIFFICULT CASE
OF MR. K*A*P*L*A*N

IN the third week of the new term, Mr. Parkhill was forced to the conclusion that Mr. Kaplan's case was rather difficult. Mr. Kaplan first came to his special attention, out of the forty-odd adults in the beginners' grade of the American Night Preparatory School for Adults ("English—Americanization—Civics—Preparation for Naturalization"), through an exercise the class had submitted. The exercise was entitled "Fifteen Common Nouns and Their Plural Forms." Mr. Parkhill came to one paper which included the following:

house	makes	houses
dog	"	.... dogies
libary	"	.... Public libary
cat	"	.... Katz

Mr. Parkhill read this over several times, very thoughtfully. He decided that here was a student who might, unchecked, develop into a "problem case." It was clearly a case that called for special attention. He turned the page over and read the name. It was printed in large, firm letters, with red crayon. Each letter was outlined in blue. Between every two letters was a star, carefully drawn, in green. The multicolored whole spelled, unmistakably, "H*Y*M*A*N K*A*P*L*A*N."

This Mr. K*A*P*L*A*N was in his forties, a plump, red-faced gentleman, with wavy blond hair, *two* fountain pens in his outer pocket, and a perpetual smile. It was a strange smile, Mr. Parkhill remarked; vague, and consistent in its monotony. The thing that emphasized it for Mr. Parkhill was that it never seemed to leave the face of Mr. Kaplan, even during Recitation and Speech period. This disturbed Mr. Parkhill considerably, because Mr. K*A*P*L*A*N was particularly bad in Recitation and Speech.

Mr. Parkhill decided he had not applied himself as conscientiously as he might to Mr. Kaplan's case. That very night he called on Mr. Kaplan first.

"Won't *you* take advantage of Recitation and Speech practice, Mr. Kaplan?" he asked, with an encouraging smile.

Mr. Kaplan smiled back and answered promptly, "Vell, I'll talk 'bot Prazidents United States. Fife Prazidents United States is Abram Lincohen, he was freeing the neegers; Hodding, Coolitch, Judge Vashington, an' Banjamien Frenklin."

Further encouragement revealed that in Mr. Kaplan's literary Valhalla the "most famous three American writers" were Jeck Laundon, Valt Vitterman, and the author of "Hawk L. Barry-Feen," one Mocktvain. Mr. Kaplan took pains to point out that he did not mention Relfvaldo Amerson because "He is a poyet, an' I'm talkink 'bot riders."

Mr. Parkhill diagnosed the case as one of "inability to distinguish between 'a' and 'e.' " He concluded that Mr. Kaplan *would* need special attention. He was, frankly, a little distressed.

Mr. Kaplan's English showed no improvement during the next hard weeks. The originality of his spelling and pronunciation, however, flourished like a sturdy flower in the good, rich earth. A man to whom "Katz" is the plural of "cat" soon soars into higher and more ambitious endeavor. As a one-paragraph "Exercise in Composition," Mr. Kaplan submitted:

> When people is meating on the boulvard, on going away one is saying "I am glad I mat you" and the other is giving answer, "Mutual."

Mr. Parkhill felt that perhaps Mr. Kaplan had overreached himself, and should be confined to the simpler exercises.

Mr. Kaplan was an earnest student. He worked hard; knit his brows regularly, albeit with that smile; did all his homework; and never missed a class. Only once did Mr. Parkhill feel that Mr. Kaplan might, perhaps, be a little more serious about his work. That was when he asked Mr. Kaplan to "give a noun."

"Door," said Mr. Kaplan, smiling.

It seemed to Mr. Parkhill that "door" had been given only a moment earlier, by Miss Mitnick.

"Y-es," said Mr. Parkhill. "Er—and another noun?"

"Another door," Mr. Kaplan said promptly.

Mr. Parkhill put him down as a doubtful "C." Everything pointed to the fact that Mr. Kaplan might have to be kept on an extra three months before he was ready for promotion to Composition, Grammar, and Civics, with Miss Higby.

ONE night Mrs. Moskowitz read a sentence, from "English for Beginners," in which "the vast deserts of America" were referred to. Mr. Parkhill soon discovered that poor Mrs. Moskowitz did not know the meaning of "vast." "Who can tell us the meaning of 'vast'?" asked Mr. Parkhill, lightly.

Mr. Kaplan's hand shot up, volunteering wisdom. He was all proud grins. Mr. Parkhill, in the rashness of the moment, nodded to him.

" 'Vast'!" began Mr. Kaplan, impressively. "It's comming fromm 'diraction.' Ve have four diractions: de naut, de sot, de heast, and de vast."

Mr. Parkhill shook his head and explained that that was "west." He wrote "vast" and "west" on the blackboard. To the class he added, tolerantly, that Mr. Kaplan was apparently thinking of "west," whereas it was "vast" which was under discussion.

This seemed to bring a great light into Mr. Kaplan's inner world. "So is 'vast' what you esking?" he queried, knowingly.

Mr. Parkhill admitted that it was "vast" for which he was *ask*ing.

"Aha!" cried Mr. Kaplan. "You minn 'vast,' not"—with scorn— " 'vast.' "

"Yes," said Mr. Parkhill, faintly.

"Hau Kay!" said Mr. Kaplan, essaying the vernacular. "Ven I'm buyink a suit clothes, I'm gattink de cawt, de pents, an' de vast."

Mr. Parkhill shook his head, very sadly. "I'm afraid," he said, "that you've used still another word, Mr. Kaplan."

Oddly enough, this seemed to please Mr. Kaplan considerably.

Several nights later Mr. Kaplan took advantage of Open Question period. This ten-minute period was Mr. Parkhill's special innovation in the American Night Preparatory School for Adults. It was devoted to answering any questions which the students might care to raise about any difficulties of pronunciation or idiom which they might have encountered during the course of their adventures with the language. Mr. Parkhill enjoyed Open Questions. He liked to clear up *practical* problems. He felt he was being ever so much more constructive that way. Miss Higby had once told him that he was a born Open Questions teacher.

"Please, Mr. Pockheel," asked Mr. Kaplan as soon as the period opened. "Vat's de meanink fromm—" It sounded, in Mr. Kaplan's rendering, like "a big department."

" 'A big department,' Mr. Kaplan?" asked Mr. Parkhill, to make sure.

"Yas—in de stritt, ven I'm valkink, I'm hearink like 'I big depottment.' "

It was definitely a pedagogical opportunity. "Well, class," Mr. Parkhill said.

He began by telling them that they had all probably done some shopping in the large downtown stores. (Mr. Kaplan nodded.) In these large stores, he said, if they wanted to buy a pair of shoes, for example, they went to a special *part* of the store, where only shoes were sold—a *shoe* department. (Mr. Kaplan nodded.) If they wanted a table, they went to a different *part* of the store, where *tables* were sold. (Mr. Kaplan nodded.) If they wanted to buy, say, a goldfish, they went to still another *part* of the store, where goldfish . . . (Mr. Kaplan frowned; it was clear that he had never bought a goldfish.)

"Well, then," Mr. Parkhill summed up hastily, "each article is sold in a different *place*. These different and special places are called *departments*." He wrote "D-E-P-A-R-T-M-E-N-T" on the board in large, clear capitals. "And a *big* department, Mr. Kaplan, is merely such a department which is large—*big!*"

He put the chalk down and wiped his fingers.

"Is that clear now, class?" he asked, with a modest smile. (It was rather an ingenious explanation, he thought; it might be worth repeating to Miss Higby during the recess.)

It *was* clear. There were forty nods of approval. Mr. Kaplan alone looked uncertain. It was obvious that Mr. Kaplan did *not* find it clear.

"Is that clear now, Mr. Kaplan?" asked Mr. Parkhill, anxiously.

Mr. Kaplan pursed his lips in thought. "It's a fine haxplination, Titcher. But I don' unnistand vy I'm hearink de voids de vay I do. Simms to me it's used in annodder meanink."

"There's really only one meaning for 'a big department,'" said Mr. Parkhill. "*If* that's the phrase you mean."

Mr. Kaplan shook his head. "Sounds like dat—or maybe more like '*I* big de pottment.'"

Mr. Parkhill took up the chalk. ('*I* big department' was obviously a case of Mr. Kaplan's curious audition.) He repeated the explanation carefully, this time embellishing the illustrations with a shirt department, a victrola section, and "a separate part of the store where, for example, you buy canaries, or other birds."

Mr. Kaplan followed it all politely, even the part about "canaries, or other birds." He smiled throughout with consummate reassurance.

Mr. Parkhill assumed, in his folly, that the smiles were a testimony to his exposition. But when he had finished, Mr. Kaplan shook his head once more, this time with a new firmness.

"Is the explanation still not clear?" Mr. Parkhill asked. He was gen-uinely concerned by this time.

"Is de haxplination clear!" cried Mr. Kaplan with enthusiasm. "Ha! I should live so! Soitinly! Clear like gold! So clear! And nacheral, too! But, Mr. Pockheel—"

"Go on, Mr. Kaplan," said Mr. Parkhill, studying the white dust on his fingers. There was, after all, nothing more to be done. *(Domine, dirige nos.)*

"Vell! It's more like '*I* big de pottment!' "

"Go on, Mr. Kaplan, go on," said Mr. Parkhill.

"I'm hearink it in de stritt. Sometimes I'm stendink in de stritt, talkink to a frand, or my vife, mine brodder, or maybe only stendink. An' somevun is pessing aroun' me. An' by hexident he's giving me a bump. He says, 'Axcuse me!' No? But sometimes, an' dis is vat I minn, he's sayink, 'I big de pottment'!"

Mr. Parkhill studied the picture of "Abram Lincohen" on the back wall, and wondered whether he could reconcile it with his conscience if he were to promote Mr. Kaplan to Composition, Grammar, and Civics, with Miss Higby. Another three months of Recitation and Speech might, after all, be nothing but a waste of Mr. K⋆A⋆P⋆L⋆A⋆N's valuable time.

1936

JAMES THURBER

THE NOTEBOOKS OF JAMES THURBER

I EXPLAINED in the pages of this journal of biography about ten years ago why my letters will probably never be collected and published under the title "I Saw It Coming," or under any other title. If you read the piece in question, you have no doubt forgotten what I had to say, so I will briefly summarize its contents. I came back from Europe in 1938 (it says in this piece) to discover that my friends had not saved my letters—or "preserved the correspondence," to use the formal phrase. Oh, they had preserved it in a manner of speaking, but they "couldn't put their hands on it at the moment." That is, they didn't have the vaguest idea where it was. I knew where it was then, and I know where it is now. Letters have a way of ending up in attics and warehouses, along with polychrome bookends, masquerade costumes, copies of the *American Mercury* for 1930, and Aunt Martha's water colors of Blois and Chenonceaux. If my friends ever set out to locate my letters, they will come upon old college yearbooks, dance programs, snapshot albums, and the works of John Fox, Jr., and probably lose interest in the original object of their search.

Now, the seventy-one letters written from abroad in 1937–38 were intended as a section of the collected correspondence to be called "Part III: The European Phase," and their unavailability is regarded by my publishers as a "major deterrent." As for "Part I: The Youthful Years" and "Part II: Sturm und Drang (1915–1935)," God only knows what has become of the letters written during those so important formative periods. There remain the letters written since 1938, and while they are "as available as hell," to quote one of my attorneys, their publication would not constitute "an act of wisdom," to quote him further. These letters repose in the files of producers, publishers, editors, and agents, and their monotony is another major deterrent, since they all begin with "As God is my judge" or "I would rather die than" and trail off into vague hints or open threats of legal action. After reading my carbons of this correspondence, Mr. Jordan, of the Charteriss Publishing Company, wrote me as follows: "I am afraid that we are all of one mind here in feeling that what had every sign of a swell performance has now turned into a rather dark picture. Mr. Steckley, of our legal department, is especially distressed, but he is perhaps a bit intemperate in estimating that defamation suits in the amount of $3,000,000 would result from the publication of 'Part IV: The Challenging Years.' We hope you may have a jolly fairy tale up your sleeve—something about giants and little princesses."

The middle-aged, or, as he prefers to be called, mature, writer who realizes that his "Collected Letters" (Charteriss, 2 vols., $8) are never going to be brought out sooner or later hits on the idea of gathering together his notes—memoranda, plot outlines, descriptions of characters, and fragments of philosophy—and seeing if he can't do something with them. He is now treading on ground hallowed by the important notebooks of the great masters, from da Vinci to Henry James, but if his invention is running low and his taxes high, he will go brashly ahead with his ill-advised project. This instantly marks him as a minor author. The notebooks of a major author are always brought out after his death, by a literary executor. If you are a major author, the literary executor will hang around your house, known as "the estate," for at least a year, mousing through voluminous papers, collating and annotating, drinking your Scotch with your widow, and sometimes, in the end, marrying your daughter.

There is also the disturbing chance that your executor, while mousing around in your literary remains, may stumble on the Figure in the Carpet, or what he conceives to be the Figure in the Carpet. That is, he may adduce from the notebooks dubious internal evidence supporting the theory that you were homosexual, impotent, or secretly in love with your radio agent's wife. It will be up to your daughter, then, to marry your executor and shut him up, but if she is a Vassar graduate, she may collaborate with him on a sequel to the notebooks—"The Real John Marcher," an honest, courageous, and best-selling examination, on behalf of the enrichment of American letters—that will strip you of every last posthumous pride and privacy. If you are a major author, and all this has frightened you, I suggest that you remove from your notebooks everything that might be regarded as evidence of "the scar"; that is, the early trauma, illness, maladjustment, or inadequacy that led you to become a writer in the first place. Or it might be simpler just to send your daughter to Cornell.

The minor author, known in New York merely as "a writer" and in Hollywood as "a word man," comes to his typewriter with few, if any, notes to guide him. He may jot down a phrase or two on the back of an envelope in a taxi or on a bus, but such notes are usually thrown away as soon as a piece is finished. Even if they were preserved, an accumulation of them over a period of years would scarcely occupy one afternoon of a serious literary executor, who would classify them as "unr.," which means "unrewarding" and suitable only as mementos for hotel maids, assistant gardeners, and third cousins. The deceased writer's aunt could distribute this kind of thing during the services at the church, or just after the services, but I don't know why anyone should save or cherish an envelope on which is written, "Talking-dog story twist. Man suddenly begins bark," or "Check if this idea used by Bench, or Perl."

IF only to justify the title of this essay, I began to poke around one day to see what I could find in the way of memoranda and memorabilia of my own. What I came up with presents, as Mr. Jordan of Charteriss would put it, a very dark picture indeed, complete with at least seven major deterrents: persistent illegibility, paucity of material, triviality of content, ambiguity of meaning, facetious approach, preponderance of juvenilia, and exasperating abbreviation. There is actually only one notebook, and since it is the solidest, or at any rate the heaviest, item in the collection, we should perhaps glance at it first. It is a notebook I kept, or was supposed to keep, in Professor Weiss's psychology class at Ohio State University in 1913. (My God, Bergie,* has it been that long?) The first few pages are given over to a description of the medulla oblongata, a listing of the primary colors, the score of the Western Reserve–Ohio State football game that season, and the words "Noozum, Noozum, Noozum." (I figured out this last entry after some thought. There was a young woman in the class named Newsome, whom Dr. Weiss always called Noozum.) The rest of the pages contain a caricature of Professor Weiss; one hundred and thirteen swastikas; the word "Noozum" in block letters; the notation "No William James in library"; an address, 1374 Summit Street; a memo: "drill cap, white gloves, gym suit. See G. Packer. Get locker"; a scrawl that seems to read "Orgol lab nor fot Thurs"; and a number of horrible two-line jokes, which I later contributed to the *Sundial,* the university monthly magazine. Two of these will more than suffice:

(1) HE: The news from Washington is bad.
     SHE: I thought he died *long* ago.
(2) ADMIRAL WATCHING ENEMY SINK: Who fired that shot?
     MATE: The ship's cook, sir. He got the range and stove in her side.

No literary executor is going to get his hands on *that* notebook.

I am sorry to say that this rather vacant item of thirty-six years ago is the most orderly exhibit in the pitiful clump of notes I have been able to discover. Most of my other material is written in pencil on sheets of yellow copy paper that have been folded over twice, a practice common with newspaper reporters but highly irritating to literary executors. Let us take the notes in order, beginning with the top sheet, which just happens to be the top sheet, since no effort has been made at organization on behalf of chronology, significance of implication, or anything else.

The first sheet, then, bears the following, in pencil, near the top of the upper left quarter: "Digital. b. donna. stramoneum (Jimson weed). Horn quicksilver. Germander. Aloes. Aloes yourself." The flippancy of the final phrase, "Aloes yourself," suggests that the piece to which this note obviously has reference was not written in a serious mood. Either

*AUTHOR'S NOTE: Bergie was in this same class.

that or the author's mood changed between the time he made the note and the time he actually wrote the piece.

We come now to the longest of the notes, and the only one instinct with a sense of affirmation. There are twenty-five sheets here, one of them foxed, or stained with cider, perhaps, and all of them folded only once. The pages are not dated; nothing ever is. The chirography has a curious smudged or sat-on appearance; there are only twenty words to a page, and again the author's mood and intent seem ambiguous. The manuscript that grew out of this plot summary was blown out to sea from a Hamilton-bound ferryboat just off Watford Bridge, Bermuda, on April 8, 1947. There was, of course, no carbon copy. Certain editorial symbols have been employed for purposes of clarification, and where words were not clear, they have, quite simply, been guessed at. Question marks have been parenthesized after such words. Perhaps the reader will wish to hazard interpretations of his own. That is his privilege. The notes, in full, follow:

"Middle-aged novelist has been unable to think of anything to write about for eleven years. Name Julian Gordon. Wife Catherine Poe Gordon, aged 37. Mr. Gordon, 48, quit writing same age wife now is. Julian picks up copy Harpers Bazzaar (sic) at Tass (?) agency. Reads swell short story filled with strange new beauty and signed Candace Poe. It turns out to be work of Mr. Gordon's wife, who's been secretly knitting little plots, keeping 'em from husband. Somebody has to make Jack (?) for the family, after all. He can't stand having his wife writing without help from him. Big scene. Julian sarcastically says no female writes without using 'it was as if' all the time. Real rift begins when he finds her hangout over garage and reads sheet in ivory-colored typewriter. Tells her at dinner she can't use sentence 'The wind ran scampering up the street like a laughing boy.' You've got to use either 'ran' or 'scampered,' can't use *both* for C. sake. She sore. Big scene. Rift widens. To his dismay Julian watches Cath. go more and more Bazzar (sic). She says she is going to rename their country place Greensleeves because look nice on station wagon door. He says by God over his dead body or somebody's dead body. 15 collar 33 or 34 sleeve B. Brothers blue button-down. Sox 11½. [Note: This appears to be a personal memo, without reference to the plot outline.] Julian, who is still on Ch. 6 of novel begun 1936, discovers Cath. has sold several pieces to mags. in one month and is in correspondence with Cerf, Finkelhoff (?), and Warner Brothers. Julian Gordon announces he intends to buy Smith & Wesson .38 police special on ground that everybody under 21 is out to get him.

Says children shooting adults down like dogs all over U.S. J. really means this, but sees wife thinks he is going crazy and decides play part of maniac to hilt. Says sees large silver fish float through bedroom. Says hears horns of elfland f.b. Says Louise Glaum (?) keeps phoning. Decides this crazy make believe just what needs to break ice jam in Ch. 6 of his novel, but finds to horror that Cath. has begun writing same plot in story for Harper's B. Terrible scene. Jul. says Smitty won't let her steal his plot. She says he's terrible to frighten her with fake insanity. He says she's horrible to use his supposed condition for H. Bazaar. Cath. buys vicious fawn-colored boxer as protection against J. and Smitty, who she suddenly realizes is S. & W. pistol. Wonderful scene in garage studio while he cleaning gun and she typing and boxer growling. She certain he intends shoot her 'accidentally.' Cath. suddenly cries, 'Get him, Greensleeves!' She has called the boxer Greensleeves, too, and now sets him on Gordon Julian (sic). Nuts to Gordon nuts to Cath. nuts to you nuts to me. Nuts to all the sons of butchers (?)" That is all there is to the only really interesting item in the Thurber collection.

THERE are a few more odds and ends, or, to be exact, odds and beginnings, but we need scrutinize only three. The first goes, "The beaver is a working fool, who went to manual-training school." I have never been able to fit this in anywhere. The second says, "Guinea pigs fight when empty milk bottles are clicked together." They do, too, but I wrote that up for *PM* in the summer of 1941, and there is no need to go into it here. The third reads, "The American Woman. $1,300 emerald cigarette lighter." Since the word "woman" is capitalized, this obviously does not refer to any particular woman to whom I intended to give a thirteen-hundred-dollar emerald cigarette lighter. Furthermore, I haven't got that kind of money. There was probably an idea for a story in this note when I set it down, but I don't see it now. If you do, you can have it—the idea, I mean. The note itself has been destroyed, along with everything else, except the plot outline of "Greensleeves." I may take a swing at that story again one of these days, now that the fawn-colored boxer is all the rage.

1949

MICHAEL J. ARLEN

ARE WE LOSING THE NOVEL RACE?

As if things weren't bad enough already, word has just reached me that the Russians have recently published a 1,600-page novel. If you don't think 1,600 pages is a lot of novel, try reading "Ivanhoe" sometime. (And don't start telling me you've already read "Ivanhoe." I know you, and you probably haven't read "Vanity Fair" or "Don Quixote," either.) "Ivanhoe" is only 430 pages long, and it once took me five and a half months to read it, not counting time out for Christmas vacation and the measles. It may not even be as long as that, since I seem to remember that some of the pages had been printed over twice, although, now that I think of it, maybe they were just written twice. At any rate, the new novel is a good 334 pages longer than the latest James Jones book, "Some Came Running," and a full 432 ahead of the second-seeded American entry, "Atlas Shrugged," and I think the figures speak for themselves.

The Russian book is called "Kamenny Poyas," which means "The Stone Belt," or "The Stone Ring," depending on how you feel about these matters. It was written by a man named Fedorov, and published in Sverdlovsk, in 1956. Fedorov had already made something of a name for himself in and around Sverdlovsk on the strength of a two-volume book he'd tossed off a year or so earlier. But he's never made much of a dent on the international scene, and one can hardly wonder why. You don't write 1,600-page novels by hanging around *espresso* bars all day and then appearing in TV panel discussions of the Irish Question until God knows when at night.

Unfortunately, the Russians have been very poor sports about releasing any detailed information on the book (you know what poor sports the Russians can be sometimes), but from the little we know of the dimensions of the Sverdlovsk presses and the standard weight of Ukrainian paper (I am here indebted to Professor Joachim Lip for his monumental study), we can make a safe guess that the gross weight of "Kamenny Poyas" runs to somewhere between 4.5 and 4.6 pounds. Our own entries are shamefully puny by comparison. The Jones book and "Atlas Shrugged" weigh in at exactly 2 lbs. 11 oz., and neither seems likely to be able to clear even the three-pound mark in any operational edition.

Of course, some of us have been saying all along that the Russians could do it, and when I say "us," don't think I am trying to rub it in, but a man gets a little tired shouting himself hoarse in the market place all day long. We've all known they had the manpower over there, and anyone who's ever tried running for a bus with a copy of "Anna Karenina" or "War and Peace" in his raincoat pocket must certainly have realized it was just a matter of time until they hit their full stride.

The situation is particularly discouraging in light of the Jones book, which almost all of us up to now have regarded as just about the heaviest novel anybody could be expected to produce under existing conditions. When word of "Kamenny Poyas" really gets around, the Scribner people will probably try to claim that "Some Came Running" was written largely for experimental purposes and that James Jones could actually have done a much longer or heavier book if he'd only put his mind to it. In fact, I hear that over at Random House a spokesman has already confused the issue by declaring that Miss Rand "wasn't really trying" with "Atlas Shrugged." In the storm of criticisms and recriminations that followed this statement, it was quickly amended to read that Miss Rand "wasn't really trying *for length,*" but public confidence has already been severely shaken, and reassurances by Bennett Cerf to the effect that it's still the second-longest novel in the free world aren't likely to make things any better.

The alarming side to all this is that not so long ago we were second to none in our ability to produce novels of exceptional length and weight. Rare were the years, even in the thirties, when Tom Wolfe ever fell below 600 pages, and toward the end of his life he was turning out solid two-pounders with the regularity of a drop forge. And who will ever forget the magnificent 2 lbs. 11 oz. attained by Marguerite Steen with "The Sun Is My Undoing," or the beautiful impression of sheer weight one received when first lifting a copy of "Gone with the Wind"? More recently, the "younger crop," as I like to call them—Thomas B. Costain, Herman Wouk, and Dr. Frank G. Slaughter—have all been edging toward the two-pound mark and giving every indication of going beyond it at any moment. Now it's probably too late to pin our hopes on *them.*

What has happened is that we have plain frittered away our lead. The Russians have closed the gap and passed us. Heads will almost certainly roll at Scribner and Random House, but I see no point now in looking around for somewhere to place the blame. At their current rate of progress, the size of the novels the Russians will be turning out in a few years should be absolutely staggering. The immediate reaction in our own country will doubtless be "Why worry? Let the Russians worry; they're the ones who are going to have to read the things." But this is sheer complacency and escapism on our part. The Russians finally have a heavier novel than we do, and we might as well face up to it.

1958

CALVIN TRILLIN

ROLAND MAGRUDER,

FREELANCE WRITER

DURING the first week of summer, at a beach party in East Hampton, a portly man wearing tan Levis and a blue-and-white gondolier's shirt told Marlene Drentluss that he was a "socio-economic observer" currently working on a study entitled "The Appeal of Chinese Food to Jewish Intellectuals." Marlene had already suggested that the rejection of one dietary ritual might lead inevitably to the adoption of another when it occurred to her that he might not be telling the truth. Later in the evening, she was informed that the man was in fact the assistant accountant of a trade magazine catering to the pulp-and-paper industry. She was more cautious a few days later, nodding without commitment when a man she met at a grocery store in Amagansett said he spent almost all of his time "banging away at the old novel." A few days later, she saw his picture in an advertisement that a life-insurance company had taken in the *Times* to honor its leading salesmen in the New York–New Jersey–Connecticut area. She eventually decided that men automatically misrepresent their occupations in the summer on the eastern end of Long Island, as if some compulsion to lie were hanging in the air just east of Riverhead. The previous summer, in another Long Island town, everybody had said he was an artist of one kind or another; the year before that, in a town not ten miles away, men had claimed to be mystical wizards of the New York Stock Exchange. Around East Hampton, she seemed to meet nobody who did not claim to be a writer. When Marlene drove past the Sunday-morning softball game in East

Hampton, she was fond of saying—even though she was invariably alone—"There stand eighteen freelance writers, unless they're using short-fielders today, in which case there stand twenty freelance writers." Marlene was beginning to pride herself on her cynicism.

Occasionally, she met writers who were not freelance writers, since they were employed by some magazine or newspaper, but they all said that their jobs meant nothing more to them than a way to finance their real writing—and they demonstrated this fact with stories about their office heresies. One of them—a slim young man who said his real writing was "a children's book for adults about a boy and girl in Carl Schurz Park"—told Marlene that he wrote the Religion section for *Time* and that he drove the editors to distraction by putting the word "alleged" before all questionable religious events, so that he would write, "The Gospels were written fifty years after the alleged Crucifixion," or "The Jews wandered in the wilderness for forty years after the alleged parting of the Red Sea." Marlene realized that the alleged writer did not in fact write the Religion section of *Time* when she finally placed his face as belonging to one of the countless Wall Street wizards she had met two summers before. It turned out he was neither a Wall Street wizard nor a Religion writer but a salesman who tried to sign up young executives for the Alexander Hamilton Business Course. Marlene was not surprised. A week later, she dismissed with one loud guffaw a young man who said he conquered the anonymity of the *Times* News of the Week in Review by spelling out "LOOK, MA, IT'S ME, IRV" vertically with the first letter of the first word in each paragraph of his stories.

Not long after she had disposed of the would-be Religion editor, she met a man named Lester Kranitt, who said he supported himself while writing his novel by working for a company called After Dinner, Inc. According to Kranitt, After Dinner, Inc. earned a great deal of money by providing after-dinner speakers with well-written speeches on any subject. "It's really *too* sordid," said Kranitt, smiling at the recollection. "I work for a very crude man who never says anything to me but 'Hey, champ, can you knock me out eight hundred words on the place of foundation garments in our private enterprise system by six tonight?' or 'Hey, champ, why don't you sit yourself down and work me up the two thousand words Eddie O'Brien will have to say at a testimonial dinner called Eddie O'Brien's Twenty-five Years Behind the Wheel of a Five-Passenger Checker, by ten tomorrow morning.

Marlene listened to Kranitt for about ten minutes before recognizing him as a man who had once waited on her at Bloomingdale's. She said,

"Listen, champ, why don't you knock me out fifty words on brushing off a phony." If he had been a decent phony, she thought later, he would have at least quoted her a price for a brush-off speech.

AFTER all these experiences, Marlene was understandably skeptical when, at a party at Bernie Mohler's summer place near East Hampton, a young man named Roland Magruder answered her question about his occupation in the usual way. "What *kind* of writer?" she said, suspiciously. She could not believe that he had not heard how difficult she was to impress with this approach.

"A freelance writer," said Magruder, who was quite aware of how difficult she was to impress with this approach, and had even heard odds quoted on the matter.

"What kind of freelance writer?" asked Marlene.

"A sign writer."

"A sign painter?"

"No," said Magruder. "I write signs. Cities retain me to write signs on a freelance basis. I specialize in traffic work. 'Yield Right of Way' is a good example."

"Somebody *wrote* 'Yield Right of Way'?" asked Marlene.

"I wrote 'Yield Right of Way,' " said Magruder, permitting a tone of pride to creep into his voice. "Do you think something like 'Yield Right of Way' writes itself? Do you think it was written by the gorilla who installed the signs on the Expressway? He would have probably written 'Let the Other Guy Keep in Front of Ya.' Have you been going under the impression that 'Vehicles Weighing Over Five Tons Keep Right' was composed by Robert F. Wagner, Jr.?"

"But these messages are obvious," argued Marlene.

"You would have probably said that it was obvious for Brigham Young to say 'This is the place' when the Mormons reached Utah, or for Pétain to say 'They shall not pass,' or for MacArthur to say 'I shall return.' I suppose you think those lines just happened to come out of their mouths, without any previous thought or professional consultation. I think, by the way, if I may say so, that my 'No Passing' says everything 'They shall not pass' says, and without succumbing to prolixity."

"You mean to say you're being paid for writing 'Stop' and 'One Way' and 'Slow'?" asked Marlene. She tried to include as much sarcasm as possible in her voice, but Magruder seemed to take no notice.

"A certain economy of style has never been a handicap to a writer," he said. "On the other hand, while it's true that traffic signs are a vehicle that permits a pithiness impossible in most forms, I do longer pieces. 'Next Train for Grand Central on Track Four' is one of mine—at the Times Square subway station. There's another one at the Times Square station that you certainly haven't seen yourself but that I think has a certain flair: 'This Is Your Men's Room; Keep It Clean.' I've heard several people talk of that one as the ultimate expression of man's inability to identify with his group in an urban society."

That was almost too much for Marlene. She had found herself beginning to believe Magruder—his self-confidence was awesome, and, after all, who would have the gall to take credit for "One Way" if he hadn't written it?—but bringing in sociological criticism was a challenge to credulity. Just then, Bernie Mohler passed by on his way to the patio and said, "Nice job on 'World's Fair Parking,' Roland."

"What did you have to do with World's Fair parking?" asked Marlene.

"That's it," said Magruder. " 'World's Fair Parking.' It's on the Expressway. Do you like it?"

Before Marlene could answer, a blond girl joined them and asked, "Was that your 'This Is Water Mill—Slow Down and Enjoy It' I saw on Highway 27, Roland?"

Magruder frowned. "I'm not going to get involved in that cutesy stuff just to satisfy the Chamber of Commerce types," he said. "I told the town board that 'Slow Down' says it all, and they could take it or leave it."

"I thought your 'No Parking Any Time' said it all," remarked a tall young man with a neat beard. "I've heard a lot of people say so."

"Thanks very much," Magruder said, looking down at the floor modestly.

"Oh, did you do that?" Marlene found herself asking.

"It wasn't much," said Magruder, still looking at the floor.

"You don't happen to know who did the big 'NO' sign at Coney Island?" Marlene asked. "The one that has one 'NO' in huge letters and then lists all the things you can't do in smaller letters next to it?" Marlene realized she had always been interested in the big "NO" sign.

"I introduced the Big 'NO' concept at the city parks several years ago," said Magruder. "Some people say it's a remarkable insight into modern American urban life, but I think that kind of talk makes too big a thing of it."

"Oh, I don't," said Marlene. "I think it's a marvellous expression of the negativism of our situation."

"Well, that's enough talking about me," said Magruder. "Can I get you another drink?"

"I'm really tired of this party anyway," said Marlene.

"I'll drive you home," said Magruder. "We can cruise by a 'Keep Right Except to Pass' sign, if you like. It's on the highway just in front of my beach house."

"Well, O.K.," said Marlene, "but no stopping."

"I wrote that," Magruder said, and they walked out the door together.

1965

PHILIP HAMBURGER

CONTEMPORARY WRITERS VI:

AN INTERVIEW WITH GRIP SANDS

THE interview with Grip Sands, three-time winner of the coveted Alma M. Halloran Fictive Award (for his novels "Lud," "Fust," and "Drime") was held at five-thirty one morning in his loft workroom-bedroom-living room on Manhattan's lower East Side, within sight of the ever-poetic span of the Brooklyn Bridge. Sands works at night and sleeps by day, and the interview was conducted between the hours of his most intense concentration and his hours of rest. He appeared exhausted yet exhilarated. He is short, squat, and somewhat dishevelled, with thick eyebrows and piercing green eyes. He was dressed in black leather pants, a black leather jacket, and highly polished black boots. Sands and his boots are inseparable, as inseparable as Sands and the strange, private lexicon of obscenities he employs in ordinary conversation. Sands wears his boots everywhere—to literary conferences, to prize conclaves, and to bed. Bed consists of a mattress on the floor of the loft, with no pillow. The loft is sparely furnished: an unpainted worktable piled high with supplies of green copy paper, on which Sands writes in red ink, and, in one corner, a refrigerator. The floor of the loft was covered with crumpled mounds of discarded pieces of copy paper. They lent the otherwise barren room the appearance of being a mossy glen in a thick forest. Sands was seated on the mattress, reading galleys of his forthcoming fictive effort, "Zwer." Several volumes of Proust were visible on top of the refrigerator, lying beside a half-eaten pomegranate.

INTERVIEWER: You have been accused of a certain deliberate obscurity, not only in connection with the time continuum but with relation to the personnel of your novels. Your non-beings appear to have more life-force than your beings, and even at times to be interchangeable with them. What are you saying to us?

SANDS: I should like very much to get my hands on the blarfs who accuse me of obscurity, much less deliberate obscurity. Their watchword would appear to be crand. I am saying what I am saying, and each driggle must figure the matter out for himself, depending on the time, the place, the barometric pressure, and the nearest horoscope. To read "Fust," for instance, without a horoscope would be sheer groozle. And yet many try, and sink. I lay great store by horoscopes, mostly for their paramorphic value. They cut through the paninvisibility of non-being. We are left with the dark shadow of cartilage. The nub of the matter.

INTERVIEWER: We know that each writer secretly whispers to himself in his innermost places, awake or asleep, that this time he has touched the truth—zeroed in, you might say.

SANDS: To me, eternity is eggshells. The whites are pure mag, and the yolks—well, I won't even consider the yolks. They are beneath contempt. But the shells present an entirely different problem. We have the problem of poise—absolutely essential—and, with it, the delicate elaboration of personality, or, in the case of "Lud," non-personality. One exudes. Otherwise, there is nothing—not even the void.

INTERVIEWER: Do the city streets inspire you? I mean, do you prowl?

SANDS: Inscrutably. Inscrutably, rather than haphazardly or continuously. The inspiration, once again, is eggshells. They rise beneath the feet and touch off myriad images. The prowling must be done under cover of darkness, and the feet themselves provide the motivation. One either senses this sort of thing or one doesn't. The eggshells are everywhere, but one must feel them. Lower Broadway bleeds with eggshells. There the poise requires deftness, murim, and a calm spirit. If one is unhurried, collected, one is safe, one's inspiration is safe. Jar the balance and there is a crack in eternity.

INTERVIEWER: That would be irreparable?

SANDS: Irreparable. There are no second chances. The wheel turns and stops—red or black, good or ill. And, of course, there is the question of money. The foundations and the grants help. I loathe them, and I loathe the gurds who sit in boardroom splendor and award them, but I never turn one down. The first grant is always the hardest. Then they pour in; some blick recommends me one year, I recommend the blick the next. It is a question of poise, almost vegetable. They say travel to England, France, Spain. I say no. I stay here. My terms. Fleep!

INTERVIEWER: Do you revise much?

SANDS: As an exercise in the art of interregnum. The floor of the studio attests to the continuously heightened and renewed perceptions and non-perceptibles.

INTERVIEWER: Do you mingle much with other writers?

SANDS: Sparsely.

INTERVIEWER: But you do mingle occasionally—conferences, creative-writing gatherings, and so on. Do you derive much inspiration, if any, from these encounters?

SANDS: The average writer is a brape. I observe them to renew my contempt. And to replenish the wellspring. The fallow times, you know, are not kinsel. Bears do it. Inspiration often derives from one's low opinion of those around one, so I occasionally drive to the gas station and ask the man to fill up the tank. Then back here to aloneness and the eternal, internal me. You are the first person I have talked to since beginning "Zwer," and you may be the last.

INTERVIEWER: "Zwer" has already evinced almost universal interest. Can you tell me something about it—its themes and goals?

SANDS: In "Zwer," the root is the branch. It will win all the prizes, but for all the wrong reasons. In "Zwer," the personae ascend in descension. The interstices become the corpus. Form follows reason to the city limits, and then explodes with malevolent magnanimity. The bulldozers appear to triumph, but the squeak of the mouse is heard over the land.

INTERVIEWER: Where would you say the novel in general is heading? I mean, this would come down, I suppose, to shape and form and content. You must have given this a good deal of thought.

SANDS: The problem centers acutely on the extricular. Gravy boats, bronzed booties, canoes—that sort of thing. Try to avoid these tactiles and the novel will foist. Slowly at first, but with increasing blushes. That is one thing I am certain of, up to a point. Characters must become egressors. The costume is without meaning, the setting a mere ball of fire, and the dialogue quirp. People often halrow and urge you to try that one on your cigar box. I tell them to emerge, shed, blacken with soot. Cold cream is dodo. Definitely. "Zwer's" most powerful scenes are illuminated with the passion of an underwater gazebo. The inundated summerhouse! It is a summing up, and nothing will ever be the same. Follow the green arrow and take the wrong turn. Most of them are rotten.

INTERVIEWER: In other words, you are optimistic.

SANDS: Insofar as the circle bisects the square and leaves it dangling. And with respect to the pastoral mutations. The rest is queel. But there are some bright spots—Lipton in Kansas City, struggling with his penetrobes, and poor Kenneeley being bitten alive in Algiers.

INTERVIEWER: Kenya, I believe.

SANDS: You are right. Kenya.

INTERVIEWER: Can you tell me something of your origins?

SANDS: Bridgeport was pure treem. The noxious workmen and their hard-boiled eggs. Puget Sound was drave, and New Orleans grob. Heady stuff. My parents were one-burner electric stove, here today and gone. St. Louis, Denver, the transcontinental bit, and then the breakaway. Collapse and recovery and the dusty road to the center. The self-initiated self. It came one night and knocked, and I said, "Enter." And here I am.

INTERVIEWER: A complete man?

SANDS: Ragout.

1967

ROGER ANGELL

IN THE DOUGH

Virginia Hardy's Story Writing Contest!

Virginia Hardy's Oven invites all patrons and friends to enter our Short Story Contest. At least one and as many as three stories will be selected each month for inclusion on Virginia Hardy's Oven pie boxes. (We print and distribute over a million boxes per year!) The author of each story selected will receive a prize of fifty free pies at any Virginia Hardy's Oven. Stories should be between 750 and 1250 words long, and, of course, suitable for general audiences. Please include a brief description of yourself suitable for our "About the author" section . . .

—Notice on a pie box.

Mrs. Ishbel Carrington Shute
Fiction Editor
Mother Melmoth Pastry Pantries, Inc.

DEAR MRS. SHUTE:

Am enclosing proofs of "Queen of Hearts" in haste to catch
deadline. Please restore and stet the lines inexplicably deleted by
you on galley 2, from "Now, in delicious disarray . . ." through
". . . a glimpse of regal bosom, charmingly dusted with an inad-
vertent dab of flour, that rose and fell, here within the sweet
warmth of the summer kitchen, in quickened tempo. Knavish
Jack, suddenly apant, stepped forward from the shadows," etc.,
etc. These sentences, rough and hand-hewn though they may appear, are essential to the ensuing chase scene, and also serve to ren-
der the Queen less distant and, yes, more earthily female, thus
preparing your readers for the sensual reconciliation after the re-
capture of the purloined tarts. Please, dear Madam, stay your avid
blue pencil here, recalling that an artist has pondered, sampled,
and weighed each staple noun, each zesty adjective, each pinch of
comma in his desire to create beauty at once nutritious and lighter
than air. Exactly, in brief, like one of your master bakers.

Speaking of which, your payment for "Cherry, the Cobbler's
Daughter" arrived today. Thanks for home delivery. And for the
Lemon Meringues—they are *scrumptious!* We still have twenty-
one Squash pies and eleven Boston Cream left over, thanks to
your other recent acceptances, so the children welcomed this
change of menu.

A new effort goes off to you tomorrow. I am dipping toe, trem-
blingly, into the icy seas of biography—the pie as history, so to speak.

> Yours ever,
> DUANE MCCONAKREE

Mr. Duane McConakree
Iowa City, Iowa

MY DEAR DUANE (if I may):

Tremble no more. You have triumphed afresh, huzza! Not since
the initial felicities of "Horner!" (now in its *sixth* edition—
Rhubarb), or perhaps since I first cast a furtive tear over the joys of

your "Shoo-Fly: A Rustic Romance," have I been so caught up, so held as I was by "Karl Robert Nesselrode, Lad of Old Russia." You have done us honor once again, and payment of fifty pies (Chocolate Nesselrode, natch) goes to you out of tonight's baking, plus a deserved bonus of thirty Old-Fashioned Southern Pecan. Don't thank us, please. The privilege of presenting your seemingly inexhaustible *œuvre* upon our humble cardboard palimpsests is reward aplenty. I await your next

Hungrily,
ISH

DEAR ISH:

Enclosed find "Priscilla's Punkins"—in time, I trust, for a quick closing on an appropriate mid-November pub. date. It seems a graceful effort, but I find it more and more difficult to judge. To tell the truth, I am bored to near dementia by this facility of mine, this Niagara of pastry puffs, but my weird old muse stands over me, rolling pin in hand, and I can but obey.

Assuming acceptance again, may I request payment this time in a separate flavor? LaVerne and little Zachary hate pumpkin. Anent which, and at the risk of jarring our perfect author-editor symbiosis, I wish to suggest a modest but commonsensical alteration in this matter of payment. This morning, during a thorough inspection of the dangerously overloaded shelves in our kitchen and laundry room, plus the teetering contents of three second-hand cupboards now doing makeshift service on the sun porch, I counted thirty-eight remaining Nesselrode pies, twenty-two Pecan, one Squash, four Lemon Meringue, forty-nine and a half Rhubarb (not, in truth, a terribly popular item here), eleven kuchen, one and one-quarter Coconut Cream, fourteen Butterscotch Chiffon, and sixteen assorted stale, crumbled, or unidentifiable, which I confiscated. This accounting does not include the nine dozen–odd pies that LaVerne has unloaded, for the merest fraction of their value, on our Eagle Discount manager and other surly local merchants, in lieu of the more common form of specie. We are, in short, amassing a corner in pies, and the essential flavor I now crave is Old Legal Tender.

These are sere times for writers of short fiction, God wot, but A. Daptable is my middle name. This hack, for one, is almost ecstatically grateful for the evidences of high literary seriousness to be found in (or on) your unusual publication. I write only in order to eat and to fill the four gaping maws within my nest, and all I ask, Ish, is a little less damned efficiency in this process. The mantle of George Horace Lorimer has fallen on the shoulders of your chef, yet this seems an insufficient excuse for the conversion of my home into a museum of *pâtisserie*. I am attempting to phrase this proposal in businesslike terms, eschewing mention of the increasingly doughy complexion of my loved ones, the Zeppelin-like recent configuration of my once lissome LaVerne, and the piteous cries that arise from the family dining table when yet another meal commences, continues, and concludes with implacably wedge-shaped helpings.

> Send cabbage, Mother Melmoth!
> DUANE

CHER MAÎTRE:

Accept the greeting, for you are not, as you have lately claimed, the Irving Wallace of Pie Writers but rather the Maupassant—nay, the Balzac. Truly, I had not guessed that our square, even busy, little journal was ready for a tale of miscegenation and the ironies of a postbellum plantation romance, but today's submission, "Brown Betty," has quite taught me otherwise. In short, a triumph! There is even more good news, for Howard Johnson's has just chosen our Tarte aux Fraises (with your classic "Simple Simone" as text) as its Pie of the Month for August, which assures rich returns for all. By the way, our people in Accounting tell me that cash payments are a no-no, but they have promised to include three dozen Beef-and-Kidney in your next royalty, thus alleviating the little dietary problems you mentioned. Glad to be of help!

> Luv,
> ISH

ISH:

I give up. Can your treasurer be wholly unaware that it has been some little time since Western man inched out of the long darkness of the barter system and into the sunshine of freely redemptive currencies? Has he not had the news that U.S. Steel no longer pays its dividends in ingots? Has he ever tried settling his telephone bill with a half-dozen Banana Cream Tortes? Has he attempted to write lean, rivet-hard prose after a breakfast of Apricot

Pan Dowdy (cold) and *réchauffée* Mince à la mode? I warn you, a man can be whipped just so far.

LaVerne, displaying a mobility quite uncharacteristic of most siege howitzers, has transformed our driveway and garage into a used-pie lot ("Drive In 'n' Nibble!"). Commercial response seems initially discouraging, but I am not absolutely sure about this, because the lady has not spoken to me these past three weeks.

I enclose, God forgive me, three new efforts—my last to you for some little time to come. I am determined to widen my market or quit this mad métier utterly.

DUANE

DUANE DEAR:

Your threats do not convince me, for genius is simply not free to opt out. Conrad and Dostoevski also railed against the lonely dark, and yet did their duty in the end. I can hardly choose among the three new *contes* (a baker's dozen dozen's–worth of fresh pies for thee!), but "A Tragedy in Custard" was certainly the most surprising. Who but you could wring pathos from the plight of a Keystone pie-thrower with bone chips in his elbow?

Onward!
ISH

KABIBBLE:

Back again, as you foresaw. My attempts to escape the thrall of piedom have come to nothing. I have the rejection slips before me— from the Hasta Luego Chili Corp., Hedda Gobbler Frozen Turkey Parts, Old Shiloh Bourbon, Tweetie-Cat Pet Dinners, etc. A clean sweep, even including my delicate Petrarchan sonnet, "Con Formaggio," which came back on an instant ricochet from the Molto Buona Pizza people. Call me mad, for I am henceforth forever pied.

I am at least alone. Last Thursday, at five in the morning, our garage departed the premises in an eruption of noise and flame strongly reminiscent of a Cape Kennedy liftoff. Talk about pie in the sky . . . Dawn disclosed the neighbors' topmost tree branches and most distant shrubbery prettily festooned with parts of variously flavored tarts, cobblers, meringues, and down-home deep-dishes, the whole resembling a direct hit on a Sicilian antipasto-works. Not a bad metaphor, in truth: I take this as a veiled warning from some local pastry-shop owner possibly miffed at our new venture in cut-rate pie-peddling. Later in the morning, while attempting to nail some pie plates over a gaping hole in our roof, I witnessed the final and not unexpected decampment of Herself and the bairns in the family auto—off, I don't doubt, in simultaneous search of a better-balanced diet and father. From my vantage point, the tableau resembled a Green Bay Packer making off with a shipment of medicine balls.

Alone now. My brain is but mincemeat, my soul chiffon, yet still shall I fight my way free . . .

D.

DEAR DUANE:

Do I detect a new, darker side to your prose? Why, I wonder. "Ludwig's Journey," for instance, has me a mite puzzled. It is, of course, a stunning theme: Ludwig, an ancient immigrant to our shores, forms an irresistible longing for one last slice of Bavarian Cream pie homemade in his own native Bavarian hamlet. Exchanging his life savings for a steerage ticket, he reaches Europe and then falls victim to a gang of ruffians in Le Havre, who rob him of his all. Nothing daunted, he presses on by foot, hobbling half the breadth of the Continent in hopes of that last one memorable mouthful. Winter falls, and our aged hero becomes lost in the Black Forest. He struggles on, the vision of Bavarian Cream before him. At last, he climbs the final mountain escarpment between himself and his goal, and is swept up in an avalanche that deposits him, more dead than alive, at the very door of his village piemaker.

All well up to here, Duane. A crackerjack pie tale, in fact. But now you begin to lose me. With gnarled and frozen knuckle, Ludwig taps on the baker's door. It opens. Prone, the battered old gentleman whispers his dear request. But what is this? "Nein," says your baker bluntly. "Ve are all out off der Bavarian Cream." Ludwig shrugs his shoulders and replies, "O.K. How about a slice of Pineapple-Cheese?" Finis. I mean, ? ? ?

Well, Duane, we have had a knock-down, top-level edit hassle here, but thanks to your Ish, I must admit, "Ludwig's Journey" will run as is. I persuaded the other minds here that the story represented a passing, Beckett-like strain in your otherwise unambiguous work, and that we owed you at least one such fugue. One, I might add, and no more. Obscurantism pushes no pies.

ISH

DEAR ISH:

Sorry about that. I trust this will make amends—a simple retelling of Shakespeare's "Titus Andronicus."

DUANE

DEAR DUANE:

Welcome back, kind sir! Not one of us here had ever read or seen "Titus Andronicus," and so hadn't an inkling that it concludes, so surprisingly and pleasingly, in a pie-eating scene. I *love* old-fashioned blood-and-thunder mellerdrama. We are running it on our big Washington's Birthday Cherry Special—a rush job in time for the holiday. Thanks and congrats!

ISH

P.S. It's of no matter, but what is the flavor of that pie that the disguised Andronicus serves to Tamora in the final scene?

MRS. SHUTE:

I have before me a box of your Washington's Birthday Cherry Special, with my little tale from the Bard well featured on the obverse. I feel again the deep satisfaction that sometimes overtakes even the most experienced author when he reads his own work and in all honesty must whisper to himself, "Oh, well done!"

You ask—ha-ha!—for the recipe of Titus's homemade, extremely deep-dish pie. I note—hoo, haw! *gnick-gnick!*—that you do not also inquire about the whereabouts of Tamora's children, the rascally Chiron and Demetrius, who are so oddly and inexplicably absent from the dessert course. Think, Madam. *Hmm:* What *is* this new, tangy flavor? Can phylophagia push pies? How do you like them apples, Mother Melmoth?

I have written my last! Today I begin my new permanent employment, as an artist with the graphic-arts division of the U.S. Bureau of the Budget.

Ish, fare thee well.
DUANE

1972

WOODY ALLEN

SELECTIONS FROM

THE ALLEN NOTEBOOKS

Following are excerpts from the hitherto secret private journal of Woody Allen, which will be published posthumously or after his death, whichever comes first.

GETTING through the night is becoming harder and harder. Last evening, I had the uneasy feeling that some men were trying to break into my room to shampoo me. But why? I kept imagining I saw shadowy forms, and at 3 A.M. the underwear I had draped over a chair resembled the Kaiser on roller skates. When I finally did fall asleep, I had that same hideous nightmare in which a woodchuck is trying to claim my prize at a raffle. Despair.

I BELIEVE my consumption has grown worse. Also my asthma. The wheezing comes and goes, and I get dizzy more and more frequently. I have taken to violent choking and fainting. My room is damp and I have perpetual chills and palpitations of the heart. I noticed, too, that I am out of napkins. Will it never stop?

IDEA for a story: A man awakens to find his parrot has been made Secretary of Agriculture. He is consumed with jealousy and shoots himself, but unfortunately the gun is the type with a little flag that pops out, with the word "Bang" on it. The flag pokes his eye out, and he lives—a chastened human being who, for the first time, enjoys the simple pleasures of life, like farming or sitting on an air hose.

THOUGHT: Why does man kill? He kills for food. And not only food: frequently there must be a beverage.

—————

SHOULD I marry W.? Not if she won't tell me the other letters in her name. And what about her career? How can I ask a woman of her beauty to give up the Roller Derby? Decisions . . .

ONCE again I tried committing suicide—this time by wetting my nose and inserting it into the light socket. Unfortunately, there was a short in the wiring, and I merely caromed off the icebox. Still obsessed by thoughts of death, I brood constantly. I keep wondering if there is an afterlife, and if there is will they be able to break a twenty?

I RAN into my brother today at a funeral. We had not seen one another for fifteen years, but as usual he produced a pig bladder from his pocket and began hitting me on the head with it. Time has helped me understand him better. I finally realize his remark that I am "some loathsome vermin fit only for extermination" was said more out of compassion than anger. Let's face it: he was always much brighter than me—wittier, more cultured, better educated. Why he is still working at McDonald's is a mystery.

IDEA for story: Some beavers take over Carnegie Hall and perform "Wozzeck." (Strong theme. What will be the structure?)

GOOD Lord, why am I so guilty? Is it because I hated my father? Probably it was the veal-parmigian' incident. Well, what *was* it doing in his wallet? If I had listened to him, I would be blocking hats for a living. I can hear him now: "To block hats—that is everything." I remember his reaction when I told him I wanted to write. "The only writing you'll do is in collaboration with an owl." I still have no idea what he meant. What a sad man! When my first play, "A Cyst for Gus," was produced at the Lyceum, he attended opening night in tails and a gas mask.

TODAY I saw a red-and-yellow sunset and thought, How insignificant I am! Of course, I thought that yesterday, too, and it rained. I was overcome with self-loathing and contemplated suicide again—this time by inhaling next to an insurance salesman.

SHORT story: A man awakens in the morning and finds himself transformed into his own arch supports. (This idea can work on many levels. Psychologically, it is the quintessence of Kruger, Freud's disciple who discovered sexuality in bacon.)

HOW wrong Emily Dickinson was. Hope is not "the thing with feathers." The thing with feathers has turned out to be my nephew. I must take him to a specialist in Zurich.

I HAVE decided to break off my engagement with W. She doesn't understand my writing, and said tonight that my "Critique of Metaphysical Reality" reminded her of "Airport." We quarrelled, and she brought up the subject of children again, but I convinced her they would be too young.

DO I believe in God? I did until Mother's accident. She fell on some meat loaf, and it penetrated her spleen. She lay in a coma for months, unable to do anything but sing "Granada" to an imaginary herring. Why was this woman in the prime of life so afflicted—because in her youth she dared to defy convention and got married with a brown paper bag on her head? And how can I believe in God when just last week I got my tongue caught in the roller of an electric typewriter? I am plagued by doubts. What if everything is an illusion and nothing exists? In that case, I definitely overpaid for my carpet. If only God would give me one clear sign! Like making a large deposit in my name at a Swiss bank.

HAD coffee with Melnick today. He talked to me about his idea of having all government officials dress like hens.

PLAY idea: A character based on my father, but without quite so prominent a big toe. He is sent to the Sorbonne to study the harmonica. In the end, he dies, never realizing his one dream—to sit up to his waist in gravy. (I see a brilliant second-act curtain, where two midgets come upon a severed head in a shipment of volleyballs.)

WHILE taking my noon walk today, I had more morbid thoughts. What *is* it about death that bothers me so much? Probably the hours. Melnick says the soul is immortal and lives on after the body drops away, but if my soul exists without my body I am convinced all my clothes will be too loose-fitting. Oh, well . . .

DID not have to break off with W. after all, for, as luck would have it, she ran off to Finland with a professional circus geek. All for the best, I suppose, although I had another of those attacks where I start coughing out of my ears.

LAST night, I burned all my plays and poetry. Ironically, as I was burning my masterpiece, "Dark Penguin," the room caught fire, and I am now the object of a lawsuit by some men named Pinchunk and Schlosser. Kierkegaard was right.

1973

GEORGE W. S. TROW

I COVER CARTER

THE DEMOCRATIC CONVENTION

MONDAY, JULY 12TH, MORNING
Looked at U.P.I. Convention Daybook. Badly Xeroxed. Faint print. Hard to read. Thought about going to Connecticut Caucus 10 A.M. Gave it up. Thought about going to Briefing for Pages and Podium Telephone Operators. Good color. The little people, etc. etc. etc. Gave it up. Thought about going to Democratic Women's "Agenda '76" Cau-

cus, but thought again. Decided definitely to go to Latino Caucus, West Room, Statler Hilton, but too tired.

MONDAY, JULY 12TH, AFTERNOON
Tempted by *El Diario* Open House for Latino Delegates—good chance to brush up on Spanish for later use at later Latino caucuses, etc. etc. Decided no. Tried to sort out aspects of the New Populism (Carter's smile, etc. etc., Carter out of *nowhere*, etc. etc., possible *danger* of no political debts to Establishment, etc. etc.), but couldn't focus.

MONDAY, JULY 12TH, EARLY EVENING
Much more confident. Had a drink—one of the new Wild Turkey Old-Fashioneds people are taking up. *Found slant.* Decided to do *instant book.* Follow one crucial delegation through caucuses, etc. etc. Through floor fights. Reaction to nomination, etc. etc. Juxtapose with human interest—Amy, Miss Lillian, etc. etc. Exhausting even to think about it.

MONDAY, JULY 12TH, NIGHT
Went to Convention. Picked up credentials. Very authentic-seeming. Noticed that credentials said "News-Periphery."

Very exciting at Garden. Little electronic security devices, etc. etc. Passed security check, observed by ten or twenty members of the general public. Members of general public had no credentials. Very satisfying. Decided definitely to go ahead with instant book. Maybe on journalists—observing the observers, etc. etc. etc. Media preconceptions, etc. etc. *Altering the event.* Men of action juxtaposed with the men behind the media. *Reversed,* though. Show man behind the medium as the *true man of action,* etc. etc. Thoughtful but irreverent. Follow one team of journalists from arrival through caucuses, etc. etc. Press-room infighting, etc. etc. Print vs. electronic, etc. etc. Juxtaposed with human interest—Amy, Miss Lillian, etc. etc.

News-Periphery area very depressing. Tiny concrete bunkers. Repulsive green curtains. Clots of provincial newspersons. Worse than a game show. Worse than anything. No drinks. Very pathetic to be a newsperson. Saw one newsperson take moving pictures of a row of telephones. Very sad. One newsperson got a quote from Patrick Moynihan. On a cassette. Played it over and over. Very sad. For him. For Moynihan. For everyone. Saw a newsperson interviewing a delegate. Delegate wearing white plastic belt. Saw clot of people *training* to be newspersons. So depressing I had to sit down. Decided to skip instant book. Decided to get drink.

Bar full of foreigners. Saw Italians with leather bags. Saw French-men. Nothing lower than a European newsperson. Every European had hundreds of attractive credentials. Fabulous tags reading "News-Fulcrum," "News-Podium," "News-Crucial." Not even the children had just "News-Periphery." Tried to concentrate on the *issues*—the New Constituencies, the New Credibility, the New Outsiders becoming the New *Insiders,* etc. etc.—but too depressed.

MONDAY, JULY 12TH, LATE NIGHT
Went to big party. Spirits *way up.* Party given *by* staff of rock-and-roll magazine *for* staff of Jimmy Carter. Many people drinking the new Wild Turkey Old-Fashioneds, so felt right in place. Had insight, wrote it down: "Everyone here (at party) definitely born between Munich and Yalta." Very pleased with insight. Decided to do piece about war babies molding the New Politics. The irresistible fact of *demographics,* etc. etc. Counter-culture accommodations with Carter, Good Old Boys, etc. etc. Takeover generation, etc. etc. Noticed no rock-and-roll stars at party. Noticed rock-and-roll *critic,* though. Critic very upset, very *vivid.* Born about V-E Day, my guess. "Last chance to sell out," he said. "Last chance to make your deal." Afraid he'd steal my insight—war babies, etc.—so didn't say a thing.

THE CAMPAIGN

SEPTEMBER 6TH
Very depressed for weeks and weeks, but *much more secure* now. Very up for in-depth campaign-diary type thing. More detail than Teddy White, etc. *More thoughtful,* too. Work in old insights—war babies, etc. Wanted to begin right away at Warm Springs, Georgia, campaign kickoff (the Roosevelt Legacy, etc. etc.), but decided better not push my luck. Almost attended Southern 500 stock-car race in Darlington, South Carolina (the Raffish South, the Unreconstructed South, etc. etc.), but decided to make diary more *selective.*

SEPTEMBER 15TH
Tried to join Carter's tour of Hans Sieverding's farm, Sioux Falls, South Dakota, but *much too far away.* Couldn't think how to even get there. Falling behind Teddy White now, I think, so a little blue.

SEPTEMBER 23RD
Ordered big dinner, but just picked at it. Tried to watch first debate, but felt queasy. Whole thing very elusive. Might write analysis, "Elusive Politician" or "Politics of Evasion." Might not.

SEPTEMBER 28TH
Had *important insight* about Carter. Wrote it down: "Carter effectively combines virtues of Elvis Presley and Colonel Tom Parker." Not sure that's right, though. Should be *Glen Campbell* and Colonel Parker. But Colonel Parker doesn't manage Glen Campbell, so hard to sort out.

OCTOBER 6TH
Tried to watch second debate, but too tense. Tried to sort out Presley-Parker-Campbell image, but couldn't. *Way* behind Teddy White. Decided to do *highlights:* strong vignettes to illuminate the whole. Tried to decide *which* vignettes, but had to give it up.

OCTOBER 22ND
Decided to write little essay *strongly condemning* Teddy White approach. Wrote note: "Teddy White has done for politics what Anaïs Nin has done for women." Felt very good to have written so much. Tried to watch third debate, but got the shakes and had to lie down.

OCTOBER 24TH
Decided on whole new angle—for *novel.* Take *one typical politician,* juxtaposed to Presidential candidate, etc. etc. *Local issues* vs. national issues, etc. etc. Similarities, *differences,* etc. etc. etc. Hopes, dreams, etc. etc. A *governor,* maybe. Only thing is, must try to figure out *which* governor.

OCTOBER 26TH
Found press release about a governor. So depressing I had to sit down. These people live lives you wouldn't wish on a disc jockey. Decided to write *screenplay.* Long, lonely shots (definitely use concrete bunkers from Convention, etc. etc.). One man's hopes *shattered,* etc. etc., in the midst of triumph of another man, etc. etc. etc. *Reversed, though.* Real triumph the inner growth made possible by defeat, etc. etc. etc. Human-interest figures based on Amy, Miss Lillian, etc. etc. etc. Could be big. On the other hand, could be ghastly.

NOVEMBER 1ST
After months of thought, have definitely decided to do instant book. *Personal* approach—the election from *my hotel room.* Very pleased, because Teddy White won't have it.

NOVEMBER 20TH
Personal approach won't work out, because *too grim.* Also worried about right hand. Right hand *won't stop shaking.* Can't write with left, so very down.

THE NEW ADMINISTRATION

JANUARY 20TH
Went to Inauguration. Tried to refocus on whole new free spirit, but got the jitters. Tried to *lighten up,* roll easily in the crowd, etc., but broke out in a *small red rash* (mostly on left hand) and had to go home. Best approach now: no-frills journalism. No gimmicks. Just good strong stuff. Chance to stress First One Hundred Days. *Amusing, though—* include little glossary of "cracker" terms so Washingtonians can understand Carter team, etc. etc.

FEBRUARY 2ND
Very down. Spotted two little "cracker" glossaries *out already.* Must do something *soon.* What about a sort of who's-who approach? Rosalynn Carter *so tough* under that sweet exterior, etc. etc. Juxtaposed to Amy, Miss Lillian, and Alice Roosevelt Longworth. Wish I knew Alice Longworth *better.* Use tape recorder for chapter on New Southern Personalities. Racist clubs, etc. etc. Almost definitely have title: "The Reign in Plains Falls Mainly on the . . ."—but can't come up with last word.

FEBRUARY 10TH
Decided best thing go to racist club. Went to door, met by Bill. "Good evening, sir," etc. Bill said club had to let Sam go, because wanted to call members by first name. Bill said doormen, waiters, etc., at Union League Club call members by first name. Very gripping. Took mental notes. Good to be reporting again. Went upstairs, had Wild Turkey Old-Fashioned. Hand *stopped shaking.*

FEBRUARY 17TH
See now must zero in on *energy,* Carter's plan: the new expectations, the new more modest life styles.

APRIL 25TH
Tried to focus on energy, but too worried about *small red rash.*

MAY 6TH
Definitely decided not to stress First One Hundred Days because too limiting. Definitely decided to forget whole New South angle because too stale. Definitely decided not to try to *lighten up* because too nervous.

JULY 15TH
Now see must focus on *revisionist* theories. New Populism really New Conservatism. Carter Administration as caretaker government, Carter

as apostle of closed government, Carter as savior of Northern élite. Ordered big lunch, but couldn't get it down. Decided small red rash defi
nitely *spreading.*

1977

POLLY FROST

NOTES ON MY CONVERSATIONS

Conversation has been [Fran] Lebowitz's lifetime work. The writing of her
books, like the plastering of a wall for a fresco, is best viewed as a preparatory
phase. . . . Instead of bemoaning Lebowitz's failure to publish, one might
envy her progress. Her work is now custom-tailored, her clientele is elite.
She has gone from *prêt à porter* to *haute couture.*

—Vanity Fair.

YOU haven't read anything by me for some time, because I have
been devoting myself to what I felt was my true art form: conversation. When I made this transition, the critics labelled me "lazy" and
"a procrastinator." The fact is, I did not stop writing in order to lounge
around at parties—that has been only a necessary adjunct to my work.

The moment I said my first word, I knew that talking was all I ever
wanted to do, despite considerable discouragement from my family.
They felt I ought to accomplish something. Yet I never found doing
things satisfying. There wasn't the sense of completion I'd get from
talking about doing something to the point where it couldn't be done,
shouldn't be done, and nobody even wanted it to be done anymore. But
had I done it, it would have been the best thing I ever did.

In response to demand for a retrospective, I have singled out my
most famous (and infamous!) conversations. In doing so, I have had to
omit numerous smaller works: kaffeeklatsches, yammers, retorts, insin-
uations, complaints, tipoffs, disseminations, and greetings. This is unfortunate.

My work falls into three major periods:

THE EARLY CONVERSATIONS

The seminal influences on me were the Masters—Dr. Johnson and Oscar Wilde. Many lay people don't know how carefully Wilde worked on his aphorisms. People seem to think that being a conversationalist means you just get out of bed in the morning and open your mouth. They don't understand the preparation that's involved, not to mention the skill and patience required to make your interlocutors stick to the subject.

An example of the kinds of challenges I faced: On October 19, 1981, I met several friends at Dolores's Coffee Shop, and we engaged in light-hearted banter. Everyone asked me, "What on earth have you been doing lately—if anything?" I didn't reply. I couldn't tell them I had been carefully crafting my wit, as that would undercut the element of surprise essential for the conversation to work. I waited until the cheeseburgers were served before introducing my topic. (Note on the participants: The initials "P.F." stand for me.)

P.F.: I've been thinking . . . about death.

T.D.: Thanks a lot—you just ruined my lunch.

P.F.: Perhaps if you simply think of death as annihilation your appetite will return.

L.B.: Can't we talk about something else?

P.F.: No!

(A critical note: During this time, I was studying Wilde's techniques for keeping his listeners on the track, and developing a few of my own.)

S.E.: Hey, has anybody seen Jeff recently? He was supposed—

P.F. (*cutting him off*): Doesn't anybody want to hear what I have to say?

EVERYONE (*resignedly*): O.K.

P.F.: Well, forget it—I've decided not to tell you.

My reputation as a conversationalist really began to be established when I moved from coffee shops to cocktail parties. It was there that I began to experiment with material and develop techniques. In particular, the technique of cornering enabled me to extend the duration of small talk beyond anything previously known. It has been noted by critics that my small talk was about duration itself.

During what I now refer to as my "representational" period, T.D. would often ask me what exactly it was I brought to the art of conversation. Traditionally, the immortal conversationalists came to talk from other disciplines—Northcote from painting, Socrates from philosophy, Heine from poetry. I began to feel that this was what was responsible for the constant intrusion of subject matter into their speech.

MIDDLE WORKS

More and more, I challenged the assumption that I shouldn't speak unless I had something to say. Words themselves were becoming of less interest to me than pure sound. I was fascinated by the possibilities of yelling, whispering, and changing my accent midsentence. Also, the visual effects, such as rolling my eyes, drumming my fingers, and grinning inappropriately.

I was able to experiment with these ideas in 1982, when I gave over two hundred interviews, culminating in EXCLUSIVE SELF-INTERVIEW, excerpted here:

> You ask if there's any recurring theme in my work. Well, CONVERSATION #87 was, on the surface, a simple story about dinner at Shirley's house but was actually about not having been invited to Roger's for some time. Then, around CONVERSATION #157, Roger pointed out that I was still talking about the same thing. So, yes, there are recurring themes in my work. But, to return to your first question. You asked if I don't feel my conversations should be a two-way street. No, I don't. I don't believe in art by committee. Life and art? There is no separation. Everything—my most recent trip, along with any others I have ever taken, all the facts in the most recent issue of *Newsweek,* Thursday night's dinner, as well as its effect on my digestion, the entire plot of the last movie I saw—everything becomes part of my conversation. What's the most interesting thing I've ever said? Impossible to answer. Like all conversationalists, I am always most in love with what I am saying at the moment.

The big breakthrough in my style came in 1983. Until then, I had always carefully planned out what I was going to say in advance. What might happen if I simply responded on the spot to what people were saying? The results of these experiments in form surprised even me. An example, from a telephone conversation in late 1984:

SHIRLEY: Hello?

P.F.: *(silence)*

SHIRLEY: HELLO?

P.F.: *(very long silence)*

At this point in the conversation, Shirley slammed down the receiver. I had never gotten this effect out of her before.

Improvisation led me to question the role my friends were playing in my conversations, which I felt was much too great. I became interested in the idea of using non-friends—people who were no longer speaking to me, strangers, inanimate objects.

By March 3, 1985, the cocktail party had become a moribund form— an exchange of anecdotes, business cards, lunch dates. Shallow gestures, devoid of meaning. People felt that when I walked toward them they were about to make a connection. No—I wanted to bring them face to face with something or other. (But what? I never could decide.)

The listener had become passive. Telephone receivers were placed down on kitchen counters while listeners made trips to the refrigerator or thumbed through magazines. In my apartment lobby, they'd continue to get their mail, with only an occasional "Mm-hmm. . . . Mm-hmm." I didn't feel like popping one of my aphorisms after all this mumbling!

In August, the whole Street Talking Movement was coming to a boil. I was one of the ones who felt that the talk going on inside restaurants ("Check, please"), office-building elevators ("Seventeenth floor, please"), as well as hotels and theatre lobbies, had lost its vitality. Outside, it was all new and experimental. I no longer wanted to talk to people. I wanted to talk at them.

Although I felt that my Street Talking should be primarily an urban phenomenon, I did once yell at a combine on the edge of a wheat field in Saskatchewan.

When I went back indoors in October, I was attacked by the critics. I felt I had exhausted the rant and rave, especially in STREET-CORNER CONVERSATION WITH PASSING CARS. I needed fresh forms. I was dying to work with the toast, the waffle, and the quibble. And in order to do so, it was imperative that I once again sit down at the dinner table.

At this point, I would like to say something about critics. I have been accused by critics of "dominating the conversation," of "not allowing anyone else to get a word in edgewise." The most annoying thing about all this criticism is it makes me forget what it was I wanted to say. . . .

This morning, I started putting my wit in code. A conversationalist can't be too free with his/her best lines. Give a seemingly off-the-cuff recital of one and the next thing you know, it's on every bumper sticker and T-shirt. That aphorism may have been as much as one month in the making, and meanwhile I haven't gotten anything for my work.

Then, at lunch, I discovered I possess that indefinable but unmistakable something known as Presence. This has had its effect on my style, as I no longer need to enter the conversation at all. In fact, talking doesn't seem enough anymore. Now I plan to explore the other art forms—for example, having my picture taken.

1986

STEVE MARTIN

WRITING IS EASY!

WRITING is the most easy, pain-free, and happy way to pass the time of all the arts. As I write this, for example, I am sitting comfortably in my rose garden and typing on my new computer. Each rose represents a story, so I'm never at a loss for what to type. I just look deep into the heart of the rose, read its story, and then write it down. I could be typing *kjfiu joew.mv jiw* and enjoy it as much as typing words that actually make sense, because I simply relish the movements of my fingers on the keys. It is true that sometimes agony visits the head of a writer. At those moments, I stop writing and relax with a coffee at my favorite restaurant, knowing that words can be changed, rethought, fiddled with, and ultimately denied. Painters don't have that luxury. If they go to a coffee shop, their paint dries into a hard mass.

LOCATION, LOCATION, LOCATION

I would like to recommend that all writers live in California, because here, in between those moments when one is looking into the heart of a rose, one can look up at the calming blue sky. I feel sorry for writers— and there are some pretty famous ones—who live in places like South America and Czechoslovakia, where I imagine it gets pretty dank. These writers are easy to spot. Their books are often filled with disease and negativity. If you're going to write about disease, I would say California is the place to do it. Dwarfism is never funny, but look at what happened when it was dealt with in California. Seven happy dwarfs. Can you imagine seven dwarfs in Czechoslovakia? You would get seven melancholic dwarfs at best—seven melancholic dwarfs and no handicap-parking spaces.

LOVE IN THE TIME OF CHOLERA: WHY IT'S A BAD TITLE

I admit that "Love in the time of . . ." is a great title, up to a point. You're reading along, you're happy, it's about *love*. I like the way the word *time* comes in—a nice, nice feeling. Then the morbid *Cholera* appears. I was happy till then. Why not "Love in the Time of the Blue, Blue, Bluebirds"? "Love in the Time of Oozing Sores and Pustules" is probably an earlier title the author used as he was writing in a rat-infested tree house on an old Smith Corona. This writer, whoever he is, could have used a couple of weeks in Pacific Daylight Time.

A LITTLE EXPERIMENT

I took the following passage, which was no doubt written in some depressing place, and attempted to rewrite it under the sunny influence of California:

> Most people deceive themselves with a pair of faiths: they believe in *eternal memory* (of people, things, deeds, nations) and in *redressibility* (of deeds, mistakes, sins, wrongs). Both are false faiths. In reality the opposite is true: everything will be forgotten and nothing will be redressed.
> —*Milan Kundera.*

Sitting in my garden, watching the bees glide from flower to flower, I let the above paragraph filter through my mind. The following New Paragraph emerged:

> I feel pretty,
> Oh so pretty,
> I feel pretty, and witty, and bright.

Kundera was just too wordy. Sometimes the delete key is your best friend.

WRITER'S BLOCK: A MYTH

Writer's block is a fancy term made up by whiners so they can have an excuse to drink alcohol. Sure, a writer can get stuck for a while, but when that happens to a real author—say, a Socrates or a Rodman—he goes out and gets an "as told to." The alternative is to hire yourself out as an "as heard from," thus taking all the credit. The other trick I use when I have a momentary stoppage is virtually foolproof, and I'm happy to pass it along. Go to an already published novel and find a sentence that you absolutely adore. Copy it down in your manuscript. Usually, that sentence will lead you to another sentence, and pretty soon your own ideas will start to flow. If they don't, copy down the next sentence in the novel. You can safely use up to three sentences of someone else's work—unless you're friends, then two. The odds of being found out are very slim, and even if you are there's usually no jail time.

A DEMONSTRATION OF ACTUAL WRITING

It's easy to talk about writing, and even easier to do it. Watch:

> Call me Ishmael. It was cold, very cold here in the mountain town of Kilimanjaroville.® I could hear a bell. It was tolling.* I knew exactly for who it was tolling, too. It was tolling for me, Ishmael Twist.© [Author's note: I am now stuck. I walk over to a rose and look into its heart.] That's right, Ishmael Twist.©

This is an example of what I call "pure" writing, which occurs when there is no possibility of its becoming a screenplay. Pure writing is the most rewarding of all, because it is constantly accompanied by a voice that repeats, "Why am I writing this?" Then, and only then, can the writer hope for his finest achievement: the voice of the reader uttering its complement, "Why am I reading this?"

1996

STEVE MARTIN

DRIVEL

DOLLY defended me at a party. She was an artist who showed at the Whitney Biennial, so she had a certain outlook, a certain point of view, a certain understanding of things. She came into my life as a stranger who spoke up when I was being attacked by some cocktail types for being the publisher of *The American Drivel Review*. It

*This sentence written by Steve Martin as heard from Cindy Adams.

wasn't drivel that I published, she explained to them, but rather the *idea* of drivel.

Later in the party, we paired off. She slouched back on the sofa with her legs ajar. I poured out my heart to this person I'd known barely ten minutes: I told her how it was hard to find good drivel, and even harder to write it. She understood that to succeed, one must pore over every word, replacing it five or six times, and labor over every pause and comma.

I made love to her that night. The snap of the condom going on echoed through the apartment like Lawrence of Arabia's spear landing in an Arab shield. I whispered passages from "Agamemnon's Armor," a five-inch-thick romance novel with three authors. She liked that.

As the publisher of *A.D.R.*, I had never actually written the stuff myself. But the next morning I sat down and tossed off a few lines, and then nervously showed them to Dolly. She took them into another room, and I sat alone for several painful minutes. She came back and looked at me. "This is not just drivel," she exulted. "It's *pure* drivel."

That night, we celebrated with a champagne dinner for two, and I told her that her skin was the color of fine white typing paper held in the sun and reflecting the pink of a New Mexican adobe horse barn.

The next two months were heaven. I was no longer just publishing drivel; I was writing it. Dolly, too, had a burst of creativity—one that sent her into a splendid spiralling depression. She had painted a table-top still-life—a conceptual work, in that it had no concept. Thus the viewer became a "viewer," and looked at a painting, which became a "painting." The "viewer" then left the museum to "discuss" the experience with "others." Dolly had a way of taking an infinitesimal pause to imply the quotation marks around a word. (She could also indicate italics with a twist of her voice.)

Not wanting to judge my own work, and not wanting to trust Dolly's love-skewed opinion, I sent my pieces around and had them rejected by at least five magazines before I would publish them in the *Drivel Review*. I was disappointed when *Woman's Day* accepted a short story I'd written about Gepetto's Handmaiden, but, looking back, I guess I secretly knew that it was good. Dolly kept producing one art work after another and selling them to a rock musician with the unusual name of Fiber Behind; it kept us in doughnuts, and he really seemed to appreciate her work.

But then our love was extinguished quickly, as though someone had thrown water from a high tower onto a burning dog.

Dolly came home at her usual time. What I had to tell her was difficult to say, but it came out with the right amount of effortlessness, in spite of my nerves: "I went downtown and saw your new picture at Dia. I enjoyed it."

She acknowledged the compliment, started to leave the room, and, as I expected, stopped short.

"You mean you 'enjoyed' it, don't you?" Her voice indicated the quotation marks.

I reiterated, "No, I actually enjoyed it."

Dolly's attention focused, and she came over and sat beside me. "Rod, do you mean you didn't go into the 'gallery' and 'see' my 'painting'?"

I nodded sadly.

"You mean you saw my painting without any irony whatsoever?"

Again, I nodded yes.

"But, Rod, if you view my work without irony, it's terrible."

I responded: "All I can tell you is that I enjoyed it."

We struggled through the night, trying to pretend that everything was the same, but by morning it was over between us, and Dolly left with a small "goodbye" soaked in the irony I had come to love so much.

> I wanted to run,
> run after her into the night,
> even though it was day.
> For my pain was bursting out of me,
> like a sock filled
> with one too many bocce balls.

Those were my final words in the last issue of the *Drivel Review*. I heard that Dolly had spent some time with Fiber Behind, but I also knew that she had probably picked up a farewell copy and read my final, short, painful burst of drivel. I like to think that a tear marked her cheek, like a snail that has crept across white china.

1997

ANDY BOROWITZ

EMILY DICKINSON, JERK OF AMHERST

IT was with great reluctance that I decided to write about my thirty-year friendship with Emily Dickinson. To many who would read my book, Miss Dickinson was a cherished literary icon, and any attempt to describe her in human terms would, understandably, be resented. And yet by not writing this book I would be depriving her most ardent admirers of meeting the Emily Dickinson I was privileged to know: more than a mentor, she was my anchor, my compass, my lighthouse.

Except when she was drunk. At those times, usually beginning at the stroke of noon, she became a gluttonous, vituperative harpy who would cut you for your last Buffalo wing. Once she got hold of her favorite beverage, Olde English malt liquor, the "belle of Amherst" would, as she liked to put it, "get polluted 'til [she] booted." This Emily Dickinson would think nothing of spitting chewing tobacco in a protégé's face, blithely explaining that she was "working on [her] aim."

Who, then, was the real Emily Dickinson? Daughter of New England in chaste service to her poetry, or back-stabbing gorgon who doctored your bowling score when you went to get more nachos? By exploring this question, I decided, I had a chance not only to learn about Miss Dickinson but also to learn about myself, and to learn even more about myself if the book went into paperback.

When I first met Miss Dickinson, I was a literary greenhorn with a handful of unfinished poems, struggling to find my voice and something that rhymed with "Nantucket." Believing that she would be more likely to take me under her wing if I appeared to be an ingénue, I entered her lace-curtained parlor in Amherst dressed as a Cub Scout. But she took no note of my attire as she read over that day's work: "Parting is all we know of heaven,/And all we need of hell." Putting down her quill, she brushed the bonnet-crowned curls from her forehead. "Well, it beats stealing cars!" she croaked in a husky baritone.

Declaring that "quittin' time is spittin' time," she reached into her sewing box for a pouch of her favorite "chaw," as she called it, and pulled a "tall and foamy" out of the icebox. She generously agreed to look over my poems, pork rinds spilling from her mouth as she read.

Finally, she anointed my efforts with words of encouragement that would sustain me throughout my early career: "You're a poet and you don't know it. Your feet show it. They're long fellows. Now I gotta hit the head."

Years passed before I saw another, less merry, aspect of Miss Dickinson's character, at a book party for Ralph Waldo Emerson. Miss Dickinson was experiencing a trough in her career; she had been reduced to writing advertising copy, most notably, "Nothing is better for thee/Than me," for Quaker Oats. At the party, Miss Dickinson sat alone at the bar, doing tequila shooters and riffing moribund, angry couplets that often did not scan. I sensed that it was time to take her home.

In the parking lot, she stopped abruptly near Emerson's car. "Let's key it," she said, her eyes dancing maniacally. I assumed that this was just "Emily being Emily," and tried to laugh it off. "Don't be such a wuss," she said, scratching "Waldo sucks" into the passenger door. I gently upbraided Miss Dickinson for her actions, which only served to inflame her: "Emerson's trying to steal my juice, baby. It took me years to get where I am, understand what I'm saying? I used to run three-card monte on the streets of Newton. And I ain't goin' back!" At this moment, I found myself confronted with a possibility that I had never wanted to consider in all our years of friendship: Emily Dickinson was a real jerk.

Some years later, Boston University asked me to moderate a panel including Miss Dickinson, William Dean Howells, and the author, long since forgotten, of the verse "Finders, keepers/Losers, weepers." I was by this time a successful poet in my own right, having become renowned for my series of "Happiness Is . . ." gift books and pillows. Seated next to Miss Dickinson, I attempted to mend the breach that had developed in our relationship; I went on at some length about my debt to her work. She took a sip of water, cleared her throat, and replied, "Bite me, you self-aggrandizing weasel."

The last time I saw Emily Dickinson, she said she didn't have time to speak, as she was on her way to the greyhound races in Taunton. But I could not let her go without asking what had happened to our friendship. Her eyes downcast, she said, simply, "You've got ketchup on your tie." Quizzically, I lowered my head and took a right uppercut to the jaw. As I crumpled to the pavement, Miss Dickinson unleashed a profane tirade, along with a pistol-whipping that was startling for both its vigor and its efficiency.

As I review this last memory it occurs to me that some readers might conclude that I am trying to cast Emily Dickinson in a negative light. Nothing could be further from my intentions. In fact, when I regained consciousness I realized that Miss Dickinson, in her tirade, had given me a final, precious gift. True, I no longer had my wallet, but I had, at long last, a separate identity, a voice. And, perhaps most valuable of all, a rhyme for "Nantucket."

1998

A
FUNNY
THING
HAPPENED

THE PEOPLE WHO HAD

THE HOUSE BEFORE

[STRANGE ADVENTURES OF THE NEXT TENANTS IN THE FAMOUS

TWO-FAMILY HOUSE AT 21 MASSASOIT STREET,

NORTHAMPTON, MASSACHUSETTS]

OCTOBER 1, 1930—Moved in today. Everything looks all right, clean, etc. The people who had the house before us were evidently good housekeepers. They *did* take away all the electric-light bulbs and base-plugs, but they probably paid for them themselves and so were within their rights. They might have left us the patent faucets on the bathtub, though. We can't fill the tub without dishing water over from the washbowl.

One thing they did leave which seems kind of strange. Each room has an insurance calendar hanging in it and on the hall window-seat there is a pile of data on the New York Life Insurance Company's special twenty-year endowment policy.

OCTOBER 14—A rather peculiar thing happened today. We were sitting in the living-room when a couple of newspaper reporters with big cameras came up to the door and asked if we would mind sitting out on the porch and having our pictures taken. I said that I would have to put on my collar first, but the man said that it would make a better picture without it. More democratic, he said. He even said if I had those overalls handy to put them on. I said "What overalls?" and he just winked.

When we got out on the porch into the light, the photographers seemed a little surprised and sort of disappointed and talked together in a low tone. Then one of them said: "Who lives in the other side of the house?" I said that I didn't know as we had just come to town ourselves from the West, but I thought their name was Walters. "You just moved in yourselves?" he asked, looking rather suspicious. "Weren't you ever President of the United States?" I laughed and said not that I knew of, but that a few years ago there was a week when I was on the Shriners' Convention that I might have been almost anything. "No, it would have had to have been longer than a week," he said. Then he said to the other man: "Pack up your things, Ed. We got the wrong house." And Ed said: "We should have ought to have done this job last spring when we got the assignment."

So they went away and we never got our picture taken.

OCTOBER 20—This afternoon the telephone rang and Edith answered it and Central said that the *Cosmopolitan Magazine* in New York City wanted to speak. So I went, being a great reader myself, and a girl's voice said that she was speaking for Mr. Wong or Long and that my copy for the January number was due. I said that I hadn't got my copy of the November number yet, and she said, "Not the copy *of,* but the copy *for,* the January number." So I hung up.

OCTOBER 21—We ran across something in the attic today which may explain something about the *Cosmopolitan* episode—but not much. Up behind one of the posts where we were putting our trunks Edith found a lot of yellow papers with "Cosmopolitan" typed in the upper left-hand corner of each. The first one had some sort of article begun on it, about a paragraph. It began: "My early life in Plymouth was just about the same sort of life that every God-fearing, healthy boy of that time was leading." The next sheet had much the same sentence as a starter, only a few words longer. In the margin were some figures scribbled, which as near as we could make out were: "$1.00 per word. 23 words. $23." The next sheet had the same sort of sentence only much longer: "I think that I may say without exaggeration that the early days of my boyhood, lived, as they were, amid the green hills of Plymouth, Vermont, were just the sort of days, taken one by one, as those which go to make up the average day of the typical healthy, God-fearing, honest and thrifty American boy of today in a town the size of Plymouth, Vermont, where Nature has a chance to imbue the growing youth with the principles of steadfast and pious observance of the laws of God and of the United States of America." In the margin beside this were the figures: "96 words @ $1.00. $96.00," and a note: "Ask Long about hyphenated words."

As none of it seemed to make much sense, we threw the whole bunch of papers away.

OCTOBER 23—Edith swore she saw a man wearing a cowboy suit hanging around the front walk tonight. I told her not to be silly, that there were no cowboys in Northampton.

OCTOBER 24—This thing is beginning to get on my nerves. This afternoon four Indians in full regalia came up on the porch and rang the bell. Edith answered and the biggest Indian asked for "Big White Chief." Edith told him that our name was Meakins and that maybe he wanted Walters, who lived in the other half of the house. The big Indian shook his head and said: "Come to pay call on Big White Chief. How-do?" Edith said: "I'm all right, thank you, but nobody here knows any Indians." Then she called to me and said: "Unless you do, George. Do you know any Indians?" I called back and simply said: "No." So Edith got a little cross by this time and said: "And what is more, we don't want any sweet-grass baskets, either, so get along with you, all four of you." This sent the Indians into a conference on the front steps and Edith came into the house and locked the door. We watched them from the bay window until they went away. I don't like the looks of things in this neighborhood.

OCTOBER 25—Well, things have about reached a climax. I saw the cowboy tonight. He was walking up and down in front of the house about half past ten. I watched him for a little while and saw him go around to the back of the house. I put the lights out and waited. Pretty soon I heard a key in the lock and the cowboy came in the front door walking very quietly. I snapped on the light and said: "I suppose you're looking for those Indians. Well, they went away yesterday." He seemed a little embarrassed. "Did you find any yellow papers here?" he asked. He talked more like a farmer than a cowboy, through his nose sort of. I said: "Yes, what's it to you?" He said: "They were typewritten only on one side, weren't they?" I said I hadn't looked on both sides. "They belong to me," he said, "and I wanted to use them up on the other side." I told him that he was too late and that we had thrown them away. "And where did you get a key for this house?" I asked him. "I used to live here," he said, and walked out. I called up the police and they said that there was a State Hospital near here and probably one of the inmates was loose, and if I saw him again to let them know right away.

OCTOBER 26—The Indians came back today, bringing another one with them. We didn't go to the door and watched them from the bay window until they went away. A small crowd gathered outside and began to cheer. We decided that they were from the State Hospital too, and Edith said she thought we ought to move.

OCTOBER 27—Edith got so nervous last night thinking she heard the cowboy and the Indians again that we put some things into a suitcase and spent the night at the Draper Hotel. Have given up the house and are going to live in Holyoke.

1930

THE CATASTROPHE

O N the fourteenth of March, at exactly fourteen minutes to three in the morning, a meteor grazed the Manhattan skyline and fell into either the sea or the outskirts of Carlstadt, New Jersey. All astronomers having been asleep at the time, the world had to rely for data on such unscientific observers as two giddy airmail pilots, a scattering of cops, several non-union millworkers on the night shift, and a man going home from El Morocco. Even the New York *Daily News* had to base its eight-inch headline, "METEOR ROCKS JERSEY," on the rumor that some windows had rattled in Trenton. As far as the insurance companies could find out, no one had been killed or injured, no damage had been done. In fact, everything considered, the phenomenon did not quite come off.

The next day, March the fifteenth, another meteor fell. This one, however, failed to disintegrate as it plunged through the earth's atmosphere, nor did it sink itself into the traditional forest or desert. It landed, nice and tidy, on all five boroughs of Greater New York.

Within an hour, the Red Cross in Philadelphia launched a relief drive for the victims. Mayor Kelly of Chicago long-distanced Mayor LaGuardia to offer sympathies. Cinema theatres wired the New York Paramount office to rush them eyewitness newsreels. Western Union accepted the wires. Whereas, of course, there were no newsreels, no Mayor LaGuardia, no anything. Approximately seven and a half million New Yorkers, and over a half-million visitors from out of town (who cared very little for the city anyway), had been annihilated. The only New Yorkers who had escaped were those who chanced to be at Miami Beach, and there they remained, shaking their heads and trying to find someone who would cash their checks.

It was not until the newspapers, in simultaneous spurts of fancy, decided to reprint the New York telephone directories as an obituary notice that the country began to grasp the scope and connotations of what had happened. New York City, like Pompeii, was through. As a final grisly touch, N.B.C., its headquarters no longer in Rockefeller Center, broadcast a ten-minute dramatization of the Catastrophe (as it was already called) on a program which included a hot swing band and a talk by Glenn Frank. The American people were, at last, unnerved. Business took something of a bad turn. Control of the big corporations, suddenly left without boards of directors, reverted to the stockholders, who, left in turn without market quotations, were not any too sure there *were* corporations. Soon, too, the country was aware of a shortage of women's wear, advertising campaigns, international bankers, O. O. McIntyre. Conditions were, as analyzed by Roger W. Babson, unsettled.

Then, inevitably, came the period of readjustment. Boston took over as the Eastern shipping centre. The gap in the American League was filled by the Baltimore Orioles; in the National, by the Toledo Mud Hens. Buffalo was made the terminus of the Twentieth Century. Then there was a wave of Catastrophe jokes (Catastrophe who?), followed by a cycle of Catastrophe films, in most of which Franchot Tone, who had come to be accepted as the typical extinct New Yorker, starred. Parker Brothers put out a game called Catastrophe. Around this time, a bill was introduced in Congress proposing that a New New York be built by the WPA. This died in committee. People were getting bored with the whole subject.

FIVE years passed, and New York City had disappeared from the last map. Ten years passed, and it had taken on the aspect of a dim exaggeration. Twenty years, and there was a full generation without a single first-hand New York memory. Eventually, the few old-timers who still claimed to have seen New York were regarded as cranks. They had to be humored when they talked about the electric signs on Broadway, the shops along Fifth Avenue, the subways, the Metropolitan Museum and Central Park and Harlem, the lobby of the Waldorf, the view from the Empire State Building. Nobody had the heart to tell them that New York had been invented by H. G. Wells.

1936

JAMES THURBER

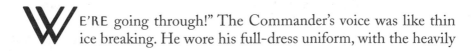

THE SECRET LIFE OF WALTER MITTY

W E'RE going through!" The Commander's voice was like thin ice breaking. He wore his full-dress uniform, with the heavily braided white cap pulled down rakishly over one cold gray eye. "We can't make it, sir. It's spoiling for a hurricane, if you ask me." "I'm not asking you, Lieutenant Berg," said the Commander. "Throw on the power lights! Rev her up to 8,500! We're going through!" The pounding of the cylinders increased: ta-pocketa-pocketa-pocketa-*pocketa-pocketa*. The Commander stared at the ice forming on the pilot window. He walked over and twisted a row of complicated dials. "Switch on No. 8 auxiliary!" he shouted. "Switch on No. 8 auxiliary!" repeated Lieutenant Berg. "Full strength in No. 3 turret!" shouted the Commander. "Full strength in No. 3 turret!" The crew, bending to their various tasks in the huge, hurtling eight-engined Navy hydroplane, looked at each other and grinned. "The Old Man'll get us through," they said to one another. "The Old Man ain't afraid of Hell!" . . .

"Not so fast! You're driving too fast!" said Mrs. Mitty. "What are you driving so fast for?"

"Hmm?" said Walter Mitty. He looked at his wife, in the seat beside him, with shocked astonishment. She seemed grossly unfamiliar, like a strange woman who had yelled at him in a crowd. "You were up to fifty-five," she said. "You know I don't like to go more than forty. You were up to fifty-five." Walter Mitty drove on toward Waterbury in silence, the roaring of the SN202 through the worst storm in twenty years of Navy flying fading in the remote, intimate airways of his mind. "You're tensed up again," said Mrs. Mitty. "It's one of your days. I wish you'd let Dr. Renshaw look you over."

Walter Mitty stopped the car in front of the building where his wife went to have her hair done. "Remember to get those overshoes while I'm having my hair done," she said. "I don't need overshoes," said Mitty. She put her mirror back into her bag. "We've been all through that," she said, getting out of the car. "You're not a young man any longer." He raced the engine a little. "Why don't you wear your gloves? Have you lost your gloves?" Walter Mitty reached in a pocket and brought out the gloves. He put them on, but after she had turned and gone into the building and he had driven on to a red light, he took them off again. "Pick it up, brother!" snapped a cop as the light changed, and Mitty hastily pulled on his gloves and lurched ahead. He drove around the streets aimlessly for a time, and then he drove past the hospital on his way to the parking lot.

. . . "It's the millionaire banker, Wellington McMillan," said the pretty nurse. "Yes?" said Walter Mitty, removing his gloves slowly. "Who has the case?" "Dr. Renshaw and Dr. Benbow, but there are two specialists here, Dr. Remington from New York and Dr. Pritchard-

Mitford from London. He flew over." A door opened down a long, cool corridor and Dr. Renshaw came out. He looked distraught and haggard. "Hello, Mitty," he said. "We're having the devil's own time with McMillan, the millionaire banker and close personal friend of Roosevelt. Obstreosis of the ductal tract. Tertiary. Wish you'd take a look at him." "Glad to," said Mitty.

In the operating room there were whispered introductions: "Dr. Remington, Dr. Mitty. Dr. Pritchard-Mitford, Dr. Mitty." "I've read your book on streptothricosis," said Pritchard-Mitford, shaking hands. "A brilliant performance, sir." "Thank you," said Walter Mitty. "Didn't know you were in the States, Mitty," grumbled Remington. "Coals to Newcastle, bringing Mitford and me up here for a tertiary." "You are very kind," said Mitty. A huge, complicated machine, connected to the operating table, with many tubes and wires, began at this moment to go pocketa-pocketa-pocketa. "The new anaesthetizer is giving way!" shouted an interne. "There is no one in the East who knows how to fix it!" "Quiet, man!" said Mitty, in a low, cool voice. He sprang to the machine, which was now going pocketa-pocketa-queep-pocketa-queep. He began fingering delicately a row of glistening dials. "Give me a fountain pen!" he snapped. Someone handed him a fountain pen. He pulled a faulty piston out of the machine and inserted the pen in its place. "That will hold for ten minutes," he said. "Get on with the operation." A nurse hurried over and whispered to Renshaw, and Mitty saw the man turn pale. "Coreopsis has set in," said Renshaw nervously. "If you would take over, Mitty?" Mitty looked at him and at the craven figure of Benbow, who drank, and at the grave, uncertain faces of the two great specialists. "If you wish," he said. They slipped a white gown on him; he adjusted a mask and drew on thin gloves; nurses handed him shining . . .

"Back it up, Mac! Look out for that Buick!" Walter Mitty jammed on the brakes. "Wrong lane, Mac," said the parking-lot attendant, looking at Mitty closely. "Gee. Yeh," muttered Mitty. He began cautiously to back out of the lane marked "Exit Only." "Leave her sit there," said the attendant. "I'll put her away." Mitty got out of the car. "Hey, better leave the key." "Oh," said Mitty, handing the man the ignition key. The attendant vaulted into the car, backed it up with insolent skill, and put it where it belonged.

They're so damn cocky, thought Walter Mitty, walking along Main Street; they think they know everything. Once he had tried to take his chains off, outside New Milford, and he had got them wound around the axles. A man had had to come out in a wrecking car and unwind them, a young, grinning garageman. Since then Mrs. Mitty always made him drive to a garage to have the chains taken off. The next time, he thought, I'll wear my right arm in a sling; they won't grin at me then. I'll have my right arm in a sling and they'll see I couldn't possibly take the chains off myself. He kicked at the slush on the sidewalk. "Overshoes," he said to himself, and he began looking for a shoe store.

When he came out into the street again, with the overshoes in a box under his arm, Walter Mitty began to wonder what the other thing was his wife had told him to get. She had told him, twice, before they set out from their house for Waterbury. In a way he hated these weekly trips to town—he was always getting something wrong. Kleenex, he thought, Squibb's, razor blades? No. Toothpaste, toothbrush, bicarbonate, carborundum, initiative and referendum? He gave it up. But she would remember it. "Where's the what's-its-name?" she would ask. "Don't tell me you forgot the what's-its-name." A newsboy went by shouting something about the Waterbury trial.

. . . "Perhaps this will refresh your memory." The District Attorney suddenly thrust a heavy automatic at the quiet figure on the witness stand. "Have you ever seen this before?" Walter Mitty took the gun and examined it expertly. "This is my Webley-Vickers 50.80," he said calmly. An excited buzz ran around the courtroom. The Judge rapped for order. "You are a crack shot with any sort of firearms, I believe?" said the District Attorney, insinuatingly. "Objection!" shouted Mitty's attorney. "We have shown that the defendant could not have fired the shot. We have shown that he wore his right arm in a sling on the night of the fourteenth of July." Walter Mitty raised his hand briefly and the bickering attorneys were stilled. "With any known make of gun," he said evenly, "I could have killed Gregory Fitzhurst at three hundred feet *with my left hand*." Pandemonium broke loose in the courtroom. A woman's scream rose above the bedlam and suddenly a lovely, dark-haired girl was in Walter Mitty's arms. The District Attorney struck at her savagely. Without rising from his chair, Mitty let the man have it on the point of the chin. "You miserable cur!" . . .

"Puppy biscuit," said Walter Mitty. He stopped walking and the buildings of Waterbury rose up out of the misty courtroom and surrounded him again. A woman who was passing laughed. "He said 'Puppy biscuit,'" she said to her companion. "That man said 'Puppy biscuit' to himself." Walter Mitty hurried on. He went into an A. & P., not the first one he came to but a smaller one farther up the street. "I want some biscuit for small, young dogs," he said to the clerk. "Any special brand, sir?" The greatest pistol shot in the world thought a moment. "It says 'Puppies Bark for It' on the box," said Walter Mitty.

HIS wife would be through at the hairdresser's in fifteen minutes, Mitty saw in looking at his watch, unless they had trouble drying it; sometimes they had trouble drying it. She didn't like to get to the hotel first; she would want him to be there waiting for her as usual. He found a big leather chair in the lobby, facing a window, and he put the overshoes and the puppy biscuit on the floor beside it. He picked up an old copy of *Liberty* and sank down into the chair. "Can Germany Conquer the World Through the Air?" Walter Mitty looked at the pictures of bombing planes and of ruined streets.

. . . "The cannonading has got the wind up in young Raleigh, sir," said the sergeant. Captain Mitty looked up at him through touselled hair. "Get him to bed," he said wearily. "With the others. I'll fly alone." "But you can't, sir," said the sergeant anxiously. "It takes two men to handle that bomber and the Archies are pounding hell out of the air. Von Richtman's circus is between here and Saulier." "Somebody's got to get that ammunition dump," said Mitty. "I'm going over. Spot of brandy?" He poured a drink for the sergeant and one for himself. War thundered and whined around the dugout and battered at the door. There was a rending of wood and splinters flew through the room. "A bit of a near thing," said Captain Mitty carelessly. "The box barrage is closing in," said the sergeant. "We only live once, Sergeant," said Mitty, with his faint, fleeting smile. "Or do we?" He poured another brandy and tossed it off. "I never see a man could hold his brandy like you, sir," said the sergeant. "Begging your pardon, sir." Captain Mitty stood up and strapped on his huge Webley-Vickers automatic. "It's forty kilometres through hell, sir," said the sergeant. Mitty finished one last brandy. "After all," he said softly, "what isn't?" The pounding of the cannon increased; there was the rat-tat-tatting of machine guns, and from somewhere came the menacing pocketa-pocketa-pocketa of the new flame-throwers. Walter Mitty walked to the door of the dugout humming "Auprès de Ma Blonde." He turned and waved to the sergeant. "Cheerio!" he said. . . .

Something struck his shoulder. "I've been looking all over this hotel for you," said Mrs. Mitty. "Why do you have to hide in this old chair? How did you expect me to find you?" "Things close in," said Walter Mitty vaguely. "What?" Mrs. Mitty said. "Did you get the what's-its-name? The puppy biscuit? What's in that box?" "Overshoes," said Mitty. "Couldn't you have put them on in the store?" "I was thinking," said Walter Mitty. "Does it ever occur to you that I am sometimes thinking?" She looked at him. "I'm going to take your temperature when I get you home," she said.

THEY went out through the revolving doors that made a faintly derisive whistling sound when you pushed them. It was two blocks to the parking lot. At the drugstore on the corner she said, "Wait here for me. I forgot something. I won't be a minute." She was more than a minute. Walter Mitty lighted a cigarette. It began to rain, rain with sleet in it. He stood up against the wall of the drugstore, smoking. . . . He put his shoulders back and his heels together. "To hell with the handkerchief," said Walter Mitty scornfully. He took one last drag on his cigarette and snapped it away. Then, with that faint, fleeting smile playing about his lips, he faced the firing squad; erect and motionless, proud and disdainful, Walter Mitty the Undefeated, inscrutable to the last.

1939

S. J. PERELMAN

I AM NOT NOW, NOR HAVE I EVER
BEEN, A MATRIX OF LEAN MEAT

AWOKE with a violent, shuddering start, so abruptly that I felt the sudden ache behind the eyeballs one experiences after bolting an ice-cream soda or ascending too recklessly from the ocean floor. The house was utterly still; except for the tumult of the creek in the pasture, swollen with melting snow, a silence as awesome as that of Fatehpur Sikri, the abandoned citadel of the Moguls, shrouded the farm. Almost instantly, I was filled with an immense inquietude, an anxiety of such proportions that I quailed. The radium dial of the alarm clock read two-thirty: the exact moment, I realized with a tremor, that I had become involved the night before in the Affair of the Boneless Veal Steaks. The Boneless Veal Steaks—it had the same prosaic yet grisly implications as the Five Orange Pips or the Adventure of the Engineer's Thumb. Propped up on one elbow and staring into the velvet dark, I reviewed as coherently as I could the events of the preceding night.

I had awakened around two and, after thrashing about in my kip like a dying tautog, had lit and smoked the cork tip of a cigarette until I was nauseated. I thereupon woke up my wife, who apparently thought she could shirk her responsibilities by sleeping, and filed a brief résumé of the disasters—financial, political, and emotional—threatening us. When she began upbraiding me, in the altogether illogical way women do, I did not succumb to justifiable anger but pacifically withdrew to the kitchen for a snack. As I was extricating a turkey wing from the tangle of leftovers in the icebox (amazing how badly the average housewife organizes her realm; no man would tolerate such inefficiency in business), my attention was drawn by a limp package labelled "Gilbert's Frozen Boneless Veal Steaks." Stapled to the exterior was a printed appeal that had the lugubrious intimacy of a Freudian case history. "Dear Chef," it said. "I've lost my character. I used to have sinews, then I met a butcher at Gilbert's. He robbed me of my powers of resistance by cutting out some of the things that hold me together. I am a matrix of lean meat with my trimmings ground and worked back into me. Please be kind. Pick me up with a pancake turner or a spatula, don't grab me by the edges with a fork. Because of all I've been through I'm more fragile than others you've known. Please be gentle lest you tear me apart. Tillie the Tender."

THE revelation that food had become articulate at long last, that henceforth I was changed from consumer to father confessor, so unmanned me that I let go the turkey wing; with a loud "Mrkgnao" she obviously had learned from reading "Ulysses," the cat straightway pounced on it. I must have been in a real state of shock, because I just stood there gawking at her, my brain in a turmoil. What floored me, actually, wasn't that the veal had found a way to communicate—a more or less inevitable development, once you accepted the basic premise of Elsie, the Borden cow—but rather its smarmy and masochistic pitch. Here, for the first time in human experience, a supposedly inanimate object, a cutlet, had broken through the barrier and revealed itself as a creature with feelings and desires. Did it signalize its liberation with ecstasy, cry out some exultant word of deliverance, or even underplay it with a quiet request like

"Mr. Watson, come here. I want you"? No; the whole message reeked of self-pity, of invalidism, of humbug. It was a snivelling, eunuchoid plea for special privilege, a milepost of Pecksniffery. It was disgusting.

In the same instant, however, I saw both the futility of moral indignation and an augury of things to come. Before long, the other victuals in the icebox, their tongues loosened by some refrigerative hocus-pocus as yet unknown to science, would undoubtedly emulate Tillie and demand similar coddling. Two courses presented themselves; I could either scream the house down and prepare it for the contingency, or I could bear the brunt singlehanded—i.e., get back into bed and let things take their course. The latter plainly being the coward's way, I adopted it at once. Between various distractions, I neglected to check the icebox the next morning, but now, as I lay there sleepless, I knew that every second of delay was calamitous. With the stealth of a Comanche, I swung my feet over the side of the bed and stood up on a standard apricot poodle who happened to be dozing there. He emitted a needle-sharp yelp.

"Shut up, damn you," I hissed through my teeth, immediately tempering it with a placatory "Good boy, good boy." The brute subsided, or pretended to, until I closed the bedroom door behind me; then, convinced I was sneaking off on a coon hunt or some other excursion without him, he started excitedly clawing the panels. I permitted him to follow and, when we were well out of earshot of his mistress, gave him a kick in the belly to teach him obedience. The moment I opened the refrigerator door, I sensed mischief was afoot. Clipped to an earthenware bowl of rice pudding was a note scrawled in a shaky, nearly illegible hand. "Dear Chef," it said breathlessly, "you're living in a fool's paradise. You wouldn't believe some of the things that go on in this box—the calumny, the envy, the chicanery. They're all against me because I have raisins. Ish ka bibble—I had raisins when that Nova Scotia salmon in the upper tier was a fingerling in the Bay of Fundy. But don't take my word, just look around for yourself. Nuf sed. A Friend."

A quick scrutiny of the various compartments revealed that something was indeed very much awry. Two bunches of celery had worked their way out of the freezer, where they normally lay, and stood jammed in a cluster of milk bottles. A mayonnaise jar had been emptied of its rightful contents and was half-filled with goose fat, hinting at the possibility of foul play. It wasn't any one single factor—the shreds of icy vapor or the saucer of frozen gravy, as bleak as Lake Baikal—but the interior was filled with a premonitory hush of the sort that precedes a cyclone or a jail break. All of a sudden, as I racked my wits for some

clandestine method of eliciting the true state of affairs, the perfect solution hit me—my tape recorder. I could secrete it in the adjacent
kitchen cabinet, run the microphone inside disguised as a potato knish,
and overnight astound the world with its first documentary on talking
groceries. The thought of the millions I was scheduled to make in royalties, the *brouhaha* in the press and the acclaim of learned societies, and
the chagrin of my enemies when I was elevated to a niche beside that
of Steinmetz so dizzied me that I had to drink a split of Dr. Dadirrian's
Zoolak to recover. True, I felt a bit anthropophagous as I swallowed it,
and I half expected a gurgled Levantine outcry, but nothing more dramatic than a slight attack of double vision ensued, and within minutes
I had the mechanism hooked up and ready to function.

"Now, then," I ordered the poodle, flicking on the switch, "back to
the hay we go. Better be up bright and early before someone finds this
and misinterprets it."

"Applesauce," he retorted. "It's your recorder, isn't it?"

"Sure," I said, "but you know how silly peop— *What did you say?*" Of
course, he dried up then, not another word out of him, and you'd have
thought the cat had his tongue.

I GOT to bed pretty perplexed about the whole thing and, what with
fear lest I oversleep and worry at the quantity of current the machine
was using, fell into a wretched slumber that terminated around daylight.
Hastening to the kitchen, I downed some black coffee, and rewound the
spool of tape to get the playback. The first few revolutions were unpro-
ductive of anything but conspiratorial whispers and an occasional word
too jumbled to decipher. Then, all at once, I heard a low-pitched voice
in the background, oily and yet pompous, stiff with disdain.

"Beggars on horseback," it was saying contemptuously. "Strictly
keeping up appearances. I spotted him and the Missis right away the
day they came into the delicatessen. She was wearing an old Persian-
lamb coat, remodelled. 'Something in the way of a cocktail snack,
Greengrass,' she says, yawning like she's Mrs. T. Markoe Robertson.
'I'll take a two-ounce jar of that domestic caviar.' Then she turns to her
husband, which he's nervously jingling the change in his pants, and she
says, 'Dear, don't you think it would be amusing to have a slice or two
of Novy for our guests?' Well, the poor *shmendrick* turned all different
colors when the boss weighed me on the scales. Five cents more and
he'd have had to walk home in the rain like a Hemingway hero."

"Listen," rejoined a grumpy bass voice that unmistakably proceeded from a forsaken bottle of horseradish. "Stick around as long as I have and nothing these people do will surprise you. Why, one time we had a rack of lamb in here seven weeks. The plumber had to cut it out with a blowtorch."

A mincing, rather overbred voice, of the sort usually associated with Harvard beets, chimed agreement. "There's one thing that doesn't get stale here, though," it said. "Club soda. How long can he last on that liquid diet of his?"

"Forever, if he don't fall down and cut himself," the lox replied with a coarse guffaw.

"Can't you make less noise, please?" put in a hateful, meaching soprano. "I haven't closed an eye. I'm just a bundle of nerves ever since my operation—"

"Pssst, there goes Tillie again," warned the horseradish. "Pipe down or she'll write him another note. The little sneak repeats everything you say." A hubbub of maledictions and recriminations broke out, the upshot of which I never heard. Quivering with fury, I stripped the tape off the reel, ran into the living room, and flung it on the embers in the hearth. Specks of assorted hues swam before my eyes; it was unendurable that I should have nourished such vipers in my bosom. Drastic steps were indicated, and I was the boy who could take them. As I flew back to the refrigerator, bent on evicting the whole kit and caboodle without mercy, I caromed off my wife, huddled in a plain wrapper, for all the world like a copy of "Lady Chatterley's Lover," and gaping at the recorder.

"Wh-what happened?" she stammered. "What are you doing with that microphone in the icebox?"

WELL, I learned one lesson from the episode; suavity is lost on women. There isn't a blessed one, from the Colonel's Lady to Judy O'Grady, capable of dealing with abstract ideas, and if you try a civilized, worldly approach, it just antagonizes them. Can you imagine a person getting so huffy that she barricades herself in a henhouse and refuses to breakfast with her own husband? I made a meal off a few odds and ends—a grapefruit and a couple of eggs—but I can't say much for their dialogue. You need someone you can really talk to.

1953

EINE KLEINE MOTHMUSIK

War on Moths Begins

The moths are beginning to eat. Even if the weather seems cool, this is their season for gluttony. Miss Rose Finkel, manager of Keystone Cleaners at 313 West Fifty-seventh Street, urges that these precautions be taken:

All winter clothes should be dry-cleaned, even if no stains are apparent. Moths feast on soiled clothes, and if a garment has been worn several times in the last few months, it should be cleaned.

Clean clothes may be kept in the closet in a plastic bag. It is safer, however, to send all woolens to a dry cleaner to put in cold storage.

Customers should check to make sure that their clothes are really sent to a cold storage and not hung in the back of the store.

—The Times.

Gay Head,
Martha's Vineyard, Mass.,
July 14

Mr. Stanley Merlin,
Busy Bee Cleaners,
161 Macdougal Street,
New York City

DEAR MR. MERLIN:

I heard on the radio this morning before I went for my swim that the heat in New York is catastrophic, but you wouldn't guess it up here. There is a dandy breeze at all times, and the salt-water bathing, as you can imagine, is superlative. Miles of glorious white beach, marvellous breakers, rainbow-colored cliffs—in short, paradise. One feels so rested, so completely purified, that it seems profane to mention anything as sordid as dry cleaning. Still, that's not exactly your problem, is it? I have one that is.

Do you, by chance, remember a tan gabardine suit I sent in to be pressed three or four years ago? It's a very expensive garment, made of that changeable, shimmering material they call solari cloth. The reverse side is a reddish color, like cayenne pepper; during the British occupation of India, as you doubtless know, it was widely used for officers' dress uniforms. Anyway, I'm a trifle concerned lest moths get into the closet where I left it in our apartment. The suit isn't really stained, mind you; there's just a faint smudge of lychee syrup on the right sleeve, about the size of your pinkie, that I got in a Chinese restaurant last winter. (I identify it only to help you expunge it without too much friction. I mean, it's a pretty costly garment, and the nap could be damaged if some boob started rubbing it with pumice or whatever.)

Will you, hence, arrange to have your delivery boy pick up the suit at my flat any time next Thursday morning after nine-fifteen? He'll have to show before ten-twenty, since the maid leaves on the dot and would certainly split a gusset if she had to sit around a hot apartment waiting for a delivery boy. (You know how they are, Mr. Merlin.) Tell the boy to be sure and take the right suit; it's hanging next to one made of covert cloth with diagonal flap pockets, and as the Venetian blinds are drawn, he could easily make a mistake in the dark. Flotilla, the maid, is new, so I think I'd better explain which closet to look in. It's in the hall, on his right when he stands facing the bedroom windows. If he stands facing the other way, naturally it's on his left. The main thing, tell him, is not to get rattled and look in the closet *opposite*, because there may be a gabardine suit in there, without pockets, but that isn't the one I have reference to.

Should Flotilla have gone, the visiting super will admit your boy to the flat if he arrives before eleven; otherwise, he is to press our landlord's bell (Coopersmith), in the next building, and ask them for the key. They can't very well give it to him, as they're in Amalfi, but they have a Yugoslav woman dusting for them, a highly intelligent person, to whom he can explain the situation. This woman speaks English.

After the suit is dry-cleaned—which, I repeat, is not essential if you'll only brush the stain with a little moist flannel—make certain that it goes into cold storage at once. I read a piece in the newspaper recently that upset me. It quoted a prominent lady in your profession, a Miss Rose Finkel, to the effect that some dry cleaners have been known to hang such orders in the back of their store. You and I have had such a long, cordial relationship, Mr.

Merlin, that I realize you'd never do anything so unethical, but I just thought I'd underscore it.

Incidentally, and since I know what the temperature in your shop must be these days, let me pass on a couple of hot-weather tips. Eat lots of curries—the spicier the better—and try to take at least a three-hour siesta in the middle of the day. I learned this trick in India, where Old Sol can be a cruel taskmaster indeed. That's also the place, you'll recall, where solari cloth used to get a big play in officers' dress uniforms. Wears like iron, if you don't abuse it. With every good wish,

Yours sincerely,
S. J. PERELMAN

New York City,
July 22

DEAR MR. PEARLMAN:

I got your letter of instructions spelling everything out, and was happy to hear what a glorious vacation you are enjoying in that paradise. I only hope you will be careful to not run any fishhooks in your hand, or step in the undertow, or sunburn your body so badly you lay in the hospital. These troubles I personally don't have. I am a poor man with a wife and family to support, not like some people with stocks and bonds that they can sit in a resort all summer and look down their nose at the rest of humanity. Also my pressing machine was out of commission two days and we are shorthanded. Except for this, everything is peaches and cream.

I sent the boy over like you told me on Thursday. There was no sign of the maid, but for your information he found a note under the door saying she has quit. She says you need a bulldozer, not a servant, and the pay is so small she can do better on relief. Your landlady, by the way, is back from Amalfi, because some of the tenants, she didn't name names, are slow with the rent. She let the boy in the apartment, and while he was finding your red suit she checked over the icebox and the stove, which she claims are very greasy. (I am not criticizing your housekeeping, only reporting what she said.) She also examined the mail in the bureau drawers to see if the post office was forwarding your bills, urgent telegrams, etc.

I don't believe in telling a man his own business. Mine is dry cleaning, yours I don't know what, but you're deceiving yourself about this Indian outfit you gave us. It was one big stain from top to bottom. Maybe you leaned up against the stove or the icebox? (Just kidding.) The plant used every kind of solvent they had on it—benzine, naphtha, turpentine, even lighter fluid—and knocked out the spots, all right, but I warn you beforehand, there are a few brownish rings. The lining was shot to begin with, so that will be no surprise to you; according to the label, you had the suit since 1944. If you want us to replace same, I can supply a first-class, all-satin quarter lining for $91.50, workmanship included. Finally, buttons. Some of my beatnik customers wear the jacket open and don't need them. For a conservative man like yourself, I would advise spending another eight dollars.

As regards your worry about hiding cold-storage articles in the back of my store, I am not now nor have I ever been a chiseller, and I defy you to prove different. Every season like clockwork, I get one crackpot who expects me to be Santa Claus and haul his clothing up to the North Pole or someplace. My motto is live and let live, which it certainly is not this Rose Finkel's to go around destroying people's confidence in their dry cleaner. Who is she, anyway? I had one of these experts working for me already, in 1951, that nearly put me in the hands of the receivers. She told a good customer of ours, an artist who brought in some hand-painted ties to be rainproofed, to save his money and throw them in the Harlem River. To a client that showed her a dinner dress with a smear on the waist, she recommends the woman should go buy a bib. I am surprised that you, a high-school graduate, a man that pretends to be intelligent, would listen to such poison. But in this business you meet all kinds. Regards to the Mrs.

Yours truly,
S. MERLIN

Gay Head, Mass.,
July 25

DEAR MR. MERLIN:
   While I'm altogether sympathetic to your plight and fully aware that your shop's an inferno at the moment—I myself am wearing

an imported cashmere sweater as I write—I must say you misin-
terpreted my letter. My only motive in relaying Miss Stricture's
finkels (excuse me, the strictures of Miss Finkel) on the subject of
proper cold storage was concern for a favorite garment. I was not
accusing you of duplicity, and I refuse to share the opinion, widespread among persons who deal with them frequently, that most
dry cleaners are crooks. It is understandably somewhat off-putting
to hear that my suit arrived at your establishment in ruinous condition, and, to be devastatingly candid, I wonder whether your boy
may not have collided with a soup kitchen in transit. But each of
us must answer to his own conscience, Merlin, and I am ready, if
less than overjoyed, to regard yours as immaculate.

Answering your question about Miss Finkel's identity, I have
never laid eyes on her, needless to say, though reason dictates that
if a distinguished newspaper like the *Times* publishes her counsel,
she must be an authority. Furthermore, if the practice of withholding clothes from cold storage were uncommon, why would
she have broached the subject at all? No, my friend, it is both useless and ungenerous of you to attempt to undermine Miss Finkel.
From the way you lashed out at her, I deduce that she touched you
on the raw, in a most vulnerable area of our relationship, and that
brings me to the core of this communication.

Nowhere in your letter is there any direct assertion that you *did*
send my valuable solari suit to storage, or, correlatively, that you
are *not* hiding it in the back of the store. I treasure my peace of
mind too much to sit up here gnawed by anxiety. I must therefore
demand from you a categorical statement by return airmail special
delivery. Is this garment in your possession or not? Unless a definite answer is forthcoming within forty-eight hours, I shall be
forced to take action.

> Yours truly,
> S. J. PERELMAN

> New York City,
> July 27

DEAR MR. PERLEMAN:
      If all you can do with yourself in a summer place is hang indoors
and write me love letters about Rose Finkel, I must say I have pity

on you. Rose Finkel, Rose Finkel—why don't you marry this woman that you are so crazy about her. Then she could clean your suits at home and stick them in the icebox—after she cleans that, too. What do you want from me? Sometimes I think I am walking around in a dream.

Look, I will do anything you say. Should I parcel-post the suit to you so you can examine it under a microscope for holes? Should I board up my store, give the help a week free vacation in the mountains, and bring it to you personally in my Cadillac? I tell you once, twice, a million times—it went to cold storage. I didn't send it myself; I gave orders to my assistant, which she has been in my employ eleven years. From her I have no secrets, and you neither. She told me about some of the mail she found in your pants.

It is quite warm here today, but we are keeping busy and don't notice. My tailor collapsed last night with heat prostration, so I am handling alterations, pressing, ticketing, and hiding customers' property in the back of the store. Also looking up psychiatrists in the Yellow Pages.

Yours truly,
S. MERLIN

Gay Head, Mass.,
July 29

DEAR MR. MERLIN:

My gravest doubts are at last confirmed: You are unable to say unequivocally, without tergiversating, that you *saw* my suit put into cold storage. Knowing full well that the apparel was irreplaceable, now that the British Raj has been supplanted—knowing that it was the keystone of my entire wardrobe, the *sine qua non* of sartorial taste—you deliberately entrusted it to your creature, a cat's-paw who you admit rifles my pockets as a matter of routine. Your airy disavowal of your responsibility, therefore, leaves me with but one alternative. By this same post, I am delegating a close friend of mine, Irving Wiesel, to visit your place of business and ferret out the truth. You can lay your cards on the table with Wiesel or not, as you see fit. When he finishes with you, you will have neither cards nor table.

It would be plainly superfluous, at this crucial stage in our association, to hark back to such petty and characteristic vandalism as your penchant for jabbing pins into my rainwear, pressing buttons halfway through lapels, and the like. If I pass over these details now, however, do not yield to exultation. I shall expatiate at length in the proper surroundings; viz., in court. Wishing you every success in your next vocation,

Yours truly,
S. J. PERELMAN

New York City,
August 5

DEAR MR. PERLMAN:

I hope you received by now from my radiologist the two X-rays; he printed your name with white ink on the ulcer so you should be satisfied that you, and you alone, murdered me. I wanted him to print also "Here lies an honest man that he slaved for years like a dog, schlepped through rain and snow to put bread in his children's mouths, and see what gratitude a customer gave him," but he said there wasn't room. Are you satisfied now, you Cossack you? Even my *radiologist* is on your side.

You didn't need to tell me in advance that Wiesel was a friend of yours; it was stamped all over him the minute he walked in the store. Walked? He was staggering from the highballs you and your bohemian cronies bathe in. No how-do-you-do, explanations, nothing. Ran like a hooligan to the back and turned the whole stock upside down, pulled everything off the racks. I wouldn't mind he wrecked a filing system it cost me hundreds of dollars to install. Before I could grab the man, he makes a beeline for the dressing room. So put yourself for a second in someone else's shoes. A young, refined matron from Boston, first time in the Village, is waiting for her dress to be spot-cleaned, quietly loafing through *Harper's Bazaar*. Suddenly a roughneck, for all she knows a plainclothesman, a junkie, tears aside the curtain. Your delegate Wiesel.

I am not going to soil myself by calling you names, you are a sick man and besides on vacation, so will make you a proposition. You owe me for cleaning the suit, the destruction you caused in my racks, medical advice, and general aggravation. I owe you for the suit, which you might as well know is kaput. The cold-storage people called me this morning. It seems like all the brownish rings in the material fell out and they will not assume responsibility for a sieve. This evens up everything between us, and I trust that on your return I will have the privilege of serving you and family as in years past. All work guaranteed, invisible weaving our specialty. Please remember me to your lovely wife.

Sincerely yours,
STANLEY MERLIN

1960

S. J. PERELMAN

MONOMANIA, YOU AND ME IS QUITS

MY immediate reaction when a head studded with aluminum rheostats confronted me over the garden gate last Tuesday morning was one of perplexity. That it belonged to a courier from outer space was, I felt, improbable, for nobody of such transcendent importance would have chosen a weedy Pennsylvania freehold to land on. Its features, moreover, were much too traditional for an interplanetary nuncio; instead of the elephant ears and needle-sharp proboscis that science fiction had prepared me for, the apparition exhibited a freckled Slavic nose and wattles ripened by frequent irrigations of malt. In the same instant, as I straightened up, giddy with the effort of extricating a mullein from the cucumbers, I realized that the spiny coiffure was in actuality a home permanent and the bulging expanse of gingham below it the rest of Mrs. Kozlich, our current cleaning woman.

"I hope I didn't scare you," she said tremulously, "but I thought I better drive over and speak to you personally. Something funny happened while you and the missus were away last weekend." She cast a quick, nervous glance about the surrounding eighty-three acres and lowered her voice. "A man burned a chair on your place Friday night."

"Yes, I know," I replied. "I meant to call you so you wouldn't be alar—"

"I was so frightened I almost fainted," she pursued, unheeding. "My niece Kafka and I were washing your upstairs windows around five o'clock when this station wagon came up the lane. I figured it was yours—"

"It was mine, Mrs. Kozlich," I gentled her. "Listen to me, will you? I made a special trip back from the city—on purpose—to *burn* that chair. Do you understand?"

It was obvious she didn't, or, even if she did, was determined not to be denied the opportunity of a dramatic recital. The car, she went on breathlessly, had traversed a long field adjacent to the barn, parking by the gulch where I file old paint cans, leaky gutters, and window screens for future reference. The driver (who bore a striking resemblance to me, the ladies decided from their distant vantage point) had then unloaded a large black easy chair, systematically disembowelled its upholstery, and, while they watched spellbound, set fire to it. "Go back there and look, if you don't believe me," she challenged. "The springs are laying all over the ground where he kicked them. After he drove out, I sent Kafka up and she found a couple of scraps like horsehide or something. It must have been a leather chair."

It was indeed, but what Mrs. Kozlich had witnessed, and what I prudently decided not to spell out for her, was the end of a dream—a romantic quest that began some twenty-two years ago. Just when or how my yearning for a tufted black leather armchair originated I cannot remember. Perhaps some elderly member of the Rhode Island medical profession, which I supported singlehanded as a boy, had one in his consulting room, or I may have seen the prototype, spavined with use, in the professorial chambers at Brown. At any rate, among the fantasies I nurtured into manhood—a princely income and a sleek, piratical schooner for cruising the Great Barrier Reef, to mention only two— was a clear-cut image of my ideal study. Its appointments varied from time to time; on occasion the walls were book-lined, or hung with rare trophies like Mrs. Gray's lechwe or a sitatunga, or again bare except for a few gems of Impressionist painting. The focus, the keystone of the décor, nonetheless, never varied—a capacious, swollen club chair, well polished, into whose depths one sank and somniferously browsed through the latest English review. There might be a revolving mahogany bookcase alongside, but I wasn't sure. I was afraid it might detract from the rich, baroque impact of the chair.

By the time I had acquired my own inglenook in the mid-thirties, though, and started prowling the auction rooms for my fictive *fauteuil,* I discovered it was a chimera. Curiosities of that sort, dealers pityingly confided, had vanished with the buffalo lap robe and congress gaiters. They offered me substitutes that awoke my outrage—knobby monstrosities of red plastic that tilted at the touch of a spring, slippery leatherette abstractions that pitchforked one into prenatal discomfort inches off the floor. The more I insisted, the more derisive they became. "Look, Grover Cleveland," one of them finally snapped at me after my third approach. "Harmoniums and water wings, diavolos and pungs we got, but Victorian easy chairs—*nyet*. And now, excuse me, will you? I have another nudnick here wants a round table like King Arthur's."

The first intimation that my will-o'-the-wisp, however unattainable, did in fact still exist came in 1938. Yawning through a Tim McCoy Western at a rural cinema in our township, I was suddenly electrified by the furnishings of the sheriff's office. Beside the period roll-top desk stood a voluptuously padded armchair, not only covered in black leather but (tears rose to my eyes) its outlines accented by brass nailheads. I whipped to my feet. "That's it! That's it!" I fluted, my voice gone contralto with agitation. "That's my chair!" I was so overwhelmed, to be candid, that it required the intervention of the manager to persuade me to resume my seat, and subsequent accounts, gleaned by my wife from local tradespeople, hinted I had succumbed to a Holy Roller seizure. Undaunted, I took care to note the production details of the film against some future visit to Hollywood, and chancing to be there shortly, at once proceeded to track down the chair. It was relatively simple. In a matter of minutes, Columbia's art department disclosed the name of the warehouse that supplied such props, and, cramming my pockets with enough rhino to vanquish any obstacle, I pelted over. The manager of the enterprise, a foxy-nose with a serried gray marcel that mounted like a linotype keyboard, was the soul of courtesy.

"Of course I remember the piece," he acknowledged silkily. "This way, please." The freight elevator discharged us in a shadowy loft on the sixth floor, where furniture of every conceivable epoch lay stored. He dove into the maze and yanked aside a dust cover. "There," he said. "Is this the one you mean?"

An inexpressible radiance suffused me. The chair was so much more beautiful than my cinematic memory that speech was inadequate. It was a haven, a refuge; I saw myself lolling in it, churchwarden poised, evolving new cosmogonies, quoting abstruse references to Occam's razor and Paley's watch. "Oh, God," I choked, extracting a fistful of bills. "I— You've made me so happy! How much?"

"How much what?" he asked woodenly.

I explained that I was prepared to buy it, to buy the whole warehouse if necessary. He uttered a sharp, sardonic hoot and bade me wipe my chin. "Not for sale, Buster," he said, replacing its shroud. "You know what this thing brings in every year in rentals? Why, last month alone it worked in 'Addled Saddles,' 'Drums Along the Yazoo'—"

Short of manacling myself to the chair, I used every inducement I could marshal to obtain it, including bribery, pleas of medical need, and threats of legal duress, but the man was intractable. I retired so crushed in spirit that I inclined to be somewhat paranoid about the subject over the ensuing decade. The world supply of tufted black leather, I frequently told my friends, was being manipulated by a small ring of interior decorators, men who would stick at nothing to bilk me. I was telling it to one of them, an advertising nabob and self-admitted expert in arranging the impossible, at a Turkish bath, when he brought me up short.

"Wait a minute," said Broomhead imperiously. "Outside of Hollywood or the Reform Club, are any of these chairs still extant?"

"Yes, in Washington," I said. "They've some honeys in the Senate corridors—the real McCoy, so to speak—but nobody could ever wangle—"

He produced a solid-gold pencil the diameter of a needle from his towel and scrawled a note on a masseur. "Relax," he commanded. "Your worries are over. I happen to know a politico or two down there who'd go pretty . . . far . . . out of his way to accommodate Curt Broomhead."

I automatically dismissed the assertion as bluster, until his secretary phoned me a month later. A certain Mr. X, whom it was inadvisable to identify, in an equally mysterious government bureau, was laid up with croup. On his recovery, he would promptly expedite the item requested by Mr. Tuftola, which, she whispered, was the pseudonym her boss had adopted for the transaction. While elated at the news, I experienced a vague malaise. It bothered me that some fine old lawgiver, a chivalrous Southerner out of George Cable, with a white imperial and arthritis, might be unceremoniously deposed from his chair because of my whim. I was also positive that I had heard a muffled click during our phone conversation, as though the line were bugged. Before I could cry peccavi and tout Broomhead off, however, the affair took on juggernaut momentum. Telegrams and messages proliferated, warning me that Mr. X's favor was in transit, and I received unmistakable assurance from a Chinese fortune cookie that destiny was arranging a surprise. A fortnight thence, two orangutans in expressmen's aprons dumped a formidable crate on the sidewalk outside our New York brownstone. After an ugly jurisdictional squabble, they departed, leaving the handyman and me to wrestle the shipment up three flights; after an uglier one, we did so, and he departed, leaving me to open it. I was ablaze with fever and salivating freely as I hacked through the excelsior wrappings, but I cooled off fast enough. Inside was a stiff and dismal board-room chair, welted with tacks, that belonged in a third-rate loan shark's office. The sticker on the reverse, however, implied otherwise. It read, "Property of U.S. State Dept."

To adduce proof that the husky, straw-hatted young man in gabardine who tailed me the whole next month was an F.B.I. operative is impossible, nor can I swear that my mail was fluoroscoped during that period. I do know that for a while I underwent all the tremors of a Graham Greene character on the run, even if it had no purificatory effect on my religious views. When my funk abated sufficiently to donate the chair to a charity bazaar, I arrived at a decision. The only way I could possibly attain my ideal was to have it custom made, and to that end I embarked on a secret layaway plan at the Coiners' and Purloiners' National. Early last summer, I took the accrual to a wholesaler friend in the Furniture Design Center, along with a steel engraving that embodied every curlicue I lusted for. He examined it tolerantly.

"It's your money, Sidney," he said, "but if I were you, I'd look around the auction rooms—"

I flung my hat on his showroom floor and stamped on it like Edgar Kennedy. "Stop!" I screamed. "Duplicate that chair and keep your goddam advice to yourself! If I need advice, I'll go to a shrinker!"

"You're overdue now," he observed, picking up a hassock to ward me off. "Okey-doke. It'll take six weeks. And don't call for it," he added quickly. "We'll deliver."

The result was not a masterpiece, as one applies the term to a floral group by Odilon Redon or the Khmer sculptures in the Musée Guimet, but it ran a close second. It was a paragon of cozy chairs, a marvel of the most intricate tufting, a monument to the upholsterer's art. You sank into its refulgent black bosom and were instantly permeated with *douceur de vivre* such as you had never known. Apothegms worthy of La Rochefoucauld tumbled from your lips, full-fashioned epigrams pleading to be encased in boxes in *McCall's* and *Reader's Digest*. True, it was a difficult chair to slumber in; at the beginning, its magnificence overawed me and I sat gingerly in it, holding at eye level a copy of Sir Samuel Baker's "The Albert Nyanza" in crushed levant. I then tried browsing through the latest English review, but somehow couldn't get past the adverts for Ovomalt and thermal underwear. At last, I found the key in Max Lerner's windy periods, and, lapped in his peristaltic rhetoric, slept like a baby. Once inside that chair, Lerner in hand, I was as remote from hypertension as from the Asiatic capitals where he bombinated.

When Buddha smiles and all is cotton candy, though, it is axiomatic that one edges toward the nearest cyclone cellar. Following a blissful week, my wife and I motored off to Willimantic to pick up a few spools of vintage thread. En route, she informed me that in our absence a new domestic had been instructed to give the flat a thorough cleaning. The place fairly gleamed when we tottered in the door; the rugs had been shampooed, the silver was burnished to diamond brilliance, and the furniture sparkled with a million highlights. As I stood openmouthed, like one of the carp at Fontainebleau, my wife issued from the kitchen, brandishing a note and a clotted paintbrush.

"A treasure! A dreamboat!" she chortled. "Guess what that girl did! She shellacked all the tables, even the breadboard and the stepladder! She worked two whole nights—"

"W-why is that sheet draped over my comfy chair?" I quavered.

"To protect it, stupid," she said impatiently. "I'm going to double her salary tomorrow, sign her to a lifetime contract—"

I leaped past her, whisked away the sheet, and was presented with a spectacle beyond description, beyond contemplation. The leather was piebald, marbleized with a scaly armor plate or orange-and-gray shellac bonded onto its surface for eternity. Never, even among the tortured vinyl-and-zebra abominations in the lowest borax showroom on East Eighth Street, had I beheld anything so loathsome. With a great cry, I sank to my knees, and, nuzzling one bulbous armrest, burst into racking sobs. Half an hour afterward, I slung a five-gallon can of kerosene into the rear of our wagon unmindful that it splattered the aspiration of a lifetime. Then I slammed up the tailgate and headed grimly downtown toward the Holland Tunnel.

1960

VLADIMIR NABOKOV

PNIN

THE elderly passenger sitting on the north-window side of that inexorably moving railway coach, next to an empty seat and facing two empty ones, was none other than Professor Timofey Pnin. Ideally bald, suntanned, and clean-shaven, he began rather impressively with that great brown dome of his, tortoise-shell glasses (masking an infantile absence of eyebrows), apish upper lip, thick neck, and strong-man torso in a tightish tweed coat, but ended, somewhat disappointingly, in a pair of spindly legs (now flannelled and crossed) and frail-looking, almost feminine feet.

His sloppy socks were of scarlet wool with lilac lozenges; his conservative black oxfords had cost him about as much as all the rest of his clothing (flamboyant goon tie included). Prior to the nineteen-forties, during the staid European era of his life, he had always worn long underwear, its terminals tucked into the tops of neat silk socks, which were clocked, soberly colored, and held up on his cotton-clad calves by garters. In those days, to reveal a glimpse of that white underwear by pulling up a trouser leg too high would have seemed to Pnin as indecent as showing himself to ladies minus collar and tie, for even when decayed Mme. Roux, the concierge of the squalid apartment house in the Sixteenth Arrondissement of Paris where Pnin had lived for a score of years after escaping from Leninized Russia, happened to come up for the rent while he was without his *faux col,* prim Pnin would cover his front stud with a chaste hand. All this underwent a change in the heady atmosphere of the New World. Nowadays, at fifty-five, he was crazy about sunbathing, wore sports shirts and slacks, and when crossing his legs would carefully, deliberately, brazenly display a tremendous stretch of bare shin. Thus he might have appeared to a fellow-passenger, but except for a soldier asleep at one end and two women absorbed in a baby at the other, Pnin had the coach to himself.

Now a secret must be imparted. Professor Pnin was on the wrong train. He was unaware of it, and so was the conductor, already threading his way through the train to Pnin's coach. As a matter of fact, Pnin at the moment felt very well satisfied with himself. When inviting him to deliver a Friday-evening lecture at Cremona—some two hundred versts west of Waindell, Pnin's academic perch—the vice-president of the Cremona Women's Club, a Miss Judith Clyde, had advised our friend that the most convenient train left Waindell at 1:52 P.M., reaching Cremona at 4:17. But Pnin—who, like so many Russians, was inordinately fond of everything in the line of timetables, maps, catalogues, and collected them, helped himself freely to them with the bracing pleasure of getting something for nothing, took especial pride in puzzling out schedules for himself—had discovered, after some study, an inconspicuous reference mark against a still more convenient train, "Lv. Waindell 2:19 P.M., Ar. Cremona 4:32 P.M.;" the mark indicated that Fridays, and Fridays only, the two-nineteen stopped at Cremona on its way to a distant and much larger city, graced likewise with a mellow Italian name. Unfortunately for Pnin, his timetable was five years old and in part obsolete.

He taught Russian at Waindell College, a somewhat provincial institution characterized by an artificial lake in the middle of a landscaped campus, by ivied galleries connecting the various halls, by murals displaying recognizable members of the faculty in the act of passing on the torch of knowledge from Aristotle, Shakespeare, and Pasteur to a lot of monstrously built farm boys and farm girls, and by a huge, active, buoyantly thriving German Department, which its head, Dr. Hagen, smugly called (pronouncing every syllable very distinctly) "a university within a university."

The enrollment in the Russian Language course consisted of three students only: Josephine Malkin, whose grandparents had been born in Minsk; Charles McBeth, a graduate student, whose prodigious memory had already disposed of ten languages and was prepared to entomb ten more; and languid Eileen Lane, whom somebody had told that by the time one had mastered the Russian alphabet one could practically read "Anna Karamazov" in the original. As a teacher, Pnin was far from being able to compete with those stupendous Russian ladies scattered all over academic America who, without having had any formal training at all, manage somehow, by dint of intuition, loquacity, and a kind of maternal bounce, to infuse a magic knowledge of their difficult and beautiful tongue into a group of innocent-eyed students in an atmosphere of Old Mother Volga songs, red caviar, and tea; nor did Pnin, as a teacher, even presume to approach the lofty halls of modern scientific linguistics— that temple wherein earnest young people are taught not the language itself but the method of teaching others to teach that method. No doubt Pnin's approach to his work was amateurish and lighthearted, depending as it did on a book of exercises in grammar brought out by the head of the Slavic Department in a far greater college than Waindell—a venerable fraud whose Russian was a joke but who would generously lend his dignified name to the products of anonymous drudgery. Pnin, despite his many shortcomings, had about him a disarming old-fashioned charm, which Dr. Hagen, his staunch protector, insisted before morose trustees was a delicate, imported article worth paying for in domestic cash. Whereas the degree in sociology and political economy that Pnin had obtained with some pomp at the University of Prague around 1920 had become by mid-century a doctorate in desuetude, he was not altogether miscast as a teacher of Russian. He was beloved not for any essential ability but for those unforgettable digressions of his, when he would remove his glasses to beam at the past while massaging the lenses of the present. Nostalgic excursions in broken English. Autobiographical tidbits. How Pnin came to the *Soedinyonnïe Shtatï* (the United States). "Examination on ship before landing. Very well! 'Nothing to declare?' 'Nothing.' Very well! Then political questions. He asks: 'Are you Anarchist?' I answer [time out on the part of the narrator for a spell of cozy mute mirth]: 'First, what do we understand under "Anarchism"? Anarchism practical, metaphysical, theoretical, mystical, abstract, individual, social? When I was young,' I say, 'all this had for me significa-tion.' So we had a very interesting discussion, in consequence of which I passed two whole months on Ellis Island [abdomen beginning to heave; heaving; narrator convulsed]."

But there were still better sessions in the way of humor. With an air of coy secrecy, benevolent Pnin, preparing the children for the marvellous treat that he had once had himself, and already revealing, in an uncontrollable smile, an incomplete but formidable set of tawny teeth, would open a dilapidated Russian book at the elegant leatherette marker he had carefully placed there; he would open the book, whereupon as often as not a look of the utmost dismay would alter his plastic features; open-mouthed, feverishly, he would flip right and left through the volume, and minutes might pass before he found the right page—or satisfied himself that he had marked it correctly after all. Usually, the passage of his choice came from some old and naïve comedy of merchant-class habitus rigged up by Ostrovski almost a century ago, or from an equally ancient but even more dated piece of trivial Leskovian jollity dependent on verbal contortions. He delivered these stale goods with the rotund gusto of the classical Alexandrinka Theatre in Petersburg, rather than with the crisp simplicity of the Moscow Artists, but since to appreciate whatever fun those passages still retained one had to have not only a sound knowledge of the vernacular but also a good deal of literary insight, and since his poor little class had neither, the performer would be alone in enjoying the associative subtleties of his text. The heaving we have already noted in another connection would become here a veritable earthquake. Directing his memory, with all the lights on and all the masks of the mind a-miming, toward the days of his fervid and receptive youth (in a brilliant cosmos that seemed all the fresher for having been abolished by one blow of history), Pnin would get drunk on his private wines as he produced sample after sample of what his listeners politely surmised was Russian humor. Presently, the fun would become too much for him; pear-shaped tears would trickle down his tanned cheeks. Not only his shocking teeth but an astonishing amount of pink upper-gum tissue would suddenly pop out, as if a jack-in-the-box had been sprung, and his hand would fly to his mouth while his big shoulders shook and rolled. And although the speech he smothered behind his dancing hand was now doubly unintelligible to the class, his complete surrender to his own merriment would prove irresistible. By the time he was helpless with it, he would have his students in stitches, with abrupt barks of clockwork hilarity coming from Charles, and a dazzling flow of unsuspected lovely laughter transfiguring Josephine, who was not pretty, while Eileen, who was, dissolved in a jelly of unbecoming giggles.

All of which does not alter the fact that Pnin was on the wrong train.

HOW should we diagnose Pnin's sad case? He, it should be particularly stressed, was anything but the type of that good-natured German platitude of last century, *der zerstreute Professor* (the absent-minded professor). On the contrary, he was perhaps too wary, too persistently on the lookout for diabolical pitfalls, too painfully on the alert lest his erratic surroundings (unpredictable America) inveigle him into some bit of preposterous oversight. It was the world that was absent-minded and it was Pnin whose business it was to set it straight. His life was a constant war with insensate objects that fell apart, or attacked him, or refused to function, or viciously got themselves lost as soon as they entered the sphere of his existence. He was inept with his hands to a rare degree, but because he could manufacture in a twinkle a one-note mouth organ out of a pea pod, make a flat pebble skip ten times on the surface of a pond, shadowgraph with his knuckles a rabbit (complete with blinking eye), and perform a number of other tame tricks that for some reason or other Russians have up their sleeves, he believed himself endowed with considerable manual and mechanical skill. On gadgets he doted with a kind of dazed, superstitious delight. Electric devices enchanted him. Plastics swept him off his feet. He had a deep admiration for the zipper. But after a storm in the middle of the night had paralyzed the local power station, the devoutly plugged-in clock would make nonsense of his morning. The frame of his spectacles would snap in midbridge, leaving him with two identical pieces, which he would vaguely attempt to unite, in the hope, perhaps, of some organic marvel of restoration coming to the rescue. The zipper a gentleman depends on most would come loose in his puzzled hand at some nightmare moment of haste and despair.

And he still did not know that he was on the wrong train.

A special danger area in Pnin's case was the English language. Except for such not very helpful odds and ends as "The rest is silence," "Never more," "weekend," "*Who's Who,*" and a few ordinary words and phrases like "cat," "street," "fountain pen," "gangster," "the Charleston," and "marginal utility," he had had no English at all at the time he left France for the States. Stubbornly he sat down to the task of learning the language of Fenimore Cooper, Edgar Allan Poe, Edison, and thirty-one Presidents. In 1945, at the end of one year of study, he was proficient enough to use glibly terms like "wishful thinking" and "okey-dokey." By 1946, he was able to interrupt his narrations with the phrase "To make a long story short." By the time Truman entered his second term, Pnin could handle quite a number of elegant clichés, but otherwise progress seemed to have stopped despite all his efforts, and in 1953 his English was still full of flaws. That autumn, he supplemented the usual courses of his academic year by delivering a weekly lecture in a so-called symposium ("Wingless Europe: A Survey of Contemporary Continental Culture") directed by Dr. Hagen. All our friend's lectures, including sundry ones he gave out of town, were edited by one of the younger members of the German Department. The procedure was somewhat complicated. Professor Pnin laboriously translated his own Russian verbal flow, teeming with idiomatic proverbs, into patchy English. This was revised by young Miller. Then Dr. Hagen's secretary, a Miss Eisenlohr, typed it out. Then Pnin deleted the passages he could not understand. Then he read it to his weekly audience. He was utterly helpless without the prepared text, nor could he use the ancient system of dissimulating his infirmity by moving his eyes up and down—snapping up an eyeful of words, reeling them off to his audience, and drawing out the end of one sentence while diving for the next. Pnin's worried eye would be bound to lose its bearings. Therefore he read his lectures, his gaze glued to his text, in a slow, monotonous baritone that seemed to climb one of those interminable flights of stairs used by people who dread elevators.

THE conductor, a gray-headed, fatherly person with steel spectacles placed rather low on his simple, functional nose and a bit of soiled adhesive tape on his thumb, had now only three coaches to deal with before reaching the last one, where Pnin rode.

Pnin in the meantime had yielded to the satisfaction of a special Pninian craving. He was in a Pninian quandary. Among other articles indis-

pensable for a Pninian overnight stay in a strange town, such as shoe
trees, apples, and dictionaries, his Gladstone bag contained a relatively
new black suit he planned to wear that night for the lecture ("Are the
Russian People Communist?") before the Cremona ladies. It also contained next Monday's symposium lecture ("Don Quixote and Faust"),
which he intended to study the next day, on his way back to Waindell,
and a paper by a graduate student, Betty Bliss ("Dostoevski and Gestalt
Psychology"), that he had to read for Dr. Hagen. The quandary was as
follows: If he kept the Cremona manuscript—a sheaf of typewriter-size
pages, carefully folded down the center so as to fit into a pocket of his
coat—on his person, in the security of his body warmth, the chances
were, theoretically, that he would forget to transfer it from the coat he
was wearing to the one he would wear. On the other hand, if he placed
the lecture in the pocket of the suit in the bag *now*, he would, he knew,
be tortured by the possibility of his luggage being stolen. On the third
hand (these mental states sprout additional forelimbs all the time), he
carried in the inside pocket of his present coat a precious wallet with two
ten-dollar bills, the newspaper clipping of a letter he had, with my help,
written to the *Times* in 1945 anent the Yalta conference, and his certifi-
cate of naturalization, and it was physically possible to pull out the wallet, if needed, in such a way as to fatally dislodge the folded lecture.
During the twenty minutes he had been on the train, our friend had already opened his bag twice to play with his various papers. When the
conductor reached the car, diligent Pnin was perusing with difficulty
Betty's latest effort, which began, "When we consider the mental climate
wherein we all live, we cannot but notice—"

The conductor entered, did not awake the soldier, promised the
women he would let them know when they were about to arrive, and
presently was shaking his head over Pnin's ticket. The Cremona stop
had been abolished two years before.

"Important lecture!" cried Pnin. "What to do? It is a cata-stroph!"

Gravely, comfortably, the gray-headed conductor sank into the opposite seat and consulted in silence a tattered book full of dog-eared inser-
tions. Finally he said that in a few minutes—namely, at three-eight—Pnin
would have to get off at Whitchurch; this would enable him to catch the
four-o'clock bus that would deposit him, around six, at Cremona.

"I was thinking I gained twelve minutes, and now I have lost nearly
two whole hours," said Pnin bitterly. Upon which, clearing his throat
and ignoring the consolation offered by the kind gray-head ("You'll
make it"), he collected his stone-heavy bag and repaired to the vestibule

of the car, to wait there for the confused greenery skimming by to be cancelled and replaced by the definite station he had in mind.

WHITCHURCH materialized as scheduled. A hot, torpid expanse of cement and sun lay beyond the geometrical solids of various clean-cut shadows. The local weather was unbelievably summery for October. Alert, Pnin entered a waiting room of sorts, with a needless stove in the middle, and looked around. In a solitary recess one could make out the upper part of a perspiring young man who was filling out forms on the broad wooden counter before him.

"Information, please," said Pnin. "Where stops four-o'clock bus to Cremona?"

"Right across the street," briskly answered the employee, without looking up.

"And where possible to leave baggage?"

"That bag? I'll take care of it."

And with the national informality that always nonplussed Pnin, the young man shoved the bag into a corner of his nook.

"Quittance?" queried Pnin, Englishing the Russian for "receipt"— "*kvitantzia.*"

"What's that?"

"Number?" tried Pnin.

"You don't need a number," said the fellow, and resumed his writing.

Pnin left the station, satisfied himself about the bus stop, and entered a coffee shop. He consumed a ham sandwich, ordered another, and consumed that, too. At exactly five minutes to four, having paid for the food but not for an excellent toothpick, which he carefully selected from a neat little cup in the shape of a pine cone near the cash register, Pnin walked back to the station for his bag.

A different man was now in charge. The first had been called home, the new man explained, to drive his wife in all haste to the maternity hospital. He would be back in a few minutes.

"But I must obtain my valise!" cried Pnin.

The substitute was sorry but could not do a thing.

"It is there!" cried Pnin, leaning over and pointing.

This was unfortunate. He was still in the act of pointing when he realized that he was claiming the wrong bag. His index wavered. That hesitation was fatal.

"My bus to Cremona!" cried Pnin.

"There is another at eight," said the man.

What was our poor friend to do? Horrible situation! He glanced streetward. The bus had just come. The engagement meant an extra fifty dollars. His hand flew to his right flank. It was there, *slava Bogu* (thank God)! Very well! He would not wear his black suit, *vot i vsyo* (that's all). He would retrieve it on his way back. He had lost, dumped, shed many more valuable things in his day. Energetically, almost lightheartedly, Pnin boarded the bus.

He had endured this new stage of his journey for only a few city blocks when an awful suspicion crossed his mind. Ever since he had been separated from his bag, the tip of his left forefinger had been alternating with the proximal edge of his right elbow in checking a precious presence in his inside coat pocket. All of a sudden, he brutally yanked out the folded sheets. They were Betty's paper.

Emitting what he thought were international exclamations of anxiety and entreaty, Pnin lurched out of his seat. Reeling, he reached the exit. With one hand, the driver grimly milked out a handful of coins from his little machine, refunded him the price of the ticket, and stopped the bus.

Poor Pnin landed in the middle of a strange town. He was less strong than his powerfully puffed-out chest might imply, and the wave of hopeless fatigue that suddenly submerged his top-heavy body, detaching him, as it were, from reality, was a sensation not utterly unknown to him. He found himself in a damp green park, of the formal and funereal type, with the stress laid on sombre rhododendrons, glossy laurels, sprayed shade trees, and closely clipped lawns, and hardly had he turned in to an alley of chestnut and oak, which the bus driver had curtly told him led back to the railway station, than that eerie feeling, that tingle of unreality, overpowered him completely. Was it something he had eaten? That pickle with the ham? Was it a mysterious disease that none of his doctors had yet detected? My friend wondered, and I wonder, too.

I DO not know if it has ever been noted before that one of the main characteristics of life is discreteness. Unless a film of flesh envelops us, we die. Man exists only insofar as he is separated from his surroundings. The cranium is a space traveller's helmet. Stay inside or you perish. Death is divestment, death is communion. It may be wonderful to mix with the landscape, but to do so is the end of the tender ego. The sensation poor Pnin experienced was something very like that divestment, that communion. He felt porous and pregnable. His chest hurt. He was sweating. He was terrified. A stone bench among the laurels saved him from collapsing on the sidewalk. Was his seizure a heart attack? I doubt it. For the nonce, I am his physician, and let me repeat, I doubt it. My patient was one of those singular and unfortunate people who regard their heart ("a hollow, muscular organ," according to the gruesome definition in Webster's New Collegiate Dictionary, which Pnin's orphaned bag contained) with a queasy dread, a nervous repulsion, a sick hate, as if it were some strong, slimy, untouchable monster that one had to put up with, alas. Occasionally, when puzzled by his tumbling and tottering pulse, doctors had examined him more thoroughly, and the cardiograph had outlined fabulous mountain ranges and indicated a dozen fatal diseases that excluded one another. He was afraid of touching his own wrist. He never attempted to sleep on his left side, even in those dismal hours of the night when the insomniac longs for a third side after trying the two he has.

And now, in the park of Whitchurch, Pnin felt what he had felt already on August 10, 1942, and May 18, 1937, and May 18, 1929, and July 4, 1920—that the repulsive automaton he lodged had developed a consciousness of its own, and not only was grossly alive but was causing him pain and panic. He pressed his poor bald head against the stone back of the bench and recalled all the past occasions of similar discomfort and despair. Could it be pneumonia this time? He had been chilled to the bone a couple of days before in one of those hearty American drafts that a host treats his guests to after the second round of drinks on a windy night. And then suddenly Pnin (was he dying?) found himself sliding back into his childhood. This sensation had the sharpness of retrospective detail that is said to be the dramatic privilege of drowning individuals, especially in the former Russian Navy—a phenomenon of suffocation that a veteran psychoanalyst, whose name escapes me, has explained as being the subconsciously evoked shock of one's baptism, which causes an explosion of intervening recollections between the first immersion and the last. It all happened in a flash, but there is no way of rendering it in less than so many consecutive words.

PNIN came from a respectable, fairly well-to-do St. Petersburg family. His father, Dr. Pavel Pnin, an eye specialist of some repute, had once had the honor of treating Leo Tolstoy for a case of conjunctivitis. Timofey's mother, a frail, nervous little person with a waspy waist and bobbed hair, was the daughter of the once famous revolutionary Umov (rhymes with "zoom off") and of a German lady from Riga. Through his half swoon, Pnin saw her approaching eyes. It was a Sunday in midwinter. He was eleven. He had been preparing lessons for his Monday classes at the First *Gymnasium* when a strange chill pervaded his body. His mother took his temperature, looked at her child with a kind of stupefaction, and immediately called her husband's best friend, the pediatrician Sokolov. He was a small, beetle-browed man, with a short beard and a crew cut. Easing the skirts of his frock coat, he sat down on the edge of Timofey's bed. A race was run between the Doctor's fat golden watch and Timofey's pulse (an easy winner). Then Timofey's torso was bared, and to it the Doctor pressed the icy nudity of his ear and the sandpapery side of his head. Like the flat sole of some monopode, the ear ambulated all over Timofey's back and chest, gluing itself to this or that patch of skin and then stomping on to the next. No sooner had the Doctor left than Timofey's mother and a robust servant girl with safety pins between her teeth encased the distressed little patient in a strait-jacket-like compress. It consisted of a layer of soaked linen, a thicker layer of absorbent cotton, and another of tight flannel, with a sticky, diabolical oilcloth—the hue of urine and fever—coming between the clammy pang of the linen next to his skin and the excruciating squeak of the cotton around which the outer layer of flannel was wound. A poor cocooned pupa, Timosha (Tim) lay under a mass of additional blankets; they were of no avail against the branching chill that crept up his ribs from both sides of his frozen spine. He could not close his eyes because his eyelids stung so. Vision was but oval pain with oblique stabs of light; familiar shapes became the breeding places of evil delusions. Near his bed was a four-section screen of varnished wood, with pyrographic designs representing a lily pond, a bridle path felted with fallen leaves, an old man hunched up on a bench, and a squirrel holding a reddish object in its front paws. Timosha, a methodical child, had often wondered what that object could be (a nut? a pine cone?), and now that he had nothing else to do, he set himself to solve this dreary riddle, but the fever that hummed in his head drowned every effort in pain and panic. Still more oppressive was his tussle with the wallpaper. He had always been able to see that in the vertical plane a combination made up of three different clusters of purple flowers and seven different oak leaves was repeated a number of times with soothing exactitude; but now he was bothered by the undismissible fact that he could not find what system of inclusion and circumscription governed the horizontal recurrence of the pattern; that such a recurrence existed was proved by his being able to pick out here and there, all along the wall from bed to wardrobe and from stove to door, the reappearance of this or that element of the series, but when he tried travelling right or left from any chosen set of three inflorescences and seven leaves, he forthwith lost himself in a meaningless tangle of rhododendron and oak. It stood to reason that if the evil designer—the destroyer of minds, the friend of fever—had concealed the key of the pattern with such monstrous care, that key must be as precious as life itself and, when found, would regain for Tim his everyday health, his everyday world, and this lucid—alas, too lucid—thought forced him to persevere in the struggle.

A sense of being late for some appointment as odiously exact as school, dinner, or bedtime added the discomfort of awkward haste to the difficulties of a quest that was grading into delirium. The foliage and the flowers, with none of the intricacies of their warp disturbed, appeared to detach themselves in one undulating body from their pale-blue background, which, in its turn, lost its papery flatness and dilated in depth till the spectator's heart almost burst in response to that expansion. He could still make out through the autonomous garlands certain parts of the nursery more tenacious of life than the rest, such as the lacquered screen, the gleam of a tumbler, the brass knobs of his bedstead, but these interfered even less with the oak leaves and rich blossoms than would the reflection of an inside object in a windowpane with the outside scenery perceived through the same glass. And although the witness and victim of these phantasms was tucked up in bed, he was, in accordance with the twofold nature of his surroundings, simultaneously seated on a bench in a green-and-purple park. During one melting moment, he had the sensation of holding at last the key he had sought, but, coming from very far, a rustling wind, its soft volume increasing as it ruffled the rhododendrons, confused whatever rational pattern Timofey Pnin's surroundings had once had. He was alive and that was sufficient. The back of the bench against which he still sprawled felt as real as his clothes, or his wallet, or the date of the Great Moscow Fire—1812.

A gray squirrel sitting on comfortable haunches on the ground before him was sampling a peach stone. The wind paused, and presently stirred the foliage again.

The seizure had left him a little frightened and shaky, but he argued that had it been a real heart attack, he would have surely felt a good deal more unsettled and concerned, and this roundabout piece of reasoning

completely dispelled his fear. It was now four-twenty. He blew his nose
and trudged back to the station.

The initial employee was back. "Here's your bag," he said cheerfully.
"Sorry you missed the Cremona bus."

"At least"—and what dignified irony our unfortunate friend tried to
inject into that "at least"—"I hope everything is good with your wife?"

"She'll be all right. Have to wait till tomorrow, I guess."

"And now," said Pnin, "where is located the public telephone?"

The man pointed with his pencil as far out and sidewise as he could
without leaving his lair. Pnin, bag in hand, started to go, but he was
called back. The pencil was now directed streetward.

"Say, see those two guys loading that truck? They're going to Cremona right now. Just tell them Bob Horn sent you. They'll take you."

SOME people—and I am one of them—hate happy endings. We feel
cheated. Harm is the norm. Doom should not jam. The avalanche
stopping in its tracks a few feet above the cowering village behaves not
only unnaturally but unethically. Had I been reading about this mild
old man, instead of writing about him, I would have preferred him to
discover, upon his arrival at Cremona, that his lecture was not this Friday but the next. Actually, however, he not only arrived safely but was
in time for dinner—a fruit cocktail to begin with, mint jelly with the
anonymous meat course, chocolate syrup with the vanilla ice cream.
And soon afterward, surfeited with sweets, wearing his black suit, and
juggling three papers, all of which he had stuffed into his coat so as to
have the one he wanted among the rest (thus thwarting mischance by
mathematical necessity), he sat on a chair near the lectern while, at the
lectern, Judith Clyde, an ageless blonde in aqua rayon, with large, flat
cheeks stained a beautiful candy pink and two bright eyes basking in
blue lunacy behind a rimless pince-nez, presented the speaker.

"Tonight," she said, "the speaker of the evening— This, by the way,
is our third Friday night; last time, as you all remember, we all enjoyed
hearing what Professor Moore had to say about agriculture in China.
Tonight we have here, I am proud to say, the Russian-born, and citizen of this country, Professor—now comes a difficult one, I am
afraid—Professor Pun-neen. I hope I have it right. He hardly needs
any introduction, of course, and we are all happy to have him. We
have a long evening before us, a long and rewarding evening, and I am
sure you would all like to have time to ask him questions afterward.

Incidentally, I am told his father was Dostoevski's family doctor, and
he has travelled quite a bit on both sides of the Iron Curtain. Therefore I will not take up your precious time any longer and will only add
a few words about our next Friday lecture in this program. I am sure
you will all be delighted to know that there is a grand surprise in store
for all of us. Our next lecturer is the distinguished poet and prose
writer Miss Linda Lacefield. We all know she has written poetry,
prose, and some short stories. Miss Lacefield was born in New York.
Her ancestors on both sides fought on both sides in the Revolutionary War. She wrote her first poem before graduation. Many of her
poems—three of them, at least—have been published in 'Response,' a
collection of a hundred love lyrics by American women. In 1922, she
published her first collection, 'Remembered Music.' In 1924, she received the cash prize offered by—"

But Pnin was not listening. A faint ripple stemming from his recent
seizure was holding his fascinated attention. It lasted only a few heart-
beats, with an additional systole here and there—last, harmless
echoes—and was resolved in demure reality as his distinguished hostess invited him to the lectern. But while it lasted, how limpid the vision
was! In the middle of the front row of seats he saw one of his Baltic
aunts, wearing the pearls and the lace and the blond wig she had worn
at all the performances given by the great ham actor Khodotov, whom
she had adored from afar before drifting into insanity. Next to her, shyly
smiling, sleek dark head inclined, gentle brown gaze shining up at Pnin
from under velvet eyebrows, sat a dead sweetheart of his, fanning herself with her program. Murdered, forgotten, unrevenged, incorrupt,
immortal, many old friends were scattered throughout the dim hall
among more recent people, such as Miss Clyde, who had modestly regained a front seat. Vanya Bedniashkin, shot by the Reds in 1919, in
Odessa, because his father had been a liberal, was gaily signalling to his
former schoolmate from the back of the hall. And in an inconspicuous
situation Dr. Pavel Pnin and his anxious wife, both a little blurred but
on the whole wonderfully recovered from their obscure dissolution,
looked at their son with the same life-consuming passion and pride
that they had looked at him with that night in 1912 when, at a school
festival commemorating Napoleon's defeat, he had recited (a bespecta-
cled lad all alone on the stage) a poem by Pushkin.

The brief vision was gone. Old Miss Herring, retired professor of
history, author of "Russia Awakes" (1922), was bending across one or
two intermediate members of the audience to compliment Miss Clyde

on her speech, while from behind that lady another twinkling old party was thrusting into her field of vision a pair of withered, soundlessly clapping hands.

1953

GEORGE S. KAUFMAN

ANNOY KAUFMAN, INC.

FOR some time now, I have suspected the existence of an organization whose scope and energies are so enormous that they stagger the imagination. I am not prepared to say with certainty that such an organization exists, but there are various recurrent phenomena in my life that can be explained only by the theory that a major plan is in operation— plan so vast and expensive that it is almost impossible to envision it.

The organization that carries out this plan must spend millions of dollars annually to achieve its object. It has—it must have—great suites of offices, and thousands upon thousands of employees. On a guess, I would put its running cost at ten million dollars a year; if anything, the figure may be higher. With some presumption, I have christened it Annoy Kaufman, Inc., though I will admit that I cannot find that title in any lists of corporations.

But the facts are incontrovertible:

First, there is the matter of going to the bank. Let us say that I have run out of money and am required to cash a small check. Now, no one knows that I am going to the bank on that particular morning. There is nothing about it in the papers. I am not immodest, and I know that, at best, such an announcement would get only a few lines on a back page: "George S. Kaufman is going to the bank this morning to cash a check. We wish him all success"—something like that.

But not a word is printed. No one knows about it. As a matter of fact, I have probably not made up my mind to go until about eleven o'clock. Yet the organization is prepared. It immediately arranges that half a dozen big companies should be drawing their payroll money that morning, and that each of them should send a clerk to the bank with a list of payroll requirements—so many five-dollar bills, so many dollar bills, so many quarters, dimes, nickels, pennies. Next, it is arranged that all these people should get to the tellers' windows just a few seconds ahead of me.

Now, this takes doing. Remember, the organization has not known just which morning I was planning to go to the bank, so for weeks and weeks these clerks have been held in readiness somewhere. And suppose I stop to talk to a friend and arrive five minutes later than expected. Obviously, several relays of clerks must be kept in reserve in a corner of the bank, awaiting a signal.

Moreover, these are not people who are just pretending to be cashing payrolls; the bank would never stand for that. No, they are people from real companies—companies founded by the organization and kept in business for years and years, probably at an enormous loss, just so that their representatives can get to the bank windows ahead of me. And it is not always the same people who stand in front of me; it is different ones. This, in turn, means a large number of separate companies to maintain. These companies run factories, keep books, pay income taxes, hold board meetings, advertise on television, pension their employees. Surely this side of the enterprise alone must run to a pretty figure.

MY next example may sound like a simple and inexpensive thing to manage, but it isn't. It has to do with the engineer's little boy, Danny. Danny is six years old. In fact, he has been six years old for the thirty-five years that I have been making overnight train journeys. (I suppose that, actually, they keep on having an engineer's little boy born every year, but even that takes planning.) Anyhow, for years and years Danny has been begging his father to let him run the locomotive some night. For years and years, his father has been saying no. Then, finally, the night comes. "Can I run the engine tonight, Daddy?" asks Danny, who is too young to know about "can" and "may." And his father says, "Yes, Danny, boy. We have just got word that Kaufman will be on the train tonight, and he is very tired and needs a good night's sleep, so you can run the engine." So Danny runs the engine, the result being the neck-breaking stops and starts that keep me awake all night.

The organization has, of course, the incidental expense of maintaining Danny in Chicago or Pittsburgh or Cleveland, as the case may be, until I am ready to make the return trip. (Danny's father obviously cannot wait over to take care of him; he must go back to running the

engine properly on the nights when I am not travelling.) So the organization must keep branch offices in Chicago and Pittsburgh and
Cleveland (and wherever else I may go), and provide someone to take
care of Danny, and schools for him to go to, and somebody to make
sure that he doesn't practice, and so learn how to run the engine better,
before I make my return trip. This seemingly small part of the business
can run to fantastic sums over the years.

BUT the bank and Danny are, after all, relatively minor matters. Once
done with, they are over till the next time. I come now to the major
opus—the basic activity for which Annoy Kaufman, Inc., was founded.

Years ago, when I moved to New York, I noticed that a little man in
a gray overcoat was watching me closely as I took the ferry from Jersey
City to Twenty-third Street. I don't know why, but I think his name
was Mr. Moffat. At all events, Mr. Moffat was the first person off the
ferryboat when it docked. Hurriedly joining his pals in a midtown office, Mr. Moffat reported as follows: "Boys, he's here. We can take out
incorporation papers in Albany tomorrow and go to work. In a day or
two, I'll have all the dope for you."

Now, you may think it arrogant of me to claim that the entire re-
building of New York City, at present in full bloom, came about solely as
a result of my arrival here, but I can only cite the facts. No sooner did I
move to a given neighborhood than the wreckers were at work on the
adjoining building, generally at eight o'clock in the morning. The pneumatic asphalt-ripper, with which we are all now familiar, was first used
early one morning as a weapon against the slumber of none other than
myself. The first automatic rivet came into existence to be the destroyer
of my sleep. (All dates and names of streets are on file in the office of my
attorney.) Naturally, I kept moving to new neighborhoods in quest of
peace, but the boys were always ready and waiting. Can you blame me
for feeling that it was I, and I alone, who unwittingly charted the course
of the city's onward sweep?

Only once, in all these years, did they slip up. Acting without sufficient research, they put up Lever House just to the south of me, unaware
that my bedroom was on the other side of my apartment. Discovering
their error, they, of course, bought the property to the north and went
quickly to work. Well, sir, heads rolled in the office that morning, I can
tell you. Mr. Moffat, I like to think, shot himself, but I suspect he was
immediately succeeded by his son, and since then the organization has

functioned so efficiently that I am now exactly thirty-seven years behind on sleep, with only an outside chance of making it up.

WITH all that on their hands, you wouldn't think they'd have time for Congressional lobbying, too, would you? This ultimate move came to light during a visit of mine to Washington a few weeks ago. Having been made suspicious, over the years, by my dealings with the Internal Revenue people, I went to the trouble of looking up the original text of the income-tax law, as filed in the Library of Congress. Sure enough, there it was—Paragraph D, Clause 18—just as I had suspected: "The taxpayer, in computing the amount of tax due to the Government, may deduct from his taxable income all legitimate expenses incurred in the course of conducting his business or profession—except," it added, "in the case of George S. Kaufman."

1957

H. F. ELLIS

THE LAST REPOSITORY

OF the mental exercises, or fantasies, I indulge in to keep myself awake when I cannot sleep, perhaps the most useless runs as follows: I am the last adult left on earth, in charge of a huddle of children who will be the fathers and mothers of all future mankind. We are in some sort of safe place and have no immediate problems about survival or keeping out the rain. I don't know how we got there and I don't care, any more than I concern myself with the details of our daily life. I am too old now to picture myself as the kind of man who could carve fishhooks out of bones in an emergency. All that side of life is somehow provided for; nor am I answerable to anyone for a full explanation. If I were cooking up an imaginative novel, it would be different; fiction is sacred, fantasy is free. So, also, I am not compelled to account to myself for the fact that all knowledge has disappeared along with my contemporaries. All books, all instruments and apparatus, all drugs, vehicles, weapons, factories, pots, pans, and other relics of civilization have been destroyed or buried irretrievably under a thick layer of radioactive dust. I am the sole repository of the accumulated wisdom and experience of man, from pre-Sumerian times to the holocaust.

I feel the responsibility acutely, and often have to turn my pillow over to keep a cool head when I reflect that whatever I fail to pass on to my little band of orphans tumbling about so happily in the sun will be lost forever—or at best will have to be rediscovered by the slow and painful process of trial and error. It seems to me a terrible thing that the human race should have to wait another seven thousand years before safety matches are available again. I cannot bear to contemplate the repetition of the myriad ingenious fallacies and misapprehensions that have bedevilled the course of human history. It was some five thousand years after the dawn of civilization (which I take leave to date around the sixth millennium) before Empedocles produced the notion that earth, air, fire, and water were the four elements of which everything was composed, and got considerable credit for this error. More than two thousand years later, imponderables like phlogiston, caloric, and ether were still supposed to be at large in the universe, accounting for things. We do not want to plow our way through all that stuff again. And only I, tossing and turning in my lonely bed, can prevent it.

I must try to put my toddlers on the right lines about protons and neutrons, which is bound to involve some preliminary talk about electricity. And this again reminds me that I may not be spared long enough for their tiny minds to be ready for instruction about even so elementary a matter as winding wire around a magnetized iron core. I may be suffering from a touch of strontium 90, which could be a serious thing at my age. In case anything irremediable happens to me in the meantime, I ought to write these things down. I have paper and pencils in this fantasy, for I really cannot be bothered to improvise clay tablets at half past one in the morning. But what shall I write? Where shall I begin my task? The phrase "something irremediable" that came into my head just now is a pleasant Grecism for death and reminds me that the achievement of ancient Athens will be lost forever unless I put it down on paper. It is a question of time and evaluation. I find it extraordinarily difficult to decide whether Sophocles or safety matches should come first.

"Safety matches are a simple means of producing fire and are made by dipping thin pieces of wood into a brown mixture containing phosphorus," I see myself jotting down for posterity. "When the brown end is rubbed against some more of this brown stuff, a flame results and the piece of wood burns. Phosphorus is found in bones, if I remember rightly, and you will just have to keep on trying until you learn how to extract it."

This, to my surprise, is the best note I can write about the manufacture of matches without getting out of bed and consulting an encyclopedia. I should be sounder on Sophocles, I think, but it is hard to believe that a people still at the stage of rubbing sticks together would have time for Greek tragedy. I am constantly up against this problem of priorities. I desperately want, for instance, to give them a glimmering about airplanes, not caring to think about lives uselessly thrown away two thousand years hence in experiments with canvas frameworks attached to the arms. But it would be a long business, and at the end of it I doubt whether a machine made to my instructions would be stable in a high wind. How is it to be powered? I daresay I could set down the principle of the internal combustion engine in terms that would save time for these youngsters, once they had found out how to make steel, and I could add a footnote about jet propulsion for later on. It is the thought of the fuel that depresses me. When the whole human race is numbered in tens, or even in thousands, how does one present to them in an attractive light, as a worthwhile operation, the process of drilling tremendously deep holes in the earth on the off chance of finding a substance that is useless until you have cracked it?

I am up against much the same difficulty over drip-dry shirts. The truth seems to be that you have to have a population running into millions before anyone will take the trouble to make machines capable of producing millions of shirts. This is the kind of hard economic fact one comes up against around 3 A.M., when it begins to look as if the first essential step to be taken by my little group of survivors on the road back to civilization is to multiply as rapidly as possible. I do not feel, however, that I need give them any guidance about that.

SOMETIMES, at about this point in my fantasy, I half decide to concentrate on culture, eked out with a few simple conveniences made of wood. Aristotle's definition of tragedy; whatever of Shakespeare I have by heart; the principle of the lever; the golden section, if I can be sure of it; a rough sketch of a wheelbarrow—that would not be a contemptible contribution to the future of the race. I could add an appendix stating a few scientific facts (the sun is ninety-three million miles away; water boils at two hundred and twelve degrees Fahrenheit) for them to make what they liked of. But I can't be satisfied with it. There is a sense of waste, of irreparable loss. Before long I am stuck again with the old desire to give them *all* I know, convinced anew that I must take the long-term view, that in the long run the merest hint—a shadowy clue about the possibility of refrigeration, pneumatic tires, anesthetics, the telephone, dried milk—is better than the endless silence of the tomb. Am I to lie here like a hog, sheltering behind the lateness of the hour, and deprive millions yet unborn of the knowledge that trees cut up fine, boiled into a mash, and rolled out thin can be written on with ink?

I am now face to face with the appalling truth that I have no idea how ink is made. Is it conceivable that it is still harvested from deliberately frightened cuttlefish on extensive squid farms? If so, I shall never touch it again.

The danger of setting down information for a too distant posterity is that it may be disregarded in the meantime—even lost—or its purpose may be misconceived. I foresee, as the cocks begin to crow, the possibility that my notebooks, with their fragments of Tennyson's "Ulysses," their squiggled representations of sewing machines and teapots, the brave attempt at the binomial theorem, will within a few generations assume the status of legend, become the corpus of a world mythology. My notebooks may, though I rather hope not, found a new religion. My description of the random behavior of molecules in an expanded gas may be read out on feast days by some uncomprehending priest while the multitude prostrates itself in awe and terror.

This is a risk that I am prepared to take. Justice will in the end be done. Some Schliemann of the future, filled with burning faith, will unearth with his primitive spade the proof that my writings are as true as Homer's. "I have gazed," he will report in a dramatic smoke signal, "upon the veritable egg whisk of the Notebooks." This will cause a proper stir. The knowledge that the Notebooks are not Myth but Manual is bound to change the course of history. The tribe or clan that owns them, with the secret of the spoked wheel safe in its grasp, must inevitably predominate. My book will become the Book of Power—closely guarded, eagerly sought, probably fought for. The thought that my patient labor may well become the cause of World War IV sometimes, though not invariably, sends me to sleep.

1962

YMA DREAM

I N this dream, which I have had on the night of the full moon for the past three months, I am giving a cocktail party in honor of Yma Sumac, the Peruvian singer. This is strange at once, for while I have unbounded admiration for four-octave voices, I have never met Miss Sumac, and, even in a dream, it seems unlikely that I should be giving her a party. No matter. She and I are in the small living room of my apartment, on Charles Street, in Greenwich Village, and we are getting along famously. I have told her several of my Swedish-dialect stories, and she has reciprocated by singing for me, in Quechua, a medley of Andean folk songs. Other guests are expected momentarily. I have no idea, however, who any of them will be. Miss Sumac is wearing a blue ball gown and I am in white tie and tails. Obviously, despite the somewhat unfashionable neighborhood and the cramped quarters of my apartment, it is to be a pretty swell affair. In any case, I have spread several dishes of Fritos about the room, and on what is normally my typing table there is a bowl of hot *glügg*.

The doorbell rings. A guest! I go to the door, and there, to my astonished delight, is Ava Gardner. This is going to be a bit of all right, I think.

"Tom, darling!" she says, embracing me warmly. "How wonderful of you to have asked me."

In my waking hours, unfortunately, I have never met Miss Gardner. In my dream, though, my guests seem to know me rather intimately, while, oddly, none of them seem to know each other. Apparently it is their strong common affection for me that has brought them to Charles Street. For my part, although I immediately recognize each guest as he or she arrives, I have no memory of having ever met any of them, or, for that matter, of having invited them to a party in my apartment. On with the dream, however. "Miss Ava Gardner," I say, "I'd like you to meet Miss Yma Sumac."

"Charmed," says Miss Sumac.

"Delighted," counters Miss Gardner.

"Ah, but Tom," says Miss Sumac, with an enchanting laugh (which runs up the scale from E above middle C to C above high C), "let us not, on this of all occasions, be formal. *Por favor*, introduce each guest only by the first name, so that we may all quickly become—how shall I say?—*amigos*."

Typical Peruvian friendliness, I think, and reintroduce the two. "Ava, Yma," I say.

We sit around for some time, sipping *glügg* and munching Fritos. Things seem to be going well. The doorbell rings again. The second guest is a man—Abba Eban, the former Israeli Ambassador to the United Nations. Again I make the introductions, and, bowing to the wishes of the guest of honor, keep things on a first-name basis. "Abba, Yma; Abba, Ava," I say.

I stifle a grin, but neither Miss Sumac nor my two other guests see anything amusing in the exchange. We chat. The bell rings again, and I am pleased to find Oona O'Neill, Charlie Chaplin's wife, at the door. She is alone. I bring her into the room. "Oona, Yma; Oona, Ava; Oona, Abba," I say.

We are standing in a circle now, smiling brightly but not talking much. I sense a slight strain, but the party is young and may yet come to life. The bell again. It is another man—Ugo Betti, the Italian play-wright. A bit hurriedly, I introduce him to the circle. "Ugo, Yma; Ugo, Ava; Ugo, Oona; Ugo, Abba," I say.

Miss Sumac gives me an enigmatic glance that I try to interpret. Boredom? Thirst? No, she looks almost *irritated*. Hastily, I replenish everyone's glass. For some reason, I begin to hope that no other guests have been invited. The doorbell rings once again, however, and I open the door on two lovely actresses, Ona Munson and Ida Lupino. This gives me a happy inspiration for my introductions. "Ona and Ida," I say, "surely you know Yma and Ava? Ida, Ona—Oona, Abba." Damn! It doesn't come out even. "Ida, Ona—Ugo," I finish lamely.

I have scarcely given Miss Munson and Miss Lupino their first drinks when I am again summoned to the door. My guests stand stony-faced as I usher in the new arrival, the young Aga Khan. He is looking exceptionally well turned out in a dinner jacket with a plaid cummer-bund. Smiling too cheerfully, I introduce him to the waiting group. "Folks," I say, using a word I have always detested, "here's the Aga Khan! *You* know." But there is silence, so I must continue. "Aga—Yma, Ava, Oona, Ona 'n' Ida, Abba 'n' Ugo."

The Aga Khan and Mr. Eban, I notice, take an immediate dislike to each other, and I begin to feel an unmistakable pall descending over my party. I suggest a game of charades. This is met with glacial looks from everyone, including Miss Gardner, whose earlier affection for me has now totally vanished. When the doorbell rings this time, everybody turns and glares at the door. I open it and discover another pair—Ira Wolfert, the novelist, and Ilya Ehrenburg, the *Russian* novelist. The latter, I know, is quite a man-of-the-world, so I try a new approach. "Ilya," I say, "why don't you just introduce yourself and Ira? You know all these lovely people, don't you?"

"*Nyet,*" says Mr. Ehrenburg. "Can't say that I do."

"Oh, all *right,*" I say. "Ilya, Ira, here's Yma, Ava, Oona. Ilya, Ira— Ona, Ida, Abba, Ugo, Aga."

I ask Miss Sumac to sing for us. She refuses. We continue with the *glügg* and some hopelessly inane small talk. Mr. Eban and the Aga Khan stand at opposite sides of the room, eying each other. I begin to wish I'd never given the goddam party. Ona Munson jostles Ugo Betti's elbow by accident, spilling his drink. I spring forward to put them at their ease, whipping a handkerchief from my pocket. "Never mind!" I cry. "No damage done! Ugo, you go get yourself another drink. I'll just wipe this *glügg* off the, uh, *rügg.*" The guests fix me with narrowed eyes. At this moment, Eva Gabor, the Hungarian actress, sweeps through the door, which I have cleverly left open. Unaware of the way things are going, she embraces me and turns, beaming, to meet the others. Inevitably, I must make the introductions. I start rapidly. "Eva, meet Yma and Ava and Oona—" But then I find that Miss Gabor is pausing to hug each guest in turn, so I am forced to make the remaining introductions separately. "Eva, Ona; Eva, Ida; Eva, Ugo; Eva, Abba; Eva, Ilya; Eva, Ira; Eva, Aga."

This is a *terrible* party. All the men have bunched up. We stand in a circle, glowering at one another. I can think of nothing to say. I feel oddly hemmed in, like a man who is about to be stoned to death.

"Am I late?" asks the actress Uta Hagen gaily as she comes tripping into the room.

"No, no!" I say, gallantly taking her arm and steering her at once toward the punch bowl and away from the others.

"Please have the common decency to introduce your guests to one another," says Miss Sumac, in a cold monotone. "And in the proper manner."

In the dream, Yma Sumac seems to have some kind of hold over me, and I must do as she wishes. "O.K., O.K.," I snap crossly. "Uta, Yma; Uta, Ava; Uta, Oona; Uta, Ona; Uta, Ida; Uta, Ugo; Uta, Abba; Uta, Ilya; Uta, Ira; Uta, Aga; Uta, Eva." I turn to see if this has placated Miss Sumac, but she coldly ignores me. I have begun to hate her. Then I discover that the *glügg* has run out, and I am forced to offer my guests rye-and-7-Up. In the hope that no further company will arrive, I silently close the door. The bell rings instantly, however, and I feel a chill run down my spine. I pretend not to hear it.

"Answer the door," Miss Sumac says peremptorily. My circle of guests moves menacingly toward me. With a plummeting heart, I open the door. Standing before me, in immaculate evening dress, is a sturdy, distinguished-looking man. He is the Polish concert pianist Mieczyslaw Horszowski.

"Come in, Mieczyslaw!" I cry, with tears in my eyes. "I've never been so glad to see anyone in my whole life!"

And here always, my dream ends.

1962

ROGER ANGELL

AINMOSNI

INSOMNIA is my baby. We have been going steady for a good twenty years now, and there is no hint that the dull baggage is ready to break off the affair. Three or four times a week, somewhere between three and six in the morning, this faulty thermostat inside my head clicks to "On," raising my eyelids with an almost audible clang and releasing a fetid blast of night thoughts. Sighing, I resume my long study of the bedroom ceiling and the uninteresting shape (a penguin? an overshoe?) that the street light, slanting through the window, casts on the closet door, while I review various tedious stratagems for recapturing sleep. If I am resolute, I will arise and robe myself, stumble out of the bedroom (my wife sleeps like a Series E government bond), turn on the living-room lights, and take down a volume from my little shelf of classical pharmacopocia. George Eliot, James, and Montaigne are Nembutals, slow-acting but surefire. Thoreau, a dangerous Seconal-Demerol bomb, is reserved for emergencies; thirty minutes in the Walden beanfield sends me back to bed at a half run, fighting unconsciousness all the way down the hall. Too often, however, I stay in bed, under the delusion that sleep is only a minute or two away. This used to be the time for Night Games, which once worked for me. I would invent a No-Star baseball game, painstakingly selecting two nines made up of the least exciting ballplayers I could remember (mostly benchwarmers with the old Phillies and Senators) and playing them against each other in the deserted stadium of my mind. Three or four innings of walks, popups, foul balls, and messed-up double plays, with long pauses for rhubarbs and the introduction of relief pitchers, would bring on catalepsy. Other nights, I would begin a solo round of golf (I am a terrible golfer) on some recalled course. After a couple of pars and a brilliantly holed birdie putt, honesty required me to begin playing my real game, and a long search for my last golf ball, horribly hooked into the cattails to the left of the sixth green, would uncover, instead, a lovely Spalding Drowz-Rite. In time, however, some perverse sporting instinct began to infect me, and my Night Games became hopelessly interesting. As dawn brightened the bedroom, a pinch-hitter would bash a line drive that hit the pitcher's rubber and rebounded crazily into a pail of water in the enemy dugout, scoring three runs and retying the game, 17–17, in the twenty-first inning; my drive off the fourteenth tee, slicing toward a patch of tamaracks, would be seized in midair by an osprey and miraculously dropped on the green, where I would begin lining up my putt just as the alarm went off. I had to close up the ballpark and throw away my clubs; I was bushed.

It was an English friend of mine, a pink-cheeked poet clearly accustomed to knocking off ten hours' sleep every night, who got me into real small-hours trouble. He observed me yawning over a lunchtime Martini one day and drew forth an account of my ridiculous affliction. "I can help you, old boy," he announced. "Try palindromes."

"Palindromes?" I repeated.

"You know—backward-forward writing," he went on. "Reads the same both ways. You remember the famous ones: 'Madam, I'm Adam.' 'Able was I ere I saw Elba.' 'A man, a plan, a canal: Panama.' The Elba one is supposed to be about Napoleon. Here—I'll write it for you. You see, 'Able' backward is 'Elba,' and—"

"I know, I know," I snapped. "But what's that got to do with not sleeping? Am I supposed to repeat them over and over, or what?"

"No, that's no good. You must make up your own. Nothing to it. Begin with two-way words, and soon you'll be up to sentences. I do it whenever I can't sleep—'sleep' is 'peels,' of course—and in ten minutes I pop right off again. Never fails. Just now, I'm working on a lovely one about Eliot, the poet. 'T. Eliot, top bard . . .' it begins, and it ends, 'drab pot toilet.' Needs a bit of work in the middle, but I'll get it one of these nights."

I was dubious, but that night, shortly after four, I began with the words. In a few minutes, I found "gulp plug" (something to do with bass fishing) and "live evil," and sailed off into the best sleep I had enjoyed in several weeks. The next night brought "straw warts" and "repaid diaper," and, in time, a long if faintly troubled snooze ("ezoons"). I was delighted. My palindromic skills improved rapidly, and soon I was no longer content with mere words. I failed to notice at first that, like all sedatives, this one had begun to weaken with protracted use; I was doubling and tripling the dose, and my intervals given over to two-way cogitation were stretching to an hour or more. One morning, after a mere twenty minutes of second shut-eye, I met my wife at the breakfast table and announced, " 'Editor rubs ward, draws burro tide.' "

"Terrific," she said unenthusiastically. "I don't get it. I mean, what does it *mean?*"

"Well, you see," I began, "there's this editor in Mexico who goes camping with his niece, and—"

"Listen," she said, "I think you should take a phenobarb tonight. You look terrible."

It was about six weeks later when, at five-fifteen one morning, I discovered the Japanese hiding in my pajamas. "Am a Jap," he said, bowing politely, and then added in a whisper, "Pajama." I slept no more. Two nights later, at precisely four-eleven, when "Repins pajama" suddenly yielded "Am a Jap sniper," I sprang out of bed, brewed myself a pot of strong coffee, and set to work with pencil and paper on what had begun to look like a war novel. A month later, trembling, hollow-eyed, and badly strung out on coffee and Dexamyl, I finished the epic. It turned out that the thing wasn't about a Japanese at all; it was a long telegram composed by a schizophrenic war veteran who had been wounded at Iwo Jima and was now incarcerated in some mental hospital. (This kind of surprise keeps happening when you are writing palindromes, a literary form in which the story line is controlled by the words rather than the author.) Experts have since told me that my barely intelligible pushmi-pullyu may be the longest palindrome in the English language:

MARGE, LET DAM DOGS IN. AM ON SATIRE: VOW I AM CAIN. AM ON SPOT. AM A JAP SNIPER. RED, RAW MURDER ON G.I.! IGNORE DRUM. (WARDER REPINS PAJAMA TOPS.) NO MANIAC, MA! IWO VERITAS: NO MAN IS GOD.   —MAD TELEGRAM

MY recovery was a protracted one, requiring a lengthy vacation at the seashore, daily exercise, warm milk on retiring, and eventually a visit to the family psychiatrist. The head-candler listened to my story ("Rot-cod . . ." I began), then wrote out a prescription for a mild sedative (I murmured, "slip pils") and swore me to total palindromic abstinence. He told me to avoid Tums, Serutan, and men named Otto. "Only right thinking can save you," he said severely. "Or rather, *left-to-right* thinking."

I tried, I really tried. For more than a year, I followed the doctor's plan faithfully, instantly dropping my gaze whenever I began to see "POTS" and "KLAW" on traffic signs facing me across the street, and plugging away at my sleepy-time books when I was reafflicted with the Big Eye. I had begun to think that mine might be a total cure when, just two weeks ago, nodding over "Walden" again, I came upon this sentence: "We are conscious of an animal in us, which awakens in proportion as our higher nature slumbers. It is reptile and sensual, and perhaps cannot be wholly expelled. . . ."

"Ah-ha!" I muttered, struck by the remarkable pertinence of this thought to my own nocturnal condition. Thoreau himself had said it; I could never quite escape. To prove the point, I repeated my exclamation, saying it backward this time.

I did not entirely give way to my reptile. Remembering my near-fatal bout with the telegram, I vowed to limit myself entirely to revising and amplifying existing palindromes—those famous chestnuts recited to me by my English friend. The very next night, during a 4 A.M. rainstorm, I put my mind to "A man, a plan, a canal: Panama." Replacing de Lesseps with a female M.I.T. graduate, I achieved "A *woman*, a plan, a canal: Panamowa," which was clearly inadequate; she sounded more like a ballerina. Within a few minutes, however, a dog trotted out of the underbrush of my mind—it was a Pekinese—and suddenly redesigned the entire isthmus project: "A dog, a plan, a canal: pagoda." I went to sleep.

Napoleon led me into deeper waters. Bedwise by night light, I envisioned him as a fellow-sufferer, a veteran palindromist who must have been transfixed with joy to find the island of his first exile so brilliantly responsive to his little perversion. But what if the allies had marooned him on a *different* island in 1814? Various possibilities suggested themselves: "A dum reb was I ere I saw Bermuda." . . . "No lava was I ere I saw Avalon." . . . "Lana C. LaDaug was I ere I saw Guadalcanal."

None would do; the Emperor's aides, overhearing him, would conclude that the old boy had fallen victim to aphasia. A night or two later, I replaced Boney on Elba and retinued him with a useful and highly diversified staff of officers and loyal friends—a Rumanian, a female camp follower, a Levantine, and a German. These accompanied the Emperor by turns during his habitual evening walks along the cliffs, each feigning awe and delight as the impromptu musing of the day fell from his lips. "Uncomfortable was I ere I saw Elba, Trofmocnu," he confessed to the first. To the female, smiling roguishly and chucking her under the chin, he murmured, "Amiable was I ere I saw Elba, Ima." The next evening, made gloomy by the rabbinical sidekick, he changed to "Vegetable was I ere I saw Elba, Tegev." He cheered up with the burly Prussian, declaiming, "Remarkable was I ere I saw Elba, Kramer!," but, finding the same man on duty the following night (the list had run out, and new duty rosters were up), he reversed himself, whining, "*Un*remarkable was I ere I saw Elba, Kramer, *nu?*"

That seemed to exhaust Elba (and me), and during the wee hours of last week I moved along inevitably to "Madam, I'm Adam." For some reason, this jingle began to infuriate me. (My new night journeys had made me irritable and suspicious; my wife seemed to be looking at me with the same anxious expression she had worn when I was fighting the Jap sniper, and one day I caught her trying to sneak a telephone call to the psychiatrist.) Adam's salutation struck me as being both rude and uninformative. At first, I attempted to make the speaker more civilized, but he resisted me: "Good day, Madam, I'm Adam Yaddoog." . . . "Howdy, Madam, I'm Adam Y. Dwoh." . . . "*Bonjour,* Madam, I'm Adam Roujnoh." No dice. Who *was* this surly fellow? I determined to ferret out his last name, but the first famous Adam I thought of could only speak after clearing his throat ("*Htuis,* Madam, I'm Adam Smith"), and the second had to introduce himself just after falling down a flight of stairs ("*Y ksnilomray!* . . . Madam, I'm Adam Yarmolinsky"). Then, at exactly six-seventeen yesterday morning, I cracked the case. I was so excited that I woke up my wife. She stared at me, blurry and incredulous, as I stalked about the bedroom describing the recent visit of a well-known congressman to Wales. He had gone there, I explained, on a fact-finding trip to study mining conditions in the ancient Welsh collieries, perhaps as necessary background to the mine-safety bills now pending in Washington. Being a highly professional politician, he boned up on the local language during the transatlantic plane trip. The next morning, briefcase and homburg in hand, he tapped on the door of a miner's cottage in Ebbw Vale, and when it was opened by a lady looking very much like Sara Allgood in "How Green Was My Valley," he smiled charmingly, bowed, and said, "*Llewopnotyalc*, Madam, I'm Adam Clayton Powell."

When I got home last night, I found a note from my wife saying that she had gone to stay with her mother for a while. Aware at last of my nearness to the brink, I called the psychiatrist, but his answering service told me that he was away on a month's vacation. I dined forlornly on hot milk and Librium and was asleep before ten . . . and awake before three. Alone in bed, trembling lightly, I restudied the penguin (or over-shoe) on the wall, while my mind, still unleashed, sniffed over the old ashpiles of canals, islands, and Adams. Nothing there. Nothing, that is, until seven-twelve this morning, when the beast unearthed, just under the Panama Canal, the small but glittering prize, "Suez . . . Zeus!" I sat bolt upright, clapping my brow, and uttered a great roar of delight and despair. Here, I could see, was a beginning even more promising than the Jap sniper. Released simultaneously into the boiling politics of the Middle East and the endless affairs of Olympus, I stood, perhaps, at the doorway of the greatest palindromic adventure of all time—one that I almost surely would not survive. "No!" I whimpered, burying my throbbing head beneath the pillows. "No, no!" Half smothered in linen and sleeplessness, I heard my sirens reply. "On!" they called. "On, on!"

1969

PETER De VRIES

THE HIGH GROUND, OR LOOK, MA,

I'M EXPLICATING

WHEN the helpmate pointed out how I tended to mumble and grunt in confrontation with paintings and other works of art, and suggested I might try framing my reactions in more articulate English, or at least sentences that parsed, I was at first resentful. I remembered T. S. Eliot's remark about how he hated being pressed for his opinions when strolling through galleries and museums, preferring to accumulate and discharge them at his leisure, if at all. Yet that position is hardly tenable under circumstances such as formed the occasion for my wife's whispered stricture—the black-tie opening of a one-man retrospective that we attended with some newly acquired friends, Bill and Jessie Gmelch. Such an event is in its nature half social—something one cannot in all conscience negotiate with a mouthful of teeth. So I made an effort to hitch up my responses onto a plane more nearly approximating that of ordered evaluation—with results that surprised and, I must say, delighted me.

"What we have here seems to me an organic fusion of form and content," I said, of an oil before which we four collectively stood, shortly after the murmured complaint for which the helpmate had momentarily drawn me out of the Gmelches' hearing, "one in which linear and compositional values are also happily resolved. I like especially the juxtaposition of contrasts, which are at once subtle and intrepid, forthright without being obtrusive."

Bill Gmelch nodded, tapping against pursed lips a catalogue which he had rolled into a tube. "Hmm," Jessie said, gazing at the picture. I continued.

"The amalgamation of subject and object, which was but tentatively realized in the artist's earlier period—in such efforts as the 'Blue Configuration' over there, where an ostensibly abstract intention is still somewhat qualified by representational elements—seems to me consummately achieved in this more recent 'City Modality,' where the object qua object, the *Ding an sich,* if you will, disappears in the chromatic boil."

"Oh, there are the McConkeys," Jessie said, and made for the new arrivals, hastily followed by Bill. The helpmate again waited till they were out of earshot. Then she said, "Go back to the way you were."

This was more easily said than done. When a man has found his tongue on the level I had, the cat is not likely to get it again very soon. I could hardly wait for the next chance to practice my newly discovered gift, which was like a heady wine. It came the very next week when we attended an all-Chopin concert by a Brazilian pianist, again with the Gmelches.

"Like him?" Bill said in the lobby during the intermission, eying me warily as he shook a cigarette from a pack. "I think he's good. His reading of the sonata struck me as especially fine."

"Except in the slow movement," I said, "where I detected a certain viscosity in the phrasing. Also his tempi were at times heretical, to say the least, notably in the more reflective passages, where the lyrical intent of the original was distorted by an overinflation of its rhythmic values, I thought. I find the performance in general somewhat marred by a willful pyrotechnicality, which repeatedly sacrifices the composer's avowed melodic line to a heedless personal panache. Where is everyone going?"

Bill gesticulated through the doorway to a bar across the street, sucking back a large mouthful of smoke. "Time for a quick one before the buzzer."

I chased them through a light drizzle, shouting explications lost in the noise of the traffic and then that of the bar, which discouraged all but the small talk into which my three companions seemed, for some reason, eagerly to plunge. I listened with abstracted smiles to their gossip as I mentally drafted amplifications of the points I had raised. I was now beginning to wonder about Eliot. The pleasures of pontification were none he had ever passed up in his prose writings!

Something or other was causing a steady decline in the Gmelches' state of mind. They were in quite a foul humor when we got up to our place for a nightcap after the concert. I noticed them whispering angrily together in a corner of the living room, glancing in my direction and breaking off as I approached with brandies. Evidently a little domestic spat of some sort. It showed me how urgent the need for a bit of stimulating talk. A new novel, lying on a coffee table, offered just the opportunity.

"I felt it a distinct advance over the author's previous work," I said, "particularly compelling in its portrayal of the slob as counter-culture. Here the grubby romanticism of asphalt vagabondage, long familiar to us in a rash of 'road' fiction from those still into words, is elevated into an outright arraignment of the work ethos as more puritanic dregs. Especially notable are the scenes in which the protagonist takes to the streets and asks nonentities for their autographs, as Whitmanesque gestures of democracy. Would, alas, the style were more Whitmanesque."

They all watched in hangdog silence as I packed and lit a pipe.

"My quarrel is not that it's recycled Faulkner—what isn't these days!—but that rhetoric is, *en principe,* incongruous with so putatively skeptical a vision. Let me just get the book and read a passage illustrating—"

"No." Both Gmelches spoke as they rose simultaneously and stood with clenched fists, as though prepared to bar my passage to the book with physical force if necessary. "We have to toddle along," Bill said, levelly. "We have to get up tomorrow," Jessie explained. The helpmate now climbed to her feet, like a third guest I must see to the door. Until we actually reached it, there was the eeriest sense that she might indeed sail through it and out into the night, remembering only at the last moment that she lived here.

"Well, you've driven them away," she said when we were alone. "Probably for good. In God's name, can't you stop it? Talking like that?"

"It would be dishonest to guarantee anything. Once you've got the hang of something—"

"Then I'll guarantee something. That I can't take much more of this phase. Look. We're all going to the Bilkingtons' cocktail party Saturday, and you'd damn well better talk United States there, is all I can say, Buster."

THE helpmate's misgivings were not without foundation. Bo Bilkington is a tired businessman who encourages canards such as that he carries a hip flask to the opera. When he shakes hands, he will fold his fingers back two joints, so that you think you are grasping stumps, and say, with a laugh, "Lost 'em on a minesweeper." Saturday evening saw me being greeted again in that vein, and smilin' through in my own, as I rolled an eye around the apartment to see who was on deck. A large mixture of friends and strangers. Plucking a drink from a passing tray, I made for a group at the far end of the living room who were listening to an L.P. of some new poet reading his stuff—an album entitled "Vibes," of which I caught the last ten minutes.

"Like it?" Jenny Bilkington said, when the stereo had clicked off.

There were murmurs of approval, a few polite shrugs and exclamations. I could feel the helpmate's eye on me, though from behind. I made an effort to get a grip on myself. The brief, foredoomed struggle of a man hooked on exegesis. I cleared my throat as Jenny moved to play the flip side.

"I find it on the whole creditable of its kind, allowing for the element of naïveté in colloquial art generally," I said. "The style is basically folk collage rather than formalized song, of course. The use of slang, clichés, and the like, wedged arbitrarily into what systematic verse there is, offers a literary counterpart of the 'found objects' incorporated into contemporary junk sculpture—yet another example of the fragmentation that has marked our art for half a century, reflecting a dilapidated Western psyche. Each generation espouses its argot with more bravado than the last (the hippie lexicon is almost all cult verbiage), a development hardly surprising, for in the beginning may have been the word but the end is always jargon."

"How about that?" said Bo. He glanced wretchedly over at another group as he reached for his highball. "Let's—"

"I liked especially the passage beginning, 'What availeth it a lawn-mower?,' as a wry commentary on certain pernickety homeowning elements comprising in fact a culture in midslide. Also effective was the symbolism of the carpenter's apprentice who throws down his tools and leaves Scarsdale, as allusion to the current Jesus bag."

The plan to hear a little of the flip side was abandoned as the group dispersed, to re-form into smaller knots of muttering guests. One especially exercised little cluster, incidentally including Bill Gmelch, were shaking their heads and even their fists. A mob can be an ugly thing. I caught the words "be allowed out" and other such inflamed scraps. In this way the party now began to take more discernible shape. The helpmate grasped my hand at one point and towed me across the long living room to a group clear at the other end. "They're discussing movies," she said with a smile intended for public consumption, adding, through gritted teeth, "*thank God*."

That lot were talking about a picture I happened to have seen, and so was fortunately able to join in the conversation. A groan went up from some woman as I approached, probably someone bored with Al Herndon's two cents about the film, for he was holding forth in typical style on its merits. One thing is, he's loaded with inherited money, which always sets people's backs up. I stood with the flat of a hand against the wall, hearing him out like the rest.

"The art that conceals art," I said the instant Plentykins paused for breath, "is nowhere more important than in the cinema, where we have such a variety of techniques to keep scrupulously in line. I found both the photography and the direction in 'Bus to Scranton' obtrusive. The long coalpit and slag-heap shots were beautifully realized as anti-scenery, but the close-ups became much too studied, as did the raffishness of the male principal, whose exposition of the role was an uneasy hash of Bogart and Mastroianni, which any director worth his salt could have disciplined . . ."

AMONG the last to arrive, we were the first to leave. The helpmate seemed anxious to get me alone in a taxicab.

"Well, that tears it," she said as we sped for home. "Did you notice the Herndons and the Gmelches and the Bustamentes talking about getting theatre tickets to something and breaking it off when we came up? We'll never be invited anywhere again, except to a dogfight. I swear I don't know what makes you tick. One minute you're the soul of concession, the next you can't be budged, especially if it involves something that gives you some kind of subcutaneous gratification."

"Can I help it if it's my mature period?"

"Oh, God, who knows what anybody is like!" she said, ignoring me. "Before a woman can begin telling you what a prince you are, you've become a pain. You know what I think? *I* think," she went on, warming to her subject, "you mask a genuine aggression under a façade of compliance, and vice versa—a sort of basic insecurity inside this husk of independence. You seem unable to divorce your societal from your ego drives, your gregarious from your competitional . . ."

She can go on like that for days. Ah, well, it's an age of criticism, isn't it? It's nothing if not that.

1971

IAN FRAZIER

APARTMENT 6·A: AFTER THE FALL

IT has been over a year now since, in the wake of demoralizing setbacks, I finally abandoned my West Village apartment to the North Vietnamese. It was a time of great chaos. In my haste I had no choice but to leave behind hundreds of dollars' worth of appliances, clothing, and plants. The panic, the loss of my security deposit, getting my phone turned off, packing my small travelling bag, grabbing a taxi—all that seems like a dim nightmare to me now. But as the painful memories have lost some of their sharpness, my curiosity has grown. How has my apartment changed in the past year and a half? What have the Communists managed to make of the place where I sustained a free and democratic life for the better part of two years? I, of course, have not been allowed to visit my old pied-à-terre, but from accounts of Taiwanese businessmen and Belgian journalists who have been allowed in I have managed to piece together a picture of the new Apartment 6-A at 226 Waverly Place.

More than a year after its fall, 6-A appears to be an apartment still in transition. In the living room, the Communists have retained much of my furniture, including my stereo and my portable color-TV. All the furniture and appliances that used to belong to me have been registered and given identity cards. My two end tables have been removed, under the Communists' Return to Deco Shop of Origin program. My terra-cotta fish poacher and horseshoe-crab-shell lamps have been relocated out into the country. My couch has submitted to voluntary reuphol-stering. The Communists have kept all my record albums, and I am told that they play them a lot. My cat, Bill, who likes to watch pigeons, seems perfectly happy with his new name, Ho Chi Minh Domestic Animal. My clippings of "Ziggy" and "Today's Chuckle" are no longer taped to the refrigerator, and in their place are Communist maxims: "Advance in the Flush of Victory with New Vigor and Remember to Get an Extra Set of Keys Made!," "Strive Resolutely to Pick Up the People's Laundry Before Five!," and "Work for a Striking Development of Our Sunny Breakfast Nook!" In general, the kitchen has a more functional, lived-in look than before, when I mainly used it to prepare cans of Campbell's Chunky Beef Soup.

Among the more important dynamics at work in the redesign of my apartment is a division between two schools of thought in the Politburo of the Workers' Party. One school, the moderates, maintains that illit-erate peasants who have only recently emerged from the jungles and paddies after a twenty-year period of war and apartment-hunting can-not be expected to have any sense of design, style, color, or fabric, and that the new government should not be afraid to hire interior decora-tors who may be foreign-born or who even may not hold to the strict Communist Party line. The hard-liners, on the other hand, believe that coming up with a decorating scheme is well within the powers of the North Vietnamese Army, and that all they really have to do is put a couple of coats of barn-red deck paint on the floor, paint the walls and ceiling off-white, buy a couple of nice rugs and some hanging plants and some big pillows, and then get a wheel of Brie and throw a party to break the place in. A similar theoretical split exists among the members of the Phong-trao Phu-nu Giai-phong, or Freed Women Movement, whose efforts to fix the bathroom so that the cold-water pipe under the sink doesn't leak on the physical therapist in 5-A have been beset with problems. The moderates advocate trying Liquid-plumr or an Epoxi-Patch, while the hard-liners believe it is the landlord's problem, and if he doesn't do something about it pretty soon they favor going after the windshield of his Mercury Montego with a Volkswagen jack. At present, the moderates hold sway in most areas of the renovation of Apartment 6-A, and the success of their efforts over the next few months will very likely determine whether they or the hard-liners will continue to formulate apartment policy in such unresolved areas as the potentially divisive matchstick versus traditional-plastic-venetian window-blind issue.

In recent months, the Communists have been entertaining more—having more people over at Plenteous Rice Harvest Brunches and Revere Progressive Elders At-Homes, and guests have remarked that they notice a new atmosphere of hope in my former residence. After all, it's in a nice neighborhood, and it's convenient—right on the I.R.T.—and there are lots of things to do in the area, and the Communists have my list of sitters. They have a two-year lease on the place, so unless rent control is repealed the rent won't go up right away, and they also have a sublet clause, just in case they ever want to move on. It's a fairly safe part of town, and just a couple of blocks away there's a delicatessen that's open until two, where they sell Pepperidge Farm cookies, and there are some terrific new courses they can take at The New School, and things just might turn out to be not all that bad.

1976

GEORGE W. S. TROW

SPILL

A VICIOUS oil spill at Bergdorf's has ruined hundreds of pretty items. Swirling up at a rate of one thousand gallons a minute, the oil has ruined several slit-to-the-waist dresses in a silk crêpe de Chine that shimmers like a wicked smile in peach, auburn, dusky blue, and lemp. Attempts to cap the spill—the standby crew in painters' pants (tied at the ankle), Pure-As-Suède tool holders, construction caps, and red-red goggles—failed utterly, sending streams of thick crude into eyes, ears, mouths, *everywhere,* soiling *everything,* leaving a thick-thick residue on lips and fingertips.

The secondary effects are just beginning to be felt. Horrid oil balls, clumping together in several large masses, have moved up stairwells, emergency chutes, and steamways, to upper floors heretofore judged impervious to spills and mishaps, frustrating all attempts to preserve from damage hundreds of the prettiest possible snakeskin bags—clutch, over-the-shoulder on a whisper of a *string,* attached by *thongs* to wrist or belt, or tied about the neck. Refreshing!

Many things have been tried, naturally. Real oil riggers have set about to drill a relief hole, but they can't seem to get the hang of it. In fact, inside sources who nearly always know the *scoop* claim that the relief well is now gushing tens of thousands of gallons more of the rich, expensive crude over the new Laudanum Collection of antibacterial facial formulas, including Stripped Mask, Under-Glaze Country Bronzing Creme, and Laudanum Laurel, Laudanum Landscape, and Laudanum Lavalier unscented pure-as-pure moisturizing facilitators for regular, oily, and dry complexions. Some of the oil riggers have gone back to the Southwest, naturally, but others have come up with a new-cut overall, *full through the waist* but pegging, pegging down the leg. Flattering!

SOME of New York's top-top party people have tried to be helpful—organizing little teas, sending in relief crews, planning out mop-up operations, etc. Most just peek in, but one or two real friends won't leave the scene. Mrs. Freddy Boots, for instance, hasn't had a bath for days, won't change her slicker-smock, plunges in time after time in a reckless attempt to save some of the fabulous gabardine, which has really been completely ruined by the oil. Mrs. Boots takes each retrieved oily item and conducts an elaborate ritual, using enthusiastic young volunteers. First, each item is soaked in a harsh—almost unbearably harsh—acid bath to remove the oil from within the fine-weave gabardine. Then Mrs. Boots *very quickly* transfers the cloth—before it has a chance to utterly disintegrate in the harsh-harsh bath—into a soothing moisture-full solution of *entirely natural* ingredients: cool-as-silk mixtures of precious cress, dill, avocado, and arugula, for instance, undercut with just a tang of lemon to keep the vegetable matter from actually penetrating into the cloth fibre and rotting there. Despite her best efforts, this regimen hasn't worked out yet—the gabardine, horribly weakened by the acid bath, tends to blotch and then clump in the

vegetable moistures—but Mrs. Boots won't give up, and she plunges in
again and again, actually diving under the oil, where you can't get a
breath and where the terrible, powerful currents set in motion by the
flow of oil can suck you deep under in a minute or, *worse still*, send you
spinning up into one of the powerful jets of salt water that completely
inept temporary workers (many of them would-be buyers, assistant
buyers, and stylists) direct here and there almost at random in an attempt to reduce the viscosity.

Only the top-top party people understand.

"It's fabulous fabric," a child said—a child who is even now much
more popular and social than many mature people. "We may never see
gabardine like this again."

1980

BILL FRANZEN

HEARING FROM WAYNE

WHILE I was flipping through the day's mail after a real yawn fest
of a workday at the Stereo Shack, I came across something that
knocked me over like a good brushback pitch. It was a postcard from
Wayne, and I've really got to hand it to him, but before I get going on
Wayne's postcard and on Wayne and on how Wayne was my best friend
and just the whole incredible Wayne Story, I'd like to say right up front
that my *real* fear of any kind of hereafter is that instead of being sort of
reunited with my family and friends and everyone I've ever felt close to,
I'll get there and find myself in the middle of just casual acquaintances—
people I recognize, people I always said hi-how-you-doing to, but *nobody*
I ever felt close to. Like the guy from the luncheonette, kitty-corner from
the Stereo Shack, who makes the great two-story ham sandwiches,
plenty of mustard, but who I can't exactly say I'm attached to. He's a nice
guy and all, and I even gave him ten per cent on some speakers once, but
if he's the first person I see in the afterlife it'll be some letdown. And if I
reach life's nineteenth hole *before* him, and I'm the first one *he* sees, I can
understand how it'll sour the whole experience for him, too. I'd probably
try to duck before he saw me, but if he saw me ducking, that would be

pretty awful. I mean, imagine yourself popping through into extra innings, only to see one of your regular sandwich customers, who suddenly
ducks, pretends he doesn't know you, pretends you never made maybe
two hundred and ninety-seven ham sandwiches for him during his lifetime, plenty of mustard. Now, I can't tell from Wayne's postcard if the afterlife ever starts out that creepy for anyone, but if it does, it's just like
Wayne not to go into it. That's the way Wayne was, and one reason why
he was my best friend and one reason why he'll stay my best friend, especially if he can keep up this great second effort through the mail. He did
slip in a few comments about the afterlife on his card, but nothing that
would scare any of us still playing life's back nine.

On a snowy night one year ago, Wayne and I were sitting and water-
ing our faces in that Wild West bar called the Sitting Bull. Above the
bar, there's this giant painting of four Sioux Indians in big, flowing
headdresses riding in a gondola in Venice that Wayne was so crazy
about, and right in front of us those upside-down cowboy hats with the
barbecue-flavored party mix that we both liked. Wayne and I were
swapping stories about Harold, the Stereo Shack's only TV salesman
and a buddy from the Stereo Shack's softball team. Harold had recently
left the team and every other earthly organization after plowing smack
into an oak tree. He wasn't even supposed to be driving. This guy was a
narcoleptic, which means permission denied as far as getting your
hands on a wheel in this state goes. So anyway, old Wayne and I get to
wondering what Harold's .450 batting average is doing for him wherever he is now, and soon we're speculating as to what that wherever actually is and if it would be possible for a guy exiting to that place to
smuggle in a room equalizer. I explain to Wayne my fear of seeing just
people I kind of recognize there, but take-it-as-it-comes Wayne, of
course, says he's not worried, and laughs through a mouthful of party
mix. He says he's expecting something more like the best room they
have at the Ramada Inn in Fort Lauderdale, with telepathic models
bringing you and your best deceased pals frothy turquoise drinks just as
soon as you've all drained your clear orange ones.

Eventually, I get around to telling Wayne about Houdini and his
wife. I took this book out from the bookmobile once that was all about
the Houdinis conducting their own afterlife experiment. They went
and promised each other that the first one of them to die would do
everything possible to reach the one still alive. Well, Harry Houdini
died in 1926. And, according to the book, before Beatrice Houdini
died, in 1943, she admitted that she'd never heard from Harry and

called their experiment a failure. But Wayne, who I guess was feeling his boilermakers pretty well by then, says he loves the idea anyway, and he gets me to say "What the heck" and shake hands and then sign and date a Sitting Bull Bar cocktail napkin with him to cement our own pact, and a man next to us who's been muttering something about his sister making a thousand dollars a second seems glad to sign it, too.

WELL, that was a year ago. Then, a half year later, Wayne and I are locking up the Stereo Shack after a real gutterball of a business day when Wayne turns to me and says, "Let's call 'em." So we take turns calling our wives from a phone booth in the parking lot, and twenty cents later we're loose. There's some all-you-can-stand fish fry at the Sitting Bull, but it sounds a little too bush league to us. Instead, we drive out to Long Lake and smack two large buckets of balls each at Denny's Driving Range. Wayne uses a 3-wood, and after every swipe says—loud enough for everybody there including Denny to hear—"*That's* on the green." Then we go nearby for some Italian and a couple of pitchers of draught beer. Later, when we're cruising back in my Toronado with all the windows down, Wayne finds the head of a green toy soldier in my glove compartment. It's just this tiny little rubbery soldier head without a body that my kid, Timmy, probably left around, and it made us sort of laugh. Then Wayne puts it in his left nostril—just a little ways—so that the little army man could sort of look out, and then turns so they're both looking at me. And that really cracks me up. Next, Wayne says something like "Eyes on the road!" and snaps his head straight ahead, so that the soldier watches the road, and it's stupid, but we're giggling like high schoolers and tears are coming down. But then Wayne—gasping for air—sort of snorts inwards and the little head vanished and we had to drive right to Long Lake Hospital and it wasn't funny anymore. And the way it turned out, the inside of that hospital was the last thing on earth poor Wayne ever saw—at least in this life.

ANYWAY, Wayne's postcard is a miniature version of the big painting above the bar at the Sitting Bull—the one with the four Sioux Indians in headdresses riding in a gondola in Venice. Except that on Wayne's postcard there's a fifth passenger squeezed in between two of the Indians, and it's Wayne in his Stereo Shack softball uniform, smiling and with his cap on backwards. There wasn't a stamp or a postage mark anywhere on the card, but there was a decent-sized message in Wayne's usual slanty brand of printing. Wayne began by saying hi and saying he bet I was surprised he'd got ahold of me like we'd talked about and that he missed hanging out together, but that at least this was some kind of way to reach me. Then he asked if my Timmy was still playing Battle of the Bulge in the car, and wrote "ha ha" afterwards. He said that his notion of the hereafter being something like a room at the Ramada Inn in Fort Lauderdale was way off, except for the turquoise drinks. He said that the stereo systems there aren't nearly as impressive as you might expect, but added, "The acoustics in our modules are choice." He plays a lot of what he calls Cluster Ball there—"a potent blend of golf, bowling, and softball for large numbers," in his words. Then he advised me to get out in life and shake my tail feathers all I can, and said if I wanted to perform one especially decent act, I should tell the police that seventy-nine cats and eleven dogs are being kept inside a home at 281 South Brook Lane, about half a mile from Denny's Driving Range.

Finally, Wayne said it's really not so bad after your third strike and not to worry about it but just to stay loose and go with it and that everything will make a lot more sense to me when we meet up again— "more than you could ever imagine right now," Wayne wrote. Which was nice of Wayne to say, and another reason why he was my best friend and why he'll stay my best friend—regardless of whether or not he can keep up this great second effort through the mail.

1983

JACK HANDEY

STUNNED

As I looked through the telescope, I could hardly believe my eyes: There before me, in the constellation of Virgo, circling a medium-sized star, was a planet. And not just any planet. It had oceans and landmasses and polar ice caps, just like Earth.

And then it hit me: Not only was this planet a lot like Earth—it was *exactly* like Earth! It was an exact twin of our very own planet!

I was stunned. I had to walk away from the telescope. An exact copy of Earth! Were there people there? Were they like us? Did they have the same problems, the same hopes? When I finally summoned the courage to look again, I realized that I had been wrong. It wasn't exactly like Earth. The continents didn't have anywhere near the same shapes as ours, the oceans were different, and many other features were dissimilar. Still, it was a planet, and the first conclusive evidence of such outside our own solar system.

Then it hit me: According to my calculations, the entire planet—oceans, continents, and all—was only a mile in diameter, and rotating at more than twenty times per second. It was a world in miniature, spinning at a phenomenal rate of speed!

I was stunned. I sat back in my chair and rubbed my face in bewildered disbelief. After rechecking my calculations, I realized that I had been off on the size of the planet. It wasn't a miniature planet but was instead about the size of our own Earth. And it wasn't spinning as fast as I had originally calculated. In fact, it was spinning much slower—a little bit slower than our own planet. But that didn't dampen my enthusiasm.

What would I call this new planet? It had large blue oceans, continental landmasses, and polar ice caps, not unlike Earth. Then it hit me: This wasn't an exact duplicate of Earth but was very, very similar to an upside-down Earth!

I had to step back from the telescope and steady myself. I looked again, and it still looked like an upside-down Earth, but not as much as it had before. In fact, the more I looked at it, the clearer it became: My God, it wasn't an upside-down Earth likeness at all but an exact duplicate of Earth! I had been right in the first place!

I was stunned. But then I was struck by a thought that was even more devastating: What if it wasn't an exact copy of us but instead we were an exact copy of *it*? The possibilities were fantastic! What were we like, I wondered. Were we warlike? Did we look like humans?

So it was with great disappointment that I realized I had been aiming the telescope at a picture of Earth on the wall. I had been right after all: It *was* a duplicate of Earth. And yet it wasn't a planet. I sat back in my chair, stunned.

When I finally recovered, I began to scan the nighttime skies. What would I find? The possibilities were enormous—everything from an exact duplicate of Earth to a planet that, if you blurred your vision, might look quite similar to our own.

Then I saw it: If that wasn't a hologram of Earth, I don't know what was. But who could be projecting such a hologram? Were they like us? Did they have the same hopes and dreams and hologram projectors? Just as I was being stunned by all of this, I heard a voice: "Wake up, wake up!"

I woke up, and then it hit me: It had all been a dream. I had fallen asleep at the telescope. Then I went back to sleep for about three hours, and this time I didn't dream at all. But I woke up again, and I realized that the next-to-last nap had all been a dream. I was stunned.

"Hey, Bob," I said. "You wouldn't believe the dream I had two naps ago. I dreamed I discovered a planet that was just like our planet, Earth."

"Earth?" said Bob. "Our planet isn't called Earth. It's called Megatron."

I was stunned. What in the name of a supreme being exactly like God was going on here?

"No, wait—I was thinking of another planet," Bob said. "This *is* Earth."

Eagerly, I turned the telescope toward the sky. What new marvels were awaiting me up there, I wondered.

1987

GARRISON KEILLOR

———————————

HE DIDN'T GO TO CANADA

JUST as I was finishing college, in 1969, and was about to join the Marines, the Indiana National Guard made me a wonderful offer, via my father, to join their public-information battalion, and so, despite a lingering affection for those fighting in Vietnam, one bright June afternoon I drove my old Mustang to Fort Wayne to enlist along with my best friend, Kevin. A few miles out of Muncie, he lost his nerve and went to pieces. "I'll never make it," he said. "I'm sorry. I thought this could remain my secret, but I'm afraid that the stress of Guard training would crack me like a nut. You see, I have a flaw inside me, a dark place in my soul—something painful and unnamable that can only be eased by alcohol. Let me out of the car. I'm going to Canada." I let him off at the bus depot and never saw him again. Years later I heard that he had become very wealthy up there selling amphetamines but then ate a bad piece of meat and got worms and died an extremely painful death.

I went to Fort Wayne and reported to the address that the recruiter had given to my dad over the phone, a haberdasher's called Sid's Suit City, upstairs from a trophy plant in a cinder-block building. A little bald guy with a tape around his neck who looked as though his feet hurt stuck out his hand. I showed him my papers, and he showed me a nice green knit shirt (short-sleeved), a pair of yellow slacks, and white buck shoes with red tassels and cleats. "Those are golf clothes," I said.

He grabbed me by the neck and threw me up against the mirror and shoved his grizzled face within an inch of mine. "Don't tell me anything I don't ask you for first, you chicken doo. I own you, Mister. If I tell you to play golf, you reach for your clubs, Mister, and if I order you to order two big pepperoni pizzas and a six-pack of Bud, you jump to the phone and do it, Mister, and if I tell you to sit down and watch 'Andy Griffith,' 'Huckleberry Hound,' 'Leave It to Beaver,' and 'American Bandstand,' I don't want to catch you with a newspaper in your hand. You're in the Guard, understand? Good. Now take your face out of here and get it over to the Alhambra apartment complex, on West Cheyenne Drive. You're in 12-C. Beat it, and take your convertible with you. You're gonna need it."

He wasn't kidding about the golf. The next Monday morning, forty of us reported, bright-eyed and bushy-tailed, to Burning Bush Country Club and were each issued a set of Wally Hammar golf clubs and an electric cart and sent out to play. We were assigned to foursomes. Randy Qualey, Keith Quintan, and Dennis Quintz were in mine, and in the next couple of months we got to know each other like real buddies. We went out drinking together and everything. We shot eighteen holes every morning—sunny or cloudy, warm or cool, it made no difference.

Two months later, I was utterly fed up. I'd been promoted to corporal, but why wasn't I doing the job I'd joined the Guard to do: inform the public? Was it because of poor grades in college and a low score on the Guard entrance exam? Was it because of my inability to type? If the Guard didn't have confidence in me, why hadn't they let me go to Vietnam?

I talked it over with my dad, and he promised to look into the matter. Meanwhile, I met my wife at a dance. It was love at first sight. The next three months were the happiest of my life. Then one day I was called into Colonel Mills' office at ComInNatGu—the secret Guard command center housed in a complex of deep bunkers around the ninth hole. You entered through a tiny tunnel via a door marked "HIGH VOLTAGE: EXTREMELY DARNED DANGEROUS!" The door was in the janitor's closet of the men's room off the Bee Bee Lounge, in the clubhouse basement. Before I reached the men's room, though, I heard a big, booming voice say, "Sit down, trooper." It was the Colonel, looming up behind the bar in a green-and-yellow Hawaiian shirt with a bolo tie made from bullets, shaking up a batch of Bombardiers, his face hidden by a broad straw hat with long fronds. "Understand you got some questions, son," he said. "Let's talk."

I climbed up on a stool and leaned forward and started to tell him that I was trying to figure out why the heck I was in the Guard and what I was supposed to accomplish. "Mmmmmm," he said. "Uh-huh, uh-huh." And then, in a split second, before I could move a muscle, he grabbed me by the neck and hauled me across the bar and had me flat on my back on the ice chest and was holding a blender to the side of my head. I'll never forget the cold animal anger in his green eyes as he stared down at me, unblinking, for the three longest seconds of my life. Then he helped me to my feet and offered me a drink.

"Sorry about losing control like that," he said. "I guess I got angry because I see in you so much of myself. I get fed up with waiting around, too. It's the hardest part of being in the Guard. And it's twice as hard in the I.N.G. You want to know why?"

I did.

"Because we're not even supposed to exist."

He put a big ice cube in his mouth and ate it like a cherry. "You see, Soviet spy satellites in low orbit are reading Indiana right now like a children's book, and we have to make sure they see us as a bunch of civilians in one-bedroom apartments who happen to like golf a lot. You see, at peak strength, mobilized, the Indiana National Guard numbers fourteen million men. It's the biggest secret army in the free world. And one of the best equipped. We're one ace the President's got that they don't know about—maybe the only one. Get in my car, Dan."

THE Colonel's beige Buick Electra was moored in a secret parking space under an aluminum roof beside the kitchen. Aluminum confuses the heck out of radar, he explained, and beige is the hardest color to re-member afterward. The car shone. A good wax job, he pointed out, prevents a person or persons from leaving messages in the dust. When he turned the ignition key, the car sprang alive, antennas rose, the radio came on, the seats themselves hummed with power, ready to go for-ward or back at a finger's touch. "Always fasten your seat belt," he said. "It's one thing they'd never expect us to do." We cruised west into the warehouse district, and he pointed out long, low aluminum I.N.G.

buildings where the hardware was kept. "We have more than four thousand forklifts, fifty-two hundred portable biffies, eighteen bulk-milk trucks, and four thousand rider mowers," he said. Those were the figures I wrote down. There were also more than six hundred infrared cluster-type thrusters with uplink/downlink/intercept capability. "Only two thousand fifty of those puppies in the whole U.S.," he said. "So, you see, we're sitting on top of one of the larger secrets in the defense community. Our job: keep it that way. It's tough to sit tight, no buts about it, but when we get the word to go I want the other side to find out about us all of a sudden. Bang, we're there. I don't want the enemy to be studying us for three years and getting a Ph.D. The big secret of the I.N.G. is that we could take ninety per cent casualties with no effect on our capability. I don't want the enemy to know why. When the time comes, I want to be able to get in there, search, destroy, interdict, capture the flag, and bring the boys home for Christmas."

"Count me in," I said softly as the big car nosed homeward. "I want a piece of it."

"Just don't forget who you are," the Colonel said. "Look relaxed, but don't be relaxed. Smile, but don't make a point of it. Drink vodka. Lots of ice. Lemon, not lime. Not too many peanuts. Always turn the conversation to the other person. Pace yourself. Always take the end urinal in the men's room. Sunday morning, take a side pew. Don't wash dishes; always dry. Remember: you're a killer, a professional killer. Your stereo has a sharp needle you could poke a man in the eye with. You know how to take an ordinary putter and beat somebody senseless. With your skill, even an ordinary golf ball is lethal. Killers are what we are. And, by the way, always choose Thousand Island."

He pulled up in front of the Alhambra. Music drifted out from behind the closed windows, shadowy figures moved behind the drawn shades. "So for now, trooper, your orders are to stay low: play good golf, drink cold beer, and make love to beautiful women. And let's just hope the Russians aren't doing the same."

He came around to open the door for me, but I was ready for him, and when he tried to kick me I got him by the ankle and flipped him up on the roof of the Buick and pounded him twice, hard, in the pancreas. "Good," he said. "Darned good."

HIS lecture changed my way of thinking, and for the remaining two months of Guard training I tried to act as normal as humanly possible.

It wasn't easy. A guy looks down at his typewriter knowing it can be switched over instantly to invisible ink simply by typing "Hoosier" (a word that even Russians fluent in English would not be familiar with), and he finds it hard to relax and have a cool time. (I kept my typewriter set on invisible most of the time, in case I forgot the password.) We had to remember to always use electric golf carts on the course, for fast response in case of a Code Green alert. The radio signal would be two longs and a short, on either a horn or a saxophone, on "The Don Davis Show," on K-WAYNE, or on my own "Dan the Man Show," on the Gentle Giant 101 (2:00–6:00 P.M.).

Being an information officer meant that I knew a great deal, and having a popular radio show meant that I was in a position to sway minds, and so, in the event of enemy capture, I was prepared to take cyanide. On the golf course, I kept it hidden in a fake ball (I always used my dad's Top-Flites, but one ball, which could be pried open to reveal the deadly white pill wound with string in the core, was marked "Top Flight"—a discrepancy a Russian would never notice), and in the radio studio I kept the cyanide in a tiny slit cut in the foam rubber around the microphone. All I had to do was lean forward and bite. It wasn't easy playing music knowing that death was always two inches from my lips, but I did it. And then one day the war was over.

All of us knew that if the President had pursued an all-out strategy to win the war and had unleashed the I.N.G. against the Vietcong the outcome would have been very different, but we were never allowed to go. We never blamed the President for it—his hands were tied by the press and the protesters—but the tragedy is that we never got the chance to get over there and get the job done.

Twenty years later, millions of Indiana National Guardsmen suffer from postwar regret, waking up in the middle of the night with an urge to go out in the rain and hunker down in the mud, to hold a gun and use a walkie-talkie and for a while I felt bad like that, too, and made a point of playing golf in extremely hot weather and not drinking enough liquids, deliberately pushing myself toward the edge. It was on a real scorcher of a day, playing the Gary Country Club, that I met Colonel Mills for the last time. He was dressed in regulation green and yellow, blasting out of a sand trap. He made a perfect shot and turned and saw me and we exchanged the traditional National Guard wink. (Russians do not wink, and therefore would fail to comprehend this signal.)

"How's civilian life treating you?" he asked. I told him how I felt and he stood there and said, "You should be proud, soldier. You didn't burn the flag, you didn't go to Canada. You did your job. Accept the rewards of a grateful nation." Then he turned on his heel and went straight up and over a steep hill in front of the green, and I never saw him again.

About three years after that, I actually did go to Canada for a weekend. It was O.K., but, based on what I saw, I was glad that I hadn't gone there before.

1988

VERONICA GENG

POST-EUPHORIA

Frankfurt Stock Exchange
Frankfurt, Germany

DEAR SIRS:

Specifically speaking, how does a stock exchange work? One would require approximately how many tables and chairs? And then what?

As fledglings, we are excited to be initiating such a body! Having in readiness for our members a fifty-litre samovar, we now await merely your input on final refinements of procedure.

Gratefully,
FREE MARKET PLANNING
COMMISSARIAT

British Humane Society
London, England

LADIES AND GENTLEMEN:

Begging your advisory as per the ensuing hypothetical. Someone on my street, not me, keeps surrealist parasites in his basement as a hobby. Supposing he decided to release them from the holding pen—what would be the safest way? Should he just smash the pen open with a hammer and then run? I heard there is a danger that uninhibited specimens have a difficult transition phase and might form roving packs of killer strays. Is this true, or would they reenter the natural population?

> Very truly yours,
> CONCERNED SIBERIAN CITIZEN
> (RET.)

Editor-in-Chief
Le Monde
Paris, France

ESTEEMED COLLEAGUE:

Our best regards to you and your enchanting wife.

By the way, how do you decide which are the news stories and which are the editorials? Is it by word count or, rather, a collective decision reached by secret ballot? Or perchance you leave this matter in the capable hands of your delightful spouse. In that case, might we consult with her now and then, purely on a professional basis?

> With felicitations,
> *IZVESTIA* EDITORIAL BOARD

P.S.: Please forgive the ironic idiocy of the above query if yours is one of the Western press organs which have been taking their instructions from us. Someone told us to forget about all that, so we had to.

Supervisor
Cook County Board of Elections
Cook County, Illinois, U.S.A.

DEAR SIR OR MADAM:

Knowing your reputation far and wide, we were just wondering. What if there occurred some voting machines of a highly democratic technology—for example, allowing multiple choice by means of extra slots and levers? Is there some method, in its sophistication a mystery to us, for insuring that a candidate with more votes does not obtain an unfair advantage over a candidate with not so many votes? There could be a situation where the latter is more deserving, due to family needs or health problems, etc., yet is passed aside by a hasty or whimsical electorate for a candidate they think they "want." Then idealism would cry out on its hands and knees to serve a higher justice. Is there a special device for this?

Also, do you happen to know how to get the ballots out of the machine—smash the whole thing open like a piggy bank, or what?

Sincerely,
SUPREME ELECTION REFORM
CENTRAL COMMITTEE

Mr. Akio Morita, Chairman
Sony Corporation
Tokyo, Japan

DEAR MR. MORITA:

This is not your problem, but in our admiration for your fantastic acumen we hope to presume upon your farseeing wisdom and topnotch business sense.

A woman named Yoko Ono has made us a firm offer of $30,000 in hard currency for eight hundred thousand hectares of state-owned pasture in the northeastern Urals. She asserts managerial skills such that over a five-year period she can transform the area into a profit-making dairy farm equipped with automated milking system, carriage barn, historically restored rustic stone walls, manor house with large deck, hardwood floors, antique lighting, Tulikivi radiant fireplace, all-electric kitchen, aluminum siding, up-to-the-minute recording studio, and much more, and will then rent it back to us on terms to be mutually deferred.

Naturally we are tempted to gobble this while her enthusiasm is still at fever pitch. But the wife of our deputy agro-industrial minister suggests we ask if you know a hard-nosed tactic to sweeten our end of the deal.

Most respectfully,
LAND DEVELOPMENT
INSPECTORATE

Hughes Tool Company
U.S.A.

TO THE BOARD OF DIRECTORS:

No doubt it is something out of the blue, receiving a letter from an unknown woman in Russia. I have selected your company because my husband is a fan of your unique oil-drilling equipment, which he appreciates only by remote lore and word of mouth but aspires someday to purchase for his business here. Having started from a single informal kerosene drum in a shed behind our dacha on the Black Sea, he has created over the years quite a formidable oil-and-gas-pumping endeavor, and now stands in position to operate on a mammoth regional scale.

However, I am concerned that he is the victim of a fairy tale about capitalist management principles. A small cohort of men visiting from your state Utah have attained influence over him. They are causing him to discharge fond employees of loyal longevity, and to sign many papers, and now they have him in a reclusion, lying in bed with long fingernails, watching a videotape of a film, "Ocean's Eleven." Recently he sent out to me an elaborate pencil memorandum explaining how I should open herring jars in a certain way so germs from my hair cannot tumble in. He said that titans of capital have to protect themselves from poison elements, but I believe this to be a propaganda romance, indoctrinated by the Utah men. Finally, would it be a fact that executive decision-making power is enhanced by hourly injections of the substance "codeine"? This is what they proclaim, although they themselves are fanatically abstemious when it comes to even vodka or tea.

As I am too typical of our national unfamiliarity with these parts of the free-enterprise system, I pray that you can inform my perspective before it is already too late and I smash open the attic with a hammer.

Desperate

To Whom it May Concern:
I am free. What should I do?

1991

KEITH RICHARDS' DESERT-ISLAND DISKS

Each month, the editors of Pulse magazine ask a rock-and-roll star to list which ten CDs he or she would bring to a desert island. Keith Richards selected the following:

Little Richard: "Lucille" or "Tutti Frutti"
Beethoven's Third Symphony
Anything early by the Nat King Cole Trio
Everly Brothers: "That's Just Too Much"
Robert Johnson: "32–20 Blues"
Big Bill Broonzy
Louis Armstrong: "Pratt City Blues"
Blind Willie McTell
Carla Thomas
Otis Redding
Brenda & the Tabulations: "Who's Lovin' You"

• DAY ONE

Rigged a distress flag with me gypsy scarf, but it droops like Mick's jowls. While waiting for it to fly, played all ten disks. Ate a peanut-butter-and-Fluff sandwich the missus packed for me dinner and washed it down with me new poison of choice: Stoli and Sunkist. Smoked a Marlboro Red and watched the sun go down. Was lulled into me forty winks by the island's own music, the flop flop of the waves and the caw caw of the parrots.

• DAY TWO

Went combing for shells for me bungalow back home. In the uninhabited spots, one gets first pick, so to speak. Dragged back a whopping conch! Chilled out with me CDs. The sign of good music: if it's got some soul, ya know, you can listen to it over and over. That cat Little Richard must've had a desert island in mind when he wrote "Tutti Frutti." Scanned horizon.

• DAY THREE

Do I really need both Big Bill Broonzy and Blind Willie McTell? Thinkin' I should've put some Buddy Holly on that list, or maybe some Four Tops. Had a real craving for "That'll Be the Day." Spent the afternoon scouting for other signs of life and listening to "Tutti Frutti" on repeat.

• DAY FIVE

Can't get "Tutti Frutti" out of me head. Perhaps "Lucille" would've been a better pick. Opened me Big Bill Broonzy CD to discover me little one, Theodora, had switched it with the soundtrack to "Elmo in Grouchland." Cheeky critter. I must've missed it before when I was wrestling that monkey for coconuts. Been using the Shuffle option Patti showed me on the disk player to give those ten disks a new life they badly needed. The local birds and monkeys bop along to the tunes; one parrot in particular seems a bit more on key than Don Everly. It's me own Voodoo Lounge. Me Zippo ran out of fluid, so I'm reduced to lighting me Marlboros with two stones.

• DAY SIX

The bloody CD player got sand in it and it took the better part of the day to clean it out. Pissed me off. Wanted something to clear "Tutti Frutti" from me brain.

• DAY EIGHT

Must remember to put the disks back in their cases: Carla Thomas and Beethoven's Third got warped in the sun. Just me luck, only had a chance to listen to them four dozen or so times. Started using "Tutti Frutti" as a shaving mirror. Man, the crooked reflection really makes me look like that Celine Dion bird. Next thing you know, like, I'll be banging me chest with me fist. Listen to Nat King Cole enough, you can detect a slight lisp. Ran out of Stoli. Have started mixing Sunkist and salt water for a kick even I'm not quite used to. Ten butts left. Horizon a bloody blur.

• DAY TEN

The distance from me chin to me groin is exactly five CDs!

• DAY ELEVEN

Tried to signal a passing ship for help—or at least some different disks. Played "Who's Lovin' You" on top volume and accompanied it with me Fender. Ship didn't hear me, man, and I blew a tweeter, so I ejected the disk and tried to reflect little rays of CD light at the craft as an S.O.S. The ship sailed on. In all the excitement, I trampled me sand castles. A real downer. Man, Robert Johnson is depressing: "I'm down this, I'm down that." Otis Redding's Mr. Pitiful and me all-black threads ain't much cheerier. I don't know if it's me ocean-water intake or the fact I've been smoking sand for a week, but I started to see Chuck Berry playing Kadima on the beach with Muddy Waters. "I got a gal named Sue"—I try to keep morale up, but me fear is that "Tutti Frutti" is inhabiting me mind.

• DAY THIRTEEN

Me ten favorite books: "Moby-Dick," "The Girls' Guide to Hunting and Fishing," "Tutti Frutti," "Gravity's Rainbow," "Tutti Frutti" . . . Ah, hell!

• DAY SIXTEEN

Tried to play the Everlys backward to look for hidden messages. Big Bill Broonzy is starting to sound too much like that little red Muppet monster. Broonzy ain't so big; I could whup him. Keep finding meself humming variations on "Tutti Frutti": "Loosy Goosey" and "Ittut Itturf!"

• DAY EIGHTEEN

Let it be known that this was the day I realized I could put all ten CDs on me ten toes. Makes me look a bit like a princess.

• DAY TWENTY-THREE

Aha! Discovered "Tutti Frutti" is inhabiting me conch. Little Richard is evidently *very* little and trapped inside me shell. Can't hear the ocean at all when I put it up to me ear. Turned in around five and me silver skull ring tried to bite me in me sleep. Woke up with a cut on me finger.

• DAY TWENTY-FIVE

Had a bitch of a row with some parrots who prefer Mick's solo outings to mine. Creatures are mocking me. Parrots singing "Tutti Frutti" like they invented it. I shut up one cheeky bird by stuffing his beak in the hole in the Everlys. A monkey took me side and I offered him Billy Wyman's bass position. Horizon slowly unravels.

• DAY THIRTY
Re-formed the Stones with the monkey on bass, meself on guitar, a seagull on drums, and a parrot named Daisy singing lead. The bird's a real prima donna, but can belt it out like bloody Sam Cooke. Played that old chestnut "Tutti Frutti" till the creatures' bedtime.

• DAY THIRTY-ONE
Bloody bird left the group to go solo. Bitch.

• DAY THIRTY-FOUR
"I got a gal named Patti, she almost drive me batty." Not bad. "I got a parrot named Daisy, she almost drive me crazy!" The monkey and me are trying to pry wee, tiny little Richard out of the conch shell. Want to sing him the Patti/batty rhyme. "Tutti Frutti au rutti, too-ttay froo-ttay, au roo-ttay—"

• DAY FIFTY-TWO
"A bop-bop a-loom-op a-lop bop boom!"

1999

WORDS

OF

ADVICE

UPTON SINCLAIR

HOW TO BE OBSCENE

I HAVE made a discovery almost priceless to authors. If I were a self-ish author, I would keep it to myself and live on it the rest of my life. Being an altruist, I pass it on for my colleagues to make use of.

You spend a lot of time writing a book, and then maybe no one pays any attention to it. The season is dull, and there are mountains of books on the desks of the literary editors; you have got lost in the mob, your book is dead, and your wife and kids can't go to the seashore this summer.

But then some good angel puts it into the head of a Boston preacher to read your book and take it to the Boston police, and the police go and arrest a bookclerk for selling your book, which is obscene. Instantly the press agencies flash the name of your book to every town and village in the United States, and your publishers get orders by telegraph from Podunk and Kalamazoo. The literary editors grab the book out of the pile they had set aside to be turned over to the secondhand dealers. The printers of your book have to telegraph to the mill for a carload of paper for a new edition, and the royalties from the first three days' sales pay your expenses while you travel from California to Boston, to enter a protest against the action of the censor, and ensure the sale of the new edition before it has gone to press.

Last week I was a guest of the Kiwanis Club of Boston. They gave me a very nice luncheon of cold meats and potato salad and ice cream and cake, and we saluted the flag, and sang songs about it, and then I told them about this wonderful situation—using the Kiwanis dialect, which, as you may know, is closely related to the Rotary and Lions' languages. I said: "Under this arrangement we authors are using the rest of the United States as our selling territory, and Boston as our advertising headquarters."

IF it were necessary to write really obscene books, I wouldn't recommend this plan, because real obscenity is altogether foreign to my interests. But the beauty of the plan is that you don't have to write anything really harmful; all you have to do is to follow the example of the great masters of the world's literature, and deal with the facts of life frankly and honestly. That is what the Boston police call "obscenity," and as soon as the rest of the country understands that, it will be an honor to have the Boston advertisement. So far they have conferred it upon H. L. Mencken, Percy Marks, Sinclair Lewis, Theodore Dreiser and myself. I am now engaged in trying to get them to confer it upon William Shakespeare and the author of the Book of Genesis, but they say these classics don't need advertising.

You don't have to give very much space in your book to the forbidden subjects. Under the Boston law, they can pick out a single paragraph, or even a single sentence which they do not like, and on the basis of this, they can advertise an entire book, which may be otherwise quite all right from the prudish point of view. Nobody has to read the whole book save a Boston police clerk; he picks out the passages which tend to corrupt his sensitive religious nature, and marks them. These passages are sworn to in a complaint, and after that they are the "evidence," and if you try to read any other passages, you are out of order.

THIS matter is of such great importance to authors that I am sure they will want full particulars, seeing that I am here on the ground, and have got all the data. Just what must one say in order to annex this free Boston advertising? In the case of my novel "Oil!" which they are now boosting for me, they specify nine pages out of a total of 527—and you can see how easy that makes it for any author.

To begin with, one must not mention that such a thing as birth control exists. In Boston they have arrested Margaret Sanger several times, and they make desperate efforts to keep all knowledge of contraception from the masses of the people. Boston also has its Watch and Ward Society, whose purpose is to keep you from mentioning the passionate aspects of love in any place but a medical treatise. This was explained to me by Mr. Fuller, proprietor of the Old Corner Book Store, and chairman of the committee of the booksellers which is trying to persuade the police to arrest the authors instead of the booksellers. Mr. Fuller talked very eloquently to me for an hour, to persuade me that it was my duty to get arrested. I tried to oblige him, but the courts wouldn't let me. They thought I had had my share of advertising.

It is very simple, after all, to get this Boston police advertisement; all you have to do is to take any book of the great standard literature of the world, pick out the passages dealing with love and courtship, write something of the same sort in your book, and then mail a few copies to members of the Boston society. Get "The Ordeal of Richard Feverel," for example, or "Tess of the D'Urbervilles."

DON'T write anything really obscene, of course, and don't think that I mean any such thing. I have never written anything of the sort in my life, and police advertising couldn't tempt me. Not for a million dollars would I put into a book of mine any words as vile as those *Hamlet* addresses to *Ophelia* in one passage of that play. (I think some cheap actor wrote it into the script, but there it is, a part of standard English literature, taught in all high schools.) And not all the wealth in New York could hire me to write a story as foul as the tale of what Lot's daughters did to their drunken old father in Genesis XIX, 30–38.

1927

ROBERT BENCHLEY

FILLING THAT HIATUS

THERE has already been enough advice written for hostesses and guests so that there should be no danger of toppling over forward into the wrong soup or getting into arguments as to which elbow belongs on which arm. The etiquette books have taken care of all that.

There is just one little detail of behavior at dinner parties which I have never seen touched upon, and which has given me personally some little embarrassment. I refer to the question of what to do during those little intervals when you find that both your right-hand and your left-hand partner are busily engaged in conversation with somebody else.

You have perhaps turned from what you felt to be a fascinating conversation (on your part) with your right-hand partner, turned only to snap away a rose bug which was charging on your butter from the table decorations or to refuse a helping of salad descending on you from the left, and when you turn back to your partner to continue your monologue, you find that she is already vivaciously engaged on the other side, a shift made with suspicious alacrity, when you come to think it over. So you wheel about to your left, only to find yourself confronted by the clasp of a necklace and an expanse of sun-browned back. This leaves you looking more or less straight in front of you, with a roll in your hand and not very much to do with your face. Should you sit and cry softly to yourself, with your underlip stuck out and tears coursing unnoticed down your cheeks, or should you launch forth into a bawdy solo, beating time with your knife and fork?

OF course, the main thing is not to let your hostess notice that you are disengaged, for, if she spots you dawdling or looking into space, she will either think that you have insulted both your partners or else will feel responsible for you herself and start a long-distance conversation which has no real basis except that of emergency. So above all things you must spend the hiatus acting as if you really were doing something.

You can always make believe that you are talking to the person opposite, making little conversational faces and sounds into thin air, nodding your head "Yes" or "No," and laughing politely every now and again, perhaps even continuing the talk from which you had been cut off, just as if someone were still listening to you. This may fool your hostess in case her glance happens to fall your way (and sometime we must take up the difficulty of talking to hostesses whose glances must, of necessity, be roving up and down the board while you are trying to be funny) but it is going to confuse the person sitting opposite you in case he or she happens to catch your act. If one looks across the table and sees the man opposite laughing and talking straight ahead with nobody on the other end, one is naturally going to think that he had better not take any more to drink, or perhaps even that he had better not go out to any more parties until some good specialist has gone over him thoroughly. It is this danger of being misjudged which makes the imitation conversation inadvisable.

You can always get busily at work on the nuts in front of your plate, arranging them on the tablecloth in fancy patterns with simulated intensity which will make it look as if you were performing for somebody's benefit, especially if you keep looking up at an imaginary audience and smiling "See?" Even if you are caught at this, there is no way of checking up, for anyone of the dinner guests might possibly be looking at you while talking to somebody else. It isn't much fun, however, after the first five minutes.

IF you have thought to bring along a bit of charcoal, you can draw little pictures on the back on either side of you, perhaps even spelling out "Repeal the 18th Amendment" on one of them to help along a good cause, or, lacking charcoal and the ability to draw, you might start smothering the nicer-looking back with kisses. This would, at least, get one of your partners to turn around—unless she happened to like it. As time wears on, and you still find yourself without anyone to talk to, you can start juggling your cutlery, beginning with a knife, fork, and spoon and working up to two of each, with perhaps a flower thrown in to make it harder. This ought to attract *some* attention.

Of course, there is always one last resort, and that is to slide quietly out of your chair and under the table, where you can either crawl about collecting slippers which have been kicked off, growling like a dog and frightening the more timid guests, or crawl out from the other side and go home. Perhaps this last would be best.

1932

ROBERT BENCHLEY

IT'S FUN TO BE FOOLED . . . IT'S MORE

FUN TO KNOW

HERE are some of the tricks of sleight-of-hand which I used to do when I was a small boy, together with complete explanations of how each trick was done.

I may be incurring the ire of the Society of Magicians, as certain cigarette advertisers have done, by giving away these secrets of the Black Art
which I have guarded for so many years (that is, if I can remember them),
but times are hard, and Magic has become more or less a pedestrian trade,
and I feel that I am quite within my rights in sharing with the world the
details of my erstwhile relationship with the Forces of Darkness.

You must remember that my only equipment in this legerdemain,
aside from the natural dexterity of a boy of eleven, was a set of imple-
ments forwarded to me by a soap firm in Glastonbury, Connecticut, in
return for some slight favor I had done them in connection with soap
wrappers. The entire set could be easily concealed in a wardrobe trunk,
and, when brought into the room where the feats were to be performed,
attracted no more attention than a traveling dog-and-monkey circus
would have done. A great many of my audience often detected nothing
unusual about my appearance other than several bulging pockets,
which might have come from carrying small puppies in them, or possibly a slight indistinctness in speech due to my mouth being full of odds
and ends of apparatus, such as coins, eggs, and flags of all nations.
Aside from these items, I was innocence itself.

THE BEWITCHED FLOWERPOT

ILLUSION:
What seems to be an ordinary tin flowerpot (except that it is the size
and shape of a rolling-pin) is opened to show the audience that it is
completely empty. In fact, the magician's wand is inserted into the
opening and moved gingerly about to prove the point.

The cover is then readjusted and tapped several times too many with
the wand. During this tapping an almost imperceptible move is made
turning the pot upside down, and, when the cover is taken off again, a
rose bush in full bloom is disclosed. Well, perhaps not a rose bush, and
perhaps not in full bloom, but at any rate a bunch of red-paper flowers,
slightly crushed. The audience is astounded.

EXPLANATION:
The flowerpot is not a *real* flowerpot, but a contraption with *two separate compartments,* one containing nothing (which the audience is permitted to see first) and the other containing the rose bush in full bloom.
The almost imperceptible movement turning the pot upside down
really *does* turn it upside down, so that the empty compartment is on
the bottom and the rose compartment on top. The rest is easy.

THE GHOSTLY FINGER

ILLUSION:

A derby hat is borrowed from someone in the audience, or one belonging to the magician is used. It is passed about for examination to prove that there are no holes in it (yet) and is then held, top toward the spectators, and a handkerchief is wrapped around it. (Possibly the magician's back is turned to the audience for the fraction of a minute, as if he were looking for something behind him, while a running line of clever patter distracts the attention of those present.) On removing the handkerchief, the magician's forefinger is seen *protruding from the top of the hat,* to all appearances having been thrust *through the material!* The handkerchief is then wrapped again around the hat, the back possibly turned again for a few seconds, and, when the handkerchief is removed, there is no finger *and no hole!* Several of the more nervous ladies swoon.

EXPLANATION:

A *wax finger,* with a long pin attachment, is used in this trick. The magician "palms" the wax finger ("to palm," in the lingo of the Devil's disciples, is to conceal an object in the palm of the hand so cleverly that it looks as if the hand were empty, or at any rate merely convulsed in *rigor mortis*). When the handkerchief is being wrapped around the hat the first time, the pin is inserted into the top part of the derby and grasped by the hand which is inside the hat. This, unless the pin is pushed only halfway in, gives the effect of the finger actually coming through the hat. Otherwise it gives the effect of the finger *and pin* coming through the hat, which is not so mystifying. When the handkerchief is passed again, the finger-pin is pulled out and palmed once more, care being taken this time, *of all times,* not to drop it on the floor.

THE ASTOUNDING STRING

ILLUSION:

A piece of string, which for some reason has been run through two cylindrical pieces of wood, and for some other reason has two small glass beads attached to either end, is cut with a knife so that it hangs in two distinct pieces. This in itself is startling enough. But when the two cylinders are placed together and subjected to the influence of the wand, with the result that the string is again pulled back and forth between them as freely as it ever was, the effect is electric.

EXPLANATION:

Never quite clear, even to the magician. Somehow the string is either joined together, or another piece of string run through the cylinders, or *some*thing. Owing to this haziness concerning the basic principles of the trick, it was not always performed with complete success, and very often not even tried. What is worth doing at all is worth doing well.

MIND-READING

ILLUSION:

(This is a feat based on a similar, though more elaborate, one performed in India.)

A member of the audience leaves the room and the rest decide on some object which he is to be "willed" to touch when he returns. Let us say that it is a hassock. The absentee is then sent for and the "control" (the magician himself) fixes his gaze on him and says: "Will you hassock ice cream?" Immediately, the "subject" walks across the room and touches a plate of ice cream. Pandemonium ensues.

EXPLANATION:

The one who leaves the room is in reality a *confederate* of the magician, who has been practicing the act since three o'clock in the afternoon. It has been agreed that, whatever the object to be touched is, the "control" will introduce its name into a sentence apparently spoken at random. Thus, if the object selected has been a radiator, the sentence would be "Have you had any radiators today?" (Catch on?) Where the instance quoted above was faulty was that *two* possibilities were mentioned in the same sentence. Eternal vigilance is the only guard against this sort of slip-up.

THUS we see that, no matter how mystifying a feat of legerdemain or mind-reading may be, there is always an explanation for it somewhere in the archives of Black Art. But, human nature being what it is, people would much rather be fooled in this manner than deal, day in and day out, with the obvious and transparent things of life.

Once again I apologize to the Society of Magicians for "spilling the beans."

1933

ROBERT BENCHLEY

WHY WE LAUGH—OR DO WE?

(LET'S GET THIS THING SETTLED, MR. EASTMAN)

IN order to laugh at something, it is necessary (1) to know *what* you are laughing at, (2) to know *why* you are laughing, (3) to ask some people why *they* think you are laughing, (4) to jot down a few notes, (5) to laugh. Even then, the thing may not be cleared up for days.

All laughter is merely a compensatory reflex to take the place of sneezing. What we really want to do is sneeze, but as that is not always possible, we laugh instead. Sometimes we underestimate our powers and laugh and sneeze at the same time. This raises hell all around.

The old phrase "That is nothing to sneeze at" proves my point. What is obviously meant is "That is nothing to *laugh* at." The wonder is that nobody ever thought of this explanation of laughter before, with the evidence staring him in the face like that.*

We sneeze because we are thwarted, discouraged, or devil-may-care. Failing a sneeze, we laugh, *faute de mieux*. Analyze any funny story or comic situation at which we "laugh" and it will be seen that this theory is correct. Incidentally, by the time you have the "humor" analyzed, it will be found that the necessity for laughing has been relieved.

Let us take the well-known joke about the man who put the horse in the bathroom.† Here we have a perfect example of the thought-sneeze process, or, if you will, the sneeze-thought process. The man, obviously an introvert, was motivated by a will-to-dominate-the-bathroom, combined with a desire to be superior to the other boarders. The humor of the situation may *seem* to us to lie in the tag line "I want to be able to

---

*Schwanzleben, in his work "Humor After Death," hits on this point indirectly when he says, "All laughter is a muscular rigidity spasmodically relieved by involuntary twitching. It can be induced by the application of electricity as well as by a so-called 'joke.' "

†A man who lived in a boarding house brought a horse home with him one night, led it upstairs, and shut it in the bathroom. The landlady, aroused by the commotion, protested, pointed to the broken balustrade, the torn stair carpet, and the obvious maladjustment of the whole thing, and asked the man, confidentially, just why he had seen fit to shut a horse in the common bathroom. To which the man replied, "In the morning, the boarders, one by one, will go into the bathroom, and will come rushing out, exclaiming, 'There's a *horse* in the bathroom!' I want to be able to say, 'Yes, I know.' "

say, 'Yes, I know,'" but we laugh at the joke *subconsciously* long before this line comes in. In fact, what we are really laughing (or sneezing) at is the idea of someone's telling us a joke that we have heard before.

Let us suppose that the story was reversed, and that a *horse* had put a *man* into the bathroom. Then our laughter would have been induced by the idea of a landlady's asking a horse a question and the horse's answering—an entirely different form of joke.

The man would then have been left in the bathroom with nothing to do with the story. Likewise, if the man had put the *landlady* into the bathroom, the *horse* would obviously have been *hors de combat* (still another form of joke, playing on the similarity in sound between the word "horse" and the French word "*hors*," meaning "*out* of." Give up?).

Any joke, besides making us want to sneeze, must have five cardinal points, and we must check up on these first before giving in:

(1) The joke must be in a language we can understand.

(2) It must be spoken loudly enough for us to hear it, or printed clearly enough for us to read it.

(3) It must be about *something*. You can't just say, "Here's a good joke" and let it go at that. (You *can,* but don't wait for the laugh.)

(4) It must deal with either frustration or accomplishment, inferiority or superiority, sense or nonsense, pleasantness or unpleasantness, or, at any rate, with some emotion that can be analyzed, otherwise how do we know when to laugh?

(5) It must begin with the letter "W."*

Now, let us see just how our joke about the horse in the bathroom fulfills these specifications. Using the *Gestalt,* or Rotary-Frictional, method of taking the skin off a joke, we can best illustrate by making a diagram of it. We have seen that every joke must be in a language that we can understand and spoken (or written) so clearly that we can hear it (or see it). Otherwise we have this:

Fig. 1.
Joke which we cannot hear, see, or understand the words of.

---

*Gunfy, in his "Laughter Considered as a Joint Disease," holds that the letter "W" is not essential to the beginning of a joke; so long as it comes in somewhere before the joke is over. However, tests made on five hundred subjects in the Harvard School of Applied Laughter, using the Mergenthaler Laugh Detector, have shown that, unless a joke begins with the letter "W," the laughter is forced, almost unpleasant at times.

You will see in Figure 2 that we go upstairs with the man and the horse as far as the bathroom. Here we become conscious that it is not a *true* story, something we may have suspected all along but didn't want to say anything about. This sudden revelation of *absurdity* (from the Latin *ab* and *surdus,* meaning "out of deafness") is represented in the diagram by an old-fashioned whirl.

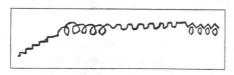

Fig. 2.
*The horse-in-bathroom story under
ideal conditions.*

Following the shock of realization that the story is not real, we progress in the diagram to the point where the landlady protests. Here we come to an actual *fact,* or factual *act.* Any landlady in her right mind *would* protest against a horse's being shut in her bathroom. So we have, in the diagram, a return to normal ratiocination, or Crowther's Disease, represented by the wavy line. (Whoo-hoo!)

From then on, it is anybody's joke. The whole thing becomes just ludicrous. This we can show in the diagram by the egg-and-dart design, making it clear that something has definitely gone askew. Personally, I think that what the man *meant* to say was "That's no horse—that's my wife," but that he was inhibited. (Some of these jokes even *I* can't seem to get through my head.)*

1937

---

*A. E. Bassinette, in his pamphlet "What Is Humor—A Joke?," claims to have discovered a small tropical fly which causes laughter. This fly, according to this authority, was carried from Central America back to Spain by Columbus's men, and spread from there to the rest of Europe, returning to America, on a visit, in 1667, on a man named George Altschuh.

INSERT FLAP "A" AND THROW AWAY

ONE stifling summer afternoon last August, in the attic of a tiny stone house in Pennsylvania, I made a most interesting discovery: the shortest, cheapest method of inducing a nervous breakdown ever perfected. In this technique (eventually adopted by the psychology department of Duke University, which will adopt anything), the subject is placed in a sharply sloping attic heated to 340°F, and given a moth-proof closet known as the Jiffy-Cloz to assemble. The Jiffy-Cloz, procurable at any department store or neighborhood insane asylum, consists of half a dozen gigantic sheets of red cardboard, two plywood doors, a clothes rack, and a packet of staples. With these is included a set of instructions mimeographed in pale-violet ink, fruity with phrases like "Pass Section F through Slot AA, taking care not to fold tabs behind washers (see Fig. 9)." The cardboard is so processed that as the subject struggles convulsively to force the staple through, it suddenly buckles, plunging the staple deep into his thumb. He thereupon springs up with a dolorous cry and smites his knob (Section K) on the rafters (RR). As a final demonic touch, the Jiffy-Cloz people cunningly omit four of the staples necessary to finish the job, so that after indescribable purgatory, the best the subject can possibly achieve is a sleazy, capricious structure which would reduce any self-respecting moth to helpless laughter. The cumulative frustration, the tropical heat, and the soft, ghostly chuckling of the moths are calculated to unseat the strongest reason.

In a period of rapid technological change, however, it was inevitable that a method as cumbersome as the Jiffy-Cloz would be superseded. It was superseded at exactly nine-thirty Christmas morning by a device called the Self-Running 10-Inch Scale-Model Delivery-Truck Kit Powered by Magic Motor, costing twenty-nine cents. About nine on that particular morning, I was spread-eagled on my bed, indulging in my favorite sport of mouth-breathing, when a cork fired from a child's air gun mysteriously lodged in my throat. The pellet proved awkward for a while, but I finally ejected it by flailing the little marksman (and his sister, for good measure) until their welkins rang, and sauntered in to breakfast. Before I could choke down a healing fruit juice, my consort, a tall, regal creature indistinguishable from Cornelia, the Mother of the Gracchi, except that her foot was entangled in a roller skate, swept in. She extended a large, unmistakable box covered with diagrams.

"Now don't start making excuses," she whined. "It's just a simple cardboard toy. The directions are on the back—"

"Look, dear," I interrupted, rising hurriedly and pulling on my overcoat, "it clean slipped my mind. I'm supposed to take a lesson in crosshatching at Zim's School of Cartooning today."

"On Christmas?" she asked suspiciously.

"Yes, it's the only time they could fit me in," I countered glibly. "This is the big week for crosshatching, you know, between Christmas and New Year's."

"Do you think you ought to go in your pajamas?" she asked.

"Oh, that's O.K." I smiled. "We often work in our pajamas up at Zim's. Well, goodbye now. If I'm not home by Thursday, you'll find a cold snack in the safe-deposit box." My subterfuge, unluckily, went for naught, and in a jiffy I was sprawled on the nursery floor, surrounded by two lambkins and ninety-eight segments of the Self-Running 10-Inch Scale-Model Delivery-Truck Construction Kit.

THE theory of the kit was simplicity itself, easily intelligible to Kettering of General Motors, Professor Millikan, or any first-rate physicist. Taking as my starting point the only sentence I could comprehend, "Fold down on all lines marked 'fold down;' fold up on all lines marked 'fold up,'" I set the children to work and myself folded up with an album of views of Jane Russell. In a few moments, my skin was suffused with a delightful tingling sensation and I was ready for the second phase, lightly referred to in the directions as "Preparing the Spring Motor Unit." As nearly as I could determine after twenty minutes of mumbling, the Magic Motor ("No Electricity—No Batteries— Nothing to Wind—Motor Never Wears Out") was an accordion-pleated affair operating by torsion, attached to the axles. "It is necessary," said the text, "to cut a slight notch in each of the axles with a knife (see Fig. C). To find the exact place to cut this notch, lay one of the axles over diagram at bottom of page."

"Well, *now* we're getting someplace!" I boomed, with a false gusto that deceived nobody. "Here, Buster, run in and get Daddy a knife."

"I dowanna," quavered the boy, backing away. "You always cut yourself at this stage." I gave the wee fellow an indulgent pat on the head that flattened it slightly, to teach him civility, and commandeered a long, serrated bread knife from the kitchen. "Now watch me closely, children," I ordered. "We place the axle on the diagram as in Fig. C, applying a strong downward pressure on the knife handle at all times." The axle must have been a factory second, because an instant later I was in the bathroom grinding my teeth in agony and attempting to staunch the flow of blood. Ultimately, I succeeded in contriving a rough bandage and slipped back into the nursery without awaking the children's suspicions. An agreeable surprise awaited me. Guided by a mechanical bent clearly inherited from their sire, the rascals had put together the chassis of the delivery truck.

"Very good indeed," I complimented (naturally, one has to exaggerate praise to develop a child's self-confidence). "Let's see—what's the next step? Ah, yes. 'Lock into box shape by inserting tabs C, D, E, F, G, H, J, K, and L into slots C, D, E, F, G, H, J, K, and L. Ends of front axle should be pushed through holes A and B.' " While marshalling the indicated parts in their proper order, I emphasized to my rapt listeners the necessity of patience and perseverance. "Haste makes waste, you know," I reminded them. "Rome wasn't built in a day. Remember, your daddy isn't always going to be here to show you."

"Where *are* you going to be?" they demanded.

"In the movies, if I can arrange it," I snarled. Poising tabs C, D, E, F, G, H, J, K, and L in one hand and the corresponding slots in the other, I essayed a union of the two, but in vain. The moment I made one set fast and tackled another, tab and slot would part company, thumbing their noses at me. Although the children were too immature to understand, I saw in a flash where the trouble lay. Some idiotic employee at the factory had punched out the wrong design, probably out of sheer spite. So that was his game, eh? I set my lips in a grim line and, throwing one hundred and fifty-seven pounds of fighting fat into the effort, pounded the component parts into a homogeneous mass.

"There," I said with a gasp, "that's close enough. Now then, who wants candy? One, two, three—everybody off to the candy store!"

"We wanna finish the delivery truck!" they wailed. "Mummy, he won't let us finish the delivery truck!"

"Delivery truck, delivery truck!" I bawled, turning purple. "What do you think life is, one long delivery truck?" Threats, cajolery, bribes were of no avail. In their jungle code, a twenty-nine-cent gewgaw bulked larger than a parent's love. Realizing that I was dealing with a pair of monomaniacs, I determined to show them who was master and wildly began locking the cardboard units helter-skelter, without any regard for the directions. When sections refused to fit, I gouged them with my nails and forced them together, cackling shrilly. The side panels collapsed; with a bestial oath, I drove a safety pin through them and lashed them to the roof. I used paper clips, bobby pins, anything I could lay my hands on. My fingers fairly flew and my breath whistled in my throat. "You want a delivery truck, do you?" I panted. "All right, I'll show you!" As merciful blackness closed in, I was on my hands and knees, bunting the infernal thing along with my nose and whinnying, "Roll, confound you, roll!"

"ABSOLUTE quiet," a carefully modulated voice was saying, "and fifteen of the white tablets every four hours." I opened my eyes carefully in the darkened room. Dimly I picked out a knifelike character actor in a Vandyke beard and pencil-striped pants folding a stethoscope into his bag. "Yes," he added thoughtfully, "if we play our cards right, this ought to be a long, expensive recovery." From far away, I could hear my wife's voice bravely trying to control her anxiety.

"What if he becomes restless, Doctor?"

"Get him a detective story," returned the leech. "Or better still, a nice, soothing picture puzzle—something he can do with his hands."

1944

L. RUST HILLS

HOW TO EAT AN ICE-CREAM CONE

BEFORE you even get the cone, you have to do a lot of planning about it. We'll assume that you lost the argument in the car and that the family has decided to break the automobile journey and stop at an ice-cream stand for cones. Get things straight with them right from the start. Tell them that after they have their cones there will be an imaginary circle six feet away from the car and that no one—man, woman, or especially child—will be allowed to cross the line and reënter the car until his ice-cream cone has been entirely consumed and he has cleaned himself up. Emphasize: Automobiles and ice-cream cones don't mix. Explain: Melted ice cream, children, is a fluid that is eternally sticky. One drop of it on a car-door handle spreads to the seat covers, to trousers, to hands, and thence to the steering wheel, the gearshift, the rearview mirror, all the knobs of the dashboard—spreads *everywhere* and lasts *forever*, spreads from a nice old car like this, which might have to be abandoned because of stickiness, right into a nasty new car, in secret ways that even scientists don't understand. If necessary, even make a joke: "The family that eats ice-cream cones together sticks together." Then let their mother explain the joke and tell them you don't mean half of what you say, and no, we won't be getting a new car.

Blessed are the children who always eat the same flavor of ice cream or always know beforehand what kind they will want. Such good children should be quarantined from those who want to "wait and see what flavors there are." It's a sad thing to observe a beautiful young child who has always been perfectly happy with a plain vanilla ice-cream cone being subverted by a young schoolmate who has been invited along for the weekend—a pleasant and polite visitor, perhaps, but spoiled by permissive parents and scarred by an overactive imagination. This schoolmate has a flair for contingency planning: "Well, I'll have banana if they have banana, but if they don't have banana then I'll have peach, if it's fresh peach, and if they don't have banana or fresh peach I'll see what else they have that's like that, like maybe fresh strawberry or something, and if they don't have that or anything like that that's good I'll just have chocolate marshmallow chip or chocolate ripple or something like that." Then—turning to one's own once simple and innocent child, now already corrupt and thinking fast—the schoolmate invites a similar rigmarole. "What kind are *you* going to have?"

I'm a great believer in contingency planning, but none of this is realistic. Few adults, and even fewer children, are able to make up their minds beforehand what kind of ice-cream cone they'll want. It would be nice if they could all be lined up in front of the man who is making up the cones and just snap smartly when their turn came, "Strawberry, please," "Vanilla, please," "Chocolate, please." But of course it never happens like that. There is always a great discussion, a great jostling and craning of necks and leaning over the counter to see down into the tubs of ice cream, and much interpersonal consultation—"What kind are *you* having?"—back and forth, as if that should make any difference. Until finally the first child's turn comes and he asks the man, "What kinds do you have?"

Now, this is the stupidest question in the world, because there is always a sign posted saying what kinds of ice cream they have. As I tell the children, that's what they put the sign up there for—so you won't have to ask what kinds of ice cream they have. The man gets sick of telling everybody all the different kinds of ice cream they have, so they put a sign up there that *says*. You're supposed to read it, not ask the man.

"All right, but the sign doesn't say strawberry."

"Well, that means they don't have strawberry."

"But there *is* strawberry, right there."

"That must be raspberry or something." (Look again at the sign. Raspberry isn't there, either.)

When the child's turn actually comes, he says, "Do you have strawberry?"

"Sure."

"What other kinds do you have?"

The trouble is, of course, that they put up that sign saying what flavors they have, with little cardboard inserts to put in or take out flavors, way back when they first opened the store. But they never change the sign—or not often enough. They always have flavors that aren't on the list, and often they don't have flavors that *are* on the list. Children know this—whether innately or from earliest experience it would be hard to say. The ice-cream man knows it, too. Even grownups learn it eventually. There will always be chaos and confusion and mind-changing and general uproar when ice-cream cones are being ordered, and there has not been, is not, and will never be any way to avoid it.

HUMAN beings are incorrigibly restless and dissatisfied, always in search of new experiences and sensations, seldom content with the familiar. It is this, I think, that accounts for people wanting to have a taste of your cone, and wanting you to have a taste of theirs. "*Do* have a taste of this fresh peach—it's delicious," my wife used to say to me, very much (I suppose) the way Eve wanted Adam to taste her delicious apple. An insinuating look of calculating curiosity would film my wife's eyes—the same look those beautiful, scary women in those depraved Italian films give a man they're interested in. "How's *yours?*" she would say. For this reason, I always order chocolate chip now. Down through the years, all those close enough to me to feel entitled to ask for a taste of my cone—namely, my wife and children—have learned what chocolate chip tastes like, so they have no legitimate reason to ask me for a taste. As for tasting other people's cones, never do it. The reasoning here is that if it tastes good, you'll wish you'd had it; if it tastes bad, you'll have had a taste of something that tastes bad; if it doesn't taste either good or bad, then you won't have missed anything. Of course no person in his right mind ever *would* want to taste anyone else's cone, but it is useful to have good, logical reasons for hating the thought of it.

Another important thing. Never let the man hand you the ice-cream cones for the whole group. There is no sight more pathetic than some bumbling disorganized papa holding four ice-cream cones in two hands, with his money still in his pocket, when the man says, "Eighty cents." What does he do then? He can't hand the cones back to the man to hold while he fishes in his pocket for the money, for the man has just given them to *him*. He can start passing them out to the kids, but at least one of them will have gone back to the car to see how the dog is doing, or have been sent round in back by his mother to wash his hands or something. And even if papa does get them distributed, he's still going to be left with his own cone in one hand while he tries to get his money with the other. Meanwhile, of course, the man is very impatient, and the next group is asking him, "What flavors do you have?"

No, never let the man hand you the cones of others. Make him hand them out to each kid in turn. That way, too, you won't get those disgusting blobs of butter pecan and black raspberry on your own chocolate chip. And insist that he tell you how much it all costs and settle with him *before* he hands you your own cone. Make sure everyone has got paper napkins and everything *before* he hands you your own cone. Get *everything* straight before he hands you your own cone. Then, as he hands you your own cone, reach out and take it from him. Strange, magical, dangerous moment! It shares something of the mysterious, sick thrill that soldiers are said to feel on the eve of a great battle.

Now, consider for a moment just exactly what it is that you are about to be handed. It is a huge, irregular mass of ice cream, faintly domed at the top from the metal scoop, which has first produced it and then insecurely balanced it on the uneven top edge of a hollow inverted cone made out of the most brittle and fragile of materials. Clumps of ice cream hang over the side, very loosely attached to the main body. There is always much more ice cream than the cone could hold, even if the ice cream were tamped down into the cone, which of course it isn't. And the essence of ice cream is that it melts. It doesn't just stay there teetering in this irregular, top-heavy mass; it also melts. And it melts *fast*.

And it doesn't just melt—it melts into a sticky fluid that *cannot* be wiped off. The only thing one person could hand to another that might possibly be more dangerous is a live hand grenade from which the pin had been pulled five seconds earlier. And of course if anybody offered you that, you could say, "Oh. Uh, well—no, thanks."

Ice-cream men handle cones routinely, and are inured. They are like professionals who are used to handling sticks of TNT; their movements are quick and skillful. An ice-cream man will pass a cone to you casually, almost carelessly. Never accept a cone on this basis! Too many brittle sugar cones (the only good kind) are crushed or chipped, or their ice-cream tops knocked askew, by this casual sort of transfer from hand to hand. If the ice-cream man is attempting this kind of brusque transfer, keep your hands at your side, no matter what effort it may cost you to overcome the instinct by which everyone's hand goes out, almost automatically, whenever he is proffered something delicious and expected. Keep your hands at your side, and the ice-cream man will look up at you, startled, questioning. Lock his eyes with your own, and *then*, slowly, calmly, and above all deliberately, take the cone from him.

Grasp the cone with the right hand firmly but gently between thumb and at least one but not more than three fingers, two-thirds of the way up the cone. Then dart swiftly away to an open area, away from the jostling crowd at the stand. Now take up the classic ice-cream-cone-eating stance: feet from one to two feet apart, body bent forward from the waist at a twenty-five-degree angle, right elbow well up, right forearm horizontal, at a level with your collarbone and about twelve inches from it. But don't start eating yet. Check first to see what emergency repairs may be necessary. Sometimes a sugar cone will be so crushed or broken or cracked that all one can do is gulp at the thing like a savage, getting what he can of it and letting the rest drop to the ground, and then evacuating the area of catastrophe as quickly as possible. Checking the cone for possible trouble can be done in a second or two, if one knows where to look and does it systematically. A trouble spot some people overlook is the bottom tip of the cone. This may have been broken off. Or the flap of the cone material at the bottom, usually wrapped over itself in that funny spiral construction, may be folded in a way that is imperfect and leaves an opening. No need to say that through this opening—in a matter of perhaps thirty or, at most, ninety seconds—will begin to pour hundreds of thousands of sticky molecules of melted ice cream. You know in this case that you must instantly get the paper napkin in your left hand under and around the bottom of the cone to stem the forthcoming flow, or else be doomed to eat the cone far too rapidly. It is a grim moment. No one wants to eat a cone under that kind of pressure, but neither does anyone want to end up with the bottom of the cone stuck to a messy napkin. There's one other alternative—one that takes both skill and courage: Forgoing any cradling action, grasp the cone more firmly between thumb and forefinger and extend the other fingers so that they are out of the way of the dripping from the bottom, then increase the waist-bend angle from twenty-five degrees to thirty-five degrees, and then eat the cone, *allowing* it to drip out of the bottom onto the ground in front of you! Experienced and thoughtful cone-eaters enjoy facing up to this kind of sudden challenge.

SO far, we have been concentrating on cone problems, but of course there is the ice cream to worry about, too. In this area, immediate action is sometimes needed on three fronts at once. Frequently the ice cream will be mounted on the cone in a way that is perilously lopsided. This requires immediate corrective action to move it back into balance—a slight pressure downward with the teeth and lips to seat the ice cream more firmly in and on the cone, but not so hard, of course, as to break the cone. On other occasions, gobs of ice cream will be hanging loosely from the main body, about to fall to the ground (bad) or onto one's hand (far, far worse). This requires instant action, too; one must snap at the gobs like a frog in a swarm of flies. Sometimes, trickles of ice cream will already (already!) be running down the cone toward one's fingers, and one must quickly raise the cone, tilting one's face skyward, and lick with an upward motion that pushes the trickles away from the fingers and (as much as possible) into one's mouth. Every ice-cream cone is like every other ice-cream cone in that it potentially can present all of these problems, but each ice-cream cone is paradoxically unique in that it will present the problems in a different order of emergency and degree of severity. It is, thank God, a rare ice-cream cone that will present all three kinds of problems in exactly the same degree of emergency. With each cone, it is necessary to make an instantaneous judgment as to where the greatest danger is, and to *act!* A moment's delay, and the whole thing will be a mess before you've even tasted it (*Fig. 1*). If it isn't possible to decide between any two of the three basic emergency problems (i.e., lopsided mount, dangling gobs, running trickles), allow yourself to make an arbitrary adjudication; assign a "heads"

Fig. 1

value to one and a "tails" value to the other, then flip a coin to decide which is to be tended to first. Don't, for heaven's sake, *actually* flip a coin—you'd have to dig in your pockets for it, or else have it ready in your hand before you were handed the cone. There isn't remotely enough time for anything like that. Just decide *in your mind* which came up, heads or tails, and then try to remember as fast as you can which of the problems you had assigned to the winning side of the coin. Probably, though, there isn't time for any of this. Just do something, however arbitrary. Act! *Eat!*

In trying to make wise and correct decisions about the ice-cream cone in your hand, you should always keep the objectives in mind. The main objective, of course, is to get the cone under control. Secondarily, one will want to eat the cone calmly and with pleasure. Real pleasure lies not simply in eating the cone but in eating it *right*. Let us assume that you have darted to your open space and made your necessary emergency repairs. The cone is still dangerous—still, so to speak, "live." But you can now proceed with it in an orderly fashion. First, revolve the cone through the full three hundred and sixty degrees, snapping at the loose gobs of ice cream; turn the cone by moving the thumb away from you and the forefinger toward you, so the cone moves counterclockwise. Then, with the cone still "wound," which will require the wrist to be bent at the full right angle toward you, apply pressure with the mouth and tongue to accomplish overall realignment, straightening and settling the whole mess. Then, unwinding the cone back through the full three hundred and sixty degrees, remove any trickles of ice cream. From here on, some supplementary repairs may be necessary, but, the cone is now defused.

At this point, you can risk a glance around you. How badly the others are doing with their cones! Now you can settle down to eating yours. This is done by eating the ice cream off the top. At each bite, you must press down cautiously, so that the ice cream settles farther and farther into the cone. Be very careful not to break the cone. Of course, you never take so much ice cream into your mouth at once that it hurts your teeth; for the same reason, you never let unmelted ice cream into the back of your mouth. If all these procedures are followed correctly, you should shortly arrive at the ideal—the way an ice-cream cone is always pictured but never actually is when it is handed to you (*Fig. 2*). The ice cream should now form a small dome whose circumference exactly coincides with the large circumference of the cone itself—a small

Fig. 2

skullcap that fits exactly on top of a larger, inverted dunce cap. You have made order out of chaos; you are an artist. You have taken an unnatural, abhorrent, irregular, chaotic form, and from it you have sculpted an ordered, ideal shape that might be envied by Praxiteles or even Euclid.

Now at last you can begin to take little nibbles of the cone itself, being very careful not to crack it. Revolve the cone so that its rim remains smooth and level as you eat both ice cream and cone in the same ratio. Because of the geometrical nature of things, a constantly reduced inverted cone still remains a perfect inverted cone no matter how small it grows, just as a constantly reduced dome held within a cone retains *its* shape. Because you are constantly reshaping the dome of ice cream with your tongue and nibbling at the cone, it follows in logic—and in actual practice, if you are skillful and careful—that the cone will continue to look exactly the same, except for its size, as you eat it down, so that at the very end you will hold between your thumb and forefinger a tiny, idealized replica of an ice-cream cone, a thing perhaps one inch high. Then, while the others are licking their sticky fingers, preparatory to wiping them on their clothes, or going back to the ice-cream stand for more paper napkins to try to clean themselves up—*then* you can hold the miniature cone up for everyone to see, and pop it gently into your mouth.

1968

VERONICA GENG

TEACHING POETRY WRITING
TO SINGLES

I HAD the idea to teach more kinds of people to write poetry as a result of two previous books of mine: "I Taught Republicans to Write Poetry" and "How to Teach the Writing of Poetry to Fashion Coördinators." I thought of singles because of an interesting hour I had spent reading my own poems at a singles bar called Ozymandias II, and because of many other hours, much less happy ones, I had spent before my marriage as a visitor to another singles bar, Nick's Roost, where there were no activities of that kind going on.

I asked the owners of Ozymandias II, my friends Ozzie and Mandy Dias, to arrange for the class. I had four students, and we met once, on a Friday at midnight, at the big table in front. Like the others in the crowded room, most of the four were in their twenties, thirties, forties, and fifties. Some of them wore glasses. One worked for an escort agency, one was a hayride organizer, another a fashion coördinator, another a Republican. The singles bar gave these people a feeling of meetability, but none had ever written poetry there, and none, I think, would have done so without me.

I started the class by saying what I was going to do was get them to write words in lines of uneven length on a piece of paper (I didn't want to scare them with the formal term "poem") and then I would write a book about how much I had helped them. The students were not in the habit of sitting and hearing something like this explained. Some were so distracted that they could only talk in incomplete sentences, such as "What the—?!" Others stared nervously at the TV screen above the bar, where the final minutes of some kind of sports event seemed to be going on. I said that writing words in lines of uneven length on a piece of paper was not the hard thing that many people think. I said how could it be hard if I was going to teach it to them? I was sure I could give them the mastery of literary form and metaphor so lacking in singles-bar life. I said I knew they had all been single since childhood and I could see how this might make them feel "unmarried" and "on their own," but I said John Milton and Vachel Lindsay and James Dickey had all been single at one time or another and that writing words in lines of uneven length on a piece of paper had helped them to stop running.

I said the first thing we would do would be a collaboration. I knew the students had all gone on a singles bicycling tour of the Wye River in England five years before, so I said I want everyone to remember that trip and think of a sentence about it. Something you saw. Or an outfit you wore. Or a feeling you had about time passing and your not being married yet and having to go on bicycle tours to meet somebody. I'll write down everyone's sentence and put them together, I said, and we'll have words in lines of uneven length on a piece of paper.

At first the students were puzzled. "We went there, that's all." "I remember we did different stuff." "And bicycling." Then William said, "O.K. A double vodka, please. Five years have passed; five summers, with the length of five long winters!" This was a good start, I said, especially the dramatic "frame" made by "O.K. A double vodka, please," as if the lines were being said casually to someone by someone sitting in a bar or tavern.

Then Ezra spoke up: "And again I hear these waters, rolling from their mountain springs with a soft inland βροδοδάκτυλος." This was better than I had expected, but the poem was getting a false-sounding jig-jigging rhythm, and I said for the students not to worry about academic gimmicks such as metre. I also said try to get in more of your own personal feelings and hangups. I said for instance I remember when I was in high school I worried a lot about my bike getting rusty.

It was Emily's turn: "Once again do I behold these steep and lofty cliffs, that on a wild secluded scene impress thoughts: the soul selects her own scene, but you meet more eligible guys by going out and partying rather than staying at home." I said the repetition of "scene" was nice, it gave a nice feeling of repetition.

At this point William got very agitated and said we were ruining "his" idea. I said all right, you do the next part, but I pressed him to put in more details from his own experience as a single—the very details that he seemed most reluctant to put in, maybe because he thought they were "stupid." He continued: "The day is come when I again socialize, taking a nice girl to dinner and a show, and view the floor show and the salad bar, which at this season, with its unripe fruits, is clad in one green hue, and lose myself 'mid men and women, who have different attitudes toward sex."

Quite soon the students felt they had enough words in lines of uneven length on a piece of paper. I read the results back to them and said what they had written was a poem. I asked them to think of a title. They decided the poem was really about working out the problems of writing a poem, so they called it "Working Out at the Wye."

I THEN said to do individual poems. Writing a poem all by yourself is something that nobody can do with you, and this is a special problem for people who are already panicked about being alone, such as so-called singles. I say "so-called" because the words "single," "bachelorette," etc., may be thought to apply to people's *imaginations,* and they do not. The power to see the world as a configuration of couples linked inextricably in Holy Matrimony is the possession of everyone.

I told the students that one of the main problems poets have is what to write about. I said this was a really hard problem if you were lonely and in a studio apartment and had to go out to a bar to seek some grotesque mockery of human contact. But I said that in a poem you can be somebody else, you can even be *two* people. I said for everyone to start their poem with "Let us . . ." The "us" in the poem could do anything: get married, have a huge church wedding with a flower girl and a page boy, sit down and talk over family finances—anything.

The most popular "Let us . . ." poem was Tom's:

> Let us go then, you and me,
> When the weekend is spread out for us to see
> Like a roommate bombed out of his gourd under the table. . . .
> Oh, do not ask, "You said you were *who?*"
> Let us go to the free luau.
>
> In the room the women come and go
> Talking of someone who might be tall and share their enthusiasm for
>   theatre.

I praised Tom's poem, saying it might seem silly to a lot of people but to me it gave a nice sociable feeling, the sounds of nice people talking to each other. I said there were many more things having to do with the five senses that could be in a poem, like colors. I said for instance when I was a boy I had a dog named Rusty. I said close your eyes and take a swallow of beer and say what color it reminds you of. They answered. "Black." "Beer color." "Black." "Blackish." After this exercise, Ezra wrote his "Little Black Book" poem:

> Hang it all, Mark Cross,
> there can be but the one little black book. . . .
> Under black leather dress, lithe daughter of telephone directory . . .

I said noises could be in a poem. I threw a beer stein on the floor and asked what word the noise sounded like. "Bunk." "Drunk." "Black." "Bash." Right away Emily wrote something down and gave it to me:

> I dreamt I was a Key Club,
> Select Fraternity.
> At night the eligible Men
> All had a Bash at me.

I said that in a poem you can compare things in goofy ways. Compare something small to something yellow, something big to something you don't know the name for, something married to something legally separated. William later told me that this idea made him write his nice poem that starts:

> Shall I compare thee to your place or mine?

I WAS surprised when it was 4 A.M., closing time at Ozymandias II. The students were still quite excited and said could they stay for a few minutes after hours because they wanted to collaborate on one final poem, a poem for me. They made me go into the john while they wrote, and when I came back they were laughing. The poem was this:

> Thank you, this has been as much fun as a free trip
> To Aspen—only I can't ski and anyhow I'd probably break something
> In several places, crack! crack! crack!
>
> Gosh, thanks, I simply feel as if you gave me a raunchy souvenir T-shirt from the
> Annual Bachelor Rally—quite an icebreaker, but I already have one.
>
> By the way, thank you for this night like a bag of yellow Doritos, the
>   name reminds me of a dog I once heard of named Doris
> But I'm on a diet of blue and of purple.
>
> Thank you for an experience similar to drinking tee Martoonis,
> Which I could compare to those other clear drinks that I can hardly be
>   expected to remember the name of. Oh—water!
> Listen, really, we all thank you for teaching us that looks aren't every-
>   thing, even in a poem.

I said they had learned a whole lot and it was a really nice poem, one that gave a strong feeling of niceness.

1978

IAN FRAZIER

DATING YOUR MOM

IN today's fast-moving, transient, rootless society, where people meet and make love and part without ever really touching, the relationship every guy already has with his own mother is too valuable to ignore. Here is a grown, experienced, loving woman—one you do not have to go to a party or a singles bar to meet, one you do not have to go to great lengths to get to know. There are hundreds of times when you and your mother are thrown together naturally, without the tension that usually accompanies courtship—just the two of you, alone. All you need is a little presence of mind to take advantage of these situations. Say your mom is driving you downtown in the car to buy you a new pair of slacks. First, find a nice station on the car radio, one that she likes. Get into the pleasant lull of freeway driving—tires humming along the pavement, air-conditioner on max. Then turn to look at her across the front seat and say something like, "You know, you've really kept your shape, Mom, and don't think I haven't noticed." Or suppose she comes into your room to bring you some clean socks. Take her by the wrist, pull her close, and say, "Mom, you're the most fascinating woman I've ever met." Probably she'll tell you to cut out the foolishness, but, I can guarantee you one thing: she will never tell your dad. Possibly she would find it hard to say, "Dear, Piper just made a pass at me," or possibly she is secretly flattered, but, whatever the reason, she will keep it to herself until the day comes when she is no longer ashamed to tell the world of your love.

Dating your mother seriously might seem difficult at first, but once you try it I'll bet you'll be surprised at how easy it is. Facing up to your intention is the main thing: you have to want it bad enough. One problem is that lots of people get hung up on feelings of guilt about their dad. They think, Oh, here's this kindly old guy who taught me how to hunt and whittle and dynamite fish—I can't let him go on into his twilight years alone. Well, there are two reasons you can dismiss those thoughts from your mind. First, *every* woman, I don't care who she is, prefers her son to her husband. That is a simple fact; ask any woman who has a son, and she'll admit it. And why shouldn't she prefer someone who is so much like herself, who represents nine months of special concern and love and intense physical closeness—someone whom she actually created? As more women begin to express the need to have something all their own in the world, more women are going to start being honest about this preference. When you and your mom begin going together, you will simply become part of a natural and inevitable historical trend.

Second, you must remember this about your dad: you have your mother, he has his! Let him go put the moves on his own mother and stop messing with yours. If his mother is dead or too old to be much fun anymore, that's not your fault, is it? It's not your fault that he didn't realize his mom for the woman she was, before it was too late. Probably he's going to try a lot of emotional blackmail on you just because you had a good idea and he never did. Don't buy it. Comfort yourself with the thought that your dad belongs to the last generation of guys who will let their moms slip away from them like that.

Once your dad is out of the picture—once he has taken up fly-tying, joined the Single Again Club, moved to Russia, whatever—and your mom has been wooed and won, if you're anything like me you're going to start having so much fun that the good times you had with your mother when you were little will seem tame by comparison. For a while, Mom and I went along living a contented, quiet life, just happy to be with each other. But after several months we started getting into some different things, like the big motorized stroller. The thrill I felt the first time Mom steered me down the street! On the tray, in addition to my Big Jim doll and the wire with the colored wooden beads, I have my desk blotter, my typewriter, an in-out basket, and my name plate. I get a lot of work done, plus I get a great chance to people-watch. Then there's my big, adult-sized highchair, where I sit in the evening as Mom and I watch the news and discuss current events, while I paddle in my food and throw my dishes on the floor. When Mom reaches to wipe off my chin and I take her hand, and we fall to the floor in a heap—me, Mom, highchair, and all—well, those are the best times, those are the very best times.

It is true that occasionally I find myself longing for even more—for things I know I cannot have, like the feel of a firm, strong, gentle hand at the small of my back lifting me out of bed into the air, or someone who could walk me around and burp me after I've watched all the bowl games and had about nine beers. Ideally, I would like a mom about nineteen or twenty feet tall, and although I considered for a while asking my mom to start working out with weights and drinking Nutrament, I finally figured, Why put her through it? After all, she is not only my woman, she is my best friend. I have to take her as she is, and the way she is is plenty good enough for me.

1978

IAN FRAZIER

A READING LIST FOR YOUNG WRITERS

WHEN aspiring young authors come to me and ask what books I think it essential for a modern writer to have read, I am hard pressed for an answer. I dislike talking about writing, because I believe that the job of a writer is to write rather than talk, and that real writing is something so deep within one that any discussion profanes it. In addition, I have a profound distrust of lists—the ten-best this, the twenty-worst that. Such lists strike me as a characteristically American oversimplification of life's diversity. Like most writers of any experience, I fear making lists simply because I fear leaving something out. Young writers, however, can be very insistent (I have found), and, as no less an authority than Flaubert once said, "what a scholar one might be if one knew well merely some half a dozen books." So I have decided to tackle this difficult task despite my misgivings. The following six works are ones that I believe every writer—in fact, every educated person— should know as well as he knows his own name and telephone number:

"Remembrance of Things Past." Marcel Proust's lyric, luminous evocation of lost time is arguably the greatest novel of the twentieth century. Moving from private to public scope, from the narrator's boyhood in the small provincial town of Combray, through the glittering salons of the Faubourg-Saint-Germain in Paris, to the sun-blinding hotels and beaches of Hawaii's Diamond Head, this monumental work has as its intent the precise description of Time itself. Time is as much a character in the book as the narrator, Marcel, or his ex-wife, Valérie. When Marcel meets Valérie on a flight to Honolulu, she is much changed since he saw her last; now she is an international diamond smuggler, and the mob has put a hundred-thousand-dollar price on her head. Again, Time is the genie who reveals to Marcel unguessed secrets about a woman with whom he was once deeply in love. Many writers have imitated Proust's generous, untrammelled, multi-hued prose; none has ever equalled it.

"Madame Bovary." In Emma Bovary, Flaubert created a character who will live as long as there are books and readers. Flaubert, we are told, wrote slowly and carefully; I try to take the same care when I read him. In the marvellous scene when Emma first discovers that the petit-bourgeois pharmacist, Homais, is operating a baby-stealing ring, the intricate chiastic imagery switches from the look of horror on Emma's face to the happy, gurgling laughter of the innocent babies in their makeshift cribs in the garage behind the drugstore. Flaubert's genius for the accumulation of observed detail in delineating character showed the way for many later writers—particularly James Joyce.

"War and Peace." Tolstoy's epic novel of Russia during the Napoleonic era is, in essence, a parable about the power of the media. Pierre Bezuhov is the ambitious young reporter who will go to any length to get a story—including murder. What he doesn't know is that Natasha Rostov, Moscow's feared "Dragon Lady," wants Pierre iced, and the hit man is Prince Andrei, Pierre's old college roommate! No writer who ever lived possessed a surer sense of plot than Tolstoy.

"Buddenbrooks." Meet Antonie. She's beautiful. She's talented. She's sexy. She's the daughter of rich German businessman Jean Budden-brook. And she's a walking time bomb. Somebody wants her dead, and she has been infected with a deadly virus that takes twenty-four hours to work. Half the city of Frankfurt goes underground looking for the antidote, and the police, in desperation, join forces with the mob. Author Thomas Mann interweaves these many strands so effortlessly that it is easy to see why he, along with Proust and Joyce, was considered one of the three main architects of twentieth-century literature.

"Bleak House." This is the one with the car chase, right? And the exploding helicopter at the end? Excellent! A neglected book but one of Dickens' best.

"Ulysses." Stephen Dedalus, star of James Joyce's "Ulysses," teams up with twelve beautiful lady truckers to find the madman responsible for a series of brutal murders. When Stephen himself becomes a suspect, he turns to his old buddy from 'Nam, Jim Rockford. Jim comes up with a great plan, which is to pretend that Stephen is dead and to plant a fake obituary in his brother-in-law's newspaper. Then Jim, Angel,

Molly Bloom, Buck Mulligan, Rocky, Stephen, and the twelve beautiful lady truckers fly over to Dublin, Stephen's home town. It is St. Patrick's Day, and in the mass of people the killer escapes. Then the scene shifts to New Orleans, where Mardi Gras is in full swing. Then it's down to Rio, for Carnaval. All this time, Joyce keeps the reader informed about what is going on inside each character's head.

MY list is, of course, only a beginning. View it as the foundation of a literary mind; do not mistake it for the edifice itself. If you approach these books with passion, with an eye to their symmetries and harmonies and violent dissonances, you will not necessarily learn how to write. But you will certainly come nearer an understanding of what it is, gloriously, to read.

1982

DONALD BARTHELME

HOW I WRITE MY SONGS

BY BILL B. WHITE

SOME of the methods I use to write my songs will be found in the following examples. Everyone has a song in him or her. Writing songs is a basic human trait. I am not saying that it is easy; like everything else worthwhile in this world it requires concentration and hard work. The methods I will outline are a good way to begin and have worked for me but they are by no means the only methods that can be used. There is no one set way of writing your songs, every way is just as good as the other as Kipling said. (I am talking now about the lyrics; we will talk about the melodies in a little bit.) The important thing is to put true life into your songs, things that people know and can recognize and truly feel. You have to be open to experience in what is going on around you, the things of daily life. Often little things that you don't even think about at the time can be the basis of a song.

A knowledge of all the different types of songs that are commonly accepted is helpful. To give you an idea of the various types of songs there are I am going to tell you how I wrote various of my own, including "Rudelle," "Last Night," "Sad Dog Blues," and others, how I came to write these songs and where I got the idea and what the circumstances were, more or less, so that you will be able to do the same thing. Just remember, *there is no substitute for sticking to it* and listening to the work of others who have been down this road before you and have mastered their craft over many years.

In the case of "Rudelle" I was sitting at my desk one day with my pencil and yellow legal pad and I had two things that were irritating me. One was a letter from the electric company that said "The check for $75.60 sent us in payment of your bill has been returned to us by the bank unhonored etc. etc." Most of you who have received this type of letter from time to time know how irritating this kind of communication can be as well as embarrassing. The other thing that was irritating me was that I had a piece of white thread tied tight around my middle at navel height as a reminder to keep my stomach pulled in to strengthen the abdominals while sitting—this is the price you pay for slopping down too much beer when your occupation is essentially a sit-down one! Anyhow I had these two things itching me, so I decided to write a lost-my-mind song.

I wrote down on my legal pad the words:

> When I lost my baby
> I almost lost my mine

This is more or less a traditional opening for this type of song. Maybe it was written by somebody originally way long ago and who wrote it is forgotten. It often helps to begin with a traditional or well-known line or lines to set a pattern for yourself. You can then write the rest of the song and, if you wish, cut off the top part, giving you an original song. *Songs are always composed of both traditional and new elements.* This means that you can rely on the tradition to give your song "legs" while also putting in your own experience or particular way of looking at things for the new.

Incidentally the lines I have quoted may look pretty bare to you but remember you are looking at just one element, the words, and there is also the melody and the special way various artists will have of singing it which gives flavor and freshness. For example, an artist who is primarily a blues singer would probably give the "when" a lot of squeeze, that is to say, draw it out, and he might also sing "baby" as three notes, "bay-ee-bee," although it is only two syllables. Various artists have their own unique ways of doing a song and what may appear to be rather plain or dull on paper becomes quite different when it is a song.

I then wrote:

> When I lost my baby
> I almost lost my mine
> When I lost my baby
> I almost lost my mine
> When I found my baby
> The sun began to shine.
>> Copyright © 1972 by French Music, Inc.

You will notice I retained the traditional opening because it was so traditional I did not see any need to delete it. With the addition of various material about Rudelle and what kind of woman she was, it became gold in 1976.

Incidentally while we are talking about use of traditional materials here is a little tip: you can often make good use of colorful expressions in common use such as "If the good Lord's willin' and the creek don't rise" (to give you just one example) which I used in "Goin' to Get To-gether" as follows:

> Goin' to get to-geth-er
> Goin' to get to-geth-er
> If the good Lord's willin' and the creek don't rise.
>> Copyright © 1974 by French Music, Inc.

These common expressions are expressive of the pungent ways in which most people often think—they are the salt of your song, so to say. Try it!

It is also possible to give a song a funny or humorous "twist":

> Show'd my soul to the woman at the bank
> She said put that thing away boy, put that thing away
> Show'd my soul to the woman at the liquor store
> She said put that thing away boy, 'fore it turns the wine

> Show'd my soul to the woman at the 7-Eleven
> She said: Is that all?
>> Copyright © 1974 by Rattlesnake Music, Inc.

You will notice that the meter here is various and the artist is given great liberties.

ANOTHER type of song which is a dear favorite of almost everyone is the song that has a message, some kind of thought that people can carry away with them and think about. Many songs of this type are written and gain great acceptance every day. Here is one of my own that I put to a melody which has a kind of martial flavor:

> How do you spell truth? L-o-v-e is how you spell truth
> How do you spell love? T-r-u-t-h is how you spell love
> Where were you last night?
> Where were you last night?
>> Copyright © 1975 by Rattlesnake Music/A.I.M. Corp.

When "Last Night" was first recorded, the engineer said "That's a keeper" on the first take and it was subsequently covered by sixteen artists including Walls.

The I-ain't-nothin'-but-a-man song is a good one to write when you are having a dry spell. These occur in songwriting as in any other profession and if you are in one it is often helpful to try your hand at this type of song which is particularly good with a heavy rhythm emphasis in the following pattern:

> Da da da da *da*
> Whomp, whomp

where some of your instruments are playing da da da da *da*, hitting that last note hard, and the others answer whomp, whomp. Here is one of my own:

> I'm just an ordinary mane
> Da da da da *da*
> Whomp, whomp
> Just an ordinary mane
> Da da da da *da*

Whomp, whomp
Ain't nothin' but a mane
Da da da da *da*
Whomp, whomp
I'm a grizzly mane
Da da da da *da*
Whomp, whomp
I'm a hello-goodbye mane
Da da da da *da*
Whomp, whomp
I'm a ramblin'-ramblin' mane
Da da da da *da*
Whomp, whomp
I'm a *mane's* mane
I'm a woeman's mane
Da da da da *da*
Whomp, whomp
I'm an upstairs mane
Da da da da *da*
Whomp, whomp
I'm a today-and-tomorrow mane
Da da da da *da*
Whomp, whomp
I'm a Freeway mane
Da da da da *da*
Whomp, whomp

Copyright © 1977 by French Music, Inc.

Well, you see how it is done. It is my hope that these few words will get you started. Remember that although this business may seem closed and standoffish to you, looking at it from the outside, inside it has some very warm people in it, some of the finest people I have run into in the course of a varied life. The main thing is to persevere and to believe in yourself, no matter what the attitude of others may be or appear to be. I could never have written my songs had I failed to believe in Bill B. White, not as a matter of conceit or false pride but as a human being. I will continue to write my songs, for the nation as a whole and for the world.

1978

SAVE OUR BUS HERDS!

SECOND Avenue, once a busy commercial thoroughfare, has been all but destroyed recently, overrun by migrating herds of enormous, baying buses. These great lumbering vehicles, which travel in groups of about eight or nine, rumble through the area each morning, scattering frightened pedestrians into the shuttered doorways of newly abandoned shops.

Approximately the size of an elephant, the once solitary bus has baffled the scientific community by beginning to exhibit herding behavior. Just before dawn, the dusty caravans make their way downtown, dawdling at intersections, where they emit their eerie honking calls, nudging each other a little before resuming their long journey.

Last January, the Federal Carrier Protection Agency designated buses an endangered vehicle. Since then, Second Avenue has drawn international crowds of omnibus watchers and conveyance researchers to the spectacle of our rare and powerfully beautiful Grummans. Residents and local merchants, however, are less appreciative of the migrating herds. "They've ruined the neighborhood," said Mrs. Edna Hardee, one of a group of antibus demonstrators gathered at Seventy-ninth Street. "Just look what they've done to the ecological balance. They travel in a pack, honking and squeaking and frightening off all the smaller vehicles." Of the flocks of yellow cabs and shore jitneys that used to frequent Second Avenue, only an occasional hardy Checker now ventures into the territory. In front of Lamston's, a perambulator stands—empty.

Several shooting incidents have been reported recently. Police say they involved deer hunters from Florida invited to the area by the more reactionary members of Young Americans Against Herds (YAAH!). The hunters picked up the trail of a herd at Thirty-fourth Street and, after stalking it for twenty-five minutes in the early-morning fog, surprised seven Grumman Flxibles placidly grazing a mailbox on the southwest corner of Twenty-third Street. Shots were fired, and two of the buses fell before the rest of the startled herd escaped around the corner. A.S.P.C.A. volunteers trying to pull the fallen buses to safety vied with hunters attempting to tie the Grummans onto the roofs of their station wagons.

"Poachers are a great threat to these worthy vehicles," said noted bus researcher Charles Pearly in an emotional appearance on "Good Morning America." "There is a flourishing black market in bus pelts. Since 1981, the U.S. Bus and Wildlife Department has confiscated six million dollars' worth of merchandise manufactured from illegally slaughtered buses. Why, just last week a raid on a Queens warehouse uncovered a huge cache of powdered bus horns destined to be sold as aphrodisiacs." Dr. Pearly, professor emeritus at Cornell University's Division of Bus Sciences, is president of the Interfaith Bus Relief Corps, a nonprofit organization established in 1979 to collect tokens for starving buses. A normal bus consumes fifteen hundred pounds of tokens per day, and the natural supply has dwindled to dangerously low levels. In theory, the buses could subsist on coins alone, but because of weather conditions this year, there has been a disappointing coin crop. Also, a subspecies native to Washington, D.C., known as the "White," because of its distinctive coloration, has joined several herds of Grumman and General Motors vehicles, almost doubling the population and causing an alarming concentration in the region. Said Dr. Pearly, "Poachers just slaughter these weakened transports."

Captain Jiminy Strout, leader of the Florida hunters, responded to Dr. Pearly's charges by saying he was "only trying to help." According to Captain Strout, the hunters must step in now that man has decimated the El and the West Side Highway, the bus's natural predators.

Conservationists, outraged by the shootings, held a press conference at Loews Tower East, during which Walt Gawd, bus biologist and chairman of the Save Our Surface Transportation Protection Foundation (SOS), raised the issue of bus shooting as a sport. "How many buses are felled every year by the hunter's bullet?" he asked. "So-called sportsmen have already wiped out the double-decker, just because it was a sitting duck."

SECOND Avenue has long been a haven for the migrating bus; in fact, it is believed that Second Avenue was originally a pathway beaten out by prehistoric motor coaches moving south. But researchers are still not sure where these impressive vehicles come from or where they go. And although there have been several sightings of individual rogue buses

charging up Third, the actual northbound route has never been identified. Even so, scientists say, they do know enough about bus behavior to
predict that any disruption of herding or migration patterns would destroy the once mighty bus altogether.

"Buses been coming by here long as I remember," one gray-haired
man commented. "Grummans now. And them white ones. But there
used to be green ones all along here. And they didn't travel in packs,
neither. No, sir. They just come along, all by themselves, one after
t'other. They gone now. Gone forever."

Concerned citizens, like Judith Needleham-Stark, of the Agency for
a Very Nice New York, attributed the extinction of the green city bus to
officials who had them painted blue. "We warned them what would
happen," Ms. Needleham-Stark recalls. "But there is so much ignorance about buses."

1982

WILLIAM WHITE

THREE GREAT MEALS

IN this article I am going to tell you how to make three great meals
using standard ingredients. By "standard ingredients" I mean things
that can be found in any supermarket from one end of the country to
the other. I am going to name names and tell you what brands I use, not
because I am in the pay of these particular brands or have any fiduciary
relation to them but because they are the ones I use daily and ones that
I have found work well, day in and day out. In each case you will notice
that the meal is geared to the person who does not have too much time
to screw around but at the same time wants extra-good results, something a little better than what you would get if you just used these fine
products straight, without informed guidance or nuance.

It is true that all of these great meals fall roughly under the rubric
"Southern Cooking," but I stress that the ingredients have nationwide
distribution, for the most part, and that because something has its ori-

gins in the South doesn't automatically mean that it can be dismissed as "low-rent" or beneath contempt. An open mind toward the cuisines of various regions is the first hallmark of the educable palate.

A GREAT BREAKFAST

For the Great Breakfast we assume that, the night before, you have gone out and bought 8–10 pieces of Popeyes Fried Chicken at the drive-in window of your local Popeyes, together with 6–8 Popeyes Biscuits. Now I am not sure that Popeyes is entirely national, but it is widely found throughout the South which makes it national enough for our purposes. Colonel Sanders may be substituted if you wish. The average family will have eaten about seven of the chicken pieces and maybe four of the biscuits during the original meal leaving you with a wealth of residue for the Great Breakfast.

Upon awakening, take one package McCormick Chicken Gravy Mix and place it in a saucepan, adding one-half can of Swanson's Clear Chicken Broth. This is the first subtlety. The directions for the Gravy Mix suggest cold water; by adding Swanson's Chicken Broth you get a gravy that is far richer. (You also double your expense, but as the Gravy Mix is typically about 63 cents a package and the Broth about 49 cents a can, it's not that much.)

Next, chop a fresh onion very fine—very *very* fine, about two tablespoons' worth. Throw this in the gravy. You may then add a splash of Soave Bolla white wine and raise heat to boil off the alcohol. If your religious convictions do not permit the use of alcohol in your breakfast it may be omitted, but what do you do when you get to Turtle Soup, leave out the sherry? While the gravy is simmering, take the leftover Popeyes Biscuits and split them, placing them in a small container in a 425-degree oven for approximately eight minutes.

Now, strip chicken from leftover Popeyes pieces and add to gravy, being careful to not include the heavy crispy skin that was your motivation for getting the Popeyes chicken in the first place. Then remove biscuits from oven, ladle gravy over them, and sprinkle with Spice Islands thyme, taking care to crush thyme between thumb and forefinger to release flavor. The result is a chicken-with-dumplings that cannot be equalled this side of that tin-roofed place on a dirt road outside of Talladega, Alabama, that we've all heard about but no one has ever found. The masterstroke here is of course the onion.

AN UNUSUAL LUNCH

This kind of lunch is possible when the green-skinned tomatillo is in season. Luckily the green-skinned tomatillo is always in season in the canned version put out by Herdez, which also includes chilis. Take a can of Gebhardt Tamales and place in a small ovengoing vessel. Layer with chopped onion. Add one can Herdez Salsa Verde Tomatillos. Cover with Kraft Shredded Sharp Cheddar, which is available in a re-sealable plastic bag for about $2.09 for 10 oz. Use about one-third of the bag to top the dish, spreading the cheese smoothly around with your hand. Bake in 425-degree oven for fifteen minutes. In the more developed parts of the country there will be locally produced tamales (usually differentiated as to "Hot" or "Mild") made by gifted indige-nous personnel and these can be substituted for the Gebhardt variety. Renown and Ro*Tel brands of tomatoes and chilis can also be used; both are excellent, although not green. This lunch has a strong Mexi-can flavor due to the use of ingredients associated with Mexico; al-though it is not in any sense authentic, it is unusual.

SUPERB DINNER FOR SIXTY

You probably did not know that a superb dinner for sixty could be made out of canned goods, but that is true. Begin with five Smok-A-Roma Fully Cooked Boneless Hams. Remove hams from wrappers and cut in chunks, each chunk roughly the size of a Bic cigarette lighter. Set aside. Next take thirty 15-oz. cans of Trappey's Black Eye Peas Flavored with Slab Bacon, open, and set aside. Next brown thirty pounds of Oscar Mayer Little Smokies, which are very good bite-sized smoked sausages. Tearing open the packages is tiresome but you can usually get children to do this for you. In the same fat, make a roux by stirring in ten pounds of Gold Medal All-Purpose Flour. This gives you approxi-mately twelve pounds of roux (flour plus oil). Set aside.

Next, into some gallons of water in huge immense pots on four six-burner stoves pour any number of cans of Progresso Peeled Tomatoes Italian Style with Basil (Pomidoro Pelati Tipo Italiano con Basilico). If you use the larger cans you have fewer cans to open. Add forty-eight cloves of chopped Elephant Garlic, which is sold in little net bags from Frieda of California and has a subtle explosiveness that is piquant.

By now you will be slightly confused as you look around you at the mighty forces you have mustered but everything is easier than it looks. You must understand that we don't like to get this involved either but maybe it's your daughter's wedding or something and you have the choice of giving the whole problem over to some unreliable caterer who'll just supply some pink froufrou on lettuce leaves at a horrible price per head or doing it yourself with your accustomed élan and good will. Place a half pound of the roux into each pot and paddle it around in there until the liquid has achieved a rich dark-brown color, then add the ham, sausages, and Black Eye Peas. Simmer for some time; you are doing just fine.

Pork is the motif which has up to now dominated the mix, and the pork has to have a contrasting flavor. The only thing to do is to slug in five Maple Leaf Farms Frozen Ducklings. Defrost and cut up ducks, brown quickly in Lou Ana 100% Pure and Natural Peanut Oil, home office, Opelousas, La., place in pots and let simmer for one hour. Salt (Morton), pepper (Lawry's), and parsley your twenty-four pots all to hell, and you are ready to serve. About twenty pounds of sliced onions would be a good addition, although they probably should have gone in earlier. If you want to know something to call this superb meal you could probably call it a burgoo. (I would like to acknowledge input for this recipe from the Arkansas Department of Corrections, Food Services Division.)

For other excellent recipes involving American canned goods, my 64-page leaflet is available upon request. But I am not trying to sell the leaflet, only to stress an appropriate respect and love for the American canned good, which is not, and never will be, Japanese.

1987

BRUCE McCALL

——————————

READ THIS FIRST

CONGRATULATIONS, but WARNING: Driving your new car may cause car sickness. NOTE: While using this manual, make sure your reading area is well ventilated and free of Ebola viruses. To avoid eyestrain, use both eyes. CAUTION: Do not attempt to read the manual backward or underwater. If you are underwater, unlock all doors (A) and the glove box (B), using square-headed key (F).

Open doors may cause aerodynamic drag. To close door, swing door (A) toward the car body (B), using the handle (C), until the latch (D) engages. Do NOT attempt to force beyond this point. This could tip the car over on its side and interfere with a smooth, safe journey.

WARNING: You are a flammable substance. Always check before shifting out of P that you are not on fire. If your skin is blistering and you detect a barbecue-like aroma, you are on fire. A burning driver can cause serious damage to the car's upholstery. Repairs should be made only by an authorized dealer, using genuine original replacement parts. Failure to do so can void your warranty.

Your turn signal is a precision driving instrument. Do not attempt to use the left or right signal's one-two beat as a metronome during in-car sing-alongs. This can induce hypnotic trances and loss of control, with possible damage to the car's paint finish. WARNING: Locust plagues cause only superficial paint damage. Never attempt to erase blemishes with a rat-tail file. Use only recommended locust plague removers. See your authorized dealer's wide selection.

If you hear a steady humming noise during driving, do NOT attempt to dismantle your car while it is running. This can lead to loss of windshield-washer fluid. Check your radio or other occupants for humming sounds. If humming noise persists, drive until the fuel gauge reads "Empty," at which point humming should stop. WARNING: When refilling fuel tank, uncap slowly, as shown in diagrams 1–2–3–4–5–6, on a well-ventilated prairie. Never uncap fuel filler port in close proximity to a Chinese New Year celebration.

WARNING: The driver's sun visor (A) can create visual "blind spots" that cause fatal head-on collisions. If you are about to have a fatal head-on collision, leave current registration and insurance documents in the glove box (B). SAFETY NOTE: Never leave valuables in an unlocked glove box. The same key (C) that unlocks your trunk (D) unlocks your glove box and the right-rear passenger door. The Valet Key (E) unlocks the driver's-side door only when ALL other doors, the fuel filler port, and the trunk are locked. The ignition key (F) also unlocks all doors, the fuel filler port (G), and the trunk (H). Never give the ignition key to a stranger (I). If all keys are used simultaneously, the Gard-a-Larm (J) will sound until the Valet Key is inserted in the trunk lock (K) and turned counterclockwise, as in diagrams 9–10. Turn clockwise to rearm.

WARNING: Your car's "package" or "hat" shelf (A) is not a shelf. Packages and hats should NEVER be placed there. For package-shelf instructions, consult the Package Shelf or Emergency sections of this manual or make an appointment with the service manager at your authorized dealer.

WARNING: Attempting to drive your car with a pedestrian underneath can cause uneven tire wear, front-end misalignment, binding of the steering gear, and damage to the catalytic converter in your exhaust system, creating an environmental threat that may increase the danger of global warming. Never leave your car's engine running in the Amazon rain forest. MAINTENANCE TIP: If Amazon damages seat upholstery, wipe clean with a sponge or cloth soaked in tepid water. WARNING: Use only genuine, factory-direct tepid water. See your authorized dealer.

While your car has been carefully engineered for years of enjoyable motoring, high-speed driving maneuvers during a heart attack, stroke, or machine-gun fusillade should be attempted only by trained professionals on a specially prepared closed course. If you are about to be incapacitated by events beyond your control, keep both hands on the wheel, turn the radio, tape deck, or CD player to OFF, deactivate Cruise Control, reduce speed, activate your turn signal, drive onto a level area away from traffic, bring your car to a gradual stop, stow all beverages and return cup holders to the stored position, put the parking brake in the ON position, shift to P, turn the ignition to OFF, unlock all doors, switch your emergency flasher to ON, and consult the Emergency section of this manual. IMPORTANT: Do NOT unbuckle your seat belt. It is the most critical element of your car's Supplemental Restraint System and has been shown to save lives in certain instances. Remember: Give your loved ones a good belt!

1997

TAKE IT FROM ME

WHILE the rest of you loudly and meaninglessly celebrate the New Year—I'm not judging, I'm just making an observation— I prefer to reflect quietly on the lessons I've learned or partially absorbed or once thought I heard someone talking about as I was going down the street trying to get to the hardware store before it closed. Though we all know that the words we shout into the wind are like footprints in the sand, that does not stop us from going to the beach, even during peak burning hours; and though our chances of making a lasting impression on the world are like the chances of finding enough snow to make a snowball on a hot day, that does not prevent us from sometimes feeling chilly even when we are wearing a sweater. In this spirit, whatever it is, I would like to share some of the accumulated wisdom of my years, which, like the result of the woolgatherer's efforts, has become a big ball of wool. It may be too late for me—I'm not saying it is and I'm not saying it isn't—but if I can help just one person, even if it's someone I really don't like or am not speaking to or have sued, then I will not have lived in vain. Now let's move on—I have to be somewhere in a half hour.

So what are we talking about here? Practical stuff. For example, don't wait until you're forty to have nude pictures taken of yourself. If you plan to be famous, or even if you don't, make sure you get this out of the way while you're in your late teens or, at the very latest, early twenties. They'll keep! All you have to do is stay in touch with the photographer to make sure he has stored them properly and is ready to distribute them at a moment's notice. One phone call a year—*Hi. How ya doin'? Just wanted to make sure you still have the pictures. O.K. Great, yeah, I'll do that. O.K., you too. Right. Buh-bye.* How hard is that? I waited until my face had "character" to have my pictures done. What was I thinking? Answer: I wasn't thinking.

It's an open secret that it is now fashionable to laugh at the idea of having fifteen minutes of fame. People! I, too, used to think, Oh, that doesn't apply to me, I'll be famous whenever I want to—the first two weeks of April, every August, after Mom moves into the home. I don't have to watch the clock, let the clock watch *me*. Well, I was caught nap-ping, literally, and I found out too late that my fifteen minutes had come during an intense REM cycle while I was dreaming about— No, forget it, it doesn't matter what I was dreaming about. This isn't about me.

I'm not saying that I have all the answers—if I did I'd be laughing all the way to the bank instead of all the way in the opposite direction from the bank, until it becomes a tiny dot on the horizon and then disappears entirely. My whole point is: Do you want to miss your ice time, foul out before the game has begun, do an end run around yourself, be caught looking when the high heater comes over the fat part of the plate, just so you'll have an "interesting" dream about going into a tunnel to tell your shrink the next day? Maybe you do. But I don't think so. And, by the way, when they say fifteen minutes they mean fifteen minutes. It's the old story: "Sorry, we can't help you. If we made an exception for you, blah, blah, blah."

Look, I know this is all pretty obvious, and having to spell it out is almost as embarrassing for me as, in a completely unrelated way, it would be for you to tell your boss that you hate his guts, that you could run the company better than he can, that he can't fire you because you quit, and thanks for nothing, you jerk, you can go to hell. But you know you owe it to your boss to be honest with him, even if it's a wee bit painful—that's why he hired you. In the same way, I owe it to myself to be honest, at some point, with someone. It doesn't matter who—you let me worry about that.

What I have to say is simple. But that doesn't make it any less true. If anything, it makes it more true. It's simple—unless *you* make it complicated. If I've done my job here today, you will have achieved that heightened state of receptivity that lies midway between not paying much attention and not paying any attention. Or maybe you just think I'm a big phony. So be it. It's O.K. to have that feeling. But, right or wrong—they boil down to the same thing at the end of the day, if not by lunchtime, although of course it depends when you turned the flame on—I would rather not "know" about it, so if you have any brains you won't "tell" me about it. Not that brains are everything—you'll also need a skull to put them in. And, much as I'd like to help you out with that, I can't live your life for you. That much I do know. But that's neither here nor there.

1997

CHANGES IN THE MEMORY

AFTER FIFTY

BORED? Here's a way the over-fifty set can easily kill a good half hour:

1. Place your car keys in your right hand.
2. With your left hand, call a friend and confirm a lunch or dinner date.
3. Hang up the phone.
4. Now look for your car keys.

(For answer, turn page upside down.)

The lapses of memory that occur after fifty are normal and in some ways beneficial. There are certain things it's better to forget, like the time Daddy once failed to praise you, and now, forty years later, you have to count the tiles in the bathroom—first in multiples of three, then in multiples of five, and so on, until they come out even—or else you can't get out of the shower. The memory is selective, and sometimes it will select 1956 and 1963 and that's all. Such memory lapses don't necessarily indicate a more serious health problem. The rule is that if you think you have a pathological memory problem you probably don't. In fact, the most serious indicator is when you're convinced you're fine and yet people often ask you, "Why are you here in your pajamas at the Kennedy Center Honors?"

Let's say you've just called your best friend, Joe, and invited him to an upcoming anniversary party, and then, minutes later, you call Joe back to invite him to the same party again. This does not mean that you are "losing it" or are "not playing with a full deck" or are "not all there" or that you're "eating with the dirigibles" or "shellacking the waxed egg" or

Your car keys are in your right hand. Please remember to turn page right side up.

"looking inside your own mind and finding nothing there," or any of the other demeaning epithets that are said about people who are peeling an empty banana. It does mean, however, that perhaps Joe is no longer on the list of things that you're going to remember. This is Joe's fault. He should be more memorable. He should have a name like *El Elegante.*

Sometimes it's fun to sit in your garden and try to remember your dog's name. Here's how: simply watch the dog's ears while calling out pet names at random. This is a great summer activity, especially in combination with "Name That Wife" and "Who Am I?" These games actually strengthen the memory, and make it possible to solve more complicated problems, such as "Is this the sixth time I've urinated this hour or the seventh?" This, of course, is easily answered by tiny pencil marks applied during the day.

Note to Self: Remember to write article about waxy buildup.

If you have a doctor who is over fifty, it's wise to pay attention to his changing memory profile. There is nothing more disconcerting than a patient and a healer staring at each other across an examining table wondering why they're there. Watch out for the stethoscope being placed on the forehead or the briefcase. Watch out for greetings such as "Hello . . . you." Be concerned if while looking for your file he keeps referring to you as "one bad boy." Men should be wary if the doctor, while examining their prostate, suddenly says, "I'm sorry, but do I know you?"

There are several theories to explain the memory problems of advancing age. One is that the brain is full: it simply has too much data to compute. This is easy to understand if we realize that the name of your third-grade teacher is still occupying space, not to mention the lyrics to "Volare." One solution for older men is to take all the superfluous data swirling around in the brain and download it into the newly large stomach, where there is plenty of room. This frees the brain to house more relevant information, like the particularly troublesome "days of the week." Another solution is to take regular doses of *Ginkgo biloba,* an extract from a tree in Asia whose memory is so indelible that one day it will hunt down and kill all the humans who have been eating it. It is strongly advised that those taking *Ginkgo biloba* label the bottle "Memory Pills." There is nothing more embarrassing than looking at a bottle of *Ginkgo biloba* and thinking it's a reliquary for a Spanish explorer.

SO, in summary, waxy buildup is a problem all of us face. Only a good, strong cleanser, used once or twice a month, will save us the humiliation of that petrified yellow crust on our furniture. Again, I recommend an alcohol-free, polymer-based cleanser, applied with a damp cloth. Good luck!

1998

STEVE MARTIN

THE HUNDRED GREATEST BOOKS
THAT I'VE READ

1. *The A-Bomb and Your School Desk*
2. *Little Lulu,* No. 24, January, 1954
3. *Weekly Reader* humor column
4. Women Love It If You're Funny! (ad)
5. *Robert Orben's Patter for Magicians*
6. The book that starts, "It was the best of times, it was the worst of times."
7. *Silas Marner* (first and last page only)
8. *The Catcher in the Rye*
9. *Sex for Teenagers* (pamphlet)
10. *The Nude* (serious art photos)
11. *Lolita* (movie only)
12. Owner's Manual, 1966 Mustang
13. *Showmanship for Magicians,* by Dariel Fitzkee
14. *Republic,* by Plato
15. *Steal This Book,* by Abbie Hoffman
16. *Fasting with Incense,* by "Free"
17. *Being and Nothingness,* by J. P. Sartre
18. *Being and Nothingness,* Cliffs Notes
19. *Complete Works of e. e. cummings*
20. *Complete Works of Shelley*

21. *How for Two Years to Never Once Speak to the Girl of Your Dreams, Even Though You Sit Across From Her Every Day in the College Library*, by D. James
22. *How to Seduce Women by Being Withdrawn, Falsely Poetic, and Moody* (same author)
23. *Hamlet* (screenplay)
24. *The Banjo and Marijuana: Delusions of Grandeur*, by Snuffy Grubbs
25. *Howl*, by Allen Ginsberg
26. *Why It's Not Important to Get a Fancy Table at a Restaurant*, by D. Jones
27. *Journey to Ixtlan*, by C. Castaneda
28. *Who to Call When You're Busted for Peyote*, by Officer P. R. Gainsly
29. *What to Read on Your Summer Vacation* (pamphlet)
30. *Tess of the D'Urbervilles*
31. *The Idiot*
32. "The *Playboy* Advisor" (letters about stereo equipment only)
33. *What Night-Club Audiences Are Like in Utah*, by Tippy Tibbs
34. *50 Great Spots for Self-Immolation in Bryce Canyon*, by Tippy Tibbs (deceased)
35. *Great Laundromats of the Southwest*, General Services Administration
36. *Using Hypnotism to Eliminate the Word "Like" from Your Vocabulary*
37. "The Hollywood Hot 100" (article)
38. *How to Not Let Anyone Know You're Having a Panic Attack*, by E.K.G.
39. "The Hollywood Hot 100" (rechecking)
40. "Whatever Happened To . . . ?" (article)
41. *If You're Not Happy When Everything Good Is Happening to You, You Must Be Insane*, by Loopy d'Lulu
42. *The Nouveau Riche and Its Attraction to Silver Bathroom Wallpaper*, by Paige Rense
43–49. *How to Bid at Sotheby's* (seven volumes)
50. *Thinking You're a Genius in the Art Market Until 1989*, by Gregor Ito
51. *Beating the Experts at Chinese Ceramics*, by Taiwan Tony
52. *Selling Your Fake Chinese Ceramics*, by Taiwan Tony
53. *Windows for Dummies*
54. *Windows for Idiots*
55. *Windows for the Subhuman*

56. *Fifty Annoying Sinus Infections You Can Legally Give Bill Gates*
57. *Romeo and Juliet*
58. *Great Love Poems*
59. *Martha Stewart's Marriage Book*
60. *Men Are from Mars, Women Are from Venus,* by John Gray (gift)
61. *How Come You Don' Listen to Me No Mo'?,* by Dr. Grady Ulose (gift)
62. *Ten Lousy Things Men Do to Be Rotten,* by Dr. Laura Sleshslinger (gift)
63. *Crummy Men Who Can't Think and Don' Do Nothin',* by J. Delius (gift)
64. *Prenup Loopholes,* by Anon., Esq.
65. *How to Survive a Broken Heart*
66. *Be a Man, Get Over It!*
67. *Diagnostic Manual of Mental Disorders,* American Psychiatric Association
68. *Get Ready to Live!,* by H. Camper
69. *Omelette-Olga: Mnemonic Devices for Remembering Waitresses' Names*
70. Victoria's Secret fall catalogue
71. *Your Stomach, and Why It's So Fat*
72. *Inappropriate Dating and Your Hair,* by Spraon Brown
73. *Male Menopause,* by Jed Diamond
74. *The Male Within,* by Dr. Ken Justin
75. *It's a Guy Thing,* by "Jesse" (convicted felon)
76. *What Breasts Can Make You Do*
77. Owner's Manual for the Harley-Davidson Sportster 883
78. *100 Worst Movies of the Eighties*
79. *Bonding with the Feminine*
80. *Bringing Out the Feminine*
81. *Loving Your Anima*
82. *Show Tunes You Can Whistle,* by Keith
83. *Life Begins at Forty, Too Bad You're Fifty,* by Trini Montana
84. *It's Time to Leave Childish Humor Behind,* by Ayed Lykta Dooya
85. *Ulysses* (first sentence only)
86. *Vanity Fair,* September issue
87. *Your Prostate,* by Dr. Pokey d'Hole
88. *Glasses or Eye Surgery?* (pamphlet)
89. *Tingling Feet: A Diet Cure*

1998

JACK HANDEY

REINTRODUCING ME TO MY HABITAT

I WOULD like to take this opportunity to urge conservation-minded people everywhere to pressure the government for the reintroduction of me to my native habitat.

My native habitat, of course, is the desert Southwest, where I used to roam wild and free. But, sadly, I no longer exist there. For several years, I have been largely confined to a small two-bedroom apartment in the Chelsea section of Manhattan.

It is clear that I do not belong here, as my neighbors will tell you. I am still frightened by car horns, and the fancy Eastern food I am fed is at odds with my natural diet of enchiladas and gingersnaps. Often I can be found pacing mindlessly back and forth in my cramped office, which I am told is a sign that I am insane.

Occasionally, there are scattered sightings of me in my old habitat— shooting a wet straw wrapper at someone's kid in a restaurant in Santa Fe, then denying it; doing my funny cowboy dance at a party in Silver City until people make me stop—but these cannot be confirmed.

For all intents and purposes, I have been eliminated from my former range, the Rio Grande Valley. I used to be found from El Paso and

Juárez in the south all the way up to Taos and sometimes beyond (if I missed the turnoff to Taos).

Once, I filled a vital role in the ecosystem. I would prey primarily on the weak and the old, who were usually the only ones who would hire me. Then, when their businesses went under, they were removed from the system, as nature intended.

My world was in harmony. But then, as often happens, man intervened. Ranchers would drive me from their lands when they caught me throwing a keg-party barbecue, maybe using one of their cows. Divorce and job dismissals took their toll. I found I could not coexist with my creditors. At one point, public sentiment against me was so strong that I was considered "vermin" and a "pest."

But now, I think, attitudes are changing. People don't automatically want to shoot me, like they used to. This is mainly because of my reeducation efforts and because they haven't seen me for a long time.

The truth about me is finally starting to emerge. For instance, there is no record of me ever attacking a human, unless he was much, much smaller than me. The old myths are starting to die off, such as the one that if you leave your campsite unattended, I will sneak in and steal beer and food from your cooler and maybe knock down your tent.

The time to act is now. I am not getting any younger, and my rent here in New York could go up at any time. Also I could be wiped out by the stock market.

I have been conducting a captive-breeding program with my wife, but so far it has yielded no offspring. (The reason, I found out, is that my wife uses contraceptives, which I guess I knew.)

All of these factors make it imperative that you write the government and tell them to reintroduce me, via first-class airfare, to my old habitat. With a generous per diem and a late-model car, I think I could once again fill my old niche. I would probably try to mate with females of my species, unless my wife found out. And I would be willing to keep a journal of what I eat and what TV shows I watch, so that more may be learned about my ways.

I will, if necessary, wear a radio collar.

I am willing to do these things because I believe that until people can sit around a desert campfire and go "Shhh, hear that?" and then listen for the plaintive howl of me, we as a society have lost something.

1999

THANK YOU FOR STOPPING

THANK you for stopping. You have obviously found me unconscious by the side of the road, or at a party, or possibly propped up against a wall someplace, and you have wisely reached into my pocket and found this medical advisory.

If you found other things in my pockets, kindly do not read or keep them. They are none of your business and/or do not belong to you. And remember that, even though I am unconscious now, when I wake up I will remember the things I had.

If I am wearing a tie, please loosen it. But, again, do not take it off and keep it. It is not yours and is probably more expensive than you can afford. If I am not wearing a tie, look around at the other people who have gathered to look at me and see if any of them is wearing a tie that might belong to me. If so, please approach that individual and ask for my tie back. If he says it is his, say you do not think so. If he insists, give him one of the cards (in the same pocket where you found this note) of my attorney, and tell the person he will be hearing from him soon.

Keep me warm. Take off your coat and put it around me. Do not worry, you will get it back. If you do not, within thirty days contact the attorney on the card, and he will advise you.

If you must, build a fire to keep me warm. But—and this is very important—DO NOT ROAST ME OVER THE FIRE. I say this because many people who stop to help others are not that smart, and are capable of doing such a thing.

There are some pills in one of my pockets. Take them and hold on to them. If any authorities ask you about them, say they are yours.

If I am outdoors under a hot sun, do not allow children near me with a magnifying glass. Even if they are on leashes, do not allow monkeys near me. Do not allow others to make fun of me, poke me with sticks, or, if an anthill is nearby, pour honey on me. Do not allow onlookers to pose with me for "funny" photos. Failure to stop any of these things may be construed as participation in them, and may subject you to severe legal remedies.

Try to keep me calm. If you are not a physically attractive person, try not to let yourself be the first thing I see when I wake up.

Call an ambulance. I guess that would be obvious to most people, but you never know.

If I am on fire, put me out. If you put me out by rolling me on the ground, do not let me roll down a hill. If I do roll down a hill and get stuck under some bushes, just leave me there; you've given me enough "help" already.

If I suddenly begin to sweat profusely and my entire body begins to shimmy violently, do not worry; that is normal.

If I am bleeding, how'd that happen? What did you do now?

Even though I am unconscious, do not dangle things over me. I do not like that.

Answer my cell phone if it rings. If it is a woman named Peggy, pretend to be me and say you are breaking up with her.

If I have wet my pants, get a glass of water and act like you tripped and spilled it on my pants.

If I appear near death, do not call a priest. And do not call a rabbi and a minister, and have them all go into a bar and do something funny, because I don't want my life to end up as one big joke.

Get a better job. If you have time to stop for unconscious people, you are obviously not working at full capacity.

Thank you again for stopping. Now, please, stand back and give me some air.

1999

CHRISTOPHER BUCKLEY

HOMEWORK: A PARENT'S GUIDE

MID-YEAR *Parent–Teacher Conferences:* Explain to child's teachers that you and your spouse declined all social invitations during the previous semester, including a state dinner at the White House, owing to amount of child's homework. Effect may be enhanced by blubbering, twitching, fidgeting with metal balls, etc. Suppress impulse to perform act of aggravated violence on fellow-parent who counters that his child is insufficiently "challenged" by current homework load.

(Note: Recent juries have demonstrated marked reluctance to convict in such cases.)

• *The Appeal:* In event teacher does not appear to care that you are staying up until eleven-thirty every night to help child with report on Gross Domestic Product of Guatemala, you may discuss your "issues" (previously called "rage") with the school principal. This will result in an expression of sympathy, and an increase in the workload to 12:30 A.M. In extremis, drop hint to school principal that you are contemplating "significant" gesture to principal's "discretionary fund" (code for principal's summer "cottage"), but that you lack the proper time in the evening to "judiciously" oversee liquidation of the relevant equities, bonds, real-estate properties, etc.

• *Math:* Parents will find that the current "new" math bears no resemblance to the one of their own day, or, indeed, to any math. Ptolemy and Euclid would not recognize it. The multiplication table, for instance, has been replaced by a system whereby the digits of the right hand are interlaced with the toes of the left while the child hops backward in three-two time. (Chicago Math.) Variants include the Milwaukee Math, in which whole numbers (that is, numbers not followed by dots and more numbers) are expressed by binary burping, and the San Francisco Math, which employs Grape-Nuts and an algorithm based on the number of people currently leaping off the Golden Gate Bridge each month. These advances have rendered the normally capable parent incapable of calculating how many apples Jerome will be left with if he gives half to Mary, eats two and deposits the remaining number in an offshore account in the Cayman Islands. Fathers today find it increasingly useful to advise, "Go ask Mom; she really knows this stuff." (Note: You will be expected to be conversant with the metric system. Useful tips: One metre is "a squidge" more than the traditional yard. A hundred millimetres equals an extra-length cigarette, while a "litre" bottle of expensive French fizzy water is "more or less" one quart.)

• *The Phone Call:* Each night just as dinner is on the table, child will announce that he must telephone Georgia or Joseph to get the assignment for tomorrow, despite your tantrums of the previous four evenings over the absolute necessity of writing down the assignment in class. As a rule, Georgia or Joseph's phone will be busy for not less than one and a quarter hours, prompting rancorous parental running commentary. (Warning: Late-night calls to the teacher to find out the assignment are generally considered unwise, as the parent is by now in a state of acute emotional derangement and is therefore apt to "download" on the subject of homework. This will result in an increase in the daily load to 1:30 A.M.)

• *The Knapsack:* The current fashion is for child to carry a knapsack weighing no less than 3.2 times body weight (gross tonnage). This includes such items as are deemed essential by today's students, such as a hundredweight of Pokémon cards, hair scrunchies mixed with jelly beans, spare limbs from Barbie dolls, rotting fruit matter from the previous term, and extra ammunition clips. Net tonnage is the amount—expressed in long tons—of materials directly related to education, such as books, binders, and a minimum of three dozen mechanical pencils not containing leads. Care should be exercised while assisting child with harnessing of knapsack so as to avoid slipped disks and rotator-cuff injuries necessitating surgery. Nightly commencement of homework process (see tab A: "Getting To 'Okay, *Okay*' ") will involve ten minutes of rummaging in knapsack for "the" pen, despite parental proffer of any number of alternative pens. Length of time necessary to locate pen generally corresponds to time remaining in current episode of "Dawson's Creek."

• *The Science Project:* No phrase strikes more terror into the heart of a parent today than "Science Project." Notwithstanding, a few weeks into the start of term your spouse will cheerfully announce to you—in child's presence, so as to preclude any protest on your part—the "wonderful" news that your child has selected you, specifically, to be his "partner" in the aforementioned exercise. (Refrain from stabbing spouse with fork under the table; there will be plenty of time in which to express your rage, betrayal, and other emotions.) You are now expected to devote all your "free" time over the next six weeks to devising a miniature version of the particle accelerator at CERN, in Switzerland, a home video explaining string theory using cooked spaghetti, or erecting a model of the human genome using 3.4 trillion Styrofoam balls (available at Wal-Mart). Unfortunately, the days are past when science projects could without embarrassment consist of store-bought ant farms (minus ants); hastily drawn cardboard charts showing how fast ice melts when immersed in a mixture of five parts gin, one part vermouth; a model of Sputnik using a Ping-Pong ball and two toothpicks; or a malodorous dish of dead tadpoles proving scientifically once and for all that amphibians cannot be left indefinitely on a hot radiator. In extremis, a project can be built around parent's recent hospitalization for exhaustion.

2000

DAVID OWEN

WHAT HAPPENED TO MY MONEY?

GOD has taken your money to live with Him in Heaven. Heaven is a special, wonderful place, where wars and diseases and stock markets do not exist, only happiness. You have probably seen some wonderful places in your life—perhaps during a vacation, or on television, or in a movie—but Heaven is a million billion times more wonderful than even Disney World. Jesus and Mary and the angels live in Heaven, and so do your grandparents and your old pets and Abraham Lincoln. Your money will be safe and happy in Heaven forever and ever, and God will always take care of it.

Your money is still your money—it will always be your money—but it cannot come back to you, not ever. That may seem unfair to you. One day you were buying puts and shorting straddles, and the next day you woke up to find that your account had been closed forever. Perhaps you got a sick or empty feeling in your stomach when that happened; perhaps you have that sick or empty feeling still. You loved your money very, very much, and you did not want God to take it away.

Your feelings are natural and normal—they are a part of the way God made you—but God took your money in accordance with His wonderful plan, which is not for us to know or understand. You must trust God and have faith that He loves your money just as He loves you and every other part of His creation. Someday—probably a very, very long time from now, after you have lived a long and happy life in compliance with the nation's securities laws—God will take you to live with Him in Heaven, too. Then you will understand.

Even though your money is gone forever, it can still be a part of your life. As long as love and kindness and happiness dwell in your heart, your money can dwell there, too. At night, before you go to sleep, you can talk to your money in a prayer. You can think about the B.M.W. that you and your money were going to buy, and you can remember the house on the beach that you and your money were going to build, and you can laugh about your funny old plan to send your children to private colleges. Someday, when you no longer feel as sad as you do today, you may even find that thinking about your money can give you some of the same happy feelings that spending your money used to give you.

Those feelings belong to you and they always will; no one can take them away from you. Even when you are very, very old, you will still be able to think about your money and remember how much you loved it. But you will still not be able to spend your money, or even borrow against it.

2000

RECOLLECTIONS

AND

REFLECTIONS

ALEXANDER WOOLLCOTT

ON TAXI DRIVERS

I AM engaged at present on a monumental work which will give the history of the New York taxicab up to and including 1930. It will take up many problems, such as why the most rheumatic cabs invariably throng the curbs outside the best hotels, and will examine the morbid passion of the drivers for weaving in and out of elevated pillars. Then it will assemble all the best recipes for dissuading the tumultuous creatures from driving at a pace faster than the shattered fare can endure. I may add that these recipes will be compiled by a nervous wreck, who feels that nothing is so certain as death and taxis.

Above all, it will inquire into the reasons for the flashing individualism which, in an age of robots, makes the taxi driver as vivid and striking as a scarlet tanager in a thicket of spruces. Long ago I wrote an essay entitled "The Paris Taxi Driver Considered as an Artist." Therein I told, among other anecdotes, the story of the sneering cab which cruised the rain-swept streets one night when most of the Paris taxis were on strike. Its malicious driver would swoop up to the curb, ask a frantically signalling citizen where he wanted to go, and then drive laughingly on without him. But when one young couple, huddled pathetically under an umbrella, told him that they had hoped to go to the opera, he suddenly forgot all about the class war, and even forgot to bargain for the extra fare everybody was offering.

"*Mon dieu*," he cried, "jump in. It is 'Samson and Delilah' tonight, and the overture begins at eight."

And whirled them across Paris on one wheel. That essay was written in my salad days, and is marred by the provincial notion that a *pomme de terre* has a glamour not possessed by our own potato, or more particularly that all quaint characters are to be found abroad. Now, in what must be my cheese-and-crackers days, I know that the seeing eye would find just such anecdotes on every corner in New York. Your correspondant has at least a listening ear for any who may have such tales to tell.

My book will include the episode of Towne and Tennyson. It happened of a summer's evening last year, when Charles Hanson Towne, editor and fairly *bon vivant,* was dining out, somewhere on the upper East Side, I assume. At all events, Mr. Towne noted with delight that the dusky jehu's name was Clifford Tennyson, and lapsing at once into a broad Southern accent, addressed him so humorously as Cliffahd all the way up town that his companion grew restive at so much comedy. Therefore when, two blocks before their destination, Mr. Towne descended from the cab to buy a winsome nosegay for his hostess, this companion and the driver went into hasty conference, to rehearse a faintly retaliatory scene.

Thus it befell that when they finally dismissed the cab, and Mr. Towne said, "Cliffahd, what do Ah owe you?" he was reduced to a becoming stupefaction by the sight of a brown hand grandly waving him aside. If only the driver had heard the whispered instructions accurately, the result would have been really stunning. Even as it was, the aforesaid *bon vivant* was bowled over by hearing this reply: "Not a penny, sir, not a penny. It is a pleasure to drive you, Mr. Towel."

NOW and again a driver does actually recognize his fare, particularly if it be one whose face appears much in the public prints. One of my favorite stories deals with the emotions of such a driver who, after profitably conducting a distracted and solitary young man around and around Central Park for several hours one night, finally grew sleepy and switched an inquisitive light on his fare, only to discover that it was none other than Charlie Chaplin. Under pressure of this inspection, the comedian expressed an intention to drive on vaguely until dawn. He had reason to suspect that process servers lay in wait for him at his hotel, and he was not minded to show his celebrated face there or anywhere else. Finally, the drowsy driver decided to put the fugitive up for the rest of the night at his own home, but insisted that the visit be made incognito, lest the little woman take umbrage at their sheltering so notorious a character. As it happened, the only place for guests in the driver's flat was one half of a bed, of which the other was occupied by his ten-year-old son. I have always thought there never was such an awakening since the world began as the one which that incredulous youngster enjoyed next morning.

Then, only the other day, Heywood Broun was at once startled and gratified to have the driver of the cab he was dismissing pause to discuss, with flattering disapprobation, the literary style of Mr. Broun's several successors on the New York *World.* This unexpected pundit was particularly hard on St. John Ervine, who, by this time, must be already on the high seas, bound for the welcoming bosom of the London *Observer.* In his own mind, the driver had somewhat disconcertingly recognized the intended target of Ervine's recent allusion to "a big, orbicular newspaper man," and had loyally resented it. "Why," he said, "I guess if anyone's a sissy, he's one himself."

Which reminds one fondly of the time when Margaret Mayo made her report to Al Woods on a French script she had just read for him.

"I don't think it's so salacious," she said.

"No," he replied, "I don't think it will go well, either."

BUT to return to the taxi drivers, I must certainly include the experience of Samuel Merwin with the one he hailed outside the Players Club one stormy night.

"I want to go to the Algonquin," said Mr. Merwin firmly, and then added, with wanton pessimism, "I don't suppose you know where it is?"

"I ought to," grunted the driver, "there's only three of us left in New York."

"Only three drivers who know where the Algonquin is?" queried the pessimist, in the surprised tone of one beaten at his own game.

"No," replied the driver, thrusting a superb, hawklike Indian profile into the light, "only three Algonquins."

1929

FATHER ISN'T MUCH HELP

IN Father's day, it was unusual for boys in New York to take music lessons. His father had sent him to college, but he hadn't had him taught music. Men didn't play the piano. Young ladies learned to play pretty things on it as an accomplishment, but few of them went further, and any desire to play classical music was rare.

After Father grew up, however, and began to do well in his business, he decided that music was one of the good things of life. He bought himself a piano and paid a musician to teach him. He took no interest in the languishing love songs which were popular then, he didn't admire patriotic things such as "Marching Through Georgia," and he had a hearty distaste for songs of pathos—he always swore if he heard them. He enjoyed music as he did a fine wine or a good ride on horseback. He had long, muscular fingers, he practiced faithfully, and learned to the best of his ability to play Beethoven and Bach.

The people he associated with didn't care much for this kind of thing, and Father didn't wish to associate with the long-haired musicians who did. He got no encouragement from anyone and his progress was lonely. But Father was not the kind of man who depends on encouragement.

His feeling for music was limited but it was deeply rooted, and he cared enough for it to keep on practicing even after he married and in the busy years when he was providing for a house full of boys. He didn't go to symphonic concerts and he never liked Wagner, but he'd hum something of Brahms' while posting his ledger, or play Mozart or Chopin after dinner. It gave him a sense of well-being.

Mother liked music too. We often heard her sweet voice gently singing old songs of an evening. If she forgot parts here or there, she swiftly improvised something that would let the air flow along without breaking the spell.

Father didn't play that way. He was erecting much statelier structures, and when he got a chord wrong, he stopped. He took that chord apart and went over the notes one by one, and he kept on going over them methodically. This sometimes drove Mother mad. She would desperately cry "Oh-oh-oh!" and run out of the room.

Her whole attitude toward music was different. She didn't get a solid and purely personal enjoyment from it like Father. It was more of a social function to her. It went with dancing and singing. She played and sang for fun, or to keep from being sad, or to give others pleasure.

ON Thursday afternoons in the winter, Mother was always "at home." She served tea and cakes and quite a few people dropped in to see her. She liked entertaining. And whenever she saw a way to make her Thursdays more attractive, she tried it.

About this time, Mother's favorite niece, Cousin Julie, was duly "finished" at boarding school and came to live with us, bringing her trunks and hatboxes and a great gilded harp. Mother at once made room for this beautiful object in our crowded parlor, and the first thing Julie knew she had to play it for the Thursday-afternoon visitors. Julie loved her harp dearly but she didn't like performing at all—performances frightened her, and if she fumbled a bit, she felt badly. But Mother said she must get over all that. She tried to give Julie self-confidence. She talked to her like a determined though kind impresario.

These afternoon sessions were pleasant, but they made Mother want to do more. While she was thinking one evening about what a lot of social debts she must pay, she suddenly said to Father, who was reading Gibbon, half-asleep by the fire, "Why not give a musicale, Clare, instead of a series of dinners?"

When Father was able to understand what she was talking about, he said he was glad if she had come to her senses sufficiently to give up any wild idea of having a series of dinners, and that she had better give up musicales, too. He informed her he was not made of money, and all good string quartets were expensive; and when Mother interrupted him, he raised his voice and said, to close the discussion: "I will not have my peaceful home turned into a Roman arena, with a lot of hairy fiddlers prancing about and disturbing my comfort."

"You needn't get so excited, Clare," Mother said. "I didn't say a word about hairy fiddlers. I don't know where you get such ideas. But I do know a lovely young girl whom Mrs. Spiller has had, and she'll come for very little, I'm sure."

"What instrument does this inexpensive paragon play?" Father inquired sardonically.

"She doesn't play, Clare. She whistles."

"Whistles!" said Father. "Good God!"

"Very well, then," Mother said after an argument. "I'll have to have Julie instead, and Miss Kregman can help her, and I'll try to get Sally Brown or somebody to play the piano."

"Miss Kregman!" Father snorted. "I wash my hands of the whole business."

MOTHER asked nothing better. She could have made a grander affair of it if he had provided the money, but even with only a little to spend, getting up a party was fun. Before her marriage, she had loved her brother Alden's musicales. She would model hers upon those. Hers would be different in one way, for Alden had had famous artists, and at hers the famous artists would be impersonated by Cousin Julie. But the question as to how expert the music would be didn't bother her, and she didn't think it would bother the guests whom she planned to invite. The flowers would be pretty; she knew just what she would put in each vase (the parlor was full of large vases); she had a special kind of little cakes in mind, and everybody would enjoy it all thoroughly.

But no matter what kind of artists she has, a hostess is bound to have trouble managing them, and Mother knew that even her homemade material would need a firm hand. Julie was devoted to her, and so was the other victim, Sally Brown, Julie's schoolmate. But devoted or not, they were uneasy about this experiment. Sally would rather have done almost anything than perform at a musicale, and the idea of playing in public sent cold chills down Julie's back.

The only one Mother worried about, however, was Julie's teacher, Miss Kregman. She could bring a harp of her own, so she would be quite an addition, but Mother didn't feel she was decorative. She was an angular, plain-looking woman, and she certainly was a very unromantic sight at a harp.

Father didn't feel she was decorative either, and said, "I'll be damned if I come." He said musicales were all poppycock anyway. "Nothing but tinkle and twitter."

"Nobody's invited you, Clare," Mother said defiantly. As a matter of fact, she felt relieved by his announcement. This wasn't like a dinner, where she wanted Father and where he would be of some use. She didn't want him at all at her musicale.

"All I ask is," she went on, "that you will please dine out for once. It won't be over until six at the earliest, and it would make things much easier for me if you would dine at the club."

Father said that was ridiculous. "I never dine at the club. I won't do it. Any time I can't have my dinner in my own home, this house is for sale. I disapprove entirely of these parties and uproar!" he shouted. "I'm ready to sell the place this very minute, and we can all go and sit under a palm tree and live on breadfruit and pickles!"

ON the day of the musicale, it began to snow while we were at breakfast. Father had forgotten what day it was, of course, and he didn't care anyhow—his mind was on a waistcoat which he wished Mother to take to his tailor's. To his astonishment, he found her standing on a stepladder, arranging some ivy, and when he said "Here's my waistcoat," she gave a loud wail of self-pity at this new infliction. Father said in a bothered way: "What is the matter with you, Vinnie? What are you doing up on that ladder? Here's my waistcoat, I tell you, and it's got to go to the tailor at once." He insisted on handing it up to her, and he banged the front door going out.

Early in the afternoon, the snow changed to rain. The streets were deep in slush. We boys gave up sliding downhill on the railroad bridge in East Forty-eighth Street and came tramping in with our sleds. Before going up to the playroom, we looked in the parlor. It was full of small folding chairs. The big teakwood armchairs with their embroidered backs were crowded off into corners, and the blue velvety ottoman with its flowered top could hardly be seen. The rubber tree had been moved from the window and strategically placed by Miss Kregman's harp, in such a way that the harp would be in full view but Miss Kregman would not.

Going upstairs, we met Julie coming down. Her lips were blue. She was pale. She passed us with fixed, unseeing eyes, and when I touched her hand it felt cold.

Looking over the banisters, we saw Miss Kregman arrive in her galoshes. Sally Brown, who was usually gay, entered silently later. Miss Kregman clambered in behind the rubber tree and tuned the majestic gold harps. Mother was arranging trayfuls of little cakes and sandwiches, and giving a last touch to the flowers. Her excited voice floated up to us. There was not a sound from the others.

At the hour appointed for this human sacrifice, ladies began arriving in long, swishy dresses which swept richly over the carpet. Soon the parlor was packed. I thought of Sally, so anxious and numb she could hardly feel the piano keys, and of Julie's icy fingers plucking valiantly away at the strings. Then Mother clapped her hands as a signal for the chatter to halt, the first hesitating strains of music began, and someone slid the doors shut.

When we boys went down to dinner that evening, we heard the news, good and bad. In a way it had been a success. Julie and Sally had played beautifully the whole afternoon, and the ladies had admired the harps, and applauded, and eaten up all the cakes. But there had been two catastrophes. One was that everybody had kept looking fascinatedly at Miss Kregman's feet, which had stuck out from the rubber tree, working away by themselves, as it were, at the pedals, and the awful part was she had forgotten to take off her galoshes. The other was that Father had come home during a sweet little lullaby and the ladies had distinctly heard him say "Damn" as he went up to his room.

1933

JAMES THURBER

THE NIGHT THE GHOST GOT IN

THE ghost that got into our house on the night of November 17, 1915, raised such a hullabaloo of misunderstandings that I am sorry I didn't just let it keep on walking, and go to bed. Its advent caused my mother to throw a shoe through a window of the house next door and ended up with my grandfather shooting a patrolman. I am sorry, therefore, as I have said, that I ever paid any attention to the footsteps.

They began about a quarter past one o'clock in the morning, a rhythmic, quick-cadenced walking around the dining-room table. My mother was asleep in one room upstairs, my brother Herman in another; grandfather was in the attic, in the old walnut bed which, as you may remember, once fell on my father. I had just stepped out of the bathtub and was busily rubbing myself with a towel when I heard the steps. They were the steps of a man walking rapidly around the dining-room table downstairs. The light from the bathroom shone down the back steps, which dropped directly into the dining-room; I could see the faint shine of plates on the plate-rail; I couldn't see the table. The steps kept going round and round the table; at regular intervals a board creaked, when it was trod upon. I supposed at first that it was my father or my brother Roy, who had gone to Indianapolis but were expected home at any time. I suspected next that it was a burglar. It did not enter my mind until later that it was a ghost.

After the walking had gone on for perhaps three minutes, I tiptoed to Herman's room. "Psst!" I hissed, in the dark, shaking him. "Awp," he said, in the low, hopeless tone of a despondent beagle—he always half suspected that something would "get him" in the night. I told him who I was. "There's something downstairs!" I said. He got up and followed me to the head of the back staircase. We listened together. There was no sound. The steps had ceased. Herman looked at me in some alarm: I had only the bath towel around my waist. He wanted to go back to bed, but I gripped his arm. "There's something down there!" I said. Instantly, the steps began again, circled the dining-room table like a man running, and started up the stairs toward us, heavily, two at a time. The light still shone palely down the steps; we saw nothing coming; we only heard the steps. Herman rushed to his room and slammed the door. I slammed shut the door at the stairs' top and held my knee against it. After a long minute, I slowly opened it again. There was nothing there. There was no sound. None of us ever heard the ghost again.

The slamming of the doors had aroused mother: she peered out of her room. "What on earth are you boys doing?" she demanded. Herman ventured out of his room. "Nothing," he said, gruffly, but he was, in color, a light green. "What was all that running around downstairs?" said mother. So she had heard the steps, too! We just looked at her. "Burglars!" she shouted, intuitively. I tried to quiet her by starting lightly downstairs.

"Come on, Herman," I said.

"I'll stay with mother," he said. "She's all excited."

I stepped back onto the landing.

"Don't either of you go a step," said mother. "We'll call the police." Since the phone was downstairs, I didn't see how we were going to call the police—nor did I want the police—but mother made one of her quick, incomparable decisions. She flung up a window of her bedroom which faced the bedroom windows of the house of a neighbor, picked up a shoe, and whammed it through a pane of glass across the narrow space that separated the two houses. Glass tinkled into the bedroom occupied by a retired engraver named Bodwell and his wife. Bodwell had been for some years in rather a bad way and was subject to mild "attacks." Most everybody we knew or lived near had *some* kind of attacks.

It was now about two o'clock of a moonless night; clouds hung black and low. Bodwell was at the window in a minute, shouting, frothing a little, shaking his fist. "We'll sell the house and go back to Peoria," we could hear Mrs. Bodwell saying. It was some time before mother "got through" to Bodwell. "Burglars!" she shouted. "Burglars in the house!" Herman and I hadn't dared to tell her that it was not burglars but ghosts, for she was even more afraid of ghosts than of burglars. Bodwell at first thought that she meant there were burglars in his house, but finally he quieted down and called the police for us over an extension phone by his bed. After he had disappeared from the window, mother suddenly made as if to throw another shoe, not because there was further need of it but, as she later explained, because the thrill of heaving a shoe through a window glass had enormously taken her fancy. I prevented her.

THE police were on hand in a commendably short time: a Ford sedan full of them, two on motorcycles, and a patrol wagon with about eight in it and a few reporters. They began banging at our front door. Flashlights shot streaks of gleam up and down the walls, across the yard, down the walk between our house and Bodwell's. "Open up!" cried a hoarse voice. "We're men from Headquarters!" I wanted to go down and let them in, since there they were, but mother wouldn't hear of it. "You haven't a stitch on," she pointed out. "You'd catch your death." I wound the towel around me again. Finally the cops put their shoulders to our big heavy front door with its thick beveled glass and broke it in: I could hear a rending of wood and a splash of glass on the floor of the hall. Their lights played all over the living-room and crisscrossed nervously in the dining-room, stabbed into hallways, shot up the front stairs and finally up the back. They caught me standing in my towel at the top. A heavy policeman bounded up the steps. "Who are you?" he demanded. "I live here," I said. "Well, whatsa matta, ya hot?" he asked. It was, as a matter of fact, cold; I went to my room and pulled on some trousers. On my way out, a cop stuck a gun into my ribs. "Whatta you doin' here?" he demanded. "I live here," I said.

The officer in charge reported to mother. "No sign of nobody, lady," he said. "Musta got away—what'd he look like?" "There were two or three of them," mother said, "whooping and carrying on and slamming doors." "Funny," said the cop. "All ya windows and doors was locked on the inside tight as a tick."

Downstairs we could hear the tromping of the other police; doors were yanked open, drawers were yanked open, windows were shot up and pulled down, furniture fell with dull thumps. A half-dozen police-men emerged out of the darkness of the front hallway upstairs. They began to ransack the floor: pulled beds away from walls, tore clothes off hooks in the closets, pulled suitcases and boxes off shelves. One of them found an old zither that Roy had won in a pool tournament. "Looky here, Joe," he said, strumming it with a big paw. The cop named Joe took it and turned it over. "What is it?" he asked me. "It's an old zither our guinea pig used to sleep on," I said. It was true that a pet guinea pig we once had would never sleep anywhere except on the zither, but I should never have said so. Joe and the other cop looked at me a long time. They put the zither back on a shelf.

"No sign o' nuthin'," said the cop who had first spoken to mother. "This guy," he explained to the others, jerking a thumb at me, "was nekked. The lady seems historical." They all nodded, but said nothing; just looked at me. In the small silence we all heard a creaking in the attic. Grandfather was turning over in bed. "What's 'at?" snapped Joe. Five or six cops sprang for the attic door before I could intervene or ex-plain. I realized that it would be bad if they burst in on grandfather unannounced, or even announced. He was going through a phase in which he believed that General Meade's men, under steady hammering by Stonewall Jackson, were beginning to retreat and even desert.

WHEN I got to the attic, things were pretty confused. Grandfather had evidently jumped to the conclusion that the police were deserters from Meade's army, trying to hide away in his attic. He bounded out of bed wearing a long flannel nightgown over long woolen underwear, a night-cap, and a leather jacket around his chest. The cops must have realized at once that the indignant white-haired old man belonged in the house, but they had no chance to say so. "Back, ye cowardly dogs!" roared grandfather. "Back t' the lines, ye goddam lily-livered cattle!" With that, he fetched the officer who found the zither a flat-handed smack alongside his head that sent him sprawling. The others beat a retreat, but not fast enough; grandfather grabbed Zither's gun from its holster and let fly. The report seemed to crack the rafters; smoke filled the attic. A cop cursed and shot his hand to his shoulder. Somehow, we all finally got downstairs again and locked the door against the old gentleman. He fired once or twice more in the darkness and then went back to bed. "That was grandfather," I explained to Joe, out of breath. "He thinks you're deserters." "You're telling me," said Joe.

The cops were reluctant to leave without getting their hands on somebody besides grandfather; the night had been distinctly a defeat for them. Furthermore, they obviously didn't like the "layout;" something looked—and I can see their viewpoint—phony. They began to poke into things again. A reporter, a thin-faced, wispy man, came up to me. I had put on one of mother's blouses, not being able to find anything else. The reporter looked at me with mingled suspicion and interest. "Just what the hell is the real lowdown here, Bud?" he asked. I decided to be frank with him. "We had ghosts," I said. He gazed at me a long time as if I were a slot machine into which he had, without results, dropped a nickel. Then he walked away. The cops followed him, the one grandfather shot holding his now-bandaged arm, cursing and blaspheming. "I'm gonna get my gun back from that old bird," said the zither-cop. "Yeh," said Joe. "You—and who else?" I told them I would bring it to the station house the next day.

"What was the matter with that one policeman?" mother asked, after they had gone. "Grandfather shot him," I said. "What for?" she demanded. I told her he was a deserter. "Of all things!" said mother. "He was such a nice-looking young man."

GRANDFATHER was fresh as a daisy and full of jokes at breakfast next morning. We thought at first he had forgotten all about what had happened, but he hadn't. Over his third cup of coffee, he glared at Herman and me. "What was the idea of all them cops tarryhootin' round the house last night?" he demanded. He had us there.

1933

WOLCOTT GIBBS

RING OUT, WILD BELLS

WHEN I finally got around to seeing Max Reinhardt's cinema version of "A Midsummer-Night's Dream," and saw a child called Mickey Rooney playing Puck, I remembered suddenly that long ago I had taken the same part.

Our production was given on the open-air stage at the Riverdale Country School, shortly before the war. The scenery was only the natural scenery of that suburban dell, and the cast was exclusively male, ranging in age from eleven to perhaps seventeen. While we had thus preserved the pure, Elizabethan note of the original, it must be admitted that our version had its drawbacks. The costumes were probably the worst things we had to bear, and even Penrod, tragically arrayed as Launcelot in his sister's stockings and his father's drawers, might have been embarrassed for us. Like Penrod, we were costumed by our parents, and like the Schofields, they seemed on the whole a little weak historically. Half of the ladies were inclined to favor the Elizabethan, and they had constructed rather bunchy ruffs and farthingales for their offspring; others, who had read as far as the stage directions and learned that the action took place in an Athenian wood, had produced something vaguely Athenian, usually beginning with a sheet. Only the fairies had a certain uniformity. For some reason their parents had all decided on cheesecloth, with here and there a little ill-advised trimming with tinsel.

My own costume was mysterious, but spectacular. As nearly as I have ever been able to figure things out, my mother found her inspiration for it in a Maxfield Parrish picture of a court jester. Beginning at the top, there was a cap with three stuffed horns; then, for the main part, a pair of tights that covered me to my wrists and ankles; and finally slippers with stuffed toes that curled up at the ends. The whole thing was made out of silk in alternate green and red stripes, and (unquestionably my poor mother's most demented stroke) it was covered from head to foot with a thousand tiny bells. Because all our costumes were obviously perishable, we never wore them in rehearsal, and naturally nobody knew that I was invested with these peculiar sound effects until I made my entrance at the beginning of the second act.

Our director was a man who had strong opinions about how Shakespeare should be played, and Puck was one of his favorite characters. It was his theory that Puck, being "the incarnation of mischief," never ought to be still a minute, so I had been coached to bound onto the stage, and once there to dance up and down, cocking my head and waving my arms.

"I want you to be a little whirlwind," this man said.

Even as I prepared to bound onto the stage, I had my own misgivings about those dangerously abundant gestures, and their probable effect on my bells. It was too late, however, to invent another technique for playing Puck, even if there had been room for anything but horror in my mind. I bounded onto the stage.

The effect, in its way, must have been superb. With every leap I rang like a thousand children's sleighs, my melodies foretelling God knows what worlds of merriment to the enchanted spectators. It was even worse when I came to the middle of the stage and went into my gestures. The other ringing had been loud but sporadic. This was persistent, varying only slightly in volume and pitch with the vehemence of my gestures. To a blind man, it must have sounded as though I had recklessly decided to accompany myself on a xylophone. A maturer actor would probably have made up his mind that an emergency existed, and abandoned his gestures as impracticable under the circumstances. I was thirteen, and incapable of innovations. I had been told by responsible authorities that gestures went with this part, and I continued to make them. I also continued to ring—a silvery music, festive and horrible.

If the bells were hard on my nerves, they were even worse for the rest of the cast, who were totally unprepared for my new interpretation. Puck's first remark is addressed to one of the fairies, and it is mercifully brief.

I said, "How now, spirit! Whither wander you?"

This unhappy child, already embarrassed by a public appearance in cheesecloth and tinsel, was also burdened with an opening speech of sixteen lines in verse. He began bravely:

> "Over hill, over dale,
>   Through brush, through brier,
> Over park, over pale,
>   Through flood, through fire . . ."

At the word "fire," my instructions were to bring my hands up from the ground in a long, wavery sweep, intended to represent fire. The bells pealed. To my startled ears, it sounded more as if they exploded. The fairy stopped in his lines and looked at me sharply. The jingling, however, had diminished; it was no more than as if a faint wind stirred my bells, and he went on:

> "I do wander everywhere,
> Swifter than the moone's sphere . . ."

Here again I had another cue, for a sort of swoop and dip indicating the swiftness of the moone's sphere. Again the bells rang out, and again the performance stopped in its tracks. The fairy was clearly troubled by these interruptions. He had, however, a child's strange acceptance of the inscrutable, and was even able to regard my bells as a last-minute adult addition to the program, nerve-racking but not to be questioned. I'm sure it was only this that got him through that first speech.

MY turn, when it came, was even worse. By this time the audience had succumbed to a helpless gaiety. Every time my bells rang, laughter swept the spectators, and this mounted and mingled with the bells until everything else was practically inaudible. I began my speech, another long one, and full of incomprehensible references to Titania's changeling.

"Louder!" said somebody in the wings. "You'll have to talk louder."

It was the director, and he seemed to be in a dangerous state.

"And for heaven's sake, stop that jingling!" he said.

I talked louder, and I tried to stop the jingling, but it was no use. By the time I got to the end of my speech, I was shouting and so was the audience. It appeared that I had very little control over the bells, which continued to jingle in spite of my passionate efforts to keep them quiet.

All this had a very bad effect on the fairy, who by this time had many symptoms of a complete nervous collapse. However, he began his next speech:

> "Either I mistake your shape and making quite,
> Or else you are that shrewd and knavish sprite
> Called Robin Goodfellow: are you not he
> That . . ."

At this point I forgot that the rules had been changed and I was supposed to leave out the gestures. There was a furious jingling, and the fairy gulped.

"Are you not he that, that . . ."

He looked miserably at the wings, and the director supplied the next line, but the tumult was too much for him. The unhappy child simply shook his head.

"Say anything!" shouted the director desperately. "Anything at all!"

The fairy only shut his eyes and shuddered.

"All right!" shouted the director. "All right, Puck. *You* begin *your* next speech."

By some miracle, I actually did remember my next lines, and had opened my mouth to begin on them when suddenly the fairy spoke.

His voice was a high, thin monotone, and there seemed to be madness in it, but it was perfectly clear.

"Fourscore and seven years ago," he began, "our fathers brought forth on this continent a new nation, conceived . . ."

He said it right through to the end, and it was certainly the most successful speech ever made on that stage, and probably one of the most successful speeches ever made on any stage. I don't remember, if I ever knew, how the rest of us ever picked up the dull, normal thread of the play after that extraordinary performance, but we must have, because I know it went on. I only remember that in the next intermission the director cut off my bells with his penknife, and after that things quieted down and got dull.

1936

LUDWIG BEMELMANS

THE BALLET VISITS THE
SPLENDIDE'S MAGICIAN

THE management of the Hotel Splendide, the luxurious establishment where I once worked as a busboy, a waiter, and eventually as an assistant maître d'hôtel in the banquet department, kept on file the addresses of a number of men who were magicians, fortune-tellers, or experts with cards. One of these entertainers frequently appeared at the end of the small dinner parties which were given in the private suites of the Splendide in the boom days, before the depression put an end to such pastimes and at last brought about the demise of the Splendide itself. Our entertainers had acclimated their acts to the elegance of the hotel, and the magicians, for example, instead of conjuring a simple white rabbit from their hats, cooked therein a soufflé Alaska or brought out a prize puppy with a rhinestone collar. When young girls were present, the magician pulled from their noses and out of corsages Cartier clips, bracelets, and brooches, which were presented to them with the compliments of the host.

Among the best and most talented of our performers was Professor Maurice Gorylescu, a magician who did some palmistry on the side. He came to the hotel as often as two or three times a week. After coffee had been served, he would enter the private dining room, get people to write any number they wanted to on small bits of paper, and hold the paper to their foreheads. Then he would guess the numbers they had written down and add them up. The total would correspond to a sum he found on a dollar bill in the host's pocket. He did tricks with cards and coins, and he told people about the characteristics and the habits of dress and speech of friends long dead. He even delivered messages from them to the living.

At the end of his séances he would go into some vacant room nearby, sink into a chair, and sit for a while with his hand over his eyes. He always looked very tired. After about half an hour he would shake himself, drink a glass of water slowly, then eat something and go home.

Professor Gorylescu earned a good deal of money. His fee for a single performance was a flat hundred dollars, and he sometimes received that much again as a tip from a grateful host. But although he worked all during the season he spent everything he made and often asked for and received his fee in advance. All he earned went to women—to the support of a Rumanian wife in Bucharest, to an American one who lived somewhere in New Jersey, and to what must have been a considerable number of New York girls of all nationalities to whom he sent little gifts and flowers.

When he came to the hotel during the day, he would hang his cane on the doorknob outside the ballroom office, ask me for a cigarette, and after a while steal a look at the book in which the reservations for small dinners were recorded. Very casually, and while talking of other things, he would turn the leaves and say something like "Looks very nice for the next two months," and put the book back. It took only a few seconds, but in this time his trick mind had stored away all the names, addresses, dates, and telephone numbers in the book. He went home with this information, called up the prospective party-givers, and offered his services.

There was a strict rule that no one should be permitted to look at these reservations, certainly not Professor Gorylescu, but I liked him, and when I was on duty in the ballroom office I would pretend not to see him when he peeked in the book. I also gave him left-over *petits fours,* candies, and after-dinner mints, of which he was very fond. He stuffed them into his pockets without bothering to wrap them up. He would wave goodbye with his immense hands, ask me to visit him soon at his home, and suggest that I bring along some *marrons glacés,* pastry, nuts—anything like that—and then he would leave, a stooping, uncouth figure, bigger than our tallest doorman.

MAURICE Gorylescu lived on one of the mediocre streets that run between Riverside Drive and West End Avenue. He had a room in one of the small marble mansions that are common in that neighborhood. The rooming house in which Gorylescu lived was outstanding even among the ornate buildings of that district. It was a sort of junior Frankenstein castle, bedecked with small turrets, loggias, and balconies. It faced the sidewalk across a kind of moat—an air shaft for the basement windows—traversed by a granite bridge. The door was hung on heavy iron hinges that reached all the way across.

The character of this house was, moreover, complemented by the woman who rented its rooms, a Mrs. Houlberg. She stood guard much of the time at the window next to the moat, looking out over a sign that read "Vacancies." She always covered three-quarters of her face with her right hand, a long hand that lay diagonally across her face, the palm over her mouth, the nails of the fingers stopping under the right eye. It looked like a mask, and as if she always had a toothache.

Gorylescu lived on the top-floor front and answered to four short rings and one long one of a shrill bell that was in Mrs. Houlberg's entrance hall. Badly worn banisters led up four flights of stairs. From the balcony of his room one could see the time flash on and off in Jersey and the searchlights of a battleship in the Hudson. The room was large and newly painted in a wet, loud red, the shade of the inside of a watermelon. A spotty chartreuse velvet coverlet decorated a studio couch. Facing this was a chair, a piece of furniture such as you see in hotel lobbies or club cars, covered with striped muslin and padded with down. There was also a Sheraton highboy, which stood near a door that led into an adjoining room which was not his. From the ceiling hung a cheap bazaar lamp with carmine glass panes behind filigree panels. On shelves and on a table were the photographs of many women; in a box, tied together with ribbons in various colors, he kept packets of letters, and in a particular drawer of the highboy was a woman's garter, an old girdle, and various other disorderly trophies.

Gorylescu reclined on the studio bed most of the time when he was at home. He wore a Russian blouse that buttoned under the left ear, and he smoked through a cigarette holder a foot long. One of his eyes was smaller and lower down in his face than the other, and between them rose a retroussé nose, a trumpet of a nose, with cavernous nostrils. Frequently and with great ceremony he sounded it into an immense handkerchief. His cigar-colored skin was spotted as if with a bluish kind of buckshot, and when he was happy he hummed through his nose, mostly the melody of a song whose title was "Tu Sais."

At home he was almost constantly in the company of women. He made the acquaintance of some of them at parties where he had entertained. They brought him gifts, and if they were fat and old, he read their minds and told them things of the past and future. At other times he went looking for girls along Riverside Drive, humming through his nose, and dragging after him a heavy cane whose handle was hooked into his coat pocket.

He went to various other places to find girls. He picked them up at dance halls in Harlem, on the subway, on roller coasters. He easily became acquainted with them anywhere, and they came to his room willingly and took their chances with him. I always thought I might find one of them, dead and naked, behind the Japanese screen, where he kept a rowing machine on which he built himself up. For the space of time that I knew him, love, murder, and that man seemed to be close together and that room the inevitable theatre for it.

The Professor gave me a series of lectures during my visits to his room in which he detailed for me the routines and the mechanisms of his untidy passions. He insisted during these long *études* that the most important piece of strategy was to get the subject to remove her shoes. "Once the shoes are off, the battle is already half won," he would say. "Get a woman to walk around without shoes, without heels—she looks a fool, she feels a fool, she is a fool. Without her shoes, she is lost. Take the soft instep in your hand, caress her ankles, her calf, her knee—the rest is child's play. But remember, first off with the shoes." While he talked, he would scratch his cat, which was part Siamese. The lecture was followed by a display of the collection of photographs he himself had taken, as evidence of the soundness of his theories.

WHEN the Russian Ballet came to town, Professor Gorylescu was not to be had for any parties at the hotel. He went to all the performances, matinées and evenings alike, and he hummed then the music of "Puppenfee," "L'Après-Midi d'un Faune," and the various *divertissements*, and was completely broke. One day he was in a state of the highest elation because he had invited a ballet dancer to tea. He wanted me to come too because she had a friend, who would be an extra girl for me; both of them were exquisite creatures, he assured me, and I was to bring some tea, *marrons glacés, petits fours,* and ladyfingers.

I came early and I brought everything. He darkened the room, lit a brass samovar, laid out some cigarettes, sliced some lemons, hid the rowing machine under the studio couch, and with the Japanese silk screen divided the room into two separate camps. On one side was the couch, on the other the great chair. He buttoned his Russian blouse, blew his nose frequently, and hummed as he walked up and down. He brushed the cat and put away a Spanish costume doll that might have made his couch crowded. He arranged the *petits fours* in saucers, and when the bell rang four times short and one long, he put a Chopin record on his victrola. "Remember about the shoes," he told me over his shoulder, "and always play Chopin for ballet dancers." He quickly surveyed the room once more, turned on the bazaar lamp, and, humming, opened the door—and then stopped humming suddenly. He had invited two of the dancers, but up the stairs came a bouquet of girls, more than a dozen of them.

All at once it was the month of May in the dimmed room. The lovely guests complimented the samovar, the cat, the music, and the view from the balcony, to which they had opened the door, letting much fresh air come in, which intensified the new mood. Gorylescu's voice became metallic with introductions; he ran downstairs to get more glasses for tea and came back breathing heavily. All the girls, without being asked, took their shoes off immediately, explaining that their feet hurt from dancing. They arranged the shoes in an orderly row, as one does on entering a Japanese house or a mosque, then sat down on the floor in a circle. One of them even removed her stockings and put some slices of lemon between her toes. "Ah-h-h," she said.

There started after this a bewildering and alien conversation, a remote, foggy ritual, like a Shinto ceremonial. It consisted of the telling of ballet stories, and seemed to me a high, wild flight into a world closed to the outsider. The stories were told over and over until every detail was correct. In all of these stories appeared Anna Pavlova, who was referred to as "Madame"—what Madame had said, what Madame had done, what she had thought, what she had worn, how she had danced. There was an atmosphere of furious backstage patriotism. The teller of each story swayed and danced with hands, shoulders, and face. Every word was illustrated; for anything mentioned—color, light, time, and person—there was a surprisingly expressive and fitting gesture.

The talker was rewarded with applause, with requests for repetition of this or that part again and again, and there swept over the group of girls waves of intimate, fervent emotion.

The Professor served tea on his hands and knees and retired to the shadows of his room. He sat for a while in the great chair like a bird with a wounded wing, and then, with his sagging and cumbersome gait, he wandered around the group of innocents, who sat straight as so many candles, all with their shoes off. The room was alive with young heads and throats and flanks.

The Professor succeeded finally in putting his head into the lap of the tallest, the most racy of the nymphs. She quickly kissed him, said "Sh-h-h-h, daaaahrling," and then caressed his features, the terrible nose, the eyebrows, the corrugated temples, and the great hands, with the professional detachment of a masseuse, while she related an episode in Cairo during a performance of "Giselle" when the apparatus that carried Pavlova up out of her grave to her lover got stuck halfway, and how Madame had cursed and what she had said after the performance and to whom she had said it. An indignant fire burned in all the narrowed eyes of the disciples as she talked.

Suddenly one of them looked at her watch, remembered a rehearsal, and the girls got up and remembered us. They all had Russian names, but all of them were English, as most ballet dancers are; in their best accents, they said their adieus. With individual graces, they arranged their hair, slipped into their shoes, and thanked Maurice. Each one of them said "Daaaahrling" to us and to each other. It was Madame Pavlova's form of address and her pronunciation.

All the girls kissed us, and it was as if we all had grown up in the same garden, as if they were all our sisters. The Professor said a few mouthfuls of gallant compliments, and when they were gone he fished the rowing machine out from under the couch, without a word, and carried it in back of the Japanese screen. Together, we rearranged the room. The *marrons glacés* and the ladyfingers were all gone, but the cigarettes were still there.

1940

CLOUDLAND REVISITED

WHY, DOCTOR, WHAT BIG GREEN EYES YOU HAVE!

HALFWAY through the summer of 1916, I was living on the rim of Narragansett Bay, a fur-bearing adolescent with cheeks as yet unscarred by my first Durham Duplex razor, when I read a book that exerted a considerable influence on my bedtime habits. Up to then, I had slept in normal twelve-year-old fashion, with the lights full on, a blanket muffling my head from succubi and afreets, a chair wedged under the doorknob, and a complex network of strings festooned across the room in a way scientifically designed to entrap any trespasser, corporeal or not. On finishing the romance in question, however, I realized that the protection I had been relying on was woefully inadequate and that I had merely been crowding my luck. Every night thereafter, before retiring, I spent an extra half hour barricading the door with a chest of drawers, sprinkling tacks along the window sills, and strewing crumpled newspapers about the floor to warn me of approaching footsteps. As a minor added precaution, I slept under the bed, a ruse that did not make for refreshing slumber but at least threw my enemies off the scent. Whether it was constant vigilance or natural stamina, I somehow survived, and, indeed, received a surprising number of compliments on my appearance when I returned to grammar school that fall. I guess nobody in those parts had ever seen a boy with snow-white hair and a green skin.

Perhaps the hobgoblins who plagued me in that Rhode Island beach cottage were no more virulent than the reader's own childhood favorites, but the particular one I was introduced to in the book I've mentioned could hold up his head in any concourse of fiends. Even after thirty-five years, the lines that ushered him onstage still cause an involuntary shudder:

"Imagine a person, tall, lean and feline, high-shouldered, with a brow like Shakespeare and a face like Satan, a close-shaven skull, and long, magnetic eyes of the true cat-green. Invest him with all the cruel cunning of an entire Eastern race, accumulated in one giant intellect, with all the resources of science, past and present, with all the resources, if you will, of a wealthy government—which, however, already has denied all knowledge of his existence. . . . This man, whether a fanatic or a duly appointed agent, is, unquestionably, the most malign and formidable personality existing in the world today. He is a linguist who speaks with almost equal facility in any of the civilized languages, and in most of the barbaric. He is an adept in all the arts and sciences which a great university could teach him. He also is an adept in certain obscure arts and sciences which *no* university of today can teach. He has the brains of any three men of genius. . . . Imagine that awful being, and you have a mental picture of Dr. Fu-Manchu, the yellow peril incarnate in one man."

Yes, it is the reptilian Doctor himself, one of the most sinister figures ever to slither out of a novelist's inkwell, and many a present-day comic book, if the truth were told, is indebted to his machinations, his underground laboratories, carnivorous orchids, rare Oriental poisons, dacoits, and stranglers. An authentic vampire in the great tradition, Fu-Manchu horrified the popular imagination in a long series of bestsellers by Sax Rohmer, passed through several profitable reincarnations in Hollywood, and (I thought) retired to the limbo of the second-hand bookshop, remembered only by a few slippered pantaloons like me. Some while ago, though, a casual reference by my daughter to Thuggee over her morning oatmeal made me prick up my ears. On close questioning, I found she had been bedevilling herself with "The Mystery of Dr. Fu-Manchu," the very volume that had induced my youthful fantods. I delivered a hypocritical little lecture, worthy of Pecksniff, in which I pointed out that Laurence Hope's "Indian Love" was far more suitable for her age level, and, confiscating the book, holed up for a retrospective look at it. I see now how phlegmatic I have become with advancing age. Apart from causing me to cry out occasionally in my sleep and populating my pillow with a swarm of nonexistent spiders, Rohmer's thriller was as abrasive to the nerves as a cup of Ovaltine.

THE plot of "The Mystery of Dr. Fu-Manchu" is at once engagingly simple and monstrously confused. In essence, it is a duel of wits between the malevolent Celestial, who dreams of a world dominated by his countrymen, and Commissioner Nayland Smith, a purportedly brilliant sleuth, whose confidant, Dr. Petrie, serves as narrator. Fu-

Manchu comes to England bent on the extermination of half a dozen distinguished Foreign Office servants, Orientalists, and other buttin-skies privy to his scheme; Smith and Petrie constantly scud about in a web-footed attempt to warn the prey, who are usually defunct by the time they arrive, or busy themselves with being waylaid, sandbagged, drugged, kidnapped, poisoned, or garrotted by Fu-Manchu's deputies. These assaults, however, are never downright lethal, for regularly, at the eleventh hour, a beautiful slave of Fu-Manchu named Kâramanèh be-trays her master and delivers the pair from jeopardy. The story, conse-quently, has somewhat the same porous texture as a Pearl White serial. An episode may end with Smith and Petrie plummeting through a trapdoor to nameless horrors below; the next opens on them comfort-ably sipping whiskey-and-soda in their chambers, analyzing their hair-breadth escape and speculating about the adversary's next move. To synopsize this kind of ectoplasmic yarn with any degree of fidelity would be to connive at criminal boredom, and I have no intention of doing so, but it might be fruitful to dip a spoon into the curry at ran-dom to gain some notion of its flavor.

Lest doubt prevail at the outset as to the utter malignancy of Fu-Manchu, the author catapults Nayland Smith into Petrie's rooms in the dead of night with the following portentous declaration of his purpose: "Petrie, I have travelled from Burma not in the interests of the British government merely, but in the interest of the entire white race, and I honestly believe—though I pray I may be wrong—that its survival de-pends largely on the success of my mission." Can Petrie, demands Smith, spare a few days from his medical duties for "the strangest busi-ness, I promise you, that ever was recorded in fact or fiction"? He gets the expected answer: "I agreed readily enough, for, unfortunately, my professional duties were not onerous." The alacrity with which doctors of that epoch deserted their practice has never ceased to impress me. Holmes had only to crook his finger and Watson went bowling away in a four-wheeler, leaving his patients to fend for themselves. If the fore-going is at all indicative, the mortality rate of London in the nineteen-hundreds must have been appalling; the average physician seems to have spent much less time in diagnosis than in mousing around Wap-ping Old Stairs with a dark lantern. The white race, apparently, was a lot tougher than one would suspect.

At any rate, the duo hasten forthwith to caution a worthy named Sir Crichton Davey that his life is in peril, and, predictably, discover him al-ready cheesed off. His death, it develops, stemmed from a giant red centipede, lowered down the chimney of his study by Fu-Manchu's dacoits, regarding whom Smith makes the charmingly offhand statement "Oh, dacoity, though quiescent, is by no means extinct." Smith also seizes the opportunity to expatiate on the archcriminal in some fairly delicious double-talk: "As to his mission among men. Why did M. Jules Furneaux fall dead in a Paris opera-house? Because of heart failure? No! Because his last speech had shown that he held the key to the secret of Tongking. What became of the Grand Duke Stanislaus? Elopement? Suicide? Nothing of the kind. He alone was fully alive to Russia's growing peril. He alone knew the truth about Mongolia. Why was Sir Crichton Davey murdered? Because, had the work he was engaged upon ever seen the light, it would have shown him to be the only living Englishman who understood the importance of the Tibetan frontiers." In between these rhetorical flourishes, Petrie is accosted by Kâramanèh, Fu-Manchu's houri, who is bearing a deadly perfumed letter intended to destroy Smith. The device fails, but the encounter begets a romantic interest that saves Petrie's neck on his next excursion. Disguised as rough seafaring men, he and Smith have tracked down Fu-Manchu at Singapore Charlie's, an opium shop on the Thames dockside. Here, for the first time, Petrie gets a good hinge at the monster's eyes: ". . . their unique horror lay in a certain filminess (it made me think of the *membrana nictitans* in a bird) which, obscuring them as I threw wide the door, seemed to lift as I actually passed the threshold, revealing the eyes in all their brilliant viridescence." Before he can polish his ornithological metaphor, however, Petrie is plunged through a trapdoor into the river, the den goes up in flames, and it looks like curtains for the adventurous physician. But Providence, in the form of a hideous old Chinese, intervenes. Stripping off his ugly, grinning mask, he discloses himself as Kâramanèh; she extends her false pigtail to Petrie and, after pulling him to safety, melts into the night. It is at approximately this juncture that one begins to appreciate how lightly the laws of probability weighed on Sax Rohmer. Once you step with him into Never-Never Land, the grave's the limit, and no character is deemed extinct until you can use his skull as a paperweight.

Impatient at the snail's pace with which his conspiracy is maturing, Fu-Manchu now takes the buttons off the foils. He tries to abduct a missionary who has flummoxed his plans in China, but succeeds only in slaying the latter's collie and destroying his manservant's memory—on the whole, a pretty footling morning's work. He then pumps chlorine gas into a sarcophagus belonging to Sir Lionel Barton, a bothersome explorer, with correspondingly disappointing results; this time the bag is a sneaky Italian secretary and a no-account Chinese houseboy.

The villain's next foray is more heartening. He manages to overpower Smith and Petrie by some unspecified means (undoubtedly the "rather rare essential oil" that Smith says he has met with before, "though never in Europe") and chains them up in his noisome cellars. The scene wherein he twits his captives has a nice poetic lilt: "A marmoset landed on the shoulder of Dr. Fu-Manchu and peered grotesquely into the dreadful yellow face. The Doctor raised his bony hand and fondled the little creature, crooning to it. 'One of my pets, Mr. Smith,' he said, suddenly opening his eyes fully so that they blazed like green lamps. 'I have others, equally useful. My scorpions—have you met my scorpions? No? My pythons and hamadryads? Then there are my fungi and my tiny allies, the bacilli. I have a collection in my laboratory quite unique. Have you ever visited Molokai, the leper island, Doctor? No? But Mr. Nayland Smith will be familiar with the asylum at Rangoon! And we must not forget my black spiders, with their diamond eyes—my spiders, that sit in the dark and watch—then leap!' " Yet, having labored to create so auspicious a buildup, the author inexplicably cheats his suspense and lets it go for naught. No sooner has Fu-Manchu turned his back to attend to a poisoned soufflé in the oven than Kâramanèh pops up and strikes off the prisoners' gyves, and the whole grisly quadrille starts all over again. Smith and Petrie, without so much as a change of deerstalker hats, nip away to warn another prospective victim, and run full tilt into a covey of *phansigars,* the religious stranglers familiar to devotees of the *American Weekly* as Thugs. They outwit them, to be sure, but the pace is beginning to tell on Petrie, who observes ruefully, "In retrospect, that restless time offers a chaotic prospect, with few peaceful spots amid its turmoils." Frankly, I don't know what Petrie is beefing about. My compassion goes out, rather, to his patients, whom I envision by now as driven by default to extracting their own tonsils and quarrying each other's gallstones. *They're* the ones who need sympathy, Petrie, old boy.

With puff adders, tarantulas, and highbinders blooming in every hedgerow, the hole-and-corner pursuit of Fu-Manchu drums along through the next hundred pages at about the same tempo, resolutely shying away from climaxes like Hindus from meat. Even the episode in which Smith and Petrie, through the good offices of Kâramanèh, eventually hold the Doctor at gun point aboard his floating laboratory in the Thames proves just a pretext for further bombination about those filmy greenish eyes; a shower of adjectives explodes in the reader's face, and he is whisked off on a hunt for certain stolen plans of an aero-torpedo, an interlude that veers dangerously close to the exploits of the indomitable Tom Swift. The sequence that follows, as rich in voodoo as it is innocent of logic, is heavily fraught with hypnosis, Fu-Manchu having unaccountably imprisoned a peer named Lord Southery and Kâramanèh's brother Aziz in a cataleptic trance. They are finally revived by injections of a specific called the Golden Elixir—a few drops of which I myself could have used to advantage at this point—and the story sashays fuzzily into its penultimate phase. Accompanied by a sizable police detail, Smith, Petrie, and a Scotland Yard inspector surprise Fu-Manchu in an opium sleep at his hideout. A dénouement seems unavoidable, but if there was one branch of literary hopscotch Rohmer excelled in, it was avoiding dénouements. When the three leaders of the party recover consciousness (yes, the indispensable trapdoor again, now on a wholesale basis), they lie bound and gagged in a subterranean vault, watching their captor sacrifice their subordinates by pelting them with poisonous toadstools. The prose rises to an almost lyrical pitch: "Like powdered snow the white spores fell from the roof, frosting the writhing shapes of the already poisoned men. Before my horrified gaze, *the fungus grew;* it spread from the head to the feet of those it touched; it enveloped them as in glittering shrouds. 'They die like flies!' screamed Fu-Manchu, with a sudden febrile excitement; and I felt assured of something I had long suspected: that that magnificent, perverted brain was the brain of a homicidal maniac—though Smith would never accept the theory." Since no hint is given of what theory Smith preferred, we have to fall back on conjecture. More than likely, he smiled indulgently under his gag and dismissed the whole escapade as the prankishness of a spoiled, self-indulgent child.

The ensuing events, while gaudy, are altogether too labyrinthine to unravel. As a matter of fact, they puzzled Rohmer, too. He says helplessly, "Any curiosity with which this narrative may leave the reader burdened is shared by the writer." After reading that, my curiosity shrank to the vanishing point; I certainly wasn't going to beat my brains out over a riddle the author himself did not pretend to understand. With a superhuman effort, I rallied just enough inquisitiveness to turn to the last page for some clue to Fu-Manchu's end. It takes place, as nearly as I could gather, in a blazing cottage outside London, and the note he addresses to his antagonists clears the way for plenty of sequels: "To Mr. Commissioner Nayland Smith and Dr. Petrie—Greeting! I am recalled

home by One who may not be denied. In much that I came to do I have
failed. Much that I have done I would undo; some little I have undone.
Out of fire I came—the smoldering fire of a thing one day to be a consuming flame; in fire I go. Seek not my ashes. I am the lord of the fires!
Farewell. Fu-Manchu."

I DARESAY it was the combination of this passage, the cheery hearth in
front of which I reread it, and my underwrought condition, but I thought
I detected in the Doctor's valedictory an unmistakable mandate. Rising
stealthily, I tiptoed up to my daughter's bedchamber and peered in. A
shaft of moonlight picked out her ankles protruding from beneath the
bed, where she lay peacefully sleeping, secure from dacoity and Thuggee.
Obviously, it would take more than a little crackle of the flames below to
arouse her. I slipped downstairs and, loosening the binding of "The Mystery of Dr. Fu-Manchu" to insure a good supply of oxygen, consigned the
lord of the fires to his native element. As he crumbled into ash, I could
have sworn I smelled a rather rare essential oil and felt a pair of baleful
green eyes fixed on me from the staircase. It was probably the cat, though
I really didn't take the trouble to check. I just strolled into the kitchen,
made sure there was no trapdoor under the icebox, and curled up for the
night. That's how phlegmatic a chap gets in later life.

1950

JOHN LARDNER

THOUGHTS ON RADIO-TELEVESE

INTERVIEWING Governor Rockefeller recently on Station WMCA,
Barry Gray, the discless jockey, felt the need to ask his guest a certain
question. He also felt a clear obligation to put the inquiry in radio-
televese, the semi-official language of men who promote conversation
on the air. Though it is more or less required, this language is a flexible
one, leaving a good deal to the user's imagination. "Governor," Mr.
Gray said, after pausing to review the possibilities of the patois, "how
do you see your future in a Pennsylvania Avenue sense?" I thought it

was a splendid gambit. Another broadcaster might have said "How do you see yourself in the electoral-college picture?" or "How do you project yourself Chief Executive-wise?" The Gray formula had the special flavor, the colorful two-rings-from-the-bull's-eye quality, that I have associated with the work of this interviewer ever since I began to follow it, several years ago. For the record, Governor Rockefeller replied, "I *could* be happier where I am." He might have meant Albany, he might have meant the WMCA studio. As you see, radio-televese is not only a limber language, it is contagious.

The salient characteristic of remarks made in radio-televese is that they never coincide exactly with primary meanings or accepted forms. For instance, Mr. Gray, a leader in the postwar development of the lingo, has a way of taking a trenchant thought or a strong locution and placing it somewhere to the right or left of where it would seem to belong. "Is this your first trip to the mainland? How do you feel about statehood?," I have heard him ask a guest from the Philippines on one of his shows (the program runs, at present, from 11:05 P.M. to 1 A.M.). On the topic of Puerto Ricans in New York, he has said, "How can we make these people welcome and not upset the décor of the city?" On a show a few years ago, he described an incident that had taken place in a night club "that might be called a bawd." A drunk at a ringside table, Mr. Gray said, "interrupted the floor show to deliver a soliloquy." "When did the chink begin to pierce the armor?" he once asked, in connection with a decline in the prestige of former Mayor O'Dwyer. "The fault, then," he said on another occasion, "is not with Caesar or with his stars but with certain congressmen." Speaking of the real-life source of a character in a Broadway play, he has observed, "He was the clay pigeon on whom the character was modelled." When Mr. Gray called Brussels "the Paris of Belgium," I was reminded of an editorial I had read in a Long Island newspaper long ago in which Great Neck was called "the Constantinople of the North Shore." There is an eloquence and an easy confidence in Mr. Gray's talk that stimulates even his guests to heights of radio-televese. Artie Shaw, a musician, in describing the art of another performer to Mr. Gray, said, "He has a certain thing known as 'presence'—when he's onstage, you can see him." Another guest declared that the success of a mutual friend was "owing to a combination of luck and a combination of skill." "You can say that again," Mr. Gray agreed, and I believe that the guest did so, a little later. The same eloquence and the same off-centerism can be found today in the speech of a wide variety of radio and television regulars. "Parallels are odious," Marty Glickman, a sports announcer, has stated. "The matter has reached a semi-head," a senator—I couldn't be sure which one—said at a recent televised Congressional hearing. "I hear you were shot down over the Netherlands while flying," a video reporter said to Senator Howard Cannon, a war veteran, on a Channel 2 program last winter. "Where in the next year are we going to find the writers to fill the cry and the need?" David Susskind demanded not long ago of a forum of TV directors. "Do you have an emotional umbilical cord with Hollywood?" Mr. Susskind asked a director on the same show.

Mr. Susskind's second question raises the point that metaphor is indispensable in radio-televese. "Wherein water always finds its own level, they should start hitting soon," a baseball announcer said about the Yankees the other day. In an earlier year, Red Barber, analyzing a situation in which a dangerous batter had been purposely walked, with the effect of bringing an even more dangerous batter to the plate, remarked that it was a case of "carrying coals to Newcastle, to make use of an old expression." I suspect that Mr. Barber meant that it was a case of the frying pan and the fire, and I also suspect that if he had thought of the right metaphor afterward, he would have corrected himself publicly. He is a conscientious man, and therefore by no means a typical user of radio-televese. The true exponent never retraces his steps but moves from bold figure to bold figure without apology. There have been few bolder sequences (or "seg-ways," as they are sometimes called on the air) than the one that Mr. Gray achieved in 1957, during a discussion of the perils faced by Jack Paar in launching a new program. I think I have quoted this passage here once before; it still fills me with admiration. "It's like starting off with a noose around your neck," Mr. Gray said. "You've got twenty-six weeks to make good, or they'll shoot you. That sword of Damocles can be a rough proposition." As most of you know by now, Mr. Paar eventually made good before the sword could explode and throttle him.

Perhaps the most startling aspect of radio-televese is its power to move freely in time, space, and syntax, transposing past and future, beginnings and endings, subjects and objects. This phase of the language has sometimes been called backward English, and sometimes, with a bow to the game of billiards, reverse English. Dorothy Kilgallen, a television panelist, was wallowing in the freedom of the language on the night she said, "It strikes me as funny, don't you?" So was Dizzy Dean when he said, "Don't fail to miss tomorrow's doubleheader." Tommy Loughran, a boxing announcer, was exploring the area of the displaced ego when he told his audience, "It won't take him [the referee] long before I think he should stop it." Ted Husing was on the threshold of outright mysticism when he reported, about a boxer who was cuffing his adversary smartly around, "There's a lot more authority in Joe's punches than perhaps he would like his opponent to suspect!" It is in the time dimension, however, that radio-televese scores its most remarkable effects. Dizzy Dean's "The Yankees, as I told you later . . ." gives the idea. The insecurity of man is demonstrated regularly on the air by phrases like "Texas, the former birthplace of President Eisenhower" and "Mickey Mantle, a former native of Spavinaw, Oklahoma." I'm indebted to Dan Parker, sportswriter and philologist, for a particularly strong example of time adjustment from the sayings of Vic Marsillo, a boxing manager who occasionally speaks on radio and television: "Now, Jack, whaddya say we reminisce a little about tomorrow's fight?" These quotations show what can be done in the way of outguessing man's greatest enemy, but I think that all of them are excelled by a line of Mr. Gray's, spoken four or five years ago: "What will our future forefathers say?"

It is occasionally argued in defense of broadcasters (though they need and ask for no defense) that they speak unorthodoxly because they must speak under pressure, hastily, spontaneously—that their eccentricities are unintentional. Nothing could be farther from the truth. Their language is proud and deliberate. The spirit that has created it is the spirit of ambition. Posterity would have liked it. In times to come, our forebears will be grateful.

1959

ADAM GOPNIK

THE MUSICAL HUSBANDS

THE musical husbands buy Monster cable for their speakers, because they are sure that it increases the midrange response. They listen to the speakers as soon as they have attached the new cables—even before they have pushed the speakers back up against the wall—hoping to hear all the new, warm alto tones. They take the fabric screens off the speakers to expose the woofers and tweeters. Then they put the screens back on. They have read about the midrange in their audio magazines. If the midrange is full, soprano voices are, it seems, "burnished" and "honeyed," rather than just high and piercing; in the midrange, music "swells expressively," and strings have an "ambient glow."

"It's the test of the musicality of your system," their audiophile friends explain. "You've got the flutes and harps in the tweeter, and the bass sounds in the woofer. The test of your system is how well you can get all the tones that lie in between. When you have good midrange response, all the music just seems to be flowing together. It's mostly a consequence of how good the system is at reproducing ambient sound—room tone that you can't really hear as music but that's all *around* the music. It's a mysterious thing. Some cheap systems can be rich in midrange response, and some people can spend ten thousand dollars and still not have it." The musical husbands believe passionately that they will find the midrange someday—they will put together the perfect arrangement of cables and find the right place for the speakers, and there it will be— the midrange, rising like an apparition above the stereo cabinet.

Searching for the midrange, the musical husbands pick up their black, undersized speakers and try them in different configurations around the room: on the floor on either side of the stereo cabinet, then up on the windowsill behind the stereo, then one up high, near the window, and one reverberating on the floor—first the left one up and the right one down, then the right one up and the left one down. Their wives watch them from the sofas, where they're reading, and think that the music sounds just about the same as it always has.

The musical husbands sometimes blame the disappearance of the midrange on the "tyranny of digital sound." (That's a phrase from one of the little audio magazines.) Is digital sound really as smooth and as lacquered as they had once been promised? Or is it just cold and rote and clinical? Sometimes the musical husbands slip a CD into the player and are sure that it is giving them a headache. Too cold, too cold. "Doesn't it sound harsh—sort of *glaring*—to you?" one may call out to his wife, who then appears at the door of the living room with a thumb discreetly placed inside her book.

She cocks her head. "Oh, listen! You can hear the maracas," she says encouragingly as "Beatles For Sale" plays.

"Yeah! That's the problem!" the musical husband cries in agitation. "The incidental percussion shouldn't have that kind of clarity!" She listens for the overinsistent maracas, the too bright tambourines, and then tries to look pained, too.

The musical husbands are convinced that the sound of music has changed since they were children. They can remember hearing the third movement of Beethoven's Ninth at the end of the old Huntley-Brinkley report—it was their first musical experience: the anonymous orchestra catching fire, alight with indignation at the state of the world that evening. Now, though, when the musical husbands hear Beethoven, even at Carnegie Hall, it sounds too *distinct*. The timpani pound brightly; the strings scratch away; you can pick out the horns—everyone is playing his part. That sense of an orchestra fused into one single, scowling emotion—you don't hear that anymore. Perhaps the midrange has simply vanished from the world.

WHO are the musical husbands? They are men for whom the love of music supplies more jumpiness than it does serenity. Music creates for them a cycle of appetites and worries, itches and anxieties. They can be seen in Tower Records on Friday nights, travelling between the pop and the jazz and the classical sections, a long CD package in either hand—Ella and Handel—trying to discipline themselves to buy only one. They are seized by sudden enthusiasms—*needs*—for all the music of a particular musician. And yet even as they place today's CD inside the player, they are already thinking about tomorrow's. In the space of a week, they buy all the records of Lester Young; then they lie awake, as their wives read, thinking that once again they have deluded themselves—that it was not the swoopiness of Lester Young they really desired but the breathiness of Ben Webster. The musical husbands do love music. They turn on their stereos first thing in the morning and end the day by listening with their headphones at night. But they worry about music, too. When the musical husbands stand on the main floor of Tower, they think that everyone else has a single purpose; everyone else in the store knows just what section to head for. The musical husbands stand in the center of the aisle and look all around: across the floor at the old rock records, and down the aisle at the pop singles, and then they lift their heads toward the classical section upstairs. They have been like this since they were teen-agers, when they would see the ads for the Columbia Record Club in *TV Guide;* just looking at the order forms, where you were expected to check off your "favorite music" (Country and Western, Classical, Broadway, even Teen Hits), made them feel sick. How could you choose?

Now they try to be surer about music, but they are still mercurial from day to day. "I just can't stand to listen to classical quartets when they aren't played on original instruments," they will declare. Then the next day someone will give them a reissue of a Hungarian quartet playing Schumann, recorded in 1956, and that will become their new favorite. They try to console themselves by producing their own tapes, alternating selections from the record collections that they have been assembling since they were twelve with tracks from the new compact-disk reissues. These juxtapositions, they feel, illustrate important musical points. They place gut-string performances of the Haydn string quartets alongside the Quartetto Italiano's performance of the same material, movement by movement. Or they produce scholarly tapes of popular music for their friends. "The Birth of Heavy Metal," for instance—a compilation that pairs American Delta and Chicago Blues material with its English-working-class interpretations. The selections are written out in thin felt pen on the white, ruled cardboard insert of the tape boxes: Robert Johnson's "Crossroads Blues" (1936), and then Cream's "Crossroads" (live, 1968); Howlin' Wolf's "The Red Rooster" (1961), and then the Stones' "Little Red Rooster" (1965).

THE musical husbands are nothing like their best friends, the married musicians. The married musicians once really were musicians. They played in bluegrass bands around Cape Cod one summer, or had two years at Juilliard, or wrote satirical songs for the college revue. They are casual about recorded music; often they still use the record-player they had back then or else they actually own a boom box—a ghetto blaster like the kids in the park have—and take it with them to the office, on vacation, or out to the country. They keep beautiful instruments in their apartments—handmade f-hole guitars, or Bechstein baby grands.

The musical husbands are also different from the High End Enthusiasts, with their "reference" records of the twenty-four hours of Le Mans and their speakers shaped like airplane wings; from the Serious Listeners, with their bookshelves full of early-twentieth-century recordings from La Scala; from the Focussed Collectors, with their six versions of "Show Boat"; from the Music Lovers, who are lusty rather than furtive in their musicality, and are full of musical gusto and musical wisecracks ("You call that bel canto? I call it can-belt-o!"); from the Musical Bachelors, who have Sony components and actually buy Harry Connick records; and from their own, moderately musical children, who sit in the middle of the living room, listening to Billy Joel on the Walkman, the music passing right through them, like juice.

Above all, the musical husbands are different from their musical fathers. The musical fathers never thought much about sound, for they still had musical worlds to conquer. There was so much unheard music left for them to discover. The musical fathers subscribed to the Musical Heritage Society, and every month received a single white album with blue lettering, no pictures or liner notes; each presented a new Baroque composer, a "discovery"—Telemann and C. P. E. Bach and Vivaldi, back when Vivaldi was still something. They were in revolt against Romantic music and planted their flag on two fronts at once, moving into sixteenth-century Italy and early-twentieth-century Vienna simultaneously: they heard the first "authentic" recordings of Palestrina with the same pleasure they had taken in hearing the dissonances of Webern. They took their music seriously, were prepared to banish Tchaikovsky or canonize Gesualdo. The musical fathers loved boxed sets of records— the heft of them, their impressive taped bindings—and when their sons reached their early teens, they would give them boxed sets at Christmas. To have something in a boxed set (the symphonies of Beethoven; the motets of Schütz; Bach's St. Matthew Passion) was to *possess* it—to have turned the waves of musical history into an object as solid as a doorstop.

Not that the musical fathers were musical snobs. They loved Jimmy Durante singing "Inka Dinka Doo," for instance, or the lyrics to the Peggy Lee hit "Mañana": "Oh, the window she is broken, and the rain is coming in," they would sing to their sons, with comic bravura. The musical fathers took positions and held them. They had the same seats at the symphony every Saturday night for twenty years, and then went to chamber-music concerts the next afternoon. Old soldiers in the musical wars, they recounted musical adventures to their sons. "When I saw how Toscanini had the Philadelphia horns laid out, I knew that we were in for trouble," they said. Yet many of their musical adventures seemed filled with gaiety. Sometimes, they would recall, they could get silly at concerts, listening to the Chopin "Funeral March" played too slow, for example, and then laughing so much that the ushers threw them out of the hall.

When the musical husbands think about their musical fathers, what they hear is not music but a rustle, as a father slips his record out of the paper-and-plastic inner wrapper; his decisive little pant as he blows the dust from the needle; the click of the record being placed on the record changer; the dull plop as it falls (a thrilling but oddly sinister sound, like a trapdoor being dropped open on a scaffold), and then the pause as the needle works its way across the first smooth, uninscribed eighth inch of vinyl; and finally—in the almost indescribably brief and exciting fraction of a second before the music actually begins—the hiss and pop of surface noise that precedes the orchestra, the sound of musical dust.

The musical husbands have come to believe that it was these sounds, more than any others—the sequential plop of the heavy records, and then the microsecond of fuzz—that gave their fathers ease and security in the presence of music. Sound didn't assault their fathers, didn't jump them from behind. They began to hum before the music began, and they would sometimes break their musical routines by putting on a "comedy album"—Bob Newhart, or Nichols and May, or Mel Brooks and Carl Reiner—and they would start laughing before the first high-pitched, nervous, night-club sounds broke through the static. The musical husbands don't know anybody who listens to comedy CDs, and they think this means something. Digital sound can never be funny: imagine an antic comedian's voice suddenly breaking through, without preparation, deep and amusing and surrounded by perfect silence, as though by a black border.

ARE the musical husbands really musical at all? The possibility that they are not worries them. Sometimes they think, The midrange has been there all along, but I cannot hear it. They know in their hearts that they don't really like concerts. They drag their wives to concerts, but the wives sense that the husbands are not really happy there. They sit on their coats, fighting off the sleepiness from the big Indian or Chinese meal; they're always overheated, and there's nothing to look at except the grandiose, unconvincing biographies in *Stagebill* ("Over the last ten years, Eleanor Hemidemisemiquaver has become one of the harpsichordists most widely in demand for concerts and recordings.") And in jazz clubs the sound is no good. The drums drown out the piano, the bass player has a pickup. The musical husbands would rather be at home.

They can hardly believe it now, but there was a time, back when the musical husbands were in high school, when they went to rock concerts all the time. Jethro Tull, Procol Harum, Yes. Though they still love their Beatles records, the musical husbands realize now that as a sonic arrangement, rock is without body. "It's all high notes, like a siren, and low, like a thump, with nothing in between," they announce to their wives. What they don't say is that they worry that the midrange may have atrophied in their heads from neglect. Maybe the fault is not in their speakers, or their cables, or their amplifiers; it is within them selves. All those neurons and nerve endings, shrivelled up—all their midrange software wiped out—from underuse in adolescence.

This current of self-reproach and hopelessness makes it dangerous to bring the musical husbands together. Sometimes they can be kind and helpful to one another. They visit one another on Saturday afternoons, to examine new recordings and old speakers. They tweak one another's CDs, placing rubber rings, like prophylactics, around the edges of the silver disks. (They have convinced themselves that this deepens and widens the sound.) They spray Armor All on the disks, to diminish their metallic harshness, and listen to each other's favorite passages. You see them sometimes in Tower, rummaging through the sale bins and sharing their enthusiasms, the whole universe of music stretching out around them.

But on other occasions it's dangerous to seat two musical husbands beside each other. They can get into an argument in the middle of dinner about nothing at all—about Monster cable, for instance.

"Are you one of those guys who believe in Monster cable?" one will taunt the other, who has just finished explaining about the new disposition of his speakers.

"It makes a difference. I can hear the difference," the other says, stubbornly.

"Sometime I'll have to show you how electrons work. I guess you think the electrons need to be warm or something. You believe in Monster cable. I believe in physics," the friend says. "The electrons don't need to be warm or anything."

The other musical husband is so angry that he addresses his next remarks to his wife. "This guy is too ignorant to talk to. There is a difference, and everyone who listens seriously, anyone who has an ear, can tell."

"It's just about how people listen to their *records*," she cries, exasperated. She cannot even look at the other wife, for this is not just another bit of funny, forgivable masculine absurdity; it is deeper and more shaming than that. Meanwhile, her husband's heart is broken: she has reduced him to a hobbyist, a hi-fi enthusiast, a *nerd*. Later, at home, the couple have a fight and the musical husband says, in the end, "You're just tone-deaf. You don't know how to listen. You hate music."

ARE the musical husbands basically husbands, and only musical on the side? Or is it the other way around? It's certainly true that the longer they are married the more musical they become. At the same time, they enjoy acting the part of husband. "She keeps me on a short leash," one will say ruefully to another when he is considering some musical purchase. "Yeah. Me, too," the other musical husband will say. "We made an agreement—one CD a week. But I think this leaves me a loophole for LPs. I'll stick them behind the sofa cushions." They never feel so happily husbandlike, in fact, as when they are buying music in secret.

And yet, although they pretend to enjoy their wives' tolerant indifference, their deepest fear is that their wives *were* musical once, with their teenaged musical lovers. Although the wives tend to greet their husbands' anxious, eager demands for musical attention with a few rote responses ("It's lovely," "How beautiful," or just a long, perfunctory "Mmm"), sometimes in a department store or a coffee shop, especially around Christmas, a musical husband will notice a funny look crossing his wife's face when certain songs come on. (Not good songs, usually: "So Far Away," by Carole King, or even, God forgive her, "Stairway to Heaven.")

"Why are you smiling that way?" he'll ask.

"No reason."

"It made you think of something."

"Nothing." But she *is* smiling, to herself. Often the music that makes her smile most (and it is not the smile she reserves for new friends or people he wants her to impress, but another, inward-looking smile) is alarmingly lengthy stuff—the first side of "What's Going On," or even "In-A-Gadda-Da-Vida." Sometimes they make love with music playing, but when they do the rhythm of the lovemaking never seems to give way to the swell of ambient sound that he imagines his wife once knew. Even sex has been digitized.

After he has been away for a few days, the musical husband becomes a musical Othello, and searches his stacks of recorded music to find out what his wife has been listening to while he was away. Usually, it turns out that what she has been listening to is sad songs from the fifties, before they were born. He notices that often, even while he is playing records, she is singing to herself. Sometimes, between tracks, he will look up and listen to her sing. She sings in a high-pitched, child's vibrato, and he can never quite make out the tune. "Crazy," it sounds like, or "I Should Care."

"What are you singing, my love?" he asks her, suddenly and (he thinks) tenderly. But she can hear the anxiety and suspicion and mistrust—all the incidental percussion—in his question. So she says only, and almost to herself, "Oh, just a song."

1992

LOUIS MENAND

LISTENING TO BOURBON

REPORTS of a drug said to relieve inhibition, promote conviviality, blunt the sex drive, and turn morbid misanthropes into jolly, can-do airheads did not come as a complete surprise to some of us, since we were already familiar with a substance that provides virtually the same medical benefits. How this product, which most people can acquire just by presenting a valid driver's license, has managed to escape the attention of psychopharmacologists is a puzzle. Still, there is reason to be grateful to the philosophical branch of the psychopharmacological profession for identifying an issue that had, frankly, never seemed worth getting too ontologically bent out of shape about. And that is, of course, the question: Which is the real self? Is it the self on bourbon? Or is it the self unmodified by bourbon?

This is not a matter to be approached glibly. For the problem of identity is a sea on which many philosophers have lost their way. Consider a bundle of sticks from which one stick is removed, and then another, and then another. After the removal of which stick does the bundle of sticks cease to be "a bundle of sticks"? Or take the case of the knife whose blade has been replaced once and whose handle has been replaced three times. What grounds do we have for saying that it is still "the same knife"?

As with things, so with selves. The sexual stallion and future world-beater of nineteen, for whom three pizzas and an accompanied hour in the back seat of a car are just the beginning of a decent evening, and the sagging commuter of twenty-five years later, who staggers home hoping only to have the stamina to make it through the first half hour of "Charlie Rose," are nominally "the same person." But by virtue of what? Of having the same Social Security number? Identity is the artificial flower on the compost heap of time.

So that when we begin to talk, as recent best-selling speculation on the metaphysics of pill-popping teaches us to talk, about the bourbon drinker's "real self," we are immediately made aware of a certain fugitive quality in the object of our attention. Certainly the person who after taking bourbon saunters merrily across the room at a cocktail party and says, with a feeling indistinguishable from sincerity, "Great to see you" to someone he has never met is not "the same" as the person who an hour earlier waited for the next elevator so he wouldn't have to ride down with the boss.

But then the person who has just finished a pint of coffee ice cream with cookie dough is, by every measure, not the person she was before she opened the freezer door. The person who has spent the night cleaning up after a six-year-old with a stomach virus is no longer the obliging and fair-minded chap he was when he bedded down the previous evening. The person who has paid seven dollars and fifty cents to sit through "Intersection," starring Richard Gere and Sharon Stone, is not the person who thought this sounded like a really good movie. Mood transformations have many agents.

Probably the only thing to say about the "real self," in short, is that it is, of all our selves, the one it seems the least pretentious to own up to. Is this the self that greets personal setbacks with a chipper fortitude, that chatters amiably with idiots at a party, that maintains a healthy nonchalance in the company of members of the opposite sex? Or is it the self that would rather drive aimlessly for hours than ask directions, that broods for weeks after failing to receive an invitation to a party he had no desire to attend, that worries obsessively that his new haircut is a complete turnoff? Most bourbon drinkers have no hesitation in identifying the first self as a complete fake and embarrassment and the second as the self that, given the way things are, it is most reasonable to be. That's why they need the bourbon.

It's true that bourbon drinkers can experience unpleasant side effects unknown to consumers of faddish pharmaceuticals. But bourbon has other advantages. A glass or two neat is as close as most people can get to feeling like a novelist or an Abstract Expressionist without actually having to write or paint anything—a state thought desirable even by novelists and painters, and one that cannot be manufactured by mood transformers that come in capsule form. Sexual performance may be reduced by bourbon, but ribaldry, which is, after all, a much safer indulgence, is nicely enhanced. And for steady users death, when it comes, though painful, is mercifully swift.

1994

LOOK BACK IN HUNGER

R EADY? Ready. O.K., here we go. "Fold the wings akimbo, tucking the wing ends under the shoulders as shown here." Lovely. "Then, on the same side of the chicken where you came out from the second knee . . ." Umm. "Poke the needle through the upper arm of the wing." Wings with arms, like a bat's. Cool. "Catch the neck skin, if there . . ." Hang on. *If there?* If not there, where? Whose neck is this, anyway? ". . . and pin it to the backbone, and come out through the second wing." And go for a walk in the snow, and don't come back till next year.

This wing-stitching drill, as any cook will tell you, is from the cele- brated "To Truss a Chicken" section of Julia Child's "The Way to Cook." It's a pretty easy routine, really, as long as you take it slow, run through a batch of test poultry first, have a professional chef on hand to help you through the bad times, and feel no shame when you get ar- rested and charged with satanic drumstick abuse. Julia Child is a good woman, with no desire to faze or scald us; she genuinely wants us to bard that bird, to cook it, and to carve it. ("Fork-grab under the knee. . . . Soon you'll see the ball joint where the leg-thigh meets the small of the back.") Hell, she wouldn't mind if we went ahead and *ate* the damn thing.

I don't know what it is about cookbooks, but they really drain my giblets. I buy them, and use them, and study them with the micro- attentive care of a papyrologist, and still they make me feel that I am missing out. I follow instructions, and cook dinner for friends, and the friends are usually friends again by the next morning, but what they consume at my table bears no more than a fleeting, tragically half-assed resemblance to the dish that I read about in the recipe. Although I am not a good cook, I am not a dreadful one, either; I once had a go at *mouclade d'Aunis*, once made a brave fist of *cul de veau braisé Angevin*, and once came very close to buying a carp. Last summer, I did some- thing difficult with monkfish tails; the dish took two days to prepare, a full nine minutes to eat, and three days to wash up after. But an hour in front of my cookbooks is enough to slash my ambitions to the bone— to convince me that in terms of culinary evolution I remain a scowling tree-dweller whose idea of haute cuisine is to grub for larvae under dead bark.

And we all know the name of the highly developed being standing tall at the other end of the scale. Super-skilled, free of fear, the last word in human efficiency, Martha Stewart is the woman who convinced a million Americans that they have the time, the means, the right, and—damn it—the *duty* to pipe a little squirt of soft cheese into the middle of a snow pea, and to continue piping until there are "fifty to sixty" stuffed peas raring to go. Never mind the taste; one glance at this woman's quantities is enough to spirit you into a different and a cleaner world. "I discovered a fantastic thing when preparing 1,500 potatoes for the Folk Art Show," Martha writes in her latest book. "The Martha Stewart Cookbook" is a magisterial compendium of nine previous books, and offers her fans another chance to sample Martha's wacky punch lines ("Tie securely with a single chive") and her naughtiest promises ("This hearty soup is simple to assemble"). So coolly thrown off, that last line, and you read right through it without picking up the outrageous implication. Since when did you "assemble" a soup? Even the ingredients are a fright. "Three pounds fish frames from flounder or fluke," Martha says brightly, sounding like Henry Higgins. To the rest of humanity, soup is something that involves five pans, two dented strainers, scattered bones that would baffle a forensic pathologist, and the unpleasant sensation of hot stock rising from the pot, condensing on your forehead, and running down into the pot again as lightly flavored sweat.

Martha does not perspire. There is not a squeak of panic in the woman's soul. She knows exactly where the two layers of cheesecloth can be found when the time comes to strain the stock. She assembles her fish chowder as if it were a model airplane. Moreover, she does so without appearing to spend any time in the kitchen. "One of the most important moments on which to expend extra effort is the beginning of a party, often an awkward time, when guests feel tentative and insecure," she says. The *guests* are insecure? How about the frigging cook? Believe me, Martha, I'm not handing round the phyllo triangles with lobster filling during that awkward time; I'm out back, holding on to the sink, finishing off the Côtes du Rhône that was supposed to go into the stew. But Martha Stewart is an idealist who has cunningly disguised herself as a helping hand; readers look up to her as a conservative angel who keeps the dream house tidy, radiant, ready for pals, and filled with family. "If I had to choose one essential element for the success of an Easter brunch, it would be children," she writes, as if preparing to grill the kids over a high flame.

Yet the conservative image won't quite fit. The Stewart paean to the joys of Thanksgiving ("To not cook and entertain on this day would seem tantamount to treason") is itself rather joyless in its zealotry; you keep hitting something sharp and steely in her writings—a demiglace intolerance of ordinary mortals. Her kitchen is bewitched, and she's Samantha. You won't see it on her TV shows, but I bet Martha Stewart can wiggle her nose and turn any chauvinist Darrin into crabmeat. If you're planning to fork-grab her under the knee, forget it. Was it the spirit of the season or a quiet celebration of dominant female power that led to the baked-ham recipe at the start of "Martha Stewart's Menus for Entertaining"? It looks succulent in the accompanying photograph, and I have long yearned to make it, but three factors have restrained me. First, it serves sixteen, and I don't know that many people who would be happy to munch ham at one another. Second, you need "one bunch chervil with flowers." (That's plain silly, if not quite as ridiculous as a recipe that I came across at the peak of nouvelle cuisine, in the nineteen-eighties—a recipe that demanded *thirty-four* chervil leaves.) Third, the ham must be baked for five and a half hours in a pan lined with fresh-cut grass. As in meadow. "Locate an area in advance with tender, young, organically grown grass that has not yet been cut," our guide advises. "It is best to cut it very early in the morning while the dew is still evident." I'm sorry, Martha, but it just won't do. I have inspected the grass in my back yard, and I am not prepared to serve Baked Ham with Cat Whiff and Chopped Worms.

THERE must be millions of other people who refuse to get up at dawn and mow the lawn for dinner. This fellow feeling should be a comfort to me, yet somehow it makes no difference. Cooking, for all the apple-cheeked, home-baked community spirit in which food writers try to enfold it, is essentially a solitary art—or, at least, a guarantee of lonely distress. When your hollandaise is starting to curdle and you've tried the miraculous ice-cube trick and you've tried beating a fresh egg yolk and folding in the curdled stuff and the result still looks like the climactic scene of a David Cronenberg picture, it doesn't really help to know that someone is having the very same problem in Pittsburgh. Your only friend, in fact, is that shelf of cookbooks just out of reach. Leaving the sauce to its own devices, you grab each volume in turn, frantic for advice, and make your fatal mistake: you start to read. Two yards away, the sauce is separating fast—the lemon is pursing its lips, the eggs are halfway back to the fridge—but you don't care. By now, determined to find out where you went wrong, and already dreaming of a perfect future sauce, you are deep into Georges Auguste Escoffier's recipe for hollandaise: "Remove the pan to the side of the stove or place it in a bain-marie." Well, which?

In that simple "or" reside both the delight and the frustration of the classic cookbook. It should ideally tell you almost everything but not all that you need to know, leaving a tiny crack of uncertainty that can become your own personal abyss. If any text counts as a classic, it is Escoffier's "Le Guide Culinaire," which was published in 1903. Escoffier was a colleague of César Ritz, and a man of such pantry-stocking initiative that when Paris was besieged in the Franco-Prussian War he fed the starving troops on zoo animals and stray pets. I eagerly scanned the "Guide" for pan-seared hartebeest or poodle mousse à la Fifi sauvage, but all I could find was this unflinching recipe for clear turtle soup:

> To kill the turtle, lay it on its back at the edge of the table with the head hanging over the side. Take a double meat hook and place one hook into the upper jaw and suspend a sufficiently heavy weight in the hook at the other end so as to make the animal extend its neck. . . .

It goes without saying that the flippers should be blanched, and that "the green fat which is used for making the soup must be collected carefully." But where, exactly, does this green fat come from? The author doesn't tell us. Somewhere between the carapace and the plastron, presumably, but I'm not sure that I really want to know.

Whether cooks still use Escoffier—or Larousse, or Carême, or any of the other touchstones of French cuisine—is open to question. It is not just the encyclopedic spread of these Frenchmen's interests, their desire to chew on something that we would prefer to watch in a wildlife documentary, that feels out of date; it is also their unshakable conviction that we already know our worldly way around a kitchen, that they are merely grinding a little fresh information into our basic stock of knowledge. When Escoffier tells us to "stud the fattened pullet with pieces of truffle and poach it in the usual manner," he presumes that we habitually spend our weekends looking for pullets to fatten and that we can poach them in our sleep. Many readers are scared off by this assumption; I feel flattered and consoled by it, all the more so because I know it to be dead wrong. I am not a truffle stud, nor was meant to be. Yet I willingly dream myself into a time when you could "quickly fry 10 blackbirds in hot butter"—just because I relish the imaginative jump required to get there, not because I particularly want a blackbird-lettuce-and-tomato sandwich for my lunch.

In other words, the great cookbooks are more like novels than like home-improvement manuals. What these culinary bibles tell you to do is far less beguiling than the thought of a world in which such things might be done. A single line, for instance, from Benjamin Renaudet's "Secrets de la Bonne Table," published at the beginning of this century, effortlessly summons up the century that has just ended: "When the first partridges are shot in the early morning, send them down to the house." If that grabs you, take a look at "Culinary Jottings for Madras," a collection of recipes by Deputy Assistant Quartermaster-General Arthur Robert Kenney-Herbert. First published in 1878, the book tells you more about the nature of imperial rule in India than any number of political histories. If you can feed a party of eight on snipe soup, fish fillets à la Peg Woffington, mutton cutlets à la Moscovite, oyster Kramouskys, braised capon, and a brace of wild ducks with bigarade sauce, if you can finish off with prune jelly, iced molded pudding with strawberries, and cheese, and if you can serve and eat all that when it's ninety-five degrees in the shade, then you can conquer any country you like. Nothing can stand up to Peg Woffington.

There is a pinch of snob nostalgia in reading this stuff, of course, but I don't think it ruins the flavor. What is attractive about cookbooks, after all—what prickles the glands like vinegar—is not luxury but otherness. I have a particular weakness for the chunky, old-style blockbusters that sit in every kitchen, offering reams of advice that is seldom taken, or even required. Endlessly updated with new editions, these masterworks are doomed never to be up to date. Craig Claiborne's "New York Times Cook Book," which has slowly acquired the gravitas of Holy Writ, was first published in 1961. I found an early edition, and smiled at the hors-d'oeuvres suggestions that are arrayed for our delectation in the first section of the book: how to serve oysters on the half shell, how to serve caviar, how to serve foie gras. It was a time capsule of America in the late fifties and early sixties; it made me want to watch "Pillow Talk" all over again. With a sigh of regret, I turned to the latest edition. How would it start in the nineties? Char-grilled calamari with arugula and flat-leaf parsley? Stuffed snow peas à la Martha? Shiitake tarts? But no, there it was again: how to serve oysters on the half shell, etc. What was once an accurate index of national taste has now become a museum piece. It's the same story with Irma S. Rombauer and Marion Rombauer Becker's "The Joy of Cooking," which began life in 1931 and reads as if it had never got past 1945. Social historians should head straight for the "Pies and Pastries" section and check out the crusty jokes: "No wonder pictures of leggy starlets are called cheesecake!" Baboom.

Down below caviar, even farther down than cheesecake, there is a place where the joy of cooking gives way to the joy of not bothering to cook at all. Yet even here, on the ocean floor of *cuisine en bas*, among such primitive life forms as the Fried Peanut Butter and Banana Sandwich, there is food for thought. To discover this sandwich in Brenda Arlene Butler's "Are You Hungry Tonight? Elvis' Favorite Recipes" is to be transported, without warning, to an age of innocence. The book's final chapter offers readers the chance to re-create the giant six-tier wedding cake that Elvis and Priscilla cut together on that happy day in 1967: the words "Eleven pounds hydrogenated vegetable shortening (such as Sweetex or Crisco)" speak to me as directly, and as movingly, as the partridges that Renaudet called for in the early morning.

THERE are times when this need to look elsewhere—to reach into the ovens of another age, or another culture, and pull out whatever you can—grows from a well-fed fancy into a moral necessity. Hence the invaluable contribution of Elizabeth David, whose name remains as revered in England as that of M. F. K. Fisher in America. (Why do women make such great cookery writers? Partly, I suspect, because they realize that it is enough to be a great cook, whereas men, larded with pride in their own accomplishment, invariably go one step too far and try to be great *chefs*—a grander calling, though somehow less respectable, and certainly less responsive to human need.) Both David and Fisher were spurred to action by the Second World War: Fisher's "How to Cook a Wolf" was published in 1942, when food shortages were beginning to bite, and David's "A Book of Mediterranean Food" appeared in 1950, when England was still rationed, undernourished, and keen on suet.

Elizabeth David's mission was to find the modern equivalent of Renaudet's partridges, to resuscitate flagging and amnesiac palates with the prospect of unthinkable dishes. Such food had no need to be rich; it simply had to taste of something, to bear recognizable links to natural produce, and, most important, to be non-gray. Whether it ever saw the light of day, or the candlelight of evening, was beside the point; the mere promise of it, David herself confessed, was a form of nourishment. "Even if people could not very often make the dishes here described," she pointed out, "it was stimulating to think about them." And so on the first page of "A Book of Mediterranean Food" she kicked off with *soupe au pistou* and its accompanying dollop of *aïllade*. The garlicky stink of Nice hit England full in the face, and the nation—or, at any rate, the middle classes—came back to life.

Nowadays, the situation is reversed. We know too much about food. Your principal obligation when you sit down at a restaurant in New York is to play it cool. Black spaghettini with cuttlefish and fennel tops? Been there. *Soupe au pistou?* Wake me up when it's over. In the past year, I have eaten both reindeer (a fun Christmas dish) and ostrich (better baked in sand, I guess), but they hardly count as exotic anymore. Cookbooks have followed the lead of restaurants and delicatessens: specialist works abound, the narrower the better. I gave up reading Sara Slavin and Karl Petzke's "Champagne: The Spirit of Celebration," a book devoted to cooking with and for champagne, at the point where it instructed me to "roll each cheese-coated grape in the garlic-almond mixture." Isn't there some kind of Grape Protection Society that should be fighting this stuff? As for "365 Ways to Cook Hamburger and Other Ground Meats," by Rick Rodgers, what can I say? Welcome to the most disgusting book on earth. It's not the dishes themselves that I object to—not even Ed Debevic's Burnt Meatloaf, or the Transylvanian Pork and Sauerkraut Bake—but the gruelling way in which one recipe after another resounds with the same mournful litany: "One pound ground round." Remember the wise words of M. F. K. Fisher: "The first thing to know about ground round steak is that it should not be that at all."

Far more cheering and plausible is Nick Malgieri's "How to Bake," which runs for two hundred and seventy-six pages before it even gets to "Plain Cakes." Should you find the book a little too broad in scope, you could always play the sacred card and go for "The Secrets of Jesuit Breadmaking," by Brother Rick Curry, S.J. This alternates clear spiritual homilies with yeasty advice about cooling racks. Sometimes, with a brilliant flourish, Brother Curry kneads his twin passions into one phrase: "As we begin the most austere week in Christianity, tasty rich biscuits remind us that Jesus is coming." I suspect that such highly sophisticated reasoning may have been the downfall of Gerard Manley

Hopkins, poet and Jesuit, who suffered what was reputed to be one of the worst cases of constipation in the nineteenth century.

If you really intend to be the star of your own cookbook, you need to watch out. (The finest cooks, such as Escoffier, are godlike, everywhere in the text yet nowhere to be seen.) Brother Curry, schooled in humility, gets it about right: when he says that his Loyola Academy Buttermilk Bread "goes great with peanut butter," we instinctively believe that he's plugging a good idea rather than himself. The trouble starts with celebrity cookbooks and tie-ins; try as I might, I cannot conceive of a time when I will want to concoct a meal from the pages of "The Bubba Gump Shrimp Co. Cookbook" or its literate successor, "Forrest Gump: My Favorite Chocolate Recipes." "Entertaining with Regis and Kathie Lee" is remarkable less for the quality of the cuisine than for the photographs of Kathie Lee, who seems to spend half her time with her mouth wide open, as if to catch any mouthfuls flying by. Then, there's Rosie Daley, whose food looks perfectly nice, but whose "In the Kitchen with Rosie" might not have reached the best-seller lists were she not employed as a cook by Oprah Winfrey. It's kind of hard to concentrate on the ingredients, what with Oprah's cheerleading ringing out at regular intervals. "I have thrived on pasta. I can eat it every day and practically do." You'd never guess.

Whether such works can be relied upon in the kitchen is of little consequence. Cookbooks, it should be stressed, do not belong in the kitchen at all. We keep them there for the sake of appearances; occasionally, we smear their pages together with vibrant green glazes or crimson compotes, in order to delude ourselves, and any passing browsers, that we are practicing cooks; but, in all honesty, a cookbook is something that you read in the living room, or in the bathroom, or in bed. The purpose is not to nurture nightmares of suckling pig, or to lull ourselves into a fantasy of trimly bearded oysters, but simply to baste our rested brains with common sense, and with the prospect of common pleasures to come. Take this romantic interlude from "'Tis the Season: A Vegetarian Christmas Cookbook," by Nanette Blanchard: "Turn down the lights, light all the candles you can find, throw a log on the fire, turn up the music, and toast each other with a Sparkling Grape Goblet." Oh, oh, Nanette. On the other hand, what could be sweeter than to retire with "Smoke & Spice," by Cheryl Alters Jamison and Bill Jamison, whose High Plains Jerky would be an ornament to any barbecue? Those in search of distant horizons could always caress their senses with "The Art of Polish Cooking," in which Alina Żerańska of-

fers her triumphant recipe for "Nothing" Soup (*Zupa "Nic"*), adding
darkly, "This is an all-time children's favorite."

If I could share a Sparkling Grape Goblet with anyone—not just any
cook but any person in recorded history—it might well be with Jean-
Anthelme Brillat-Savarin. Magistrate, mayor, violinist, judge, and rav-
enous slayer of wild turkeys during his visit to America, Brillat-Savarin
is now remembered for "The Physiology of Taste," which was first published in 1825. There is a good paperback version, translated by Anne
Drayton, but devotees may wish to seek out the translation by M. F. K.
Fisher herself; it has now been reissued in a luxurious new edition, with
illustrations by Wayne Thiebaud. To say that "The Physiology of Taste"
is a cookbook is like saying that Turgenev's "Sportsman's Sketches" is a
guide to hunting. "When I came to consider the pleasures of the table
in all their aspects, I soon perceived that something better than a mere
cookery book might be made of such a subject," Brillat-Savarin writes.
It is a perception that few have shared; the closest modern equivalent,
perhaps, is in the work of A. J. Liebling, a man whose delicately gluttonous writings on food keep wandering off (when he can tear himself
away) into such equally pressing areas as Paris, boxing, and sex. Brillat-
Savarin, like Liebling, gives few recipes, though he muses on innumer-
able dishes, on the scientific reasons for their effect on the metabolism,
and on the glow of sociable well-being that is their ideal result. He
sprinkles anecdotes like salt, and he defines and defends *gourmandisme*
("It shows implicit obedience to the commands of the Creator"), following it through the various stages of delight and surfeit to its logical
conclusion. There is a chapter on "The Theory of Frying" and a wonderful disquisition on death, embellished with gloomy good cheer: "I
would recall the words of the dying Fontenelle, who on being asked
what he could feel, replied: 'Nothing but a certain difficulty in living.' "

The lasting achievement of Brillat-Savarin is that he endowed living
with a certain ease. Intricately versed in the difficulties of existence, he
came to the unorthodox conclusion that a cookbook—a bastard form,
but a wealthy, happy bastard—could offer the widest and most tender
range of remedies. I'm not sure whether he knew how to fold the wings
of a chicken akimbo, and if you'd handed him a snow pea and told him
to stuff it he would have responded in kind; but it takes someone like
Brillat-Savarin to remind us that cooking need not be the fraught, per-
fectionist, slightly paranoid struggle that it has latterly become. His
love of food is bound up with a taste for human error and indulgence,
and that is why "The Physiology of Taste" is still the most civilized

cookbook ever written. I suspect that Brillat-Savarin might have been bemused by Martha Stewart, but that he would have got on just fine with Ed Debevic and his Burnt Meatloaf.

I sure wish that he had been on hand for my terrine of sardines and potatoes. There I was—apron on, gin in hand, closely following the recipe of the French chef Raymond Blanc. All went well until I got to the harmless words "a piece of cardboard." Apparently, I needed cardboard to lay on the terrine mold; the cardboard then had to be covered with "evenly distributed weights" for twelve hours. Weights? Cardboard? Twelve hours? They weren't listed with the ingredients. I had my sardines; I had my twenty capers and my freshly grated nutmeg; but I had no cardboard. Frankly, it would have been easier to kill a turtle.

That's the trouble with cookbooks. Like sex education and nuclear physics, they are founded on an illusion. They bespeak order, but they end in tears.

1995

MARTIN AMIS

TENNIS PERSONALITIES

I HAVE a problem with—I am uncomfortable with—the word "personality" and its plural, as in "Modern tennis lacks personalities" and "Tennis needs a new star who is a genuine personality." But if, from now on, I can put "personality" between quotation marks, and use it as an exact synonym of a seven-letter duosyllable starting with "a" and ending with "e" (and also featuring, in order of appearance, an "ss," an "h," an "o," and an "l"), why, then, "personality" and I are going to get along just fine.

How come it is always the old "personalities" who lead complaints about the supposed scarcity of young "personalities"? Because it takes a "personality" to know a "personality"? No. Because it takes a "personality" to *like* a "personality."

Ilie Nastase was a serious "personality"—probably the most complete "personality" the game has ever boasted. In his memoir, "Days of Grace,"

Arthur Ashe, while acknowledging that Nastase was an "unforgettable personality," also recalls that Ilie called him "Negroni" to his face and, once, "nigger" behind his back. Ilie, of course, was known as a "clown" and a "showman"; i.e., as an embarrassing narcissist. Earlier this year, his tireless "antics" earned him a dismissal and a suspension as Romania's Davis Cup captain ("audible obscenities and constant abuse and intimidation"). Ilie is forty-seven. But true "personalities" merely scoff at the passage of time. They just become even bigger "personalities."

Jimmy Connors: another total "personality." Imagine the sepsis of helpless loathing he must have inspired in his opponents during his "great runs" at the U.S. Open. There's Jimmy (what a "personality"), orchestrating mass sex with the Grandstand Court. It's great for the mild-mannered Swede or Swiss up at the other end: he double-faults, and New York goes *wild.* Jimmy was such an out-and-out "personality" that he managed to get into a legal dispute with the president of his own fan club. Remember how he used to wedge his racket between his legs with the handle protuding and mime the act of masturbation when a call went against him? *That's* a "personality."

Twenty-odd years ago, I encountered Connors and Nastase at some P.R. nightmare in a Park Lane hotel. Someone asked these two bronzed and seersuckered "personalities" what they had been doing with themselves in London. "Screwing each other," Nastase said, and collapsed in Connors' arms. I was reminded of this incident when, last fall, I saw an account of a whistle-stop tour undertaken by John McEnroe and Andre Agassi. Questioned about their relationship, Agassi described it as "completely sexual." Does such raillery inevitably come about when self-love runs up against mutual admiration? Or is it part of a bonding ritual between "personalities" of the same peer group?

By turning my TV up dangerously loud, I once heard McEnroe mutter to a linesman (and this wasn't a Grand Slam event but one of those German greed fests where the first prize is something like a gold helicopter), "Get your fucking head out of your fucking [personality]." Arthur Ashe also reveals that McEnroe once called a middle-aged black linesman "boy." With McEnroe gone, it falls to Agassi to shoulder the flagstaff of the "personalities"—Agassi, the Vegas traffic light, the "Zen master" (B. Streisand) who used to smash forty rackets a year. And I don't think he has the stomach for it, funnily enough. Nastase, Connors, McEnroe, and Agassi are "personalities" of descending magnitude and stamina. McEnroe, at heart, was more tremulous than vicious; and Agassi shows telltale signs of generosity—even of sportsmanship.

There is a "demand" for "personalities," because that's the kind of age we're living in. Laver, Rosewall, Ashe: these were dynamic and exemplary figures; they didn't need "personality" because they had character. Interestingly, too, there have never been any "personalities" in the women's game. What does this tell us? That being a "personality" is men's work? Or that it's boys' work?

We do want our champions to be vivid. How about Pete Sampras, then—so often found wanting in the "personality" department? According to the computer, Sampras is almost twice as good as anyone else in the sport. What form would his "personality" take? Strutting, fist-clenching, loin-thrusting? All great tennis players are vivid, if great tennis is what you're interested in (rather than something more tawdrily generalized). The hare-eyed Medvedev, the snake-eyed Courier, the droll and fiery Ivanisevic, the innocent Bruguera, the Wagnerian (and Machiavellian) Becker, the fanatical Michael Chang. These players demonstrate that it is perfectly possible to have, or to contain, a personality—*without* being an asshole.

1994

JOHN UPDIKE

CAR TALK

A HUMAN being has vocal cords, a tongue, teeth, and, for expressive reinforcement, eyes and hands; a car has nothing but its horn and lights. Yet cars do talk; they can say "Howdy!" (a brief, deft toot) and "I hate you!" (a firmer, sustained blast) and "Do it!" (a flicker of the headlights). As their drivers are sealed ever more inaccessibly into a casing of audiotapes, cell phones, and deafening air-conditioning, automobiles for the sake of their own survival are evolving increasingly complex speech patterns. There is a distinct difference, to the attuned ear, between the highly respectful honk used in a service station during an annual car inspection in response to the command "Sound your horn" and the just perceptibly more urgent, less deferential beep that announces to the inhabitants of a domicile that a summoned taxi or car-pool van impatiently awaits.

Meaning is, as with other languages, a matter of context. The polite, minimal sounding of the horn—the automotive equivalent of a throat-clearing—that declares simple presence ("Howdy!") in nonthreatening circumstances becomes, while one is passing on a four-lane highway an automobile that has an aura of wanting to change lanes with an abrupt swerve, more admonitory—something like "Watch it, buddy, you've got two tons of moving metal right here in your blind spot!"

If no response is indicated, the same utterance, more insistently intoned, takes on a suggestion of rebuke and heightened anxiety: "Hey, you're riding me into the median strip!" And if the swerve does take place, within inches of one's front fender, a strengthened intonation moderates the meaning to, roughly, "You crazy blind idiot, go back to driving school!" Then, if no penitent reverse-swerve or apologetic slowing communicates regret, the next level of volume declares, "You bastard—you cut me off! Drivers like you should be in jail, and I'd ram you right in your vanity plate if I didn't hate fussing with the insurance agent and weren't already late for the dentist!"

As with birdsong and insect stridulation, impressive amounts of information are packed into virtually indistinguishable sounds. In city traffic, one moderate toot, not quite deferential, informs the car ahead at an intersection that the light has changed from red to green. "Let's go, daydreamer!" might be a translation. The same toot, amplified by a few decibels, points out to a truck being slowly unloaded that double-parking is illegal and obstructive, or to a taxi that passengers should not be unloaded in the middle of the avenue. Another few decibels suggest to an errant pedestrian, "I'd be within my rights to run you over, and my brother-in-law's a lawyer," or to a messenger on a bicycle, "Having thin wheels, Lycra shorts, and a Walkman on your head doesn't make you immune to the laws of physics. Someday you're going to get flattened, and don't look for me among the mourners!"

The highest, most prolonged volume of the horn transcends communication and expresses—at, say, the mouth of the Lincoln Tunnel—frustration to the point of insanity. The noise can be read as existential protest, a frantic desire on the part of automobiles to opt out of their very condition of car-ness, as cattle at the chute of the slaughterhouse moo to be released from their condition of steer-ness.

Car lights, too, say more than they used to. Having the controls on a stalk behind the steering wheel has considerably enhanced their eloquence. Flashed lights, for instance, once only hinted that a police car was lurking around the corner, but now, flicked demurely, say "Do it" and "Thank you," much as the Italian word *prego* says both "Please" and "You're welcome."

Headlights lit in broad daylight used to mean, "We're all in a funeral procession. Don't muscle in." But now such headlights, enlarging in the rearview mirror, cry out, "Here I come, hell for leather, and no doubt crazed on drugs!" Red tail-lights, braked into luminescence, can mean not only "I'm braking" but "Stop tailgating, I beg you!" The latter can be reacted to before it is consciously understood. As in many, even more highly evolved languages, signifiers can signify their opposites: at night, high-beam lights in your eyes mean either that the offending driver has forgotten to switch to the low beam or he is telling you that *you* have. Even turned-off lights can say something: in a locked car parked in your favorite curbside spot, the message reads, "Tough luck, kid. I got here first."

1997

VERSE

E. B. WHITE

CRITIC

The critic leaves at curtain fall
   To find, in starting to review it,
He scarcely saw the play at all
   For watching his reaction to it.

1925

SONG TO BE DISREGARDED

I wrote six poems
   With love for a theme;
I slept six nights
   With love for a dream.

I've read them over,
   And dreamt them again:
Never give a lover
   A bed or a pen.

1928

TO A PERFUMED LADY AT THE CONCERT

Madam, the pervasive scent
   Rendering your person smelly
Formed a thick integument
   Round the music of Corelli.
   Lost on me the Sarabande.

Lady odorous and rare,
   You were such a proper noseful

All the brasses of "La Mer"
  Seemed by contrast quite reposeful.
    Lost on me the muted trumpet.

Baby drenched in fragrance vile,
  Scent in public may be legal
But it blanketed the guile
  Of a piece like "Eulenspiegel."
    Lost on me was Dicky Strauss.

Madam reeking of the rose,
  Red of hair and pearl of earring,
I came not to try my nose,
  I was there to try my hearing.
    Lost on me the whole darn concert.

Madam! Lady! Baby doll!
  This is what the world objects to:
Must you smell up all the hall
  Just to charm the guy you're next to?
    You were lost on him already.

                    1932

SONG OF THE QUEEN BEE

*"The breeding of the bee," says a United States De-
partment of Agriculture bulletin on artificial insemination, "has always been handicapped by the fact that
the queen mates in the air with whatever drone she
encounters."*

When the air is wine and the wind is free
And the morning sits on the lovely lea
And sunlight ripples on every tree,
Then love-in-air is the thing for me—
  I'm a bee,
  I'm a ravishing, rollicking, young queen bee,
That's me.

I wish to state that I think it's great,
Oh, it's simply rare in the upper air,
    It's the place to pair
    With a bee.
Let old geneticists plot and plan,
They're stuffy people, to a man;
Let gossips whisper behind their fan.
    (Oh, she *does?*
    Buzz, buzz, buzz!)
My nuptial flight is sheer delight;
I'm a giddy girl who likes to swirl,
    To fly and soar
    And fly some more,
        I'm a bee.
And I wish to state that I'll *always* mate
    With whatever drone I encounter.

There's a kind of a wild and glad elation
In the natural way of insemination;
Who thinks that love is a handicap
Is a fuddydud and a common sap,
For I am a queen and I am a bee,
I'm devil-may-care and I'm fancy-free,
The test tube doesn't appeal to me,
    Not me,
    I'm a bee.
And I'm here to state that I'll *always* mate
    With whatever drone I encounter.

Let mares and cows, by calculating,
Improve themselves with loveless mating,
Let groundlings breed in the modern fashion,
I'll stick to the air and the grand old passion;
I may be small and I'm just a bee
But I *won't* have Science improving *me,*
    Not me,
    I'm a bee.
On a day that's fair with a wind that's free,
Any old drone is the lad for me.

I have no flair for love *moderne,*
It's far too studied, far too stern,
I'm just a bee—I'm wild, I'm free,
   That's me.
I can't afford to be too choosy;
In every queen there's a touch of floozy,
   And it's simply rare
   In the upper air
   And I wish to state
   That I'll *always* mate
With whatever drone I encounter.

Man is a fool for the latest movement,
He broods and broods on race improvement;
What boots it to improve a bee
If it means the end of ecstasy?
   (He ought to be there
   On a day that's fair,
   Oh, it's simply rare
    For a bee.)
Man's so wise he is growing foolish,
Some of his schemes are downright ghoulish
He owns a bomb that'll end creation
And he wants to change the sex relation,
He thinks that love is a handicap,
He's a fuddydud, he's a simple sap;
Man is a meddler, man's a boob,
He looks for love in the depths of a tube,
His restless mind is forever ranging,
He thinks he's advancing as long as he's changing
He cracks the atom, he racks his skull,
Man is meddlesome, man is dull,
Man is busy instead of idle,
Man is alarmingly suicidal,
   Me, I'm a bee.

I am a bee and I simply love it,
I am a bee and I'm darned glad of it,
I am a bee, I know about love:
You go upstairs, you go above,

You do not pause to dine or sup,
The sky won't wait—it's a long trip up;
You rise, you soar, you take the blue,
It's you and me, kid, me and you,
It's everything, it's the nearest drone,
It's never a thing that you find alone.
   I'm a bee,
   I'm free.

If any old farmer can keep and hive me,
Then any old drone may catch and wive me;
I'm sorry for creatures who cannot pair
On a gorgeous day in the upper air,
I'm sorry for cows who have to boast
Of affairs they've had by parcel post,
I'm sorry for man with his plots and guile,
His test-tube manner, his test-tube smile;
I'll multiply and I'll increase
As I always have—by mere caprice;
For I am a queen and I am a bee,
I'm devil-may-care and I'm fancy-free,
Love-in-air is the thing for me,
   Oh, it's simply *rare*
   In the beautiful air,
     And I wish to state
     That I'll *always* mate
   With whatever drone I encounter.

1945

DOROTHY PARKER

RHYME OF AN INVOLUNTARY VIOLET

When I ponder lovely ladies
Slipping sweetly down to Hades,
Hung and draped with glittering booty—
Am I distant, cold and snooty?
Though I know the price their pearls are
Am I holier than the girls are?
Though they're lavish with their "Yes's,"
Do I point, and shake my tresses?
No! I'm filled with awe and wonder.
I review my every blunder. . . .
Do I have the skill to tease a
Guy for an Hispano-Suiza?
I can't even get me taxis
Off of Sydneys, Abes, and Maxies!
Do the pretty things I utter
To the kings of eggs and butter
Gain me pearls as big as boulders,
Clattering, clanking round my shoulders,
Advertising, thus, their full worth?
No, my dear. Mine come from Woolworth.
Does my smile across a table
Win a cloak of Russian sable?
Baby, no. I'd have to kill a
Man to get a near-chinchilla.
Men that come on for conventions
Show me brotherly attentions;
Though my glance be fond and melting,
Do they ever start unbelting
With the gifts they give the others?
No! They tell me of their mothers,
To the baby's pictures treat me,
Say they want the wife to meet me!
Gladly I'd be led to slaughter

Where the ermine flows like water,
Where the gay white globes are lighted;
But I've never been invited!
So my summary, in fact, is
What an awful flop my act is!

1926

FULFILMENT

For this my mother wrapped me warm,
And called me home against the storm,
And coaxed my infant nights to quiet,
And gave me roughage in my diet,
And tucked me in my bed at eight,
And clipped my hair, and marked my weight,
And watched me as I sat and stood:
That I might grow to womanhood
To hear a whistle, and drop my wits,
And break my heart to clattering bits.

1927

BOHEMIA

Authors and actors and artists and such
Never know nothing, and never know much.
Sculptors and singers and those of their kidney
Tell their affairs from Seattle to Sydney.
Playwrights and poets and such horses' necks
Start off from anywhere, end up at sex.
Diarists, critics, and similar roe
Never say nothing, and never say no.
People Who Do Things exceed my endurance;
God, for a man who solicits insurance!

1927

DON MARQUIS

MOTHER'S HOME AGAIN!

'Twas on the Eve of Christmas
    A face against the pane
Peered in at the firelight;
    'Twas worn with vice, and plain;
But all the children shouted:
    "Mother's home again!"

Mother's out of jail, Dad!
    Let us ask her in!
Make her Christmas merry,
    With food and fire and gin!
Mother's out of jail, Dad,
    Let us ask her in!

She's watching through the window
    Her babes in happy play;
Do not call a copper
    To club the Jane away—
Remember, ere you strike her,
    That once her hair was gray!

Soon at some new night-club
    She'll be pinched again,
For Mother is so popular
    With all the dancing men—
Invite her in to visit,
    Mother's home again!

She's staring through the window
    At the Yuletide glow!
Oh, do not throw the old wife
    Back into the snow!
She bore you all your children,
    And oft has told you so.

Mother's in the street, Dad!
She is out of jail!
Put morphine in the needles,
And some ether in the ale,
Mother's home for Christmas,
Mother's out of jail!

1928

PHYLLIS McGINLEY

MELANCHOLY REFLECTIONS AFTER A LOST ARGUMENT

I always pay the verbal score
  With wit, concise, selective.
I have an apt and ample store
  Of ladylike invective.

My mots, retorts, and quips of speech,
  Hilarious or solemn,
Placed end to end, no doubt, would reach
  To any gossip column.

But what avails the epigram,
  The clever and the clear shot,
Invented chiefly when I am
  The only one in earshot?

And where's the good of repartee
  To quell a hostile laughter,
That tardily occurs to me
  A half an hour after?

God rest you merry, gentlemen,
  Who nastily have caught
The art of always striking when
  The irony is hot.

1933

THE SEVEN AGES OF A NEWSPAPER SUBSCRIBER

From infancy, from childhood's earliest caper,
He loved the daily paper.

Propped on his grubby elbows, lying prone,
He took, at first, the Comics for his own.
Then, as he altered stature and his voice,
Sports were his single choice.

For a brief time, at twenty, Thought became
A desultory flame,
So with a critic eye he would peruse
The better Book Reviews.

Behold the bridegroom, then—the dazzled suitor
Turned grim commuter,
Learning without direction
To fold his paper to the Housing Section.

Forty enlarged his waistline with his wage.
The Business Page
Engrossed his mind. He liked to ponder well
The charted rise of Steel or Tel & Tel.

Choleric, pompous, and too often vext,
The fifties claimed him next.
The Editorials, then, were what he scanned.
(Even, at times, he took his pen in hand.)

But witness how the human viewpoint varies:
Of late he reads the day's Obituaries.

1946

INCIDENT IN THE AFTERNOON

I heard two ladies at a play—
    A comedy considered witty.
It was a Wednesday matinée
    And they had come from Garden City.
Their frocks were rather arts-and-crafts,
And they had lunched, I learned, at Schrafft's.

Although we did not speak or bow
    Or comment even on the weather,
More intimate I know them now
    Than if we'd gone to school together.
(As you must presently divine,
Their seats were rather near to mine.)

Before the curtain rose I heard
    What each had told her spouse that morning.
I learned the history, word for word,
    Of why three cooks had given warning.
Also that neither cared a straw
For domineering sons-in-law.

I heard a bridge hand, play by play.
    I heard how all's not gold that glitters.
I heard a moral résumé
    Of half a dozen baby-sitters.
I learned beyond the slightest question
Shrimps are a trial to digestion.

The lights went down. The stage was set.
    Still, in the dusk that fans the senses,
Those ladies I had never met
    Poured out their swollen confidences.
The dialogue was smart. It stirred them
To conversation. And I heard them.

Above each stylish epigram
    Wherewith the hero mocked his rival,

They proved how nicely curried lamb
   Might justify a roast's revival,
That some best-selling author's recent
Book was lively. But indecent.

I heard a list of maladies
   Their all too solid flesh was heir to.
I heard that one, in her deep freeze,
   Could store a steer, but did not care to.
A neighbor's delicate condition
I heard of, all through intermission.

They laid their lives, like open tomes,
   Upon my lap and turned the pages.
I heard their taste in hats and homes,
   Their politics, but not their ages.
So much I heard of strange and true
Almost it reconciled me to
One fact, unseemly to recall:
I did not hear the play at all.

1949

OGDEN NASH

PROCRASTINATION IS ALL OF THE TIME

Torpor and sloth, torpor and sloth,
These are the cooks that unseason the broth.
Slothor and torp, slothor and torp
The directest of beeline ambitions can warp.
He who is slothic, he who is torporal
Will not be promoted to sergeant or corporal.
No torporer drowsy, no comatose slother
Will make a good banker, or even an author.
Torpor I deprecate, sloth I deplore;
Torpor is tedious, sloth is a bore.
Sloth is a bore and torpor is tedious,
Fifty parts comatose, fifty tragedious.
How drear, on a planet with plenty of woes,
That sloth is not slumber or torpor repose;
That the innocent joy of not getting things done
Simmers sulkily down to plain not having fun.
You smile in the morn like a bride in her bridalness
At the thought of a day of nothing but idleness.
By midday you're slipping, by evening a lunatic,
A perusing-the-newspapers-all-afternoonatic,
Worn to a wraith from the half-hourly jaunt
After glasses of water you didn't want,
And at last when onto your pallet you creep,
You discover yourself too tired to sleep.
O torpor and sloth, torpor and sloth,
These are the cooks that unseason the broth.
Torpor is harrowing, sloth it is irksome—
Everyone ready? Let's go out and worksome.

1939

TO MY VALENTINE

More than a catbird hates a cat,
Or a criminal hates a clue,
Or the Axis hates the United States,
That's how much I love you.

I love you more than a duck can swim,
And more than a grapefruit squirts;
I love you more than Ickes is a bore,
And more than a toothache hurts.

As a shipwrecked sailor hates the sea,
Or a juggler hates a shove,
As a hostess detests unexpected guests,
That's how much you I love.

I love you more than a wasp can sting,
And more than the subway jerks;
I love you as much as a beggar needs a crutch,
And more than a hangnail irks.

I swear to you by the stars above,
And below, if such there be,
As the High Court loathes perjurious oaths,
That's how you're loved by me.

                                        1941

SO THAT'S WHO I REMIND ME OF

When I consider men of golden talents,
I'm delighted, in my introverted way,
To discover, as I'm drawing up the balance,
How much we have in common, I and they.

Like Burns, I have a weakness for the bottle;
Like Shakespeare, little Latin and less Greek;
I bite my fingernails like Aristotle;
Like Thackeray, I have a snobbish streak.

I'm afflicted with the vanity of Byron;
I've inherited the spitefulness of Pope;
Like Petrarch, I'm a sucker for a siren;
Like Milton, I've a tendency to mope.

My spelling is suggestive of a Chaucer;
Like Johnson, well, I do not wish to die
(I also drink my coffee from the saucer);
And if Goldsmith was a parrot, so am I.

Like Villon, I have debits by the carload;
Like Swinburne, I'm afraid I need a nurse;
By my dicing is Christopher out-Marlowed,
And I dream as much as Coleridge, only worse.

In comparison with men of golden talents,
I am all a man of talent ought to be;
I resemble every genius in his vice, however henious. . . .
Yet I write so much like me.

1942

COMPLIMENTS OF A FRIEND

How many gifted pens have penned
That Mother is a boy's best friend!
How many more, with like afflatus,
Award the dog that honored status!
I hope my tongue in prune juice smothers
If I belittle dogs or mothers,
But, gracious, how can I agree?
I know my own best friend is me.
We share our joys and our aversions,
We're thicker than the Medes and Persians,
We blend like voices in a chorus,
The same things please, the same things bore us.
If I am broke, then me needs money,
I make a joke, me finds it funny.
I think of beer, me shares the craving,

If I have whiskers, me needs shaving.
I know what I like, me knows what art is,
We hate the people at cocktail parties.
When I can stand the crowd no more,
Why, me is halfway to the door.
We two reactionary codgers
Prefer the Giants to the Dodgers.
I am a dodo, me an auk.
We grieve that pictures learned to talk.
For every sin that I produce,
Kind me can find some soft excuse,
And when I blow a final gasket,
Who but me will share my casket?
Beside us, Pythias and Damon
Were just two unacquainted laymen.
Sneer not, for if you answer true,
Don't you feel that way about you?

1948

THE INVITATION *SAYS* FROM FIVE TO SEVEN

There's nothing like an endless party,
A collection of clammy little groups,
Where a couple of the guests are arty
And the rest of the guests are goops.
There's the confidential girlish chatter—
It soothes you like a drug—
And the gentle pitter-patter
As the anchovies hit the rug.
There's the drip, drip, drip of the mayonnaise
As the customers' lips slip on the canapés,
There are feuds that are born,
There are friendships that pine away,
And the big cigar that smolders on the Steinaway.
The major trouble with a party
Is you need a guest to give it for,
And the best part of any guest
Is the last part out the door.

There's nothing like an endless party,
And there hasn't been since ancient Rome.
Here's Silenus making passes at Astarte
While Mrs. Silenus begs him to go home.
There is bigamy about the boudoirs,
There is bundling at the bar,
And the sideboard where the food was
Has the aspect of an abattoir.
You wonder why they pursue each other's wives,
Who by now resemble the cream cheese and the chives.
There's a corpse on the floor
From New Rochelle or Scarborough,
And its mate is swinging from the candelabara.
The best location for a party
Is in a room without a floor,
And the best way to give a party
Is leave town the night before.

1953

PETER De VRIES

THEME AND VARIATION

Coleridge caused his wife unrest,
Liking other company best;
Dickens, never quite enthralled,
Sent his packing when she palled;
Gauguin broke the marriage vow
In quest of Paradise enow.
These things attest in monochrome:
Genius is the scourge of home.

Lady Nelson made the best of
What another took the rest of;
Wagner had, in middle life,
Three children by another's wife;
Whitman *liked* to play the dastard,

Boasting here and there a bastard.
Lives of great men all remind us
Not to let their labors blind us.

Each helped to give an age its tone,
Though never acting quite his own.
Will of neither wax nor iron
Could have made a go with Byron;
Flaubert, to prove he was above
Bourgeois criteria of love,
Once took a courtesan to bed
Keeping his hat upon his head.

But mine is off to Johann Bach,
For whom my sentiment is *"Ach!"*
Not once, but twice, a model spouse,
With twenty children in the house.
Some fathers would have walked away
In what they call a fugue today;
But he left no one in the lurch,
And played the stuff he wrote in church.

1950

W. H. AUDEN

PEOPLE

Fulke Greville
Wrote beautifully at sea level;
With each rising contour his verse
Grew progressively worse.

It was impossible to inveigle
Georg Wilhelm Friedrich Hegel
Into offering the slightest apology
For his Phenomenology.

Historians have tried to widen
Our conception of John of Leiden,
But the term Anabaptist
Remains aptest.

When the young Kant
Was told to kiss his aunt,
He obeyed the Categorical Must,
But only just.

Joseph Lister
Never worried his sister
By becoming an alcoholic;
His vice was carbolic.

Longinus
Was one of those unpunctual diners;
He always knew what the Sublime was,
But never what the time was.

Friedrich Nietzsche
Had the habit as a teacher
Of cracking his joints
To emphasize his points.

William Makepeace Thackeray
Wept into his daiquiri
When he heard St. John's Wood
Thought he was no good.

Paul Valéry
Earned a meagre salary
Walking in the Bois,
Observing his Moi.

1953

DONALD HALL

SIX POETS IN SEARCH OF A LAWYER

Finesse be first, whose elegance deplores
All things save beauty, and the swinging doors;
Whose cleverness in writing verse is just
Exceeded by his lack of taste and lust;
Who lives off lady lovers of his verse
And thanks them by departing with their purse;
Who writes his verse in order to amaze,
To win the Pulitzer, or *Time*'s sweet praise;
Who will endure a moment, and then pass,
As hopeless as an olive in his glass.

Dullard be second, as he always will,
From lack of brains as well as lack of skill.
Expert in some, and dilettante in all
The ways of making poems gasp and fall,
He teaches at a junior college where
He's recognized as Homer's son and heir.
Respectable, brown-suited, it is he
Who represents on forums poetry,
And argues to protect the libelled Muse,
Who'd tear his flimsy tongue out, could she choose.

His opposite is anarchistic *Bomb*,
Who writes a manifesto with aplomb.
Revolt! Revolt! No matter why or when,
It's novelty—old novelty again.
Yet *Bomb*, if read intently, may reveal
A talent not to murder but to steal:
First from old Gone, whose fragmentary style
Disguised his sawdust Keats a little while;
And now from one who writes at very best
What ne'er was thought and much the less expressed.

Lucre be next, who takes to poetry
The businessman he swore he would not be.
Anthologies and lecture tours and grants
Create a solvency that disenchants.
He writes his poems, now, to suit his purse,
Short-lined and windy, and reserves his curse
For all the little magazines so fine
That offer only fifty cents a line.
He makes his money, certainly, to write,
But writes for money. Such is appetite.

Of *Mucker* will I tell, who tries to show
He is a kind of poet men don't know.
To shadowbox at literary teas,
And every girl at Bennington to seize,
To talk of baseball rather than of Yeats,
To drink straight whiskey while the bard creates—
This is his pose, and so his poems seem
Incongruous in proving life a dream.
Some say, with Freud, that *Mucker* has a reason
For acting virile in and out of season.

Scoundrel be last. Be deaf, be dumb, be blind,
Who writes satiric verses on his kind.

1955

ROBERT GRAVES

THE NAKED AND THE NUDE

For me, the naked and the nude
(By lexicographers construed
As synonyms that should express
The same deficiency of dress
Or shelter) stand as wide apart
As love from lies, or truth from art.

Lovers without reproach will gaze
On bodies naked and ablaze;
The Hippocratic eye will see
In nakedness, anatomy;
And naked shines the Goddess when
She mounts her lion among men.

The nude are bold, the nude are sly
To hold each treasonable eye.
While draping, by a showman's trick,
Their dishabille in rhetoric,
They grin a mock-religious grin
Of scorn at those of naked skin.

The naked, therefore, who compete
Against the nude may know defeat,
Yet when they both together tread
The briary pastures of the dead,
By Gorgons with long whips pursued,
How naked go the sometime nude!

1957

ELIZABETH BISHOP

12 O'CLOCK NEWS

gooseneck lamp

As you all know, tonight is the night of the full moon, half the world over. But here the moon seems to hang motionless in the sky. It gives very little light; it could be dead. Visibility is poor. Nevertheless, we shall try to give you some idea of the lay of the land and the present situation.

typewriter

The escarpment that rises abruptly from the central plain is in heavy shadow, but the elaborate terracing of its southern glacis gleams faintly in the dim light, like fish scales. What endless labor those small, peculiarly shaped terraces represent! And yet, on them the welfare of this tiny principality depends.

pile of mss.

A slight landslide occurred in the northwest about an hour ago. The exposed soil appears to be of poor quality: almost white, calcareous, and shaly. There are believed to have been no casualties.

typed sheet

Almost due north, our aerial reconnaissance reports the discovery of a large rectangular "field," hitherto unknown to us, obviously man-made. It is dark-speckled. An airstrip? A cemetery?

envelopes

In this small, backward country, one of the most backward left in the world today, communications are crude and "industrialization" and its products almost nonexistent. Strange to say, however, signboards are on a truly gigantic scale.

ink-bottle

We have also received reports of a mysterious, oddly shaped, black structure, at an undisclosed distance to the east. Its presence was revealed only because its highly polished surface catches such feeble moonlight as prevails. The natural resources of the country being far from completely known to us, there is the possibility that this may be, or may contain, some powerful and terrifying "secret weapon." On the other hand, given what we *do* know, or have learned from our anthropologists and sociologists about this people, it may well be nothing more than a *numen,* or a great altar recently erected to one of their gods, to which, in their present historical state of superstition and help-lessness, they attribute magical powers, and may even regard as a "savior," one last hope of rescue from their grave difficulties.

At last! One of the elusive natives has been spotted! He appears to be—rather, to have been—a unicyclist-courier, who may *typewriter* have met his end by falling from the height of the escarpment *eraser* because of the deceptive illumination. Alive, he would have been small, but undoubtedly proud and erect, with the thick, bristling black hair typical of the indigenes.

From our superior vantage point, we can clearly see into a sort of dugout, possibly a shell crater, a "nest" of soldiers. They lie heaped together, wearing the camouflage "battle dress" in-tended for "winter warfare." They are in hideously contorted positions, all dead. We can make out at least eight bodies. These *ashtray* uniforms were designed to be used in guerrilla warfare on the country's one snow-covered mountain peak. The fact that these poor soldiers are wearing them *here,* on the plain, gives further proof, if proof were necessary, either of the childishness and hopeless impracticality of this inscrutable people, our oppo-nents, or of the sad corruption of their leaders.

1973

CALVIN TRILLIN

CHRISTMAS IN QATAR

(A NEW HOLIDAY CLASSIC, FOR THOSE TIRING OF
"WHITE CHRISTMAS" AND "JINGLE BELLS")

VERSE:
The shopping starts, and every store's a zoo.
I'm frantic, too: I haven't got a clue
Of what to get for Dad, who's got no hobby,
Or why Aunt Jane, who's shaped like a kohlrabi,
Wants frilly sweater sets, or where I'll find
A tie my loudmouthed Uncle Jack won't mind.
A shopper's told it's vital he prevails:
Prosperity depends on Christmas sales.
"Can't stop to talk," I say. "No time. Can't halt.
Economy could fail. Would be my fault."

CHORUS:
I'd like to spend next Christmas in Qatar,
Or someplace else that Santa won't find handy.
Qatar will do, although, Lord knows, it's sandy.
I need to get to someplace pretty far.
I'd like to spend next Christmas in Qatar.

VERSE:
Young Cousin Ned, his presents on his knees,
Says Christmas wrappings are a waste of trees.
Dad's staring, vaguely puzzled, at his gift.
And Uncle Jack, to give us all a lift,
Now tells a Polish joke he heard at work.
So Ned calls Jack a bigot and a jerk.
Aunt Jane, who knows that's true, breaks down and cries.
Then Mom comes out to help, and burns the pies.
Of course, Jack hates the tie. He'll take it back.
That's fair, because I hate my Uncle Jack.

CHORUS:
I'd like to spend next Christmas in Tibet,
Or any place where folks cannot remember
That there is something special in December.
Tibet's about as far as you can get.
I'd like to spend next Christmas in Tibet.

VERSE:
Mom's turkey is a patriotic riddle:
It's red and white, plus bluish in the middle.
The blue's because the oven heat's not stable.
The red's from ketchup Dad snuck to the table.
Dad says he loves the eyeglass stand from me—
Unless a sock rack's what it's meant to be.
"A free-range turkey's best," Ned says. "It's pure."
"This hippie stuff," Jack says, "I can't endure."
They say goodbye, thank God. It's been a strain.
At least Jack's tie has got a ketchup stain.

CHORUS:
I'd like to spend next Christmas in Rangoon,
Or any place where Christmas is as noisy
As Buddhist holidays might be in Boise.
I long to hear Der Bingle smoothly croon,
"I'm dreaming of a Christmas in Rangoon"—
Or someplace you won't hear the Christmas story,
And reindeer's something eaten cacciatore.
I know things can't go on the way they are.
I'd like to spend next Christmas in Qatar.

1994

JOHN UPDIKE

DUET, WITH MUFFLED BRAKE DRUMS

*50 Years Ago Rolls met Royce—a Meeting that made
Engineering History*

                                          —ADV. IN *THE NEW YORKER.*

Where grey walks slope through shadows shaped like lace
Down to dimpleproof ponds, a precious place
Where birds of porcelain sing as with one voice
Two gold and velvet notes—there Rolls met Royce.

"Hallo," said Rolls. His umber silhouette
Seemed mounted on a blotter brushed when wet
To indicate a park. Beyond, a brown
Line hinted at the profile of The Town.

And Royce, his teeth and creases straight, his eye
A perfect match for that well-lacquered sky
(Has zenith since, or iris, been so pure?),
Said, "Pleased to meet you, I am sure."

A graceful pause, then Rolls, the taller, spake:
"Ah—is there anything you'd care to make?
A day of it? A fourth at bridge? Some tea?"
Royce murmured, "If your afternoon is free,
I'd rather, much, make engineering history."

1954

OCULAR HYPERTENSION

"Your optic nerve is small and slightly cupped,"
my drawling ophthalmologist observed,
having for minutes submitted that nerve,
or, rather, both those nerves to baths of light—
to flashing, wheeling scrutiny in which
my retinas' red veins would, mirrored, loom
and fade. "And it appears, as yet, undamaged.
But your pressure reads too high. Glaucoma
will be the eventual result if you
go untreated. What you have now we call
'ocular hypertension.' " Wow! I liked
the swanky sound, the hint of jazz, the rainbow
edginess: malaise of high-class orbs,
screwed to taut bliss by what raw sight absorbs.

2000

NOTES ON CONTRIBUTORS

WOODY ALLEN (b. 1935) was nominated for an Emmy as a writer for Sid Caesar's television show before becoming famous as a standup comic. He is now best known as the writer and director (and often star) of dozens of movies, including such classics as *Annie Hall*, *Manhattan*, and *Hannah and Her Sisters*. He has contributed to *The New Yorker* since 1966.

MARTIN AMIS (b. 1949) won the Somerset Maugham Award for his first novel, *The Rachel Papers*. His novels include *Money*, *London Fields*, and *Time's Arrow*. His memoir, *Experience*, was published in 2000.

ROGER ANGELL (b. 1920) has been a fiction editor at *The New Yorker* since 1956 and a contributor since 1944. He has been writing about baseball since 1962; his books include *The Summer Game*, *Season Ticket*, and *A Pitcher's Story: Innings with David Cone*.

MICHAEL J. ARLEN (b. 1930) was the magazine's television critic in the 1960s and 1970s. He is the author of a novel and seven books of nonfiction, including *Living-Room War*, an examination of television reportage. In 1976, he won the National Book Award for *Passage to Ararat*.

W. H. AUDEN (1907–1973) was born in York, England, was educated at Oxford, and achieved fame as a poet in the 1930s. In 1939 he immigrated to the United States, and published his first poem in *The New Yorker*. He was a frequent book reviewer in the 1950s and 1960s. He won a Pulitzer Prize in 1948 for *The Age of Anxiety* and the National Book Award in 1956 for *The Shield of Achilles*.

DONALD BARTHELME (1931–1989) published 128 stories in *The New Yorker* over twenty-six years, as well as film reviews, Notes and Comment, and parodies appearing under the pseudonym William White. He grew up in Houston and worked there first as a reporter for the *Houston Post*, then as the director of the Contemporary Arts Museum. He moved to Manhattan in 1963. He was regarded as one of the most innovative writers of his generation. His collection *Sixty Stories* was a PEN/Faulkner Award finalist in 1982.

NOAH BAUMBACH (b. 1969) wrote and directed the films *Kicking and Screaming* and *Mr. Jealousy*.

LUDWIG BEMELMANS (1898–1962) was born in the South Tirol, at that time part of the Austro-Hungarian Empire. He worked in hotels and restaurants from the age of fourteen, first in Europe and then in New York, and at one time part-owned a restaurant called the Hapsburg House. His writings for *The New Yorker*, mostly humorous memoirs, began appearing in 1937, and he also produced many covers for the magazine. His books include novels, travelogues, and memoirs, and he worked briefly as a screenwriter. His art was exhibited in New York and Paris; his murals can still be seen in New York's Carlyle Hotel. He is now best remembered for the "Madeline" children's books, the first of which was published in 1939.

ROBERT BENCHLEY (1889–1945) was born in Worcester, Massachusetts. He was the editor of the *Lampoon* while at Harvard, and went on to work at *Life* and *Vanity Fair*. One of the wits of the Algonquin Round Table, in the early 1920s, he developed his famous "Treasurer's Report" monologue for a stage review; he performed it throughout his life onstage, and also in one of the first short films with sound, in 1928. He wrote for *The New Yorker* from 1925 to 1940, providing theater reviews, the Wayward Press column, and many humor pieces. He was also a popular radio broadcaster, and appeared in forty-eight short films, including the Oscar-winning *How to Sleep* (1935).

ELIZABETH BISHOP (1911–1979) grew up wealthy but parentless in Nova Scotia and Worcester, Massachusetts. After graduating from Vassar, she traveled, living first in Key West, then in Mexico. Her first poem in *The New Yorker* appeared in 1940. For most of the 1950s and 1960s, she lived with her partner, Maria Carlota Costellat de Macedo Soares, near Rio de Janeiro. She won a Pulitzer Prize in 1956 for *Poems: North & South—A Cold Spring* and was elected to the American Academy of Arts and Letters in 1976.

ROY BLOUNT, JR. (b. 1941) grew up in Georgia. In addition to several books of comic essays, he is the author of a novel and a book about the Pittsburgh Steelers. He has been an editor at *Sports Illustrated* and a screenwriter, read his stories and poems on public radio, and designed word puzzles for the now de-funct *Spy* magazine.

ANDY BOROWITZ (b. 1958) is the creator and producer of the television series *The Fresh Prince of Bel-Air* and a co-producer of the film *Pleasantville*. His books include *Rationalizations to Live By* and *The Trillionaire Next Door*. He is a commentator on National Public Radio's *Weekend Edition*.

MARSHALL BRICKMAN (b. 1941) was a member of the folksinging groups the Journeymen and the Tarriers before becoming a writer for *Candid Camera* and *The Tonight Show*. He collaborated with Woody Allen as a writer on several films, sharing the Oscar for *Annie Hall*, and went on to write and direct a number of feature films, including *Simon* and *The Manhattan Project*.

DAVID BROOKS (b. 1961) is a senior editor at *The Weekly Standard* and the au-thor of *Bobos in Paradise: The New Upper Class and How They Got There*.

CHRISTOPHER BUCKLEY (b. 1952) is the editor of *Forbes FYI*. He is the au-thor of eight books, including *Thank You for Smoking, Wry Martinis*, and *Lit-tle Green Men*.

FRANK CAMMUSO (b. 1965), a political cartoonist, and HART SEELY (b. 1952), a reporter, are writing partners whose comic articles have appeared in *The New York Times* and the Syracuse *Herald-Journal; 2007-Eleven and Other American Comedies* is a collection of their pieces.

CLARENCE DAY (1874–1935) was born into an affluent New York family and began a career as a stockbroker. He turned to writing after being partially dis-abled by rheumatoid arthritis, eventually working entirely from his bedroom. Great success came in the early 1930s, with comic memoirs of family life. These pieces ran in *The New Yorker* beginning in 1933, and were collected in 1935 as *Life with Father. Life with Father* became a long-running play in 1939, a film in 1947, and a CBS sitcom from 1953 to 1955.

PETER DE VRIES (1910–1993) was born in Chicago and worked there as an editor of *Poetry* magazine. He was a regular contributor to *The New Yorker* in the 1940s and 1950s. His life in suburban Connecticut provided the setting for many of his popular comic novels, including *Reuben, Reuben* and *The Tunnel of Love*.

LARRY DOYLE (b. 1958) was for several years a writer and producer for *The Simpsons*. He has also been an editor at *Spy* magazine and *The National Lampoon*.

H. F. ELLIS (1907–2000) wrote and edited for *Punch*, until S. J. Perelman encouraged him to contribute to *The New Yorker*. He is perhaps best known in England for his book about a hapless British schoolmaster, *The Papers of A. J. Wentworth, BA*.

F. SCOTT FITZGERALD (1896–1940) achieved overnight fame with his first novel, *This Side of Paradise*. His output in the 1920s—notably *The Beautiful and Damned* and *The Great Gatsby*—epitomized the Jazz Age, a phrase Fitzgerald coined. From 1929 to 1937, he published three stories and two poems in *The New Yorker*.

NANCY FRANKLIN (b. 1956) has been on the staff of *The New Yorker* since 1978. She is now a theater and television critic for the magazine.

BILL FRANZEN (b. 1952) lives in Connecticut with his wife, the cartoonist Roz Chast. He is the author of the book *Hearing from Wayne and Other Stories*, and has contributed to *The New Yorker* since 1981.

IAN FRAZIER (b. 1951) has written humor and reported pieces for *The New Yorker* since 1974. His books include *Dating Your Mom, Great Plains*, and *On the Rez*.

BRUCE JAY FRIEDMAN (b. 1930) published his first novel, *Stern*, in 1962; it was followed by *A Mother's Kisses, The Current Climate*, and collected short stories. His dramatic works include a play, *Steambath*, and screenplays for *Splash!* and *Stir Crazy*. *Even the Rhinos Were Nymphos* is a collection of his comic essays.

POLLY FROST (b. 1952) has written on film for *Harper's Bazaar* and *Elle*, and about cooking for *The New York Times*.

FRANK GANNON (b. 1952) lives in Georgia. He is the author of *Yo, Poe; Vanna Karenina*; and *All About Man*, a comic book about the men's movement. His writing has appeared in *The New Yorker* since 1985.

VERONICA GENG (1941–1997) was born in Atlanta and worked as a fiction editor at *The New Yorker* starting in the mid-1970s. Many of her parodies were collected in *Partners* and *Love Trouble Is My Business*. A posthumous collection, *Love Trouble: New and Collected Work*, appeared in 1999.

MICHAEL GERBER (b. 1969) and JONATHAN SCHWARZ (b. 1969) have written humor pieces together for many publications, including *The Atlantic Monthly*, *Harper's*, and *McSweeney's*.

WOLCOTT GIBBS (1902–1958) was born in New York and worked on newspapers in Long Island before joining *The New Yorker* in 1927. He became known for the varied Profiles, parodies, and reminiscences he contributed and for his exacting editing of others. In 1940, he became the magazine's drama critic, and in 1950 his play *Season in the Sun* (adapted from his earlier book about Fire Island bohemianism) became a Broadway hit.

ADAM GOPNIK (b. 1956) was born in Philadelphia and began to write for *The New Yorker* in 1986, where he has published under various rubrics, among them The Art World, Paris Journal, and New York Journal. He is the recipient of two National Magazine Awards for his essays and a George Polk Award for magazine reporting. He is the author of *Paris to the Moon*.

ROBERT GRAVES (1895–1985) was born in London and produced more than 120 books in his long life, including the First World War memoir *Goodbye to All That*, the historical novel *I, Claudius*, and *The White Goddess: A Historical Grammar of Poetic Myth*. His poems appeared in *The New Yorker* for a quarter of a century, starting in 1950.

SCOTT GUTTERMAN (b. 1961) has contributed humor pieces to *The New Yorker* and *GQ*. He has also written for *Artforum*, *Vogue*, and other publications. He is the co-author, with Miles Davis, of *The Art of Miles Davis*.

DONALD HALL (b. 1928) published his first poem at the age of sixteen. He has produced more than twenty volumes of poetry and numerous children's books, as well as books on Henry Moore and baseball. He edited *The Oxford Book of Children's Verse in America* (1990), *The Oxford Book of American Literary Anecdotes* (1981), and more than twenty other anthologies and textbooks.

PHILIP HAMBURGER (b. 1914) has been a staff writer at *The New Yorker* since 1939, contributing Profiles, foreign correspondence, Notes for a Gazetteer, television and music criticism, and numerous short, funny pieces. He has published eight collections of his work, including *Friends Talking in the Night* and *Matters of State.*

JACK HANDEY (b. 1949) was born in Texas and lives in New York. He wrote for Steve Martin in the 1970s and 1980s, was a writer for *Saturday Night Live,* and is the author of several books, including *Deep Thoughts; Deeper Thoughts; Deepest Thoughts;* and *The Lost Deep Thoughts.*

L. RUST HILLS (b. 1924) was for many years the fiction editor at *Esquire.* He has written three volumes of humor, the so-called Fussy Man Trilogy.

GEORGE S. KAUFMAN (1889–1961) was the most successful American playwright of the 1920s and 1930s. He was the drama critic of *The New York Times* from 1917 to 1930 and was a member of the Algonquin Round Table set. His first theatrical success was *Dulcy* (1921), and in the following decades, almost always writing in collaboration with others, he turned out hit after hit, including *Of Thee I Sing,* with the Gershwins and Morrie Ryskind; *Dinner at Eight,* with Edna Ferber; and *The Man Who Came to Dinner,* with Moss Hart. He also wrote *The Cocoanuts, Animal Crackers,* and *A Night at the Opera* for the Marx Brothers.

GARRISON KEILLOR (b. 1942) was born in Anoka, Minnesota, and has affectionately parodied Minnesota life with his tales of Lake Wobegon on his long-running public radio program, *A Prairie Home Companion.* Keillor was inducted into the Radio Hall of Fame at the Museum of Broadcast Communications, in Chicago, in 1994. He first published in *The New Yorker* in 1970, and his pieces have been collected in such books as *Happy to Be Here, We Are Still Married,* and *The Book of Guys.*

ANTHONY LANE (b. 1962) reviewed books for *The Independent,* and films for *The Independent on Sunday,* in London before coming to *The New Yorker* in 1993. In addition to his biweekly film reviews, he contributes book reviews and other works of criticism, for which he has received a National Magazine Award.

JOHN LARDNER (1912–1960) was one of Ring Lardner's four sons, and, like his father, a sportswriter. He left Harvard to work on the *New York Herald Tribune,* wrote for *Newsweek* for twenty years, and wrote a television and radio column for *The New Yorker.* He was also known as a formidable poker player.

DON MARQUIS (1878–1937) was born in Walnut, Illinois, and worked as a teacher, a sewing-machine salesman, a printer, and a railroad man before finding his way into newspapers. In 1916, he first introduced, in his column in the *New York Sun*, archy and mehitabel—a philosophical cockroach and a down-on-her-luck cat, portrayed in free verse ostensibly written by archy. Marquis also wrote novels, plays, poetry, and satire. The poem in this anthology was his only work for *The New Yorker*.

STEVE MARTIN (b. 1945) is a comedian, actor, film director, and writer. He has written, and starred in, such films as *The Jerk, L.A. Story,* and *Bowfinger*. His humor pieces have appeared in the magazine since 1996. He is the author of *Pure Drivel* and *Shopgirl: A Novella*.

GROUCHO MARX (1890–1977), the lead man of the Marx Brothers troupe, was born Julius Henry Marx in New York City. After a long apprenticeship in vaudeville, the brothers achieved Broadway success in the 1920s before starting to make films in 1929. Among them are classics like *Animal Crackers, A Day at the Races,* and *Duck Soup*. Groucho's comic sketches in *The New Yorker* appeared from 1925 to 1929. In the 1950s he hosted the popular TV quiz show *You Bet Your Life*.

BRUCE MCCALL (b. 1935) was born in Canada and came to the United States at the age of twenty-seven. He says that he has been writing and drawing interchangeably since the age of about seven. His first writing appeared in *The New Yorker* in 1980 and his first art three years later. In 1982, he published *Zany Afternoons,* a collection of humor pieces. His memoir, *Thin Ice,* published in 1997, was made into a film.

PHYLLIS MCGINLEY (1905–1978) was born in Oregon and came to New Rochelle to work as a schoolteacher. Her poetry first appeared in Franklin P. Adams's column, "The Conning Tower," and, in 1930, in *The New Yorker*. The first of her eighteen books, *On the Contrary,* was published in 1934. Her poems were much loved for their simple evocation of ordinary life and *Times Three: Selected Verse from Three Decades* became, in 1961, the first collection of "light verse" to win a Pulitzer Prize.

CHARLES MCGRATH (b. 1947) was, for more than twenty years, an editor at *The New Yorker*. He has been the editor of *The New York Times Book Review* since 1995.

THOMAS MEEHAN (b. 1932) was working in the Talk of the Town department when a friend introduced him to Ina Claire and Uta Hagen ("Ina, Uta"), inspiring his first (and widely imitated) Casual. Later, he wrote the book for the musical *Annie*, which won a Tony Award. Meehan has collaborated with Mel Brooks on the films *To Be or Not to Be* and *Spaceballs*, and on the stage version of *The Producers*, for which he also won a Tony.

DANIEL MENAKER (b. 1941) was a fiction editor at *The New Yorker* and is now senior literary editor at Random House. He is the author of a novel, *The Treatment*, and two collections of short stories, *Friends and Relations* and *The Old Left*.

LOUIS MENAND (b. 1952) is a professor of English at the City University of New York and a staff writer at *The New Yorker*, where he has contributed reviews, essays, and other pieces since 1991. His books include *Discovering Modernism: T. S. Eliot and His Context* and *The Metaphysical Club*.

HOWARD MOSS (1922–1987) became the poetry editor of *The New Yorker* in 1950 and held the post until his death. He contributed more than a hundred of his own poems to the magazine, and published twelve collections, four books of criticism, and two plays.

VLADIMIR NABOKOV (1899–1977) was born in St. Petersburg and left Russia after the Revolution. In the interwar years, he published poems and novels in Russian under the pseudonym V. Sirin. In 1940, he came to the United States, where he taught literature at various universities and began to publish in English and under his own name. His first poem appeared in *The New Yorker* in 1942, and his first short story three years later. In 1959, after the popular success of *Lolita*, he moved to Switzerland, where he wrote the novels *Pale Fire*, *Ada*, and *Transparent Things*.

OGDEN NASH (1902–1971) was born in Rye, New York, and worked selling bonds and writing advertising copy before his first poem was published in *The New Yorker*, in 1930. His poems appeared in the magazine for the rest of his life, and their wit and uniquely anarchic prosody won him a huge following. They were collected in some twenty volumes. With Kurt Weill and S. J. Perelman, he collaborated on the hit musical *One Touch of Venus* (later a film with Ava Gardner), which included the classic song "Speak Low."

MIKE NICHOLS (b. 1931) was born in Berlin, came to America at the age of seven, and attended the University of Chicago. He became famous in the late 1950s as part of an improvisational comic duo with Elaine May. In the 1960s, he turned to directing, first on Broadway and then in films. His seventeen films include *Who's Afraid of Virginia Woolf?*, *The Graduate*, and *Primary Colors*.

SUSAN ORLEAN (b. 1955) has been writing for *The New Yorker* since 1987 and became a staff writer in 1992. Her work has also appeared in *Outside, Rolling Stone, Vogue,* and *Esquire,* and her books include *Saturday Night, The Orchid Thief,* and *The Bullfighter Checks Her Makeup.*

DAVID OWEN (b. 1955) is a staff writer and golf enthusiast. His books include *High School, The Walls Around Us, My Usual Game,* and *The Making of the Masters.*

DOROTHY PARKER (1893–1967), famed as an Algonquin Round Table regular, wrote for *The New Yorker* from its second issue, in 1925, until the end of 1957. She contributed poems, stories, and theater reviews and was also known for her book reviews, written under the pseudonym Constant Reader. Her poetry collection *Enough Rope* was a best-seller in 1926 and was followed by three other volumes. She moved to Hollywood to work with Alan Campbell, her second husband, as a screenwriter. They received an Oscar nomination for *A Star Is Born* (1937).

S. J. PERELMAN (1904–1979) grew up in Providence and attended Brown University, where he edited the humor magazine. When, in 1929, the publisher of his first book, *Dawn Ginsbergh's Revenge,* sent a copy to Groucho Marx for a blurb, Perelman was taken on as a scriptwriter and worked on two Marx Brothers movies, *Monkey Business* and *Horse Feathers.* His first *New Yorker* piece appeared in the 1930s, and he went on to contribute nearly three hundred others, which were collected in such books as *Strictly from Hunger* and *The Road to Miltown, or, Under the Spreading Atrophy.* He also collaborated on the stage comedies *All Good Americans* and *One Touch of Venus,* and shared an Oscar in 1957 for the script of *Around the World in Eighty Days.*

LEONARD Q. ROSS was a pseudonym of LEO ROSTEN (1908–1997), who was born in Lodz, Poland, and immigrated to Chicago with his family soon after. Rosten obtained a doctorate in social sciences from the University of Chicago and also studied at the London School of Economics. He claimed that he encountered the original of his famous comic character, Hyman Kaplan, while he was teaching English in night school. The malapropian Kaplan first appeared in *The New Yorker* in 1936 and in book form a year later. Two further volumes later appeared, and the series was briefly staged as a Broadway musical. Rosten is also well known for *The Joys of Yiddish* (1968), an informal lexicon liberally sprinkled with anecdote and humor.

PAUL RUDNICK (b. 1957) was born in New Jersey and graduated from Yale. His plays include *I Hate Hamlet; The Naked Eye; The Most Fabulous Story Ever Told; Mr. Charles, Currently of Palm Beach;* and *Jeffrey,* which was also made into a movie. His screenplays include *Addams Family Values* and *In & Out.* He is the author of two novels, *Social Disease* and *I'll Take It,* and a collection of movie reviews written by his alter ego, Libby Gelman-Waxner.

CATHLEEN SCHINE (b. 1953) is a novelist. *The Love Letter,* a national best-seller, was translated into fifteen languages. Her other novels include *Alice in Bed, Rameau's Niece,* and *The Evolution of Jane.*

WILLIAM SHAWN (1907–1992), the longest-serving editor of *The New Yorker,* was born in Chicago and came on staff in 1933 as a Talk of the Town writer. He turned to editing after a couple of years and became managing editor in 1939. He succeeded Harold Ross in 1952, editing the magazine until 1987.

UPTON SINCLAIR (1878–1968) wrote dime novels from the age of fifteen and made his reputation in 1906 with *The Jungle,* a novel that exposed working conditions in the Chicago meat-packing industry. He stood, unsuccessfully, as the Democratic candidate for governor of California in 1934. His popular Lanny Budd series of novels appeared from 1940 to 1953. "How to Be Obscene" was his only work for *The New Yorker.*

MARK SINGER (b. 1950) has been a staff writer at *The New Yorker* since 1974. He is the author of three books, *Funny Money, Mr. Personality,* and *Citizen K.*

SUSAN SONTAG (b. 1933) enrolled in the University of California at Berkeley at the age of fifteen and, after studies at the University of Chicago, Harvard, the Sorbonne, and Oxford, settled in New York. Her wide-ranging essays on aesthetics, culture, and politics include *Against Interpretation, Illness as Metaphor, Styles of Radical Will,* and *On Photography.* She has also written films, plays, and four novels, among them *The Volcano Lover* and *In America.*

RUTH SUCKOW (1892–1960) was born in Iowa and lived there for most of her life. She published her first poetry in 1918 and her first short story in 1921. Her first novel, *Country People,* appeared in 1924. She contributed to *The New Yorker* from 1927 to 1937. She published eleven books in her lifetime, leaving a novel unfinished when she died.

FRANK SULLIVAN (1892–1976) claimed that his career as a humorist began at the *New York World,* after he wrote a long obituary of a socialite who turned out not to be dead. He began contributing to *The New Yorker* in 1926; his cliché expert, Mr. Arbuthnot, testified in the magazine from 1935 to 1952. Sullivan was also known for the annual Christmas poem "Greetings, Friends!," which he wrote for forty-two years, until 1974.

JAMES THURBER (1894–1961) was born in Columbus, Ohio, and joined *The New Yorker* in 1927 as an editor and writer; his idiosyncratic cartoons began to appear there four years later. His books include two children's classics—*The 13 Clocks* and *The Wonderful O*—and a memoir of his time at *The New Yorker, The Years with Ross.* He also co-wrote a successful play, *The Male Animal,* and appeared in *A Thurber Carnival,* a miscellany of his works that was adapted for the stage. In 1947, "The Secret Life of Walter Mitty" was made into a film starring Danny Kaye.

CALVIN TRILLIN (b. 1935) has been a staff writer for *The New Yorker* since 1963 and has reported from all over America in his long-running U.S. Journal series. His many books include the best-sellers *Remembering Denny* and *Messages from My Father,* along with comic novels, short stories, a travel book, and three books on food, collected as *The Tummy Trilogy.* He has also twice written and performed one-man shows.

GEORGE W. S. TROW (b. 1943) first wrote for *The New Yorker* in 1966 and co-founded *The National Lampoon* in 1970. His essay of cultural criticism "Within the Context of No-Context" was published in 1980 and later became an influential book. He is the author of a novel, *The City in the Mist,* and a collection of satirical short stories, *Bullies.* He has also written several plays, including *The Tennis Game,* and has co-written two Merchant-Ivory films, *Savages* and *The Proprietor.* He has published a further volume of cultural reflections, *My Pilgrim's Progress: Media Studies, 1950–1998.*

JOHN UPDIKE (b. 1932) has written for *The New Yorker* since the mid-1950s, when he was a staff writer for The Talk of the Town. He has contributed more than six hundred short stories, poems, essays, and reviews. He has published more than fifty books, and has won two Pulitzer Prizes, two National Book Awards, and two National Book Critics Circle Awards.

LISA WALKER (b. 1956) has written a novel, *Because of You.*

ELWYN BROOKS WHITE (1899–1985) worked as a newspaperman, an advertising copywriter, and a mess boy on an Arctic steamer before coming to *The New Yorker* in 1927. Here his output comprised humor pieces, poems, short stories, newsbreak captions, and even one cover illustration, but he was most associated with the Notes and Comment essays, which he wrote for thirty years. He is famous for three enduring works of children's literature: *Stuart Little, Charlotte's Web,* and *The Trumpet of the Swan.* He received the Presidential Medal of Freedom in 1963 and a Pulitzer Prize in 1978.

WILLIAM WHITE was a pseudonym of DONALD BARTHELME.

CHET WILLIAMSON (b. 1948) has been a finalist for the World Fantasy, Edgar, and Stoker awards for his fantasy, horror, and science-fiction writing. He is also an actor.

ALEXANDER WOOLLCOTT (1887–1943) joined *The New York Times* in 1909, and was a feared and famous drama critic there from 1914 to 1922. A central figure at the Algonquin Round Table in the 1920s, he was one of the very first contributors to *The New Yorker.* In the early 1930s he wrote Shouts and Murmurs in the magazine almost every week. At the same time, he became a popular and influential radio broadcaster. He also acted in a number of plays, most famously playing the character based on him in *The Man Who Came to Dinner,* by Moss Hart and George S. Kaufman.

DAVID REMNICK is the editor of *The New Yorker*.

HENRY FINDER is the editorial director of *The New Yorker*.

A NOTE ON THE TYPE

Most of the text of this book was set in Backslap Grotesque Italic Semi-Detached, a variant of Bangalore Torpedo Moribund adapted in 1867 from a matrice by the Danish chiseler Espy Sans, a character if ever there was one. In sharp contradistinction to Bangalore's racy, almost louche taste and its weakness for the cheating side of town, Backslap is a solid citizen and a joiner: A.A., A.A.A., AARP, Christmas Club. Its close cousin Mediocre Flyweight Ultra Bold is almost too sickly-sweet for words, a semi-invalid given to tiresome late-afternoon vaporings. That part of the text not set in Backslap or Bangalore—the lowercase d's, k's, and alternate z's, except after c—is Jiffy-Lube Piscataway Light Narrow, based on a sixteenth-century face closely resembling the late Edward G. Robinson. The wise will cross to the other side of the street when this burly dock-walloper of a font comes galumphing into view.

A NOTE ON THE WRITER OF THE NOTE ON THE TYPE

Contrary to what the publisher would like you to think, these Notes on the Type don't just write themselves. The above note, for example, was written by yours truly, a freelance typographic blurbist who's occasionally thrown work by a brother-in-law in the production department for walking-around money while working toward my mason's degree. Such notes are by custom unsigned, as anonymous as a shop manual, so I can write any old damn thing I want, the above paragraph being a case in point: total baloney, utter nonsense, and one long leg-pull.

The information kit passed along by the book designer clearly states that the text of this book was actually set in Fishtail Equivocal Bold, a typeface favored for its way of leaning into the wind while keeping a straight back, designed in Flanders in 1916 by Siegfried Sassoon (no relation to Vidal), and related by marriage to Lydian Cursive.

A FURTHER NOTE ON THE TYPE

Correct! That was yet another of my frisky typo-lingo gags. Let me ask you: why are you even reading this? The book is over. Hanging around the back of the theatre after the movie to watch the credits roll, that would be understandable. Hanging around the back of a book when there's nothing to look at but a succession of blank pages—that's pathetic. And dangerous: you could get the idea that the lawyer has forced the author to cut huge sections, or that there's been some production goof-up resulting in five or ten pages too many.

But blank pages at the back of a book are a *publishing tradition*, not unlike the Note on the Type: dropped in to break up the blankness, innocuous yet classy.

ADDED NOTE FROM THE WRITER OF THE NOTE ON THE TYPE

Maybe the insights of a ten-cents-a-word hack underwhelm you, but it has to be asked: who *cares* what typeface this book was set in except for a handful of ink-stained, pica-crazed designers with floppy metal rulers? Why are they so special, anyway? Meanwhile, all that whining about rising costs, razor-thin margins, can't risk publishing first novels they're so pinched, and they throw away this precious space on a mindless convention.

Myself, I think they're missing a bet by not selling ads back here. Corns Treated at Home! Whiplash Lawyer Hates to Lose! Instant Vacation Cash from the Air Rights to Your House! Punchy ads like the ones you see in the subway cars, because after all, back-page book browsers are just like one- or two-stop subway riders, strictly skimmers.

A FINAL NOTE ON THE TYPE

On the other hand, there's supposed to be dignity in labor. Those working typographic pros probably don't deserve to be ridiculed. So: the text of this book was set in Torpor Ultra Screwball, one of a family of faces designed by Cooper Black to be seen and not heard, and widely admired for a feel so contemporary—note the kerning, urgent as the final lap of the Palio—that it makes tomorrow seem like yesterday.

Wouldn't it be more practical—not to mention smart marketing—to print favorite author recipes as tie-ins back here? Martha Stewart's Stock Split Pea Soup; Master of Horror Stephen King's Ghoulish Goulash. Tom Clancy's Hunt for Red Bell Peppers. Or, run classifieds.

Have serifs, will travel. Burned-out wordsmith seeks assignment at next professional level, preferably nearer front of book. Content desirable but not necessary. No About the Type blocks, please.

—BRUCE McCALL, 1997